AN AGENDA FOR ANTIQUITY

History of American Science and Technology Series

General Editor, LESTER D. STEPHENS

AN AGENDA FOR ANTIQUITY

Henry Fairfield Osborn
& Vertebrate Paleontology
at the American Museum
of Natural History,
1890–1935

RONALD RAINGER

The University of Alabama Press

Tuscaloosa and London

Library of Congress Cataloging-in-Publication Data

Rainger, Ronald, 1949–
    An agenda for antiquity : Henry Fairfield Osborn
and vertebrate paleontology at the American Museum
of Natural History, 1890–1935 / Ronald Rainger.
    p.   cm.—(History of American science and
technology series)
    Includes bibliographical references and index.
    ISBN 0-8173-0536-X   (alk. paper)
    1. Vertebrates, Fossil—Research—United States—
History.   2. Vertebrates—Anatomy—Research—United
States—History.   3. American Museum of Natural
History—History.   4. Osborn, Henry Fairfield,
1857–1935.   5. Paleontologists—United States—
Biography.
    I. Title.   II. Series.
    QE841.R24   1991
    566'.072073—dc20
                                        90-25167

British Library Cataloguing-in-Publication Data available

For Judy

Contents

Illustrations

Acknowledgments

During the years in which I have worked on this project, my research has been facilitated by librarians and archivists at several institutions. I would especially like to thank Nina J. Root, Librarian of the American Museum of Natural History, and her staff. Over the past several years she has given me access to the museum's archival and manuscript collections, has put up with my questions and quibbles, and has always done so with the utmost courtesy and support. Other members of the library staff, notably Valerie Wheat, Andrea La Sala, Mary Genett, Russel Rak, Carman Collazo, and Barbara Matté, have generously provided me with the opportunity to examine materials, quote from archival sources, and use the photographs contained in this book. I am grateful for their help. All photographs are published by courtesy of the Department of Library Services, American Museum of Natural History.

In the American Museum's Department of Vertebrate Paleontology, Richard Tedford, Michael Novacek, and others have encouraged my work, talked with me about the department and its history, allowed me to examine departmental records and manuscript collections. I would also like to thank the following individuals for their assistance and for allowing me to examine and quote from manuscripts in their possession: at Harvard University Clark A. Elliott; at Yale University Judith A. Schiff and Barbara Narendra; at Princeton University Jean F. Preston, Earle Coleman, and Donald Baird; at Columbia University Marion Jemmott, Bernard M. Crystal, and Corinne H. Rider; at the New-York Historical Society Thomas Dunnings and James E. Mooney; at the New

York Public Library Anastacio Teodoro; at the Academy of Natural Sciences of Philadelphia Carol M. Spawn, Marsha Gross, and William Gagliardi; at the American Philosophical Society Elizabeth Carroll-Horrocks and Martin Levitt; at the University of Pennsylvania Gail M. Pietrzyk; and librarians at Haverford College and the Earth Sciences Library, University of California at Berkeley.

Sections of this work were previously published in different sources. I am grateful to Kluwer Academic Publishers, the *Proceedings of the American Philosophical Society*, *Earth Sciences History*, and the University of Pennsylvania Press for permission to reprint portions of work that previously appeared in their publications.

My research on American vertebrate paleontology has received financial support from a number of sources. I am indebted to the History and Philosophy of Science Program of the National Science Foundation and its director Dr. Ronald Overmann for a grant for dissertation research and two subsequent grants that enabled me to do this work. A Mellon Postdoctoral Fellowship in the Humanities at the University of Pennsylvania enabled me to complete research at a number of institutions and to finish a draft of the manuscript. Jack E. Reece and Maggie Morris of the University of Pennsylvania were most helpful during my postdoctoral year. My work was also aided by a grant from the Texas State Organized Research Fund and support from the Dean's Office, College of Arts and Sciences, Texas Tech University.

I have incurred many intellectual debts in writing this work. My study of the history of vertebrate paleontology began as a dissertation under Frederick B. Churchill at Indiana University. Not only have he and my colleague Jane Maienschein been thoughtful critics and supporters of my research, but their work has served as a model for emulation. My views on Henry Fairfield Osborn, the history of vertebrate paleontology, and the history of American science have benefited from comments and criticisms from Garland Allen, John Beatty, Keith Benson, Richard W. Burkhardt, Jr., Edwin H. Colbert, Joseph T. Gregory, Joel Hagen, Lily Kay, Sally Gregory Kohlstedt, Léo Laporte, Timothy Lenoir, Edward Lurie, Ernst Mayr, John H. Ostrom, Diane Paul, Philip Pauly, Clayton Ray, Michael Ruse, and Molly Sutphen. I would like to thank Gale Avrith, Linnda Caporael, George Flynn, Gregg Mitman, Benjamin Newcomb, David Troyansky, and an anonymous referee for their comments on an earlier draft of the work. Although I have not incorporated all their suggestions, I have benefited from their insights. A year as a postdoctoral fellow at the University of Pennsylvania provided many opportunities to discuss my work with a number of colleagues. I am grateful to Mark

Adams, William Altimari, Gerald J. Cassidy, Peter Dodson, Anthony Fiorello, William Gagliardi, Lily Kay, and Robert Kohler who made the year enjoyable, challenging, and productive. Irene Meynarez and my wife, Judy, assisted with the bibliography. I am also indebted to Judy for her help with proofreading, editing, selecting photographs, and many other tasks.

Working on this project with The University of Alabama Press has been a rewarding experience. Lester Stephens, the editor of the series, and Malcolm MacDonald, the director of the University Press, have enthusiastically supported this project and have given generously of their time and energy in an effort to improve the work. I also thank the staff of the University Press for advice and help. An author could ask for no better or more committed group of people.

Finally, I thank the members of my family who have remained faithful, patient, and understanding while I have worked to complete this book. I am especially grateful to my wife Judy who not only has put up with all the trials and tribulations that go along with such a project but has been a constant source of encouragement and support. This book is for her.

Introduction

In 1905 William Diller Matthew, a vertebrate paleontologist at New York's American Museum of Natural History, sent a catalogue of that institution's newest fossil displays to Charles Schuchert of Yale University. Acknowledging the leaflet, Schuchert stated that "the Department of Vertebrate Paleontology of the American Museum of Natural History is attracting to it the eyes of all paleontologists, and especially Vertebrate Zoologists. I am thankful that we have in America a man able to make it possible for himself and his staff to bring into the light of the world the wonderful treasures of our country."[1] After having "worshipped at [his] shrine," Schuchert went on to chastise Matthew and the museum for not fully recognizing the significance of other museums. But even in criticism Schuchert was pointing to important features of early twentieth-century American vertebrate paleontology: the dominance of the American Museum in scientific research and public display, and the role that one man, Henry Fairfield Osborn, played in centralizing the science at that institution.

Osborn was a leading figure in early twentieth-century American science, but this study is not a biography of Osborn. It does not pretend to cover his entire career, nor does it examine all aspects of his work at the American Museum. Instead it is an analysis of how and why Osborn developed the leading center for vertebrate paleontology in the United States and what kind of program he created. As a scientist trained in the tradition of late nineteenth-century morphology, Osborn developed an interest in a wide range of problems pertaining to vertebrate paleon-

I

tology. Questions of variation, evolution, development, and inheritance all captured his attention. So too did geological problems concerning biostratigraphy and correlation. At Princeton, and later on a much larger scale at the American Museum, Osborn was able to establish his interests as the basis for active programs of research in vertebrate paleontology.

But Osborn was more than a scientist, and developing a successful program in vertebrate paleontology entailed more than just the examination of scientific research problems. Throughout the nineteenth century, the description and classification of extinct animals had been a specialized and legitimate area of inquiry, but during Osborn's lifetime vertebrate paleontology became an expensive and marginal field of research. In the 1870s and 1880s the activities of two aggressive entrepreneurs, Edward Drinker Cope and Othniel Charles Marsh, transformed American vertebrate paleontology into an expensive and far-flung endeavor. Going after fossils in the western states and territories with a vengeance, they established large specimen collections of bizarre but scientifically important remains. The federal government sustained their work for a time, but vertebrate paleontology had few direct economic or social benefits and eventually the government withdrew most of its support for the subject. Many colleges and universities possessed small collections of extinct animals and offered courses that included the study of fossil vertebrates, but few had the resources to finance expeditions or to maintain large collections.

Prior to the early twentieth century, vertebrate paleontology had commanded popular as well as scientific interest. The discovery of large extinct animals captured public attention and raised important questions about the history of the earth and the history of life. Charles Darwin's theory of evolution spurred the search for "missing links." In addition, vertebrate paleontology was part of a program of morphological research that emphasized documenting and describing the occurrence of evolution.

The late nineteenth century witnessed the rise and rapid expansion of experimental biology, and vertebrate paleontology became increasingly uninteresting and insignificant to most scientists. Central to the work in vertebrate paleontology was systematics: the description of structural characters and the classification of extinct organisms. The major theoretical issues concerned the evolution, extinction, and geographical distribution of once-living animals. Those problems were difficult to break down into specific, testable hypotheses. Vertebrate paleontology did not readily meet new explanatory criteria, nor did it employ the powerful tools that were offering new insights into inheritance, development, and biochemical processes. As an expensive and increasingly peripheral field of inquiry, vertebrate paleontology generated little interest among biologists and geologists in the emerging system of higher education. Instead it became based primarily in museums and was dependent on wealthy patrons whose interest in extinct animals reflected sociocultural and political aims more than scientific objectives.

Osborn succeeded in developing a program in vertebrate paleontology by relying on and appealing to those interests. Osborn came from a wealthy and prominent New York family, and he actively cultivated resources and opportunities to promote himself and his field of science. Like Cope and Marsh, he was eager to dominate vertebrate paleontology, but he did not squander his or his family's fortune in pursuit of fossil remains. Rather he solicited support from a wide network of associates in the scientific and social communities to which he belonged. As a student and later a faculty member at Princeton in the 1880s, he became an important figure in the nascent American zoological community. Through his ties to scientists and administrators at Princeton and elsewhere, Osborn was able to establish a small program in vertebrate paleontology.

In later years he drew upon friendships and associations beyond the scientific community to gain support for more ambitious projects in biology and paleontology. In New York, Osborn was not only a curator at the American Museum; he also joined a number of the city's prominent social clubs. He played an important role in the transformation of Columbia College into Columbia University. He was also actively involved in creating and administering the Bronx Zoo. In all those contexts he sought out and gained the confidence and backing of many of the city's, and the nation's, most powerful financial and political figures. In addition to relying on close personal friendships with those individuals, Osborn operated as a salesman who promoted new projects to museum administrators, authored popular articles in leading newspapers and magazines, and employed rhetoric, exaggeration, and supreme confidence to acquire economic and political support for major projects in what was otherwise an expensive, non-practical, and peripheral field of inquiry.

Osborn also embraced the ideas and objectives that motivated those with whom he was closely associated. The museum's trustees were for the most part members of the upper-class elites of late nineteenth-century New York City.[2] In addition to creating the museum, men such as J. P. Morgan, William E. Dodge, and Morris K. Jesup were responsible for establishing a number of cultural institutions as well as philanthropic organizations for the spiritual, social, and economic welfare of the populace. The development of the American Museum, the YMCA, and other institutions were not only manifestations of their interest in social and moral stewardship but also means for establishing and maintaining hegemony. In the 1880s and 1890s, some of the museum's trustees and curators also expressed a concern for the preservation of America's rapidly disappearing flora and fauna. Although Jesup, Joel A. Allen, and Frank M. Chapman did not make nature preservation a formal museum program or policy, they promoted it through publications and displays.

Osborn embraced that interest and fashioned it into an ideology. His concern for the preservation of nature, which he expanded to include the preservation of class and of race, was incorporated into both his scientific research and the public education work of his program in vertebrate paleontology. Osborn's affiliation with the museum did not in and of itself *cause* him to develop such interpretations. He was a member of an upper class elite and shared the social values and beliefs of many of his associates. At the American Museum he shaped those views into an ideology that was expressed through his evolutionary interpretations, a worldwide program of exploration and research, and massive exhibits of extinct animals. In Osborn's hands vertebrate paleontology was not only a field of scientific inquiry; it also embodied a commitment to traditional values and institutions. In that respect it served as a bulwark against increasing urbanization, industrialization, and ethnic pluralism, and it appealed to many among the upper class.

With support from museum trustees and other associates, Osborn created a program in vertebrate paleontology that dominated the field. Between 1890 and 1935, Osborn expanded his interests from paleomammalogy to dinosaurs to paleoanthropology. With the assistance of a large, diversified group of assistants, he was able to publish prolifically on a wide variety of topics. He and his associates at the museum sponsored vast expeditions, developed major collections, and promoted displays on a grand scale. Geographically, his Department of Vertebrate Paleontology expanded from a center limited to research on North American fauna and horizons to a program whose efforts covered the globe.

That department reflected Osborn's social and scientific interests. Osborn's emphasis on public displays was a manifestation of his and the trustees' interest in public education. Osborn directed his departmental assistants to develop innovative preparation and mounting techniques in order to exhibit extinct vertebrates as once-living creatures. Those displays embodied his interpretations. The department's scientific research emphasized his theoretical interests. Few of Osborn's assistants accepted his scientific interpretations or political and social beliefs. His two leading associates, William Diller Matthew and William King Gregory, developed ideas on evolution and inheritance that differed markedly from Osborn's. Their work, more than his, offered new perspectives for understanding the fossil record that influenced the next generation of vertebrate paleontologists. But the research by Matthew, Gregory, and their students rested on the economic and institutional foundation that Osborn had created. Their work also emphasized the theoretical problems that he considered important. As their mentor, department head, and later president of the museum, Osborn defined the research projects that his associates pursued. Under his direction, work on fossil vertebrates at the American Museum served social and political as well as scientific interests. On that basis Osborn was able to construct the largest and most significant program for vertebrate paleontology in the country.

Vertebrate Paleontology and American Science, 1850–1900

Henry Fairfield Osborn's career began at a time when vertebrate paleontology was an exciting and important field of scientific inquiry. In the late 1870s explorations for fossils in the western states and territories still embodied the thrill of romantic adventure. The recent discoveries of dinosaurs and large fossil mammals by the Americans Edward Drinker Cope and O. C. Marsh captured the attention of scientists throughout the world. The federal government, which was sponsoring expeditions to the trans-Mississippi West, subsidized fieldwork and the publication of studies on extinct animals. The subject was also closely tied to the contemporary enthusiasm for evolution. In addition to the interest in "missing links," paleontology was part of a morphological tradition that emphasized the study of structure as a means for documenting and describing the course of evolutionary change. Osborn's interest in the study of extinct animals drew upon the enthusiasm, questions, and methods that characterized work in mid-nineteenth-century vertebrate paleontology.

But Osborn's career continued into the 1930s, and by that time vertebrate paleontology had little interest to most biologists or geologists. The federal government was no longer a major supporter of the subject; rather it was dependent on wealthy patrons. Conceptually and methodologically the study of fossil vertebrates was peripheral to the most important work being done in the biological and geological sciences. With the rise of experimental biology, the study of evolution took a back seat to research in genetics, biochemistry, and physiology. Experimental

7

tests carried out on invertebrates in laboratories, not fieldwork and the study of large specimen collections, were the basis for important break-throughs in understanding inheritance or the biochemical processes that influenced function and behavior. In the expanding system of higher education, which became the center of American scientific and intellectual life, few students pursued graduate study in vertebrate paleontology. Work in vertebrate paleontology was based primarily in large public museums.

The developments in American vertebrate paleontology, while influenced by the famous Cope-Marsh feud, were also a consequence of the changing character of American science in the late nineteenth century. Prior to 1870 science was primarily an academic pursuit that supported both a religious tradition and an educational philosophy based on training the mental faculties. After the Civil War, as America changed from a rural, agricultural nation to one that was increasingly urban and industrial, American science was also transformed. Education was geared to providing training for an industrial economy and society that emphasized standardized tasks and techniques and that required certification. The federal government, interested in developing and taking advantage of natural resources, required scientists to man surveys or new agricultural experiment stations. By the early twentieth century, business and industry needed scientists and engineers who could aid in developing technological innovations that would facilitate the control of markets. Scientists, too, demanded changes in the educational system, and in the 1870s Harvard and the new Johns Hopkins University launched graduate programs in the sciences that emphasized specialized training and research. The sciences were compartmentalized in departments, and in the biological sciences lectures and laboratories gradually became more important than fieldwork. In that changing environment, vertebrate paleontology had a difficult time surviving. Osborn was one of the few who succeeded in sustaining that field of study.

Throughout much of the nineteenth century, vertebrate paleontology was an active, exciting field of inquiry. Studies by the French scientist Georges Cuvier demonstrated that fossils were the remains of once-living organisms and laid the foundation for future work in the science. By the 1850s most geologists and paleontologists defined fossils, not rocks, as the markers that determined strata and the relative age of the earth. The study of fossils was readily integrated into the emphasis on description and classification that characterized much of early nineteenth-century zoology and botany. Fossils also raised theoretical questions. They provided evidence of extinction, hence efforts to explain the history of the earth and life on the earth had to take fossils into account. British and American scientists employed the evidence of the fossil record to substantiate their belief that the history of the earth was a series of catastrophes followed by separate, divine creations. The English geologist Charles Lyell, who argued that present day causal agents operating at known rates explained the changes that characterized the earth's history, used invertebrate fossil remains to support his uniformitarian theory.[1]

Fossils were also attention-getters. Throughout the early nineteenth century, geology was a highly popular activity. The "romance of the field," the chance to get outdoors and study the flora, fauna, and physical environment appealed to scientists and enthusiasts alike.[2] The discoveries associated with vertebrate paleontology were also intriguing. The fossil fish, bizarre mammals, and dinosaurs found in the early years of the century not only posed new and interesting questions, they also captured public interest. Scientists and showmen placed mounted skeletons of extinct animals on display, and in Paris and Philadelphia crowds flocked to see the remains of mastodons. In the 1850s the dinosaurs constructed by Benjamin Waterhouse Hawkins under the direction of the English anatomist Richard Owen were a popular attraction at the Crystal Palace Exhibition. Fifteen years later Hawkins's mounted specimen of the dinosaur *Hadrosaurus foulkii* greatly boosted attendance at Philadelphia's Academy of Natural Sciences.[3]

Vertebrate paleontology also profited from Charles Darwin's theory of evolution. In *On the Origin of Species*, published in 1859, Darwin argued that the process of extinction and thus fossil remains were a consequence of evolution. According to his theory, evolution was a gradual process that occurred by the natural selection of random variations. Those organisms that possessed advantageous variations, particularly the ability to leave large numbers of offspring, took advantage of opportunities and evolved. Organisms that did not possess those advantages, or did not adapt to changing conditions, became extinct. According to Darwin, a historical connection existed between older and more recent forms. His theory also suggested that since evolution was a gradual process of change and replacement, geological strata should contain the remains of transitional forms. Darwin went to great lengths to explain why such missing links were scarce. But his theory provided a new interpretation of the history of life that spurred the search for fossils.[4]

From the 1860s to the 1890s paleontology was an important dimension of the work done in evolutionary biology. The discovery of missing links like *Archeopteryx*, a bird with reptilian characters, provided documentary evidence that was fitted into an evolutionary framework. Scientists employed the discovery of large numbers of ammonites or fossil horses from different geological horizons to chart the history of evolutionary change in particular families of organisms.[5] Paleontologists participated in a tradition of morphological research designed to document the occurrence of evolution. Through comparative analysis of organic structure, paleontologists, as well as embryologists and anatomists, sought to define homologies, morphological similarities that were interpreted as evidence of evolutionary relationship. The discovery of ancestral and intermediate forms, and the construction of phylogenies, the lines of descent that indicated evolutionary connections, were an important feature of much biological research in the years immediately following Darwin's work.[6]

American scientists enthusiastically participated in the study of fossils. In the first half of the nineteenth century, James E. DeKay of New York and Richard Harlan of Philadelphia published on mastodons, extinct bison, and fossil reptiles. Through their researches DeKay, Harlan, and others made European scientists aware of work being done in American science and helped to establish vertebrate paleontology as an international field of activity. The learned societies with which those men were affiliated, the New York Lyceum and Philadelphia's Academy of Natural Sciences, developed collections that included vertebrate remains. Naturalists at colleges throughout the country did the same. The collection of fossils also became a regular feature of expanding state geological surveys as well as federal government expeditions.[7]

After 1850 much of the work in the field became centralized around a few individuals and institutions. Joseph Leidy (1823–91), a Philadelphia physician and naturalist, became the first dominant figure in American vertebrate paleontology. Building on an already existing interest in fossils at the Academy of Natural Sciences, he became an authority on vertebrate remains. Through his association with Spencer Fullerton Baird of the Smithsonian Institution and other scientists and government officials, Leidy was sent remains by explorers and collectors throughout the country.[8] At the Academy of Natural Sciences he supervised a growing collection of specimens and encouraged others to pursue work in geology and paleontology. He also participated in efforts to develop displays, including the mounting of the first dinosaur specimen placed on exhibit in the United States.[9]

Leidy was also an active researcher in vertebrate paleontology. He was first and foremost a systematist who described and classified fossil specimens. With an expanding body of data he was able to revise classifications of extinct cats and oxen made by his predecessor Harlan. Leidy's "Ancient Fauna of Nebraska" (1854) included the first detailed descriptions of oreodonts, extinct rhinoceroses, titanotheres, and other mammals discovered by collectors in midwestern states and territories. His later studies of extinct reptiles and a large monograph on fossil mammals were important contributions to the literature.[10]

Leidy's work was also influenced by Darwin's theory and contributed to the expanding interest in evolution. Prior to 1860 he had discerned relationships among extinct organisms, but Leidy did not believe in the transmutation of species and was unable to explain the similarities he saw. In 1860 Darwin's work brought him "out of the darkness" like "a meteor [that] flashed upon the skies."[11] Leidy did not attempt to explain the causes of evolution or to construct phylogenies and describe patterns of evolutionary change. However, he pursued research within an evolutionary context by documenting evidence for descent with modification. He maintained that the extinct species *Bison latifrons* had affinities to the modern *Bison bison*. The even-toed oreodonts were "one of the links necessary to fill up the very wide gap between existing ruminants and that exceedingly aberrant form of the same family, the extinct *Anoplotherium* of Europe and Asia." Although Leidy claimed that his work was "intended as a record of facts," his papers on ancient proboscideans, ungulates, and other fossil mammals provided evidence of evolutionary change.[12]

An enthusiasm for paleontology also characterized the work of Leidy's two younger contemporaries, Edward Drinker Cope (1840–97) and O. C. Marsh (1832–99). As a former student of Leidy's and a member of the Academy of Natural Sciences, Cope was well aware of the hundreds of fossil specimens that collectors brought to Leidy's attention. For a time Cope, Leidy, and Marsh, a student and later professor at Yale College, all concentrated on describing fossil reptiles from Cretaceous deposits along the Atlantic seaboard.[13] Cope and Marsh also realized that Leidy was dependent on his collectors; he did not have the financial resources to explore the western or midwestern fossil fields himself. Cope and Marsh did, and as two wealthy and ambitious men they moved quickly to take advantage of that opportunity. From the late 1860s to the early 1890s, each man spent thousands of dollars collecting and paying collectors to ransack the western United States in search of fossils. Their resources and aggressiveness eventually forced Leidy to the sidelines. In the process Cope and Marsh each discovered and described hundreds of new fossil vertebrates. In an empirical sense at least, their worked moved America to the forefront of vertebrate paleontology.[14]

Although Cope and Marsh used their own money for work in vertebrate paleontology, they also received support for their endeavors. Cope, who inherited a fortune from his father, was employed by the government surveys headed by Ferdinand Vandiveer Hayden and Lieutenant George Montgomery Wheeler in the 1870s. Marsh, whose wealthy uncle George Peabody provided money for a museum at Yale as well as a personal income for his nephew, also benefited from federal government sponsorship. Clarence King, the flamboyant director of the government survey of the fortieth parallel, sponsored the publication of Marsh's monograph on extinct toothed birds found in Kansas. From 1882 to 1892 Marsh was government vertebrate paleontologist during John Wesley Powell's years as director of the U.S. Geological Survey. That position, which included an annual appropriation that reached $16,000, enabled Marsh to maintain not only many collectors in the field but also a large laboratory of preparators, artists, and other assistants at the Peabody Museum in New Haven.[15] Personal connections underscored that support. Cope had good relations with Hayden, who had often relied on Leidy and other Philadelphia scientists to promote his interests. Marsh, like King, was a product of Yale's Sheffield Scientific School, and throughout the 1870s they worked with Powell and others to bring a new order to power in government science. But in addition to the ties that Cope and Marsh cultivated, the fossils they discovered were among the important resources from the trans-Mississippi West. During the 1870s an interest in almost all western resources and an enthusiasm for government sponsorship of science provided support for research in vertebrate paleontology.[16]

The work of Cope and Marsh also interested scientists of the time. Cope conducted expeditions throughout the 1860s and 1870s and brought back remains of carnivorous dinosaurs, extinct sea serpents, and flying reptiles. He presented his discoveries and interpretations, often accompanied with graphic descriptions and imaginative restorations, to the Academy of Natural Sciences and the American Philosophical Society, two of the leading scientific organizations in the country. During his career Cope identified over one thousand new fossil species and genera. His descriptions, though often hasty and inaccurate, produced revised classifications and new interpretations of the habits, habitats, and evolution of fossil vertebrates.[17]

Cope also tackled evolutionary questions and developed a non-Darwinian evolutionary theory. He approached evolution by trying to understand what caused variation, a topic that he claimed Darwin had not investigated. Beginning with a series of papers in the early 1870s, Cope argued that evolution was caused by will or choice that led organisms to make certain movements or to use certain parts. The inheritance of those choices, habits, and acquired characteristics constituted evolution. Changes in the rate of individual development, particularly an acceleration of that process, allowed acquired changes to be added on at the end of an inherited ontogeny. Cope called his theory kinetogenesis, the mechanical use of parts that created change. Applying his interpretations to the fossil fragments he was discovering, he explained the evolution of the feet, teeth, and other parts of vertebrates. The mammalian molar tooth, he maintained, had evolved from a simple reptilian cone. The mammalian foot had evolved from a five-toed plantigrade form to a digitigrade form. Eventually Cope explained the entire vertebrate skeleton in terms of the mechanical stresses and strains produced through the use of parts and the inheritance of acquired characteristics. He also described evolutionary trends. Cope's theory provided an explanation for adaptation and divergence, but he defined evolution as an additive, cumulative process that resulted in linear patterns of change.[18]

Cope's views had an impact on his contemporaries. Although Darwin claimed he had trouble understanding Cope's ideas, his work was well received by a number of American and European scientists and social scientists. Princeton scientist Arnold Henry Guyot as well as the British paleontologists Richard Owen and H. G. Seeley praised Cope's discoveries and interpretations.[19] Cope, along with the invertebrate paleontologist Alpheus Hyatt, was one of the first Americans to put forth a comprehensive evolutionary theory. Cope's neo-Lamarckian interpretation provided an explanation for variation, evolution, and inheritance. He constructed meaningful phylogenies for the vast amount of fossil material he discovered. Cope also provided an alternative explanation of the causes of evolution that, unlike Darwin's, was not based on random change and did not smack of materialism. Cope's theory was grounded in a commitment to philosophical idealism and religious belief. His interpretation of evolution as caused by a non-material agent that gave rise to a series of orderly, progressive changes appealed to many late nineteenth-century scientists. Cope's peculiar terminology and specific features of his theory were not widely adopted, but he was the nominal head of a school of American neo-Lamarckians.[20]

Marsh's work attracted even more attention. At Yale College he sponsored fossil-hunting expeditions that yielded magnificent results. In the early 1870s Marsh and student collecting parties discovered birds with teeth, a find that "does much to break down the old distinction between Birds and Reptiles." Leidy referred to Marsh's find as "a most wonderful discovery, and certainly the most interesting yet made in American paleontology."[21] In the 1880s John Bell Hatcher, one of Marsh's leading collectors, found remains of small and rare Mesozoic mammals. Hatcher and other Marsh field hands also found the remains of dinosaurs including *Stegosaurus, Triceratops,* and the huge sauropods *Apatosaurus* and *Diplodocus.* Those were animals unlike any others previously known, and the discoveries enhanced Marsh's reputation and the status of American vertebrate paleontology.[22]

Marsh published descriptions of those specimens that were known for their detail. His monograph on birds with teeth was literally a bone-by-bone description of the specimens *Ichthyornis* and *Hesperornis regalis.* So too were his discussions of the type species *Dinoceras mirabile* in his monograph on the *Dinocerata* (1886) or the specimens in "The Dinosaurs of North America" (1896). His restorations also received much praise. Speaking of Marsh's 1880 monograph on birds with teeth, the Scottish geologist Archibald Geikie claimed: "Never before has it been possible . . . to reconstruct so perfectly so ancient an organism."[23]

Marsh's work also stood out because of its bearing on evolution. Marsh, like Leidy, was primarily a systematist and he rarely examined questions concerning the process or pattern of evolution. Yet the specimens he found and described substantiated evolution. Cope had suggested that birds evolved from reptiles, but Marsh's discoveries of birds with teeth provided the best evidence on that score. His discoveries of fossil horses were even more notable. Between 1870 and 1874 Marsh and student collectors from Yale found over thirty specimens of fossil horses from deposits in the western states and territories. According to Marsh, those fossils indicated "a natural line of descent . . . through the following genera: *Orohippus* of the Eocene; *Miohippus* and *Anchitherium* of the Miocene; *Anchippus, Hipparion, Protohippus,* and *Pliohippus* of the Pliocene; and *Equus.* . . ."[24] It was his collection that led Thomas Henry Huxley, Darwin's most famous advocate, to revise his interpretation and define America, not Europe, as the center of horse evolution. In 1880 Darwin himself proclaimed that Marsh's work was "the best support to the theory of evolution which has appeared within the last 20 years."[25]

Although Leidy, Cope, and Marsh made notable scientific contributions, by the end of the nineteenth century vertebrate paleontology was stagnating. Certainly the deposits they discovered, the collections they amassed, and the studies they produced remained important sources of information for future researchers. But none of those men was able to sustain the level of scientific research and productivity that characterized their work in the 1870s. Although Leidy published some papers on vertebrate paleontology in the last fifteen years of his life, most of his work focused on invertebrates. By the late 1880s Cope was teaching at the University of Pennsylvania, but during that decade and the next he did almost no new fieldwork. For the most part he examined theoretical questions pertaining to evolution and inheritance. Marsh too experienced problems that affected his work. In the 1880s he was the head of the country's largest paleontological laboratory. But by the early 1890s he had lost his government position and his program was considerably reduced.

There were few other individuals who took up where those men left off. Leidy and Cope taught classes at the University of Pennsylvania, but few of their students or associates concentrated on vertebrate paleontology. Marsh did not teach, and only a few of his assistants pursued careers in that field. In addition, the institutions with which these figures were associated, Yale College and the Academy of Natural Sciences, did not provide financial or administrative support for vertebrate paleontology, further reducing the incentive for others to pursue the subject.[26]

The declining status of vertebrate paleontology was in part a result of personality. Cope and Marsh were aggressive individuals and their ambitions to obtain fossils and to dominate vertebrate paleontology resulted in a feud that affected the field for over twenty years.[27] Their strong individualistic tendencies not only produced a head-on clash but also created problems with others at the institutions with which they were associated. For many years Cope was an active member of the Academy of Natural Sciences and the American Philosophical Society, but he had a testy relationship with members of both organizations and kept his fossil collections at his home in Philadelphia. In the 1870s and 1880s he became embroiled in a bitter controversy when he tried to change the academy into a research institution that would support paid professionals. A falling out with the academy leadership led Cope to limit his participation in the organization and reduced his opportunities to publish in its journals. Those problems had a bearing on the academy's failure to purchase his collections or to use the money he left to the institution to appoint a vertebrate paleontologist after his death. By the 1890s the academy, which had been a center for the science three decades before, had become a paleontological backwater.[28]

Marsh had serious troubles with the staff of the large paleontological operation that he ran at the Peabody Museum. In the 1880s some of his collectors, men such as William H. Reed and Fred Brown, complained that Marsh failed to pay them promptly or give them credit in his publications.[29] Marsh's laboratory assistants, principally George Baur and Samuel Wendell Williston, charged that they and other assistants had done much of the research and writing of the government monographs that appeared under Marsh's name. There were complaints that Marsh provided few opportunities for his assistants to publish or to pursue their own careers in vertebrate paleontology. Williston, a student with a bachelor's degree and fieldwork experience from Kansas, came to Yale to do graduate study in vertebrate paleontology. Although he told Marsh that "money is not my object in working[,] but knowledge," Marsh did not permit Williston to publish or pursue independent research and kept him employed as a paid collector. In 1884 Marsh had him removed from the government payroll when Williston complained to Powell that Marsh failed to pay his assistants promptly.[30] John Bell Hatcher experienced similar problems. Hatcher, who provided Marsh with excellent specimens and stratigraphic data, wanted the opportunity to work up his collections and to publish. But from 1884 to 1892 Hatcher spent his years with Marsh in the field. Those incidents and others created resentment toward Marsh, and many of his assistants left New Haven when Cope published their complaints in a newspaper exposé in 1890.[31]

Economics had a bearing on the status of the science. Prior to 1870 most scientists focused their attention on remains from nearby localities. Some like Leidy received specimens at no charge from collectors. The entrance of Cope and Marsh into the field changed all that. Both men had the resources to collect fossils on a full-time basis and to buy specimens. That situation had an impact on Leidy's career. As he told Archibald Geikie, "Formerly, every fossil one found in the states came to me, for nobody else cared about such things; but now Professors Marsh and Cope, with long purses, offer money for what used to come to me for nothing, and in that respect I cannot compete with them." Leidy had also relied on a network of correspondents and collectors, but with few resources those connections dried up. A fossil hunting expedition up the Missouri River in 1873 did not "repay our trouble," he noted. He published on fossils from Florida and other southern states, but those were specimens he received gratis through Francis S. Holmes, Joseph Willcox, and John Wesley Powell. Leidy had little taste for the ambition and combativeness of Cope and Marsh. But, more importantly, economics and the decreasing availability of specimens led him to reduce his research in vertebrate paleontology.[32]

Cope and Marsh covered great distances in examining fossil vertebrate deposits in western states and territories. Travel to and from those locations was expensive, and unearthing, packing, and shipping specimens back to institutions in the East added to the cost. Facilities for the cleaning, preparation, and storage of specimens were also necessary. There were additional costs in producing publications. Many naturalists continued to collect, describe, and display specimens on a limited scale. But few could compete with Cope and Marsh whose far-flung activities were expensive, labor-intensive undertakings.

The Cope-Marsh rivalry had serious economic consequences for Cope. Throughout the 1870s, his private fortune and the opportunities made available through Hayden's survey enabled him to hire collectors and pursue fieldwork. Eventually, however, he ran out of money. Discoveries of dinosaurs by his and Marsh's collectors in Colorado and Wyoming in the late 1870s resulted in a costly rush to obtain specimens. Cope also made a series of poor investments that further depleted his resources.[33] In addition, the creation of the U.S. Geological Survey in 1879 undermined Cope's work. Marsh played a central role in establishing that agency and profited from his association with it. Cope, Marsh's hated rival, had no opportunity to participate in government surveys and, with the demise of Hayden's survey and his *Paleontological Bulletin*, had no ready outlet for publication. To compensate, Cope purchased the *American Naturalist*, but that investment created additional financial strain. By the early 1880s Cope could no longer afford to pay collectors Charles Sternberg or Jacob L. Wortman and was forced to abandon fieldwork. He continued to publish, but on specimens he had already collected and on theoretical issues in biology and paleontology. Although the Academy of Natural Sciences and the Texas Geological Survey provided him with some support for fieldwork in the 1890s, Cope was forced to curtail his paleontological activities.[34]

Economic factors had a crippling impact on Marsh also. In 1892 Congress launched an investigation of government science that brought down Powell's survey and Marsh. Although he was a government scientist, Marsh had been allowed to keep his specimens at Yale, a private institution. Many considered that overt favoritism. In a time of recession, an economy-minded, utilitarian Congress viewed a field like vertebrate paleontology as an unnecessary luxury. While perhaps scientifically interesting, it had no practical applications and therefore no place in government-sponsored science. The 1892 investigation condemned Powell's management and drastically cut the Geological Survey's budget, including Marsh's appropriation. Although Marsh retained a position and small stipend as honorary government vertebrate paleontologist, he had to release most of his assistants and was unable to maintain fieldwork or laboratory work in vertebrate paleontology. He continued to publish, but Marsh's paleontological empire in the 1890s was a shadow of what it had been a decade before.[35]

Marsh had few other personal or institutional resources to fall back on. In addition to the reduction of his government salary, his own finances were in poor shape by the 1890s. The money that the Peabody donation had set aside for research and museum maintenance remained. But Marsh had virtually no personal income. As his cousin Robert Singleton Peabody put it in 1891, the "'estate' is now like a squeezed orange."[36] Since 1866 Marsh had been professor of paleontology, but without salary. In 1896 Marsh for the first time was put on salary by Yale College. That enabled him to supervise some graduate work and to purchase some fossil specimens. But Marsh's salary and benefits came at considerable cost: he had to mortgage his sumptuous home and estate to Yale.[37] As aggressive entrepreneurs, Cope and Marsh had changed the character of vertebrate paleontology, but in their efforts to dominate the field both eventually squandered their fortunes.

Marsh's difficulties point to another factor that affected vertebrate paleontology: it was an expensive, non-utilitarian study that had trouble maintaining a niche in the changing structure of late nineteenth-century American science. Federal sponsorship of science and technology emphasized practical, utilitarian considerations. The new land-grant colleges and agricultural experiment stations created by the Morrill Act in 1862 would use the nation's natural resources to foster economic development through agriculture, mining, and engineering. With the creation of the U.S. Department of Agriculture in that same year, the government promoted research in botany, horticulture, and soil sciences as a means to achieve greater productivity.[38] Geology, too, stressed empirical science and practical needs. From 1867 to 1878 four competing government surveys gathered information on minerals, land forms, average rainfall, and other data that might have a bearing on settlement and economic development. Under Clarence King, and again after the downfall of John Wesley Powell, the U.S. Geological Survey emphasized economic geology, mining, and hydrology. Vertebrate paleontology was important in relationship to taxonomy and evolutionary biology. There was little reason for the government to support such a field, and after 1892 it did so only through the Smithsonian Institution and, for a time, when Osborn and his supporters at the American Museum bore much of the expense for the work in the science.[39]

Vertebrate paleontology also failed to gain a strong foothold in the changing system of American higher education. Many colleges and universities possessed collections that included extinct animals and offered courses in geology or biology that included paleontology. But few schools had the resources or the interest to finance field parties to travel to important deposits or to maintain large collections. With the creation of new departments and disciplines, the question of where or whether to include vertebrate paleontology was a problem in some academic institutions. [40]

In addition, educational developments emphasized utilitarian objectives. The land-grant colleges emphasized applied sciences. Other institutions like Harvard, Johns Hopkins, and the University of Chicago did not explicitly emphasize practical studies but still catered to the interests of their constituents, who were frequently philanthropists with business interests. Such emphases influenced the development of the science curriculum. MIT, Yale's Sheffield Scientific School, and Columbia's School of Mines established flourishing programs in economic geology, petrology, and invertebrate paleontology. New biology departments were created at Hopkins, Columbia, and Chicago. In those contexts vertebrate paleontology had limited pedagogical relevance. A course in historical geology was valuable for budding geologists or invertebrate paleontologists. Courses on evolution and comparative anatomy benefited biology students and those intent on a career in medicine. Beyond these possibilities, however, vertebrate paleontology had no other applications and was largely ancillary to emerging educational interests and emphases. [41]

Perhaps most important in explaining the declining fortunes of vertebrate paleontology were the changes occurring in the biological sciences. In the years 1860–80 vertebrate paleontology was one of the chief supports of morphology. Leidy, Cope, and Marsh all contributed to the effort to document structural change, define ancestral and intermediate forms, and suggest phylogenetic relationships. By the late nineteenth century, however, morphology was being challenged by experimental biology, a very different sort of enterprise. Paleontologists relied on fieldwork, collections, and comparative analysis of organic structure to document changes. Those scientists and other morphologists employed historical explanations, either evolution or the presumed relationship between development and evolution, to account for change. To experimentalists, however, those were not adequate explanations. Experimental biology, derived largely from work in physics, chemistry, and physiology, employed different materials, methods, and forms of explanation. Experimentalists emphasized the testing of specific questions or hypotheses through the manipulation of organisms or conditions. Rather than relying on fieldwork or the study of large specimen collections, they experimented with easily manipulable organisms in laboratories. [42] Experimental biology did not overthrow or entirely supplant morphology;

questions about structure remained important to research in experimental embryology and other fields. Problems pertaining to taxonomy and evolution continued to interest a number of scientists. But biologists coming to the fore in the late nineteenth century increasingly emphasized new approaches. In newly emerging university departments and new disciplinary societies, morphology, including paleontology, was pushed to the periphery.[43]

Experimental biology, in contrast to more traditional fields, expanded because it provided new insights into biological problems. By posing specific hypotheses that could be tested, biologists were able to obtain specific answers. By puncturing developing embryos or exposing them to changing conditions, embryologists were able to isolate factors that influenced individual growth. Scientists using improved microscopes and aniline dyes were able to determine the stages of cellular replication and division. Using carefully cultured plants or animals, scientists conducted breeding experiments that laid the foundations for classical genetics. In those areas and others, experimental biology yielded exciting and important breakthroughs that provided the means for understanding many basic biological processes.[44]

Those same developments did not occur in paleontology. It was difficult to separate the study of evolution and extinction into discrete questions that could readily be tested by experiment. As research in experimental biology indicated that hormones, or chromosomes, or proteins were responsible for important biological processes, scientists claimed that the examination of external structural characters, in the case of paleontology fossilized skeletal hard parts, had little significance. Experimental biologists were interested in causal, not historical, explanations, and by the early twentieth century some viewed the evolutionary interpretations of paleontologists as speculative and untenable. Systematics, the description and classification of specimens, held little interest for the new generation of biologists. The claims of some experimentalists like T. H. Morgan were exaggerated and a number of biologists retained an interest in the study of structure as well as function. But with a lack of testable ideas, the use of old tools, and an emphasis on external characters that entailed inference or speculation in accounting for biological processes, research that focused exclusively on morphology held little explanatory value or promise.[45]

Vertebrate paleontology was not able to compete effectively with the new emphases in biology. Many colleges maintained their collections, and around the turn of the century a number of new college museums were established. Yet it is questionable to what extent the collections in those museums were used by students. Courses on biology and geology included material on fossil vertebrates, but few students chose or were encouraged to choose that subject as a field of specialization. At Yale, where over fifty students obtained Ph.D. degrees in geology between 1900 and 1925, only three specialized in vertebrate paleontology. At Columbia University where 144 Ph.D. degrees were granted in zoology in the years 1895–1942, fourteen were in vertebrate paleontology. The story was much the same at Princeton, the University of Chicago, the University of California at Berkeley, and other schools. As an expensive, impractical, and traditional field that did not meet the changing methodological and explanatory demands of science, vertebrate paleontology became a marginal subject at institutions of American higher education.[46]

By the early twentieth century, vertebrate paleontology continued only at a few institutions where it had financial support and served social and political objectives. At Yale, where money from George Peabody's donation provided research and maintenance funds for the subject, Marsh's successors Charles Emerson Beecher, Charles Schuchert, and Richard Swann Lull made the Peabody Museum a center for public education through the exhibition of fossil specimens. At Kansas, which possessed good fossiliferous deposits, research for fossil vertebrates received support because those specimens demonstrated the historical and scientific significance of the products of the state. At the University of Nebraska, E. H. Barbour developed an active program in vertebrate paleontology, but support for it rested on Barbour's research on mineral and geological deposits in the state. Funding for Barbour's program and a museum came largely from Charles H. Morrill, a University of Nebraska regent who emphasized the significance of fossils as important examples of the state's history. At the University of California at Berkeley, Annie Montague Alexander, amateur naturalist who was also heiress to a sugar fortune, supported John C. Merriam's researches in vertebrate paleontology for some of the same reasons.[47]

Large public museums equipped with financial support and dedicated to public education became the most important centers for vertebrate paleontology. In the 1890s two of the nation's wealthiest men, Andrew Carnegie and Marshall Field, established museums in Pittsburgh and Chicago, respectively. Both were interested in public education, and Carnegie wanted to develop a large museum with dramatic mountings of dinosaurs. Having read of the reopening of Marsh's quarries near Como Bluff, Wyoming, Carnegie devoted money and manpower to finding one of the gigantic sauropods from those deposits. The discovery of *Di-*

plodocus carnegiei in 1899 amply fulfilled that objective, and Carnegie channeled thousands of dollars toward mounting the specimen and having duplicate casts made for museums around the world. At the Carnegie and other museums, vertebrate paleontology served a social objective: to educate and entertain the public. That was the bedrock on which a program of fieldwork and research in vertebrate paleontology was sustained.[48]

Osborn established a program that surpassed all of those, though his success illustrates that a concern with more than scientific questions was necessary to sustain vertebrate paleontology. Starting at Princeton in the 1880s, Osborn focused on vertebrate paleontology as a dimension of morphology that could provide insights into evolution. But he developed a program that drew upon and appealed to existing interests and resources at that institution. Ties to wealthy friends, scientific colleagues, and a college president interested in evolution as a support for religion, provided backing for vertebrate paleontology. In later years, when vertebrate paleontology was more marginal, Osborn was even more successful. At New York's American Museum of Natural History he developed a program that encompassed the study of fossil mammals and reptiles from throughout the world. In his own work Osborn was able to examine a wide range of biological and geological questions pertaining to vertebrate paleontology.

Osborn's program flourished not because of an inherent scientific interest in vertebrate paleontology but because of who he was and how he promoted himself and his interests. Osborn was a wealthy man who realized that extensive financial support was necessary to pursue vertebrate paleontology on a large scale. Unlike Cope and Marsh he did not rely entirely on his or his family's money to develop the field. Rather he cultivated close personal relationships with many of the museum's leading patrons, administrators, and scientists. He also adopted the values and ideals of Morris K. Jesup, J. P. Morgan, and other leaders of the American Museum.

Osborn was not alone in developing a program in vertebrate paleontology. Nor was he unique in developing a program that reflected the interests of wealthy and powerful entrepreneurs; the Carnegie Museum emphasized dinosaur paleontology because of Andrew Carnegie's enthusiasm for the subject. Osborn, however, developed a much larger and more multifaceted program than vertebrate paleontologists elsewhere. It was a program that embodied not only his scientific interests, but also the social and political values of a New York elite to which he belonged. For the American Museum trustees, fossil vertebrates were important because they were rare, valuable, and visible facts. Jesup and others hoped that, in addition to providing entertainment, fossils could convey to the public important lessons about nature. Osborn embraced those objectives and directed his department and his own research along those lines. In that way he was able to develop a major program in what had become a peripheral field of scientific inquiry.

2 Osborn, Scott, and Paleontology at Princeton

Henry Fairfield Osborn first developed an interest in science, including vertebrate paleontology and evolutionary biology, at Princeton College. As a student and later a professor at Princeton in the 1870s and 1880s, he participated in the expanding interest in and opportunities for science at the college. Under the leadership of the president, James McCosh, Princeton developed undergraduate and graduate programs in the sciences as well as increased facilities for scientific research. McCosh was a deeply religious man who sought to integrate science with religion both in the Princeton curriculum and in his own studies in psychology and evolution. His social and religious emphases reinforced the training that Osborn had received at home, and his interest in scientific and philosophical questions whetted Osborn's intellectual appetite. The ethos for scientific study at Princeton had an important bearing on Osborn's work. In addition, he looked to administrators, family, and friends to support that work. At Princeton, Osborn established networks that would promote him and his science and developed a means of operating that would influence his later efforts in New York.

Osborn: Education and Opportunity at Princeton

Osborn was born in 1857 into a wealthy and prominent New York family. His mother, Virginia Reed Sturges, was the daughter of Jonathan Sturges, a prosperous New York merchant. Osborn's father, William Henry Osborn, was an enterprising man who had made a fortune in the shipping business at the age of thirty-one. In the early 1850s he joined with Sturges in taking control of the Illinois Central Railroad. As president of the company, William Osborn transformed a business that was in bad financial straits into one of the country's leading and most important railroads. In the process he acquired a fortune and became a well-known figure in New York business circles. The railroad, as well as Castle Rock, the palatial home that he constructed at Garrison in the Hudson River highlands, were William Osborn's monuments to a successful business career.[1]

The Osborns were a religious family and raised their children with a strong sense of moral and social obligation. Osborn's parents were both brought up on strict Scottish Presbyterianism, and Osborn's mother maintained that tradition in her household. The young Osborn grew up in a family that studied the Bible, attended church regularly, and endowed its social activities with religious commitment. Virginia Osborn was active in a number of charitable organizations and viewed her efforts as a form of moral stewardship. When Henry inherited $30,000 from his maternal grandfather at age twenty-one, his mother impressed upon him the importance of using that money in socially and religiously constructive ways.[2]

William Osborn had an equally strong impact on his son. Though less religious than his wife, William Osborn instructed his son in the social obligations that went along with great wealth. Osborn wanted Henry to learn about business and hoped that eventually his son would take command of the railroad system he had developed. William Osborn, who donated money to hospitals, nursing schools, and other causes, tried to impress upon his son the importance of using wealth and position in ways that were socially constructive.[3] By the 1880s, when it became apparent that Henry would pursue a career in science, not business, his father still emphasized the need for him to engage in activities that would win community support and respect.

Osborn's education reflected his family's interests. Following his early training at New York preparatory schools, Osborn entered the College of New Jersey (subsequently Princeton University) in 1873. Founded in 1746, Princeton was a conservative institution both socially and intellectually. Drawing from a population of students of Scottish and English ancestry whose families had settled in New York, New Jersey, and the southern states, Princeton had a homogeneous social composition. It was also a bastion of Scottish Calvinism.[4] Those traditions persisted throughout the nineteenth century and were evident in the administration of James McCosh.

James McCosh came to Princeton from Scotland where he was raised in a Protestant evangelical tradition. Following his early training, he became a popular and respected Presbyterian minister. In the 1850s he published a study in natural theology that explained animal form and function in terms of the creator's handiwork. His commitment to Presbyterian religious traditions fit in with the priorities at Princeton. As president of the college from 1868 to 1888, McCosh retained the school's emphasis on religious instruction and daily attendance at chapel. He even brought revivals to campus.[5]

McCosh was also a philosopher in the Scottish Enlightenment tradition who examined questions about government, education, and science. In addition to his work in natural theology, he pursued studies on the mind, vision, and the nature of the educational process. As his most recent biographer, J. David Hoeveler, Jr., has noted: "McCosh inherited from his Scottish philosophical predecessors not only the introspective method of that school but the faculty psychology that characterized its analysis of the human constitution. By this approach the mind was divided into its several components or 'faculties,' and mental philosophy became the science of these faculties, the nature of each and its interaction with the other parts."[6] McCosh believed in the traditional view that education entailed disciplining and improving a student's mental and moral faculties.

McCosh was not a reformer in the same manner as contemporary college presidents Charles W. Eliot at Harvard or Daniel Coit Gilman at Johns Hopkins.[7] Still McCosh instituted a number of reforms that affected academic life at Princeton and influenced Osborn. Soon after becoming president, McCosh launched an investigation of the college and found it sorely lacking in many areas. Not only was the Princeton faculty inbred and underpaid, but campus buildings and physical facilities were "positively unhealthy."[8] He examined the curriculum and emphasized the need to develop a modern educational program that included courses in language, literature, history, and the sciences. He did not follow Eliot in doing away with a core curriculum, but McCosh developed a program based on "a groundwork of required courses with a super-structure of electives for training in special fields."[9] The elective system went into effect at Princeton in the 1870s, and by the end of the decade McCosh had established postgraduate courses.[10]

McCosh also promoted the sciences at Princeton. The noted American physicist Joseph Henry began his work at Princeton, and Arnold Henry Guyot, a leading geographer and geologist, was a member of the faculty when McCosh became president. But McCosh claimed that the physical facilities for science were "in a very defective state," and science classes continued to be taught by recitation without experiments or laboratory work.[11] He hired several new faculty members, including Charles Macloskie in biology, Cyrus Fogg Brackett in physics, and Charles Augustus Young in astronomy. McCosh's emphasis on specialized training in the sciences led a wealthy alumnus, John C. Green, to establish a school of science in 1873.

The Green School was not a separate institution designed for professional education; rather it was closely tied to the academic department at Princeton.[12] Maintaining that education must be "fitted to enlarge the mind and to keep it from becoming narrow and one sided," McCosh made certain that the program leading to a bachelor of science degree included classes from the traditional course, and vice versa. His courses on philosophy, psychology, and physiological psychology examined conceptual and scientific issues in the context of religious belief. Guyot's courses on geography and geology emphasized how science could be employed to support the biblical account of creation. McCosh's and Guyot's conviction that a modern education must include sound training in religion ensured that the work in the sciences was tempered by humanistic study.[13]

McCosh's initiatives spurred additional efforts to promote science at Princeton. In 1873 William Libbey, a New York banker and Princeton trustee, donated money for a natural history museum and made Arnold Guyot its director. Libbey's contribution enabled Guyot to expand his research and develop a center for science at Princeton.[14] Guyot had amassed a collection of boulders from Switzerland, as well as fossils and artifacts from Europe and America. With the money from Libbey, he began to collect more specimens and to arrange them systematically.

Like other college administrators and teachers of the time, Guyot purchased specimens from Henry A. Ward, the natural history dealer in Rochester, New York. Guyot wanted synoptic collections that could be used to instruct students and to provide an overview of the earth's geological and biological history.[15] Guyot also wanted the museum to include large displays, and in 1874 he brought to Princeton the artist Benjamin Waterhouse Hawkins, who had constructed the first dinosaur restorations in England in 1854. Hawkins had recently mounted a specimen of the dinosaur *Hadrosaurus foulki* at the Academy of Natural Sciences. At Princeton he put up a cast of *Hadrosaurus* and produced seventeen water color paintings of prehistoric life.[16] In addition, Guyot hired Franklin C. Hill, a naturalist trained at Ward's and well versed in the preparation and mounting of specimens. From 1876 to 1890 Hill served as the museum curator and mounted over thirty specimens of fossil vertebrates.[17]

The new opportunities at Princeton had a significant impact on Osborn and his classmate William Berryman Scott. Neither Osborn nor Scott had planned a scientific career, and they did not follow the course of study leading to a bachelor of science degree. But both benefited from the elective system that made science classes available to students in the traditional program of study. Scott claimed that his junior year was a "complete change of atmosphere from the lower class . . . and I seemed to be entering new and more spacious worlds when I took up physics with Dr. Brackett, psychology with Dr. McCosh, logic with Dr. Atwater, geology with Dr. Guyot, and, above all, English literature with Dr. Murray."[18] Guyot's geology course, which Osborn and Scott took in the Spring of 1876, inspired them to make their first geological expedition through the Catskill Mountains that summer. Soon after they took part in a larger endeavor: the Princeton Scientific Expedition of 1877. Osborn and Scott initiated the idea for such a trip, McCosh officially sanctioned it, and Libbey provided most of the financial backing. After the trip Libbey offered additional sponsorship. The collections from the expedition of 1877 and another in 1878 required room for storage and study, and with Libbey's support the museum obtained additional space in Princeton's Nassau Hall. Libbey also underwrote a project to subsidize new faculty positions and graduate followships in science.[19]

McCosh had long been interested in expanding and improving the Princeton faculty. At first he hoped to hire professors who had earned degrees elsewhere, but that scheme met with opposition from the trustees. He then set his sights on preparing Princeton students for academic careers. In 1877 he inaugurated a postgraduate course in philosophy. He also encouraged students to pursue additional coursework, preferably in Europe, with the possibility that postgraduate study might lead to a faculty position at Princeton. Osborn, Scott, and Libbey's son, William Libbey, Jr., were members of that first postgraduate class. To promote his son's interests and further opportunities for science at Princeton, Libbey built a university hotel whose profits would create a permanent endowment for the museum, faculty positions, and student fellowships. The plan eventually failed, largely because the hotel was a financial loss. However, in the late 1870s Libbey's money allowed for expansion of the E. M. Museum of Geology and Archaeology and endowed a position for Libbey, Jr., as vice director of the museum.[20] McCosh's reforms and Libbey's donations also benefited Scott and Osborn.

Osborn, Scott, and McCosh

Following their graduation in 1877, Scott and Osborn became more closely associated with McCosh. In addition to spending that academic year preparing the specimens from the scientific expedition, they took McCosh's postgraduate course and participated in informal discussion groups "which Dr. McCosh employed to raise the level of intellectual life at Princeton to a truly university standard."[21] Scott noted that McCosh's overbearing manner toward them as undergraduates quickly disappeared and was replaced by warm affection and a close working relationship. As members of the first postgraduate class, Scott and Osborn were among those "bright young men" whom McCosh hoped to prepare for faculty positions at Princeton.[22]

Scott profited first from McCosh's efforts. Following a year of postgraduate work at Princeton, he went abroad and studied comparative anatomy with T. H. Huxley in London and embryology with Francis Maitland Balfour in Cambridge. He later completed a Ph.D. degree in comparative anatomy at Carl Gegenbaur's laboratory in Heidelberg, Germany. Osborn's father contributed financially to Scott's education abroad, but it was McCosh who had encouraged Scott to pursue graduate study and prodded him to complete the Ph.D. With money from the Libbey endowment, McCosh and Guyot appointed Scott as Guyot's assistant in geology in 1880.[23]

Osborn also took advantage of those opportunities. At McCosh's urging he spent the academic year 1877–78 doing postgraduate study and completing work on the specimens collected during the 1877 expedition. In 1878 he took courses in anatomy and physiology from William Henry Welch and John Call Dalton in New York. Early the next year he joined Scott in England and gained a sound training in embryology and comparative anatomy from Balfour and Huxley. Osborn's postgraduate education was interrupted in the spring of 1880, but eventually McCosh and Scott were able to bring him back to Princeton. Offered the first E. M. Fellowship in Biology and promised a faculty position, Osborn quickly completed his Sc.D. degree at Princeton and was appointed assistant professor of natural science in 1881.[24]

Osborn developed a close relationship with McCosh that influenced his academic career and scientific work. He participated in the scientific discussion and interest groups that McCosh promoted, and from 1883 to 1886 Osborn and Scott participated with McCosh in teaching a course on physiological psychology. Osborn and McCosh also collaborated on studies of the brain, vision, and memory. McCosh encouraged research and promoted research opportunities that enabled Osborn to carve out a scientific career.[25]

William Osborn also had an impact on his son's career. He had fully expected Henry to go into the family business and for a time opposed his son's interest in pursuing a scientific career. In 1877 the two quarreled over Henry's decision to continue scientific work after graduation. When Princeton planned a second scientific expedition for the summer of 1878, William Osborn refused to let his son participate unless a prominent scientist were appointed to lead the trip.[26] When Scott, studying in England, wrote and asked Osborn to join him, William Osborn accused Scott of "interferring with his plans for his son and in making mischief generally." Entreaties from a family friend and the English anatomist W. Kitchen Parker convinced Osborn's father to allow Henry to study abroad. But in the spring of 1880 Osborn was called home to help administer his father's recent acquisition of the Chicago, Nashville, and New Orleans Railroad. Eventually McCosh's overtures and the offers of the E. M. Fellowship and a faculty position at Princeton led William Osborn to accede to his son's plans, although he continued to exert his influence.[27]

Although William Osborn had little interest in Princeton or the educational reforms occurring there, he contributed to his son's new career. He provided financial support for McCosh's efforts to improve the college library and to create student and faculty discussion clubs.[28] The elder Osborn also apparently paid at least part of his son's salary. In his first two years as a faculty member, Osborn continued to hold the E. M. Fellowship in Biology, but his salary of $1,000 was far below Scott's. More than once he asked his father to change the arrangement concerning his salary so that he would be on a par with other faculty. At one point he even threatened to resign over the issue.[29] In 1884 when Libbey's university hotel project failed and money was no longer available to maintain the fellowships, faculty positions, and possibly the museum Libbey had endowed, William Osborn apparently took over full payment of his son's salary. That money and Osborn's income from his grandfather's legacy sustained his academic position. It also enabled him to finance work in vertebrate paleontology after the collapse of the Libbey endowment.[30]

William Osborn had some influence on what kind of scientific career his son should pursue. William Osborn was uncertain about Henry's decision to become an academic in Princeton, both an occupation and a location where he had few contacts and little influence. He wanted to make sure his son developed a career that would be socially useful and maintain the family prestige. As benefactor and counselor, William Osborn encouraged his son to develop a career in which he would be more than just a common tiller of the scientific soil. In addition to teaching and research, his son should use his financial resources and position to create networks of support, develop new large-scale projects, and coordinate the work of others on those projects. That way of thinking and operating, perhaps as much as his academic education, influenced Osborn's scientific career in Princeton and later in New York.[31]

Osborn and Science at Princeton

As new faculty members in the early 1880s, Osborn and Scott sought to promote themselves, their field of science, and their college. Both identified themselves as biologists and in addition to developing new courses at Princeton they became actively involved with the small but expanding group of American biologists. Older figures such as Alexander Agassiz and E. L. Mark at Harvard and A. E. Verrill at Yale had held positions in biology for several years. But the educational reforms of the 1870s produced the first group of American students trained specifically in biology. Under the leadership of William Keith Brooks and H. Newell Martin, the biology department at Johns Hopkins created a leading program and graduated the first American Ph.D.s in the science.[32] Osborn and Scott worked with those and other individuals to establish new foundations for biology. In 1883 both answered the invitation from Samuel F. Clarke to become charter members of the Eastern Society of Naturalists, later the American Society of Naturalists. By 1884 Osborn was helping to run that organization and the biology section of the American Association for the Advancement of Science.[33] Osborn and Scott also hoped to use the money from William Libbey to develop a biological journal, to assist Spencer Fullerton Baird in establishing a biological station and aquarium at Woods Hole, Massachusetts, and to promote other ventures.[34] When Libbey's endowment plan collapsed in 1884, Osborn played a major role in financing and promoting those developments. An effort to inaugurate a morphological journal attests to his objectives.

In 1884 Osborn told the English biologist E. B. Poulton that he was interested in starting a journal of morphology. At the time there were few opportunities to publish in that field. The *American Journal of Science* and *Science* were general periodicals that reported on developments in all the sciences. The *Journal of the American Microscopical Society* was a specialized technical publication, while the *American Naturalist* published papers on almost any subject in the broad domain of natural history. Osborn, with support from Scott and financial backing from his father, proposed a journal that would publish articles on comparative anatomy, plant and animal morphology, paleontology, histology, and embryology "but will exclude all systematic, historical, and purely descriptive work."[35] He approached a number of scientists on the subject including E. L. Mark who, along with Alexander Agassiz's assistant Charles Otis Whitman, was trying to establish an organization for "cooperation in embryological work between a few persons who have its interests most at heart." Although Osborn's journal plans, which presented difficulties for Mark and Whitman, foundered, in the late 1880s Osborn enthusiastically supported Whitman's ventures for developing the *Journal of Morphology* and the Marine Biological Laboratory at Woods Hole.[36]

Osborn and Scott had greater success in developing opportunities for their interests at Princeton. Scott's appointment was in geology and Osborn's in comparative anatomy, and each taught a variety of courses in those subjects. They also collaborated in teaching. Osborn's introductory course in embryology complemented Scott's advanced class on that subject. Osborn performed anatomical demonstrations and dissections on recent vertebrates that were part of Scott's paleontology class. Both taught physiological psychology, a course that originated from one of Osborn's presentations to the Wundt Club, an organization for the study of problems in psychology. They were also members of the Princeton Scientific Club, an organization established in 1877, and both participated in library, discussion, and artistic clubs on campus. Through their involvement in teaching, research, and a variety of informal activities, Osborn and Scott took an active part in the scientific and intellectual life at Princeton.[37]

Osborn was also successful in developing new facilities for the sciences at Princeton. Although George Macloskie had taught biology at the college since 1873, it was only in 1881, Osborn's first year on the job, that a small building referred to as the morphological laboratory was set up for teaching and research in biology. Osborn played a role in obtaining a larger laboratory. In 1886 he wrote to Moses Taylor Pyne, the president of the Princeton Board of Trustees and a close friend and classmate who took an interest in Osborn's and Scott's activities. Osborn pointed out that the science faculty needed a larger, more modern, and better equipped facility. In 1887 the Class of 1877 Biological Laboratory was completed and included lecture rooms and laboratory facilities for morphology, embryology, and physiological psychology. As Scott once noted, the laboratory was designed especially for those subjects that Osborn taught and on which he and his students conducted research.[38]

Osborn developed and supervised research programs on the subjects that captured his interest. Much of Osborn's early work was in embryology. Trained by Huxley and Balfour, he was interested in the morphological issues that dominated biology in the 1870s and 1880s. Like so many other biologists of the time, he concentrated on describing and tracing the development of the germ layers as a means for determining homologies and establishing the phylogenetic relationships that underscored evolution.[39] Part of his work focused on establishing homologies among the cranial nerves and commissures of vertebrates. In another line of research he employed embryology to document the evolutionary relationship between marsupials and placental mammals. He maintained that the embryonic marsupial yolk sac performed the same function as the allantois among placental mammals, and that villi distributed over the yolk sac conveyed nutriments from the mother to the fetus. However, his work was not very successful.

In 1886, in light of other investigations, Osborn retracted his views on the marsupial yolk sac and admitted that he did not possess the technical facility for doing research in embryology and neuroanatomy.[40] Although Osborn formally abandoned research in those fields in the mid 1880s, he continued to maintain an interest in embryology and neuroanatomy. At Princeton he supervised graduate students, including Henry Orr, Isaac Nakagawa, Oliver S. Strong, and Charles F. W. Maclure, who focused their research on the development and evolution of cranial nerves.[41] The study of embryology, which led Osborn to recognize that individual development followed well defined patterns, also had a bearing on the interpretation of evolution that he put forth in later years.

Although Osborn continued to direct his students' investigations in embryology and neuroanatomy, he increasingly focused his attention on vertebrate paleontology. He had previously done research and published articles in that subject,[42] but in his early years Osborn was not committed to devoting his career to vertebrate paleontology. In 1878, when Osborn first began to consider a career in science, Albert Bickmore, a family friend and the superintendent of the American Museum of Natural History, offered him a position as assistant curator in the museum's geology department. Osborn turned down the position, claiming that Cope and Marsh stood like Scylla and Charybdis over the field.[43] Instead he pursued graduate work in morphology and became interested in the study of development. At Princeton it was Scott, not Osborn, who taught paleontology and conducted fossil hunting expeditions. Although Osborn provided anatomical demonstrations for Scott's courses, other problems occupied his time and interest. But in 1885, recognizing his limitations for doing effective research in embryology and neuro-anatomy, Osborn turned his attention to vertebrate paleontology. Moving into another field of inquiry, he sought to develop a program of research by relying on his access to financial resources and by establishing a close working relationship with Scott and Cope.

Osborn, Scott, and Cope

In 1885 when Osborn shifted his attention to vertebrate paleontology, he took advantage of resources to establish himself as an important figure in the field. One of the first things he did was to establish a closer working relationship with Scott. By the mid-1880s Osborn and Scott had had a close personal and professional relationship for almost a decade. As students at Princeton and abroad they had worked together in classes, in the laboratory, and in the field. As faculty members they had cooperated in teaching classes, participating in discussion groups, and in general promoting science at Princeton. As young professional biologists they had reached out to others in the field and sought to establish new institutions. When he turned to vertebrate paleontology, Osborn proposed that he and Scott coauthor a textbook on North American fossil vertebrates.[44] By that time Scott had begun to acquire a reputation in the field. In addition to teaching the subject and conducting successful field operations, he had published a number of papers on extinct animals. Osborn, who had less of a background and reputation in vertebrate paleontology, would profit from a partnership with Scott.

In order to concentrate on and obtain more training in vertebrate paleontology, Osborn reduced his academic commitments. In 1885–86 he took a leave of absence from Princeton and studied in Karl Alfred von Zittel's paleontological laboratory in Munich. Working with Max Schlosser, one of von Zittel's recent Ph.D. students, Osborn gained experience in mammalian paleontology.[45] Toward the end of his time abroad, Osborn, acting on advice from his father, decided that on his return to Princeton he would devote less time to teaching and more to research. In May 1886 he asked the board of trustees for a reduction in his teaching load and for improved laboratory facilities. He continued to teach advanced courses, but Osborn's "salary" now went to assistants who took responsibility for the laboratory and demonstration work in those courses.[46]

Osborn's financial resources enabled him not only to reduce his teaching obligations but also to employ others to aid his work in vertebrate paleontology. Although Scott had successfully conducted courses and summer expeditions since the early 1880s, the collapse of the Libbey endowment raised questions about Scott's salary and the employment of the museum preparator Franklin C. Hill. With money from Osborn and Osborn's family, Princeton retained Hill's services. In addition, Osborn made modest increases in the facilities and staff necessary to do work in vertebrate paleontology. On his return from Germany, Osborn brought with him Rudolph Weber, an artist and preparator whom he hired to do the line drawings of specimens, a task Osborn had previously done himself. He also hired collectors to obtain specimens from western states and territories.[47]

At Princeton, Osborn developed a small program in vertebrate paleontology in which he operated in a supervisory capacity. Just as he directed the research of graduate students in neuroanatomy, he oversaw the work of Hill, Weber, and others. He rarely participated in field expeditions, but examined specimens collected by Scott, Scott's students, and paid collectors. Osborn's work in vertebrate paleontology consisted almost entirely of research and publication. He studied fossil materials collected and prepared by others and played a limited role in associated work in the field, laboratory, and classroom. In establishing a career in vertebrate paleontology, Osborn drew upon the source materials and expertise that Scott and various paid assistants could provide.[48]

Osborn also developed a closer working relationship with Cope, one of the leading vertebrate paleontologists in the United States. Through Guyot, who had good relations with Cope, Leidy, and other Philadelphia scientists, Osborn and Scott had received some assistance from Cope early on in their careers.[49] But Osborn's association and correspondence with Cope really date from 1885, when he seriously began to devote his attention to vertebrate paleontology. In the spring of that year Osborn consulted with Cope on questions concerning the hiring of collectors, new discoveries in vertebrate paleontology, and a variety of other issues pertaining to work in that field.[50] For Osborn, Cope, even more than Scott, represented an experienced figure whose knowledge and expertise would serve him well as he sought to pursue research in vertebrate paleontology. Indeed, Osborn and Scott became disciples of Cope: they investigated the questions that Cope considered important and for a time adopted his interpretation of evolution and inheritance. The Princetonians also supported Cope in his ongoing feud with Marsh.

By the mid-1880s Marsh had effectively beaten Cope in the battle to achieve predominance in American vertebrate paleontology. Appointed government paleontologist of the U.S. Geological Survey in 1882, Marsh augmented his personal fortune with a hefty government appropriation. At Yale he directed a laboratory of well over a dozen assistants and maintained several paid collectors in the field. The federal government supported his research projects and provided him a ready outlet for his publications. By contrast, Cope's financial resources were depleted and he had no basis of institutional support. A bitter, frustrated man, he grasped at any opportunity to defame Marsh. Thus in the summer of 1885, when he learned that Marsh's assistants were complaining of the lack of opportunities to pursue their own work and the lack of credit they received for work published under Marsh's name, Cope initiated an attack against Marsh and the Geological Survey.[51] Cope engaged Osborn and Scott in that effort.

The Princetonians willingly assisted Cope in his campaign against Marsh. Both Scott and Osborn claimed that Marsh, unlike Cope, had rebuffed their request for assistance on paleontological work in the late 1870s. Scott also claimed that Marsh had once paid a railroad agent to ship a carload of fossils, originally bound for Princeton, to New Haven.[52] In the fall of 1885, soon after Cope had informed Osborn and Scott of the problems at Yale, Scott traveled to New Haven and interviewed Marsh's assistants. At the time, Osborn was studying in Munich where he obtained additional information with which to defame "the great man."

The previous year von Zittel, in response to a request from Marsh, had sent three recent graduates to New Haven, all of whom had problems with their host. Two of those assistants, George Baur and Otto Meyer, were still at Yale. The third, Max Schlosser, had returned to Munich and told von Zittel, Osborn, and others of his complaints against Marsh. Through von Zittel and through Baur's parents, Osborn learned of Baur's financial indebtedness to Marsh and its impact on his work and state of mind.[53]

Scott and Cope hoped that Osborn could provide economic and political assistance in the fight against Marsh. Scott told Osborn that Princeton could certainly profit by hiring Berger, Marsh's principal artist, and Baur, an expert on fossil reptiles. Cope hoped that Osborn could prevail upon William B. Allison, an Osborn family friend and the Iowa senator on the congressional committee investigating the Geological Survey, to wield his political influence to undermine Marsh.[54]

Osborn's role in the attack on Marsh would have short- as well as long-term consequences. Cope and Scott were eager to bring out a pamphlet or statement exposing Marsh, but Osborn urged caution. Osborn was not supportive of Marsh, but he realized the potential hazards of attacking the man who was president of the National Academy of Sciences and vertebrate paleontologist of the Geological Survey. Rather than publishing an exposé, he wrote a private letter on Cope's behalf in 1886.[55] He offered moral, but not financial, support to Baur and established good relations with Alexander Agassiz, director of Harvard's Museum of Comparative Zoology, who disliked Marsh.[56] Osborn did not play an overt role in the effort to undermine Marsh, and for a year or so the men exchanged information and specimens. But by 1887, when Marsh learned of Osborn's behind-the-scenes activities, they had a serious falling out. In later years, as Osborn became better established and attempted to gain a dominant position in American vertebrate paleontology, he worked to bring down Marsh.

Osborn, Scott, and Evolution

Osborn worked closely with Scott and Cope to develop a program of scientific research. Much of his embryological work had focused on amphibians and reptiles, but Osborn now joined Scott in pursuing research on fossil mammals. In addition to their project for a textbook on fossil mammals, the two collaborated on researching and writing several articles. For a paper on fossil mammals from the White River Miocene they journeyed together to Philadelphia and Cambridge to examine collections. They divided material for study and analyzed each other's work for joint publication. They also authored a joint monograph on the fossil mammalia of the Uintah formation: Scott wrote the sections on geology and the systematics of artiodactyls (even-toed ungulate mammals); Osborn wrote on perissodactyls (odd-toed ungulate mammals).[57] While each provided morphological and taxonomic information on the extinct animals they examined, Osborn and Scott concentrated on the study of evolutionary questions pertaining to fossil vertebrates.

Osborn's and Scott's interest in the theoretical problems of vertebrate paleontology derived from the influence of their mentors. Evolutionary questions were central to the training they had received from Huxley and Balfour. Most of their coursework with Huxley focused on comparative morphology, but the underlying emphasis was on determining homologies, hence establishing evolutionary relationships. Balfour's course also entailed the study of evolutionary problems. Balfour, like many other nineteenth-century biologists, accepted the doctrine that ontogeny recapitulates phylogeny. Consequently, evolutionary concerns were central to Osborn's training in and study of embryology.[58]

McCosh too had an impact on their views. McCosh was a philosopher and a divine more than a scientist, but he had studied morphology and organic change. His work was in the natural theology tradition of William Paley. In an early paper on plant morphology and in a more ambitious study, *Typical Forms and Special Ends in Creation* (1855), McCosh sought to demonstrate the evidence of God's handiwork in individual form. He also claimed that there existed an overall pattern of design: the history of organic life demonstrated progressive adaptation and change that testified to God's role in nature. *Typical Forms* was a pre-Darwinian work, and in the 1850s McCosh did not believe in evolution. In later years, however, his views changed and he devoted much attention to evolutionary questions.[59]

McCosh played a leading role in the effort to reconcile evolution with Christian theism. At Princeton that was a difficult task. The college was a center of conservative Presbyterian thought, and some, including Scott's grandfather Charles Hodge, were hostile to Darwin's theory and its dissemination. Hodge, the director of the Princeton Theological Seminary, opposed the naturalism and materialism inherent in Darwin's theory and found the non-teleological character of Darwin's views repugnant.[60] McCosh, however, argued that the order and succession of natural forms indicated God's plan. He did not accept the idea that man had evolved, nor did he adopt Darwin's concept of random variations. But McCosh understood evolution by natural selection as a beneficent law of continuous development and progress that demonstrated order and purpose in the universe. "The doctrine of evolution does not undermine the argument from Final Cause," he claimed, "but rather strengthens it by furnishing new illustrations of the wisdom and goodness of God." McCosh's interpretation was not Darwin's, and in his later writings he adopted a neo-Lamarckian interpretation of evolution that was compatible with design, progress, and purpose.[61] He promulgated those views in his classes as well as in his writings. In courses on philosophy and physiological psychology, McCosh emphasized that an understanding of secondary causes and natural laws did not undermine religion.

McCosh's evolutionary views had a significant impact at Princeton. Although some older teachers continued to condemn evolution, McCosh's interpretation placed evolution in a religious framework and made it acceptable to many with strong religious convictions. Several Princetonians, including A. A. Hodge, Benjamin B. Warfield, and George Macloskie, were influenced by McCosh and adopted interpretations very similar to his.[62] So too did Osborn and Scott. That they examined the causal mechanisms of evolution and, denying random variation, adopted explanations that emphasized the orderly, continuous, and progressive nature of evolution, was due at least in part to McCosh's influence.[63]

Equally influential was Cope. In his early years Cope, a Quaker, had interpreted evolution in theistic terms. In an 1868 essay entitled "On the Origin of Genera," he had explained that the process and the pattern of evolution were "conceived by the Creator according to His own plan." Although Cope later developed a different interpretation, he continued to maintain that mind or consciousness initiated and guided evolution.[64] Raised in a devout Quaker household and educated at Quaker schools, Cope examined theoretical problems in biology and paleontology in the context of philosophical idealism and religious commitment. Osborn and Scott were not only interested in similar questions but prepared to accept similar explanations. They followed Cope's lead in examining problems of variation, evolution, and inheritance. For a time they also adopted his neo-Lamarckian interpretation.

In several studies on fossil mammals published in the late 1880s, Osborn and Scott held that the fossil record demonstrated that evolution was an orderly, regular process. Claiming that Darwin's theory could not account for that evidence, they adopted Cope's interpretation based on the use and disuse of parts and the inheritance of acquired characteristics. Beginning in the mid-1880s Scott interpreted structural changes in terms of Cope's doctrine of kinetogenesis.[65] In an 1888 study on Mesozoic mammals, Osborn noted that two hypotheses could explain the evolution of molar cusps in different genera: "The first is that the type has been acquired by the selection of accidental variations in the production of new cusps and modelling of old ones. The second is, that the interaction of the upper and lower molars in the movements of the jaws has resulted in local increase of growth at certain points, resulting first in new cusps, then in a change of position and of form in the cusps. . . . The balance of evidence in tritubercular evolution seems to favor the second or kinetogenesis theory."[66] For Osborn, the evidence from the evolution of tooth structure in reptiles and mammals supported Cope's explanation that movements, stresses, and strains had produced structural changes in skeletal hard parts.

Osborn interpreted many of the details of the evolution of vertebrate structure in terms similar to Cope's. In his analysis of Mesozoic mammals, Osborn adopted Cope's tritubercular theory that the mammalian molar tooth had evolved from an earlier reptilian cone. He accepted Cope's interpretation of the evolution of the foot bones as a result of displacement.[67] Osborn did not slavishly follow Cope but made some contributions of his own. He produced morphological descriptions of new and different perissodactyl specimens. He did not fully accept Cope's views on the evolution of foot and tooth structure. Osborn agreed that Cope's interpretations of foot displacement applied to the carpal and tarsal bones, but he claimed that Cope did not adequately explain the evolution of the podials and metapodials, structures that Osborn considered more important. Osborn also revised and expanded Cope's theory of the evolution of molar teeth. In contrast to Cope, he maintained that the tritubercular molar had evolved independently in different mammalian groups from a hypothetical ancestor. Osborn also developed a nomenclature that defined the stages of that evolution.[68] In the late 1880s Osborn offered some new ideas for explaining the evolution of vertebrate structure, but he did so within the interpretive framework defined by Cope.

By the early 1890s Osborn and Scott had abandoned Cope's theory and were putting forth a different interpretation of evolution. That was due in part to Osborn's changing ideas on inheritance. Cope's theory was based on the traditional doctrine of the inheritance of acquired characteristics. But Osborn became impressed with the views of August Weismann, a German zoologist whose work refuted the Lamarckian interpretation of inheritance. According to Weismann, organisms possessed a germ plasm and a soma plasm, and hereditary characteristics were passed on only through the germ plasm, which was isolated from the effects of the environment. Osborn did not fully accept Weismann's ideas: he tried to carve out a middle ground by claiming that Weismann's work explained inheritance, but not evolution.[69] Nevertheless, Osborn abandoned neo-Lamarckism in the early 1890s.

Scott put forth a new interpretation of evolution, one that Osborn accepted and later expanded upon. Osborn and Scott, more than Cope, discerned regular patterns of change in the fossil record. Whereas Cope had recognized the significance of adaptation and evolutionary divergence, Scott explained evolution as an orthogenetic process "advancing steadily in a definite direction, though with slight deviations."[70]

That interpretation was in part a consequence of the method for classifying organisms and constructing phylogenies that the Princetonians employed. While Cope had followed traditional methods, Osborn and Scott adopted a vertical system of classification whereby they separated specimens, even among related organisms, into distinct lines of descent at the first sign of morphological difference. Relying on that method, Scott, in two suggestive papers published in the *Journal of Morphology* in 1891, described mammalian evolution in what he called polyphyletic terms: as numerous separate and individual lines of descent. Discussing the camel and oreodont families, he claimed "that all the great groups of selenodont artiodactyls when traced back are seen to arise independently from the abundant and widespread Eocene type, which may be called the Buno-Selenodont; and which forms, as it were, a lake from which several streams, flowing in partly parallel, partly divergent directions, are derived."[71] Osborn also interpreted the history of the Mesozoic mammals in polyphyletic terms, but it was Scott who most fully examined the use of vertical classification and its consequences for interpreting the evolution of mammals. He, and later Osborn, defined evolution not in terms of a branching tree of life, but rather as a bush composed of many independent and parallel lines.

The Princeton paleontologists, again primarily Scott at first, also claimed that mammalian evolution was an orthogenetic and irreversible process. According to Scott, evolution proceeded in definite directions and yielded rectilinear, even predictable, trends. Darwin's claim that evolution was the result of the natural selection of random variations could not account for the widespread evolutionary parallelism that Scott discerned in the fossil record. Neither could Cope's theory of kinetogenesis.

For Scott, the linear, parallel patterns of descent among the families of mammals were the result of predetermined mutations, a concept that in 1891 he adopted from the German invertebrate paleontologist Wilhelm Waagen. Scott stated that "as a matter of fact, when examining an extensive series of fossils reaching through many horizons, it is difficult to escape the suspicion that individual variations are not the material with which natural selection works, so steadily does the series advance toward what seems almost like a predetermined goal. This slowness and steadiness of reduction, together with other facts already mentioned, render the question as to whether mutilations are or are not transmissible a matter of relatively small importance; for only those direct effects of the environment which similarly modify many individuals and are long continued can be of real significance in the work of transformation."[72] Scott defined Waagen's small, continuous mutations as the means for explaining the process and pattern of evolution.

Scott and Osborn were not alone in their commitment to non-Darwinian mechanisms for explaining evolution. Alpheus Hyatt, an American invertebrate paleontologist, had long explained evolution in orthogenetic terms: evolution paralleled the stages of individual development and eventually resulted in racial senescence and species extinction. Theodor Eimer and others held that internal biological mechanisms or guiding principles directed evolutionary change along linear paths.[73] But the Princetonians were about the only vertebrate paleontologists to adopt Waagen's concept of mutations and apply it to the fossil record.

Osborn's and Scott's work was influenced by more than just the empirical study of the fossil record. As two ambitious young biologists, Osborn and Scott were eager to make their mark in the scientific community. What better way to do so than by developing their own distinctive interpretation of evolution, the most popular law of the age? Scientists throughout Europe and America had put forth a variety of neo-Lamarckian and orthogenetic interpretations to account for the linear trends they observed in the fossil record. Employing a vertical system of classification and Waagen's concept of mutations, Scott and Osborn advanced their own unique explanation for the process and pattern of vertebrate evolution.

In addition, Scott was influenced by the conservative ethos at Princeton, where science reinforced religious belief. Guyot believed that the bond that connected organisms was "of an immaterial nature; the marvelous unity of plan which we observe in the mind of the Creator." He had supported the hiring of Scott on the understanding that scientific study had not undermined Scott's faith in God, and that in teaching he would concentrate on the facts and omit reference to doubtful theories, in other words "the doctrine of evolution in its extreme forms."[74] Scott had worked with McCosh on the latter's book *The Religious Aspect of Evolution*. Not surprisingly, his conception of evolution as a series of parallel lines leading inexorably in definite directions met with McCosh's wholehearted approval.[75] Osborn worked in the same context. Drawing on the collaborative, religious framework for scientific inquiry at Princeton, Osborn in the 1890s developed an evolutionary theory that reflected McCosh's influence and amplified Scott's ideas.

By 1890 Princeton had a small but active program in vertebrate paleontology. The college sponsored annual expeditions to the western fossil fields. It possessed a museum and a staff skilled in the preservation and mounting of fossil vertebrate specimens. It also boasted productive programs of teaching and research in the subject. Both Scott and Osborn had published several descriptive and systematic studies of fossil mammals, and Scott was articulating new theoretical views on evolution. Their efforts did not have the visibility of the work of Marsh and Cope, just as Osborn's program in neuroanatomy did not rival the biological research programs of William Keith Brooks or Charles Otis Whitman.[76] But in a limited sense Princeton emerged as a fruitful context for scientific research, and Osborn and Scott were making their mark as biologists and vertebrate paleontologists.

McCosh played a major role in making possible those developments.

Although not a scientist himself, he was instrumental in establishing a school of science, developing graduate education, encouraging independent study and publication, and inaugurating new research and teaching opportunities at the college. He also provided an intellectual justification for pursuing work in vertebrate paleontology. While Osborn and Scott were inspired by the important paleontological discoveries being made by Cope and Marsh, they were also influenced by Guyot's ideas and McCosh's interest in promoting studies that would reconcile evolution and religion. Osborn and Scott published technical studies on fossil mammals, but they emphasized that the evolution of those animals, which was caused by nonmaterial agents and which followed orderly trends, demonstrated plan and purpose in the world.

The developments at Princeton also revealed Osborn's facility for drawing on the ideas and resources of others. Scott taught vertebrate paleontology, led field expeditions, and published technical and theoretical analyses of the subject. But Osborn helped to make that work possible. It was Osborn and Osborn's family who, after the collapse of the Libbey endowment, provided much of the financial wherewithal necessary to pursue fieldwork and research in vertebrate paleontology. It was Osborn, more than Scott, who developed the personal connections that promoted scientific research. Eager to pursue a career in science, Osborn developed a close working relationship with a college president who encouraged such endeavors. Seeking to shift his responsibilities from teaching to research, he turned to wealthy friends who supported the development of new and improved facilities. In an effort to establish a scientific reputation, he consolidated his ties to Cope and Scott. In 1885 Osborn, unsure of his abilities, his academic position, and what program of research to pursue, had joined with Cope and Scott to achieve status in vertebrate paleontology. For Osborn, perhaps more than for Cope, Marsh, or Scott, a well-organized, cooperative research center was an important means for obtaining success. Through the development of the museum, the morphological laboratory, and other collaborative arrangements, he was able not only to pursue scientific studies but to draw upon the research and insights of others more experienced and more talented than himself. By those means he promoted his own work and ambitions, first on a limited basis at Princeton and later on a much grander scale in New York.

3　Osborn, Science, and Society in New York City

By 1890 Osborn had carved out a position for himself at Princeton, but he was eager for opportunities in a larger arena. While Princeton had provided him with a morphological laboratory, a small staff, and the chance to work in vertebrate paleontology, those efforts had not translated into major developments on a grand scale. Despite certain important reforms and new developments for the sciences, Princeton was not the equal of Harvard or Johns Hopkins. In terms of support for scientific research and education, it also yielded ground to the newly established Clark University in Worcester, Massachusetts. Princeton had never provided Osborn with a substantial salary and, as his father pointed out, it was not a major center either socially or scientifically.[1]

Osborn was searching out other opportunities in his field as early as 1888. A brief trip to Washington indicated that the National Museum had much fossil material ready and waiting to be described. But Marsh, as government vertebrate paleontologist, was nominally the curator of fossil vertebrates at that institution. By the late 1880s Osborn also knew that the American Museum of Natural History in New York was interested in developing a program in vertebrate paleontology. That possibility was intriguing, and although there is no evidence of overtures on Osborn's part in the late 1880s, by 1890 he was actively negotiating for that position. Within a year he had received a joint appointment at the American Museum and Columbia College.[2]

The chance to move to New York City had a personal appeal for Osborn. He was born and reared in New York City, and his parents as well

44

as many friends and associates still lived there. While at Princeton in the 1880s Osborn and his wife, Lucretia Perry Osborn, frequently visited and stayed with his parents. Castle Rock mansion at Garrison-on-the-Hudson was a center for family and social gatherings where the Osborns mixed with their neighbors Frederic Edwin Church, J. Pierpont Morgan, and others among New York's upper class. New York, more than Princeton, also offered greater educational and social opportunities for Osborn's growing family of four young children.[3]

Although Osborn was devoted to his family and kept their interests in mind, he directed his energies toward developing professional opportunities, and in that respect too New York had great potential. Osborn was first approached about returning to New York by Seth Low, the new president of Columbia College. In 1890 Low wrote to Osborn about joining the Columbia faculty, but he was interested in Osborn for more than his academic credentials. His family, especially his father, had connections to a wide range of important people; Osborn was a scientist who also belonged to one of New York's elites.[4] Osborn's socioeconomic status had a bearing on his appointment to Columbia. It also had an influence in gradually leading him to subordinate academics for work in a different context.

Osborn had ties to some of New York's wealthiest and most powerful figures, and while those individuals had some interest in Columbia, they were actively involved in other institutions like the American Museum of Natural History or the New York Zoological Society (Bronx Zoo). Hence, those institutions, more than the university, could offer Osborn greater possibilities for promoting himself and his field of vertebrate paleontology. Osborn continued to teach at Columbia and to participate in academic science, but by the late 1890s his primary allegiance had shifted to public centers for biology where rich and powerful friends would help him fulfill his scientific and administrative ambitions.

New York City

The late nineteenth century was a time of great social and economic change in New York City. In the words of David Hammack: "In 1880 Greater New York was still a mercantile city, with a largely German-, Irish-, and American-born population of two million engaged in the financial, commercial, and manufacturing activities appropriate to the *entrepot* that handled the lion's share of America's trade with the Atlantic world. By 1910 the metropolis was more extensively involved in the management of American industry than in the Atlantic trade, and while its own manufacturing sector remained healthy, it produced a considerably narrower range of goods. The five million people engaged in these activities were Russian-Jewish, Italian, and Austro-Hungarian as well as German, Irish, and American-born."[5] By the early twentieth century New York was a pluralistic society. It was also characterized by an economy in which railroads, law, banking, and mining had overtaken shipping, merchandising, and manufacturing as "more effective ways to wealth."[6]

Despite the transformation taking place in New York, many of the older families remained closely allied with the emerging industrialists and retained a good deal of power. While an industrial elite gradually gained precedence over an older mercantile elite, there were ties between the two groups. In some cases merchants expanded into new industrial activities. Families like the Dodges and the Phelpses had begun in merchandising early in the century but by the late 1860s had shifted their interests to railroading and mining. According to Hammack, the new investment, banking, and law firms that proliferated at the end of the century hired approximately 60 percent of their leaders from among the sons of merchant families. Frequently, too, members of the new financial-industrial elite married into older mercantile families.[7]

The Osborns were one of the families that maintained close ties with both the merchandising and industrial elites. Osborn's father and grandfather had originally made their fortunes in trading. Jonathan Sturges was a prominent merchant who was well known to the manufacturer William E. Dodge and the department store magnate A. T. Stewart. William Osborn's ventures in overseas trade brought him into close contact with Dodge, A. A. Low, and other leading shipping merchants. Sturges and Osborn were also among the leading merchants who had expanded their interests into the burgeoning railroad industry. As the leader who transformed the Illinois Central Railroad into one of the nation's largest and most important lines, William Osborn became well acquainted with other railroad entrepreneurs. E. H. Harriman, later president of Union Pacific, began his career as the treasurer of Osborn's railroad. Osborn knew Cornelius Vanderbilt and Jay Gould, two of his principal competitors. He also had business dealings with J. Pierpont Morgan and Morris K. Jesup, bankers whose financial interests included the nation's expanding railroad industry.[8]

Economic associations fostered close social relationships among those individuals. William Osborn belonged to some of the same clubs as Harriman, Morgan, and others. He had a home in the Hudson River Highlands and an apartment at 850 Madison Avenue, the same neighborhood as many other wealthy New Yorkers. The Osborn family participated in many of the same religious, philanthropic, and social activities as others among the city's Anglo-Saxon, Protestant elite.[9] William and Virginia Osborn's interests in institutions for the destitute and physically impaired paralleled Jesup's concern with similar problems. Henry Fairfield Osborn, although raised a Presbyterian, eventually became a member of St. George's Episcopal Church, the same church that counted Morgan and Abram S. Hewitt, a prominent New York businessman and politician, as two of its most faithful members and supporters.[10]

Friendships further solidified the Osborns' ties to the New York upper class. Frederick Osborn, one of Henry's younger brothers, took a serious interest in natural history and in the early 1870s developed a close friendship with another young naturalist from a prominent family: Theodore Roosevelt. The two boys often explored together and became frequent visitors to the American Museum of Natural History. Roosevelt's father, as well as many of William Osborn's close business associates, were trustees of that institution. Frederick's interests captured the attention of Albert Bickmore, one of the museum's founders and leading officials. Although Frederick died in 1875 at the age of 15, Bickmore remained close to the Osborn family. When Henry developed an interest in science, Bickmore was ready and willing to provide assistance. In later years, Roosevelt became an enthusiastic supporter of Osborn's scientific research and institutional objectives for the American Museum.[11]

The Osborns also established family ties with other prominent New Yorkers. In the mid 1850s William Osborn married one of the daughters of Jonathan Sturges, his business partner. A few years later another business associate, J. Pierpont Morgan, who had become intimate with the Osborn and Sturges families, married another Sturges daughter, Amelia. Although Morgan's young bride died in 1862, he remained very close to the Osborns and the Osborn children. Morgan later built a home in the Hudson River Highlands in close proximity to the Osborn mansion, Castle Rock. In the early 1880s William Church Osborn, another of Henry's younger brothers, married Alice Dodge, daughter of the prominent merchant and American Museum trustee William Dodge and sister of Osborn's Princeton classmates William and Cleveland H. Dodge.[12] The Osborns, Dodges, Morgans, and others were thus part of a closely connected socioeconomic network whose families intermarried and whose members held similar religious, social, and often political commitments.

The members of New York's upper class had little interest in science or vertebrate paleontology per se, but they did support activities that encompassed Henry Fairfield Osborn's work. The elites of the post–Civil War period, like their antebellum predecessors, had established many hospitals and charities for the sick and needy. They supported the development of cultural centers such as the Metropolitan Museum of Art and the New York Public Library.[13]

The emerging industrial elite also expanded the domain of philanthropic activities in at least two respects. They were "more open to the claims of intellect alone than the older gentry of the rich and well-born." Consequently, they supported efforts for academic reform. Many contributed to the development of a new campus and new facilities for Columbia College.[14] They also promoted the development of public institutions such as the American Museum and the Bronx Zoo that were designed to provide educational and recreational outlets for the burgeoning urban populace. Promoting education and science became a symbol of cultural pride and brought merchants, industrialists, and financiers into contact with political and academic interests. John Strong Newberry, a geologist at the Columbia School of Mines, received support from business and civic leaders in his efforts to expand scientific institutions and promote public education.[15] So too did Osborn, who was especially well placed to take advantage of the financial backing and cultural interests of many among New York's upper class.

Columbia University

Those connections first had a bearing on the role that Osborn would play in helping to transform Columbia College into Columbia University. That effort was spearheaded by Seth Low. A scion of one of New York's most affluent merchant families, Low was a businessman and politician who became an advocate of "scientific expertise, guided social management, and large-scale centralized organization" as the means for dealing with the problems of an urban, industrialized society. In the 1880s that philosophy had guided his actions as mayor of Brooklyn. It also directed his efforts to change Columbia from a small college with a negligible reputation into a first-class university.[16]

For Low, the development of Columbia depended on educational reform. The wave of academic reform that hit several institutions of higher education in the 1870s and 1880s did not at first affect Columbia. It remained a liberal arts institution with a number of professional schools that had only nominal ties to the college. Built originally around a School of Arts, Columbia had added a School of Medicine in 1814, a School of Mines in 1864, and a School of Political Science in 1880. Each school was an autonomous body with its own curriculum and admission and graduation requirements. Columbia in 1889 was "a jigsaw of Schools, groping toward universityhood without any feeling of unity or common purpose. The Faculties were torn by dissension and suspicion rooted in competing and conflicting ideologies and interests. The central issues of administrative governance and academic direction were confused and unresolved."[17] In 1871 Columbia graduated only thirty-one students and in the words of one scholar had "failed as a classical college." From Low's perspective the college remained rooted to an old philosophy and inefficient structure that hampered efforts to create a modern university. To develop an institution worthy of the nation's leading commercial center required extensive changes. In his first year as president, Low moved quickly to create a central administration, a coordinated curriculum, and an educational philosophy that promoted graduate study and research in all fields.[18]

The reform of the college was more than an issue in educational change; it was a program for civil and moral improvement as well. "From what quarter," Low asked, "are the trained intellect and the consecrated purpose to come which are to grapple successfully with these problems in the coming time, if not out of New York itself, and out of the schools and colleges of New York?"[19] The transformation of Columbia, in Low's eyes, had important consequences for the people and problems of New York City. Consequently, Columbia needed close ties to the city, and Low established cooperative relationships with many of New York's libraries, schools, and museums. The creation of a university also required support from local government and powerful business interests.

With a vision of academic reform that had far-reaching consequences, Low needed leading scholars as well as political and economic support. Henry Fairfield Osborn possessed those assets. As an academic at Princeton he had published in biology and vertebrate paleontology. He had been successful in developing facilities and supervising research programs in those subjects. In addition, he came from a wealthy and socially prominent family that had extensive connections in New York City. Low's father and uncle, the proprietors of A. A. Low and Brothers, were the leaders in the Far Eastern trade market in the 1840s and no doubt aware of their principal competitors, including William Henry Osborn. Seth Low also knew William Osborn; they moved in the same social network and shared many mutual acquaintances.[20] Low realized that hiring Henry Fairfield Osborn, a figure of growing academic importance and a wealthy, well-connected New Yorker, would aid in his campaign to transform Columbia.

Low's correspondence with Osborn indicates that he was interested in Osborn for more than his scientific reputation. Writing in April 1890, Low expressed an interest in hiring Osborn as a professor of physiological psychology. As Osborn put it, Low's "first thought was to complete the philosophy department by psychology and psycho-physics, and . . . you have given less consideration to the matter of Biology."[21] Low's overture reflected a lack of knowledge of Osborn's research. Osborn still taught physiological psychology at Princeton, but since 1885 his scientific work had focused on vertebrate paleontology. But the precise nature of Osborn's scientific work apparently was not Low's overriding concern; getting Osborn was. Rejecting Low's original offer, Osborn indicated that he would be interested if Columbia decided to develop a first-rate department of biology. Low proceeded to negotiate with Osborn on those grounds, and over the next year he worked closely, and confidentially, with Osborn and the Columbia Board of Trustees to lay the foundation for a new biology department that Osborn would organize and administer.[22]

Both Low and Osborn sensed the importance of establishing a biology department at Columbia. The creation of a strong biology department was an important objective in its own right. In the late nineteenth century biology was gaining a foothold in many of the nation's leading colleges and universities.[23] The development of such a program could also promote the integrated curriculum and educational as well as vocational opportunities that Low envisioned. It would help to improve a mediocre medical school and bring that school under the control of the central administration of the university. In the words of the special committee headed by Low, it was important to develop a biology program "in connection with the work already being conducted by the College and Medical School, into a symmetrical department, working harmoniously with its allied subjects to a common end."[24]

In April 1891 Osborn, with Low's backing, presented to the Columbia Board of Trustees a plan for "the Department [that] was founded very deliberately to take its place in the whole educational scheme of the University" (see figure 1).[25] According to Low and Osborn, biology had a direct relationship to existing courses and professional opportunities already available at Columbia. It would expand the science curriculum

FIGURE 1. The Relations of Biology to Other Studies

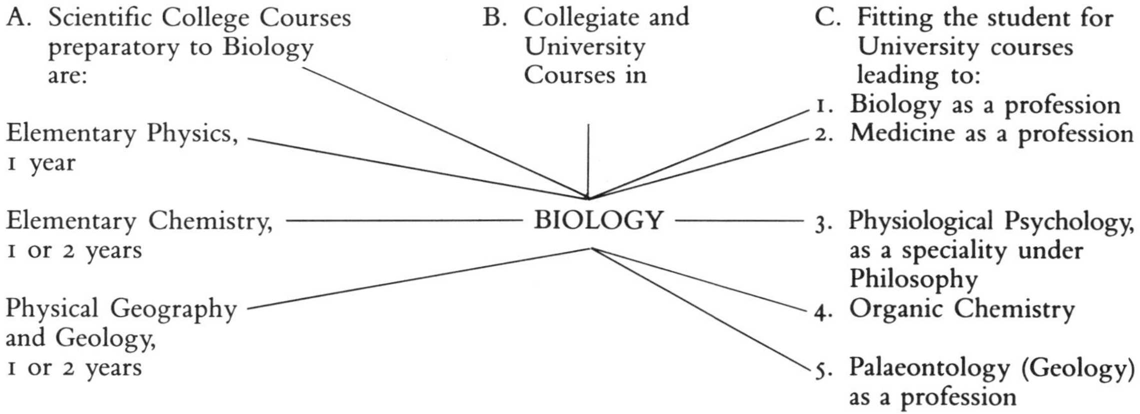

A. Scientific College Courses preparatory to Biology are:

Elementary Physics, 1 year

Elementary Chemistry, 1 or 2 years

Physical Geography and Geology, 1 or 2 years

B. Collegiate and University Courses in

BIOLOGY

C. Fitting the student for University courses leading to:

1. Biology as a profession
2. Medicine as a profession
3. Physiological Psychology, as a speciality under Philosophy
4. Organic Chemistry
5. Palaeontology (Geology) as a profession

within the college. It would be a key link in connecting the college to the separate schools of mines and medicine.[26]

Following his appointment as DaCosta Professor of Biology, Osborn worked to establish those ties. The new biology department offered no courses in 1891–92, but in that year Osborn delivered the Cartwright Lectures at the College of Physicians and Surgeons. He met the physiologists John G. Curtis and Frederick S. Lee and two years later invited Lee to deliver a series of lectures to the biology department on the comparative physiology of the nervous system. He also became more closely acquainted with the anatomist George S. Huntington and on occasion used specimens in Huntington's small anatomy museum for courses and research.[27] Two of Osborn's new colleagues in the biology department, Bashford Dean and John I. Northrup, were instructors in the School of Mines. Their appointments established ties between that school and the College's new Faculty of Pure Sciences.[28]

Osborn's plan also reflected his concept of the structure of the biological sciences. Osborn recognized that biology was related to other fields, but he sought to define a specific department with its own program of study. For him botany, physiology, and bacteriology were distinct from biology and best pursued in their own departments or in the School of Medicine. In his program, Osborn emphasized the study of zoology. It was not until 1896 that he and his colleagues substituted the title Department of Zoology for Department of Biology, but the study of zoology dominated the department's program from the start.[29] According to Osborn, the subject "naturally divides into two *parallel* branches of study:" vertebrate zoology, morphology, and embryology; and invertebrate zoology, morphology, and embryology. Osborn and Dean were responsible for the study of vertebrates, and Osborn hired E. B. Wilson from Bryn Mawr to conduct courses and research in invertebrate zoology. Osborn promoted graduate education and the development of a Ph.D. program for biology, but within the context of a broad, morphological orientation.[30]

In addition to teaching a variety of courses in vertebrate morphology and paleontology at Columbia, Osborn worked in an administrative capacity. After defining the program and hiring the faculty, he obtained financial backing and developed facilities for the department. He was partly responsible for raising money for graduate fellowships, a library, and the development of a new biological laboratory, Schermerhorn Hall.[31]

Osborn had a good working knowledge of the important developments occurring in biology and sought to establish ties to institutions that he considered crucial for the program at Columbia. Osborn's work was on vertebrates, but he was also well aware of the breakthroughs in physiology, cytology, and embryology associated with work in marine biology. During the 1890s he worked to get Columbia associated with the leading marine stations. Through his Princeton classmates Cleveland and William E. Dodge, Osborn gained support for a Columbia research table at Anton Dohrn's marine zoology station in Naples.[32] The department was also "co-operating with Professor Whitman of the University of Chicago in the endeavor to place the Marine Biological Laboratory upon a permanent footing." During the 1890s many Columbia students, including Osborn's own students in vertebrate morphology, spent summers doing research at Woods Hole.[33] Osborn and Dean had hopes of rivaling other programs in marine biology and briefly maintained a summer biology school for teachers and students at Cold Spring Harbor, New York. They also convinced Low and Charles Senff, a wealthy banker and the uncle of John Northrup, to sponsor Columbia University biological expeditions to Puget Sound and Alaska in 1896 and 1897.[34]

Osborn also played a role in strengthening the college's offerings in the sciences. In addition to his position as head of biology, Osborn was the first dean of the new Faculty of Pure Sciences from 1892 to 1896. In that position he lobbied successfully for a three-year Ph.D. degree program.[35] In the early 1890s, Low appointed him a member of the board of trustees of the new Columbia University Press. Osborn, who was already developing a lecture series in his department, used his position on the board to develop the prestigious Columbia University publication series in biology.[36] From 1892 to 1909 Osborn taught and directed research at Columbia, and William Diller Matthew, William King Gregory, Richard Swann Lull, and Francis B. Sumner were but a few of his many graduate students. But at Columbia, as at Princeton, Osborn worked primarily to establish, administer, and finance institutional foundations for the biological sciences.

Although Osborn maintained an academic position and close ties to Columbia throughout his career, beginning in the mid 1890s he directed his energies elsewhere. In 1895 he stepped down as Dean of the Faculty of Pure Sciences, and the following year he resigned as chairman of the Zoology Department. In 1899 Osborn informed Low that he intended to reduce his commitments at Columbia and turned over his lectures on vertebrate zoology to Bashford Dean and a younger faculty member, James H. McGregor.[37]

Osborn had accomplished much at Columbia in five years, but he also understood that in New York there were greater opportunities outside academe. Through his family, his ties to Low, and other connections, he realized that philanthropists and civic and business leaders were promoting developments to enhance the status of science and bring it to the attention of the public. Osborn continued to play an active role in scientific circles: in the early 1890s he became a member of the New York Academy of Sciences, the Linnaean Society of New York, the Biological Society of Washington, and other organizations. But he also belonged to the Century Association, the University Club, the Metropolitan Club, and other exclusive organizations that included many of the city's wealthiest and most powerful figures. Through his association with those individuals, Osborn realized that he could promote himself and his work in ways that were not possible through the university and that would have an important impact on New York society.[38]

One of the first organizations on which he made his mark was the New York Zoological Society. Established in 1893, the society was composed of prominent New Yorkers interested in creating a zoological park for public education and entertainment. Its leaders included Madison Grant, a lawyer trained at Columbia, C. Grant LaFarge, a prominent architect, and Elihu Root, a lawyer who would later serve as secretary of war and secretary of state. Osborn, as a biologist, had a scientific interest in such an organization, but he also realized that the development of a zoological park would provide the opportunity to expand his social and political influence. He joined the society in 1893 and, employing his ability for organizing and defining needs and opportunities, quickly became president of its executive committee. In that capacity he negotiated with political leaders to gain the city's support for the park. He also took the lead in selecting the site for the park and appointing its first director, William Temple Hornaday.[39] A number of prominent figures in New York had an interest in a public biology facility, but Osborn drew upon his scientific and social status and threw his energies into establishing himself as one of the leaders of that new institution.

The American Museum of Natural History

Even more than the Zoological Society, another institution, the American Museum of Natural History, became the focus of Osborn's interest. It too was a center that emphasized public education. It was also dominated by several of New York's political and business leaders, and with their support Osborn would seek to establish himself as a leading figure in American science.

Founded in 1869, the museum was the brainchild of Albert Bickmore, a student of Louis Agassiz's who was well acquainted with science museums in the United States and abroad. Following the Civil War, Bickmore became convinced that a natural history museum would enhance New York's status as a cultural and educational center. He approached some of the city's richest and most powerful men. Negotiating with William E. Dodge, at one time the president of the New York State Chamber of Commerce, he was soon introduced to the elder Theodore Roosevelt, who endorsed the project. Others, including J. Pierpont Morgan, Isaac N. Phelps, and Morris K. Jesup, lent their assistance. Joseph H. Choate, a prominent lawyer and politician, was influential in obtaining the support of the New York boss William M. Tweed and Superintendent of Parks Andrew H. Green. The museum was organized as a public institution that received maintenance and operating expenses from the city's Department of Public Parks. But philanthropists on its board of trustees were responsible for the acquisition of collections and the management of the institution.[40]

The museum's original board of trustees constituted a cross section of at least two of New York's elites and mirrored the changes taking place in upper class New York society. Some trustees, like William E. Dodge, Isaac N. Phelps, and A. T. Stewart, belonged to old New York families and represented New York's mid-nineteenth-century mercantile elite.[41] Equally prominent were members of the financial-industrial elite emerging in the post–Civil War period. Choate, Morgan, and Jesup were transplanted New Englanders who in the mid-nineteenth century had come to New York to make their fortunes. Despite their recent arrival, they became wealthy through banking and railroads and quickly moved into New York's leading social, economic, and political circles.[42]

A number of the trustees played an active part in local politics. Both Jesup and Dodge served as president of the New York State Chamber of Commerce. Abram S. Hewitt was mayor of New York for one term. Choate and Levi P. Morton were prominent political figures on a national scale. Many of the trustees opposed the political corruption and immigrant support associated with New York's Tammany Hall; some took part in the effort to bring down William M. Tweed's political ring.[43] But beyond that the trustees varied in their political affiliations and their positions on particular issues. As Frederic C. Jaher and other social historians have argued, the New York elites participated in politics in order to promote their commercial interests and to consolidate their "upper-class civil hegemony."[44]

The trustees shared other commitments, some of which had an impact on the development and orientation of the museum. A number of the trustees were involved in promoting philanthropic activities. Jesup, for example, was the founder of both the Society for the Suppression of Vice and the Society for the Relief of Half Orphan and Destitute Children; he was president of the Five Points House of Industry. Jesup, in conjunction with Dodge, Morgan, and Charles Lanier, another member of the museum board, was one of the original organizers and promoters of the YMCA. Those men also sponsored a number of social welfare, religious, and missionary organizations.[45] Most of the trustees were Protestants, and the institutions they established reflected their interest in disseminating religious values. Their efforts addressed the problems of poverty, vice, and broken families, all threats to the established social order and the position of the upper class. For Jesup, Dodge, and Morgan those institutions were not only statements of their moral and social commitments, but also means for maintaining the status quo. "Social control, community leadership, and the stewardship of wealth . . . motivated these elites" to develop a network of religious and social welfare organizations.[46]

The museum embodied the trustees' interest in social welfare. Although one early museum curator noted that there was no rhyme or reason to the purchase of collections, the museum did have certain generalized objectives. As an "instructive and acceptable resort for the people of the city," it was designed to entertain the public. The museum, like other institutions sponsored by the trustees, was also supposed to promote public education and spiritual welfare. Although its early collections were neither well displayed nor effectively labeled, the museum's hundreds of birds, animal skins, insects, molluscs, and fossils suggested the bounty of nature. The museum emphasized no specific program of education or ideology in its early years, but implicitly it was a testament to the wonders of creation.[47]

The museum reflected the trustees' cultural interests. With the exception of Bickmore, none of the museum's directors had a background in science. But several had an interest in collecting. William A. Haines, D. Jackson Steward, and Robert L. Stuart possessed large private collections of shells or minerals. Others, notably J. Pierpont Morgan and H. O. Havemeyer, developed outstanding art collections. They ransacked European museums to create their own private collections and to build up the new Metropolitan Museum of Art. As trustees of the American Museum they were likewise interested in "securing a rare and very valuable collection." The acquisition of natural history specimens would enable those men to extend their proprietary interests to the possession of factual knowledge.[48]

Despite the trustees' interest and support, the museum suffered serious problems in its early years. The museum had acquired a number of valuable collections, including over four thousand animal skins from Daniel G. Elliott and eight thousand coleoptera specimens from the collection of F. A. Witthaus. But they were poorly cared for. An internal survey in 1880 indicated no systematic program for storing, cataloging, or displaying and labeling specimens.[49] In 1876 the museum purchased geologist James Hall's immense collection of invertebrate fossils and hired its first curators, Robert Parr Whitfield and L. P. Gratacap, to organize and take care of the specimens. But the acquisition of Hall's collection also put the museum $26,000 in debt. In Gratacap's words the museum was little more than "a chronicle of acquisition, increased or diminished revenues, increased attendance. No element of educational intention, speculative inquiry, or any serious participation in scientific discussion had been developed." Social and cultural objectives may have motivated the trustees, but those objectives had not been translated into an effectively organized and operating institution. Within ten years of its founding, the museum served the interests of neither its benefactors nor the public.[50]

Jesup and the American Museum

Significant changes occurred when Morris K. Jesup was selected as museum president in 1881. A railroad broker who had no knowledge of science, Jesup had a great deal of interest in the museum and its state of affairs. Prior to becoming president he had headed the internal survey that found serious deficiencies in the museum's operations. After his election he personally inspected the collections, displays, and labels and called for wholesale changes. Jesup made some changes himself. But more importantly he assembled a skilled staff to improve the museum's appearance. In 1885 he hired Jenness Richardson as the museum's taxidermist. For a time in the mid 1880s the museum employed the well-known bird artists and preparators Mrs. E. S. Mogridge and her brother Henry Minturn. Jesup also hired two new curators, Joel Asaph Allen and Frank M. Chapman, to care for the mammal and bird collections. Their efforts had important consequences: Allen systematized the cataloging and labeling of specimens, and Chapman developed innovative techniques for the preparation and display of birds.[51]

On another front, Jesup promoted a project inaugurated by the museum's superintendent Albert Bickmore to provide lectures on nature for the state's school teachers. Those lectures were highly popular among the teachers. The program provided the museum with much-needed exposure and resulted in additional funds from the state superintendent of education and the legislature. By 1887 the trustees had to enlarge the building in order to construct a lecture hall for Bickmore's classes. That program, the efforts of the new curators, and the trustees' decision to accept city money by opening the museum on Sundays boosted attendance, eliminated the debt, and reinstilled the trustees' confidence in the institution.[52]

Jesup's initiatives also expanded the museum's objectives to include scientific research. When the museum hired Allen in 1885, it obtained an experienced curator who had worked at Harvard's Museum of Comparative Zoology. Allen was also one of the country's leading experts on birds and mammals. Since the late 1860s he had studied birds and mammals throughout North America. In addition to having published dozens of descriptive, taxonomic studies, Allen had investigated questions concerning variation, evolution, and geographic distribution. He was interested in understanding the factors that affected variations in organism size and color. In a number of classic papers he defined the impact of climate, elevation, and land mass on variation. Reflecting on the status of mammalian research in 1891, Allen claimed that "at the present time the relation of forms to each other, geographically and phylogenetically, and to their environment, is the one interesting problem underlying the whole subject. There is no more fascinating or profitable work for the student of the present mammalian fauna of North America than the tracing out of the habitats, and the determining of the intergradation or non-intergradation of such forms as compose many of our leading genera of mammals."[53]

As an academic scientist, Allen emphasized the significance of developing resources and facilities for research. In his first report as curator, Allen, noting that the museum possessed the nucleus of a fine collection of bird and mammal specimens, recognized the need for developing improved cataloging and preparation techniques to benefit the public. But he also claimed that study collections for students and researchers were a vital necessity.[54] He was instrumental in expanding and improving the museum's study collections, and his work attracted much support. Beginning in 1887 a number of the wealthy sportsmen associated with New York's Boone and Crockett Club contributed bird and mammal specimens to the museum. In 1889 they supported Allen's, and the museum's, first expedition to acquire North American mammals. Others who knew and respected Allen's work donated specimens, thereby expanding the museum's holdings and enhancing its importance among scientists.[55]

Allen also turned the *Bulletin of the American Museum of Natural History* into an important scientific publication. In 1881, prior to Allen's appointment, Robert Parr Whitfield, the geology curator, had established the *Bulletin*. However, no volumes of the periodical had been published by the time Allen came on the scene. He took over the editorship of the *Bulletin* and began publication on a regular basis. Many of the early contributions were his own, but Allen also made the *Bulletin* an important vehicle for describing the museum's holdings and a publication outlet for the museum's growing scientific staff.[56]

To Jesup and other trustees, Allen's work was important, but primarily insofar as it contributed to the improvement of displays and the development of the museum as a center for public education. Jesup recognized that evolution was an important generalization and that "discovering the laws of nature is one of the great tasks of our age." Consequently, he supported and promoted efforts by Allen or others that emphasized evolution.[57] But Jesup also maintained that "evolution simply confirms morality," and thus evolutionary studies reinforced his conception of the museum's primary purpose as providing for the educational and spiritual welfare of the public. From his perspective, one of the most important features of evolutionary studies was that they conveyed moral lessons.[58]

By the late 1880s Jesup was in a position to expand the museum's programs. The institution was popular and on a sound economic footing, and the president supported efforts to develop new departments in archeology and ethnology, entomology, and other fields.[59] However, he gave first priority to developing a program in vertebrate paleontology. In 1887 Jesup took the lead in advocating that the museum acquire a mounted mastodon skeleton. After sending Whitfield to examine a specimen at Ward's Scientific Establishment in Rochester, Jesup convinced the trustees to purchase the mastodon. He was impressed by the public's response to the mount and recommended to the trustees that the "one very important need of the collections in this [the Geology] department is in the direction of Vertebrate Palaeontology, remains of large fishes, reptiles, and mammals, a want which ought to be supplied with every opportunity which may offer. The extreme interest which the skeleton of the

Mastodon excites is an indication of this necessity, and it seems to me that expenditures in this direction would be of greater benefit to the Museum than those of any other department of natural objects."[60] Jesup and others on the museum's board and staff understood that extinct fossil specimens had entertainment and proprietary value. As Whitfield emphasized, the evidences of vertebrate paleontology were rare and highly valuable acquisitions. They were also large and obvious facts, the kind that would attract public attention and elicit support from individual trustees who were interested in making visible, concrete contributions to the museum.[61]

Jesup also probably knew that exciting developments were occurring in vertebrate paleontology. He had little understanding of science, but it was well known that Cope and Marsh were making exciting discoveries of the remains of large extinct animals. The fossils they uncovered were unlike any others found elsewhere, and through the work of Cope and Marsh vertebrate paleontology was one of the few fields in which the United States was surpassing Europe.[62] Jesup, probably through Whitfield and Allen, knew that fossils were the best documentary evidence of evolution.[63] Consequently, vertebrate paleontology was not only a significant field of scientific inquiry but one that could provide the public with visible means for understanding nature's laws and lessons. By 1887–88 Jesup was eager to launch a program in that field.

Although a number of paleontologists, including Cope, George Baur, and E. H. Barbour, applied for the new position at the museum, the trustees were probably predisposed toward Osborn.[64] In the late 1880s Osborn was not the leading paleontologist in the country. Marsh arguably held that distinction. Cope and Scott had more experience in fieldwork and had made more significant scientific contributions than Osborn. But Osborn was emerging as a recognized figure in the field. He had investigated problems of fossil systematics as well as evolutionary questions. He was a man of religious convictions and was socially acceptable to the trustees. Joel Allen pointed out that Osborn was a man "of gracious manners."[65] Most important, he had a social and economic background similar to the trustees, and he and his family were well known to many of the museum's leaders. Once Jesup announced that the museum would hire a vertebrate paleontologist, it is likely that Morgan or Abram Hewitt or even William Osborn made it known to their associates that Osborn's son was a scholar in that field. Because of his ties to a number of the trustees, Henry Fairfield Osborn, unlike Cope or Barbour, would not be entirely dependent on the museum to support a program in vertebrate paleontology. Osborn's selection was not predetermined; in fact, Jesup originally hoped to obtain Marsh, but was turned down. A number of factors weighed heavily in Osborn's favor.[66]

Osborn and the American Museum

Osborn realized the potential of being associated with the museum, and he actively pursued that goal. Soon after Low approached him about joining the Columbia faculty in the spring of 1890, Osborn, who knew that the college could not support preparation, displays, or fieldwork in vertebrate paleontology, was maneuvering for the museum curatorship. In the summer of 1890, when he was still at Princeton, he informed his colleague William Berryman Scott that he might be taking a position in New York. With Scott's help, Osborn began to inquire whether John Bell Hatcher, Marsh's leading collector, was interested in becoming Osborn's chief assistant. Those negotiations continued through December 1890 when Hatcher, upset at learning that Osborn was offering him a position at an institution where Osborn himself did not yet have a formal appointment, broke off the discussions.[67]

Osborn may also have had an influence in establishing a cooperative arrangement between Columbia and the museum. Low was very much interested in establishing alliances between Columbia and other institutions. In August 1890 Low suggested to Jesup that "in the direction of biology, especially, . . . the collections of your Museum might be made of great value to our students and instructors."[68] But Low was a businessman and politician with little knowledge of the wants or needs of paleontology. It was possibly through Osborn, with whom Low was in close contact throughout 1890, that he became better acquainted with the facilities and resources needed to do work in that field. It was also perhaps at Osborn's suggestion that Low realized the financial advantage of having the museum, rather than Columbia, house specimens and support expeditions. The arrangements that Low and Jesup agreed upon, whereby Osborn would teach vertebrate morphology and evolution at Columbia, and the museum would serve as the center for the college's advanced research in vertebrate paleontology, were designed with Osborn's interests and objectives in mind.[69]

Osborn also had a hand in laying the groundwork for a program in vertebrate paleontology at the museum. When Low suggested a cooperative arrangement between Columbia and the museum, Jesup supported it but other trustees were hesitant. They were uncertain about reserving the museum's facilities for just one college and thought that use of museum collections by Columbia's faculty might interfere with the work of the museum's staff. The trustees' reservations were resolved when Osborn joined the museum staff in October 1890.[70] Osborn did not receive a curatorial appointment until mid-April 1891, one week after his appointment at Columbia, but for several months in advance he had played a part in the negotiations for the museum's new position in vertebrate paleontology.

By the time Osborn was appointed curator, a well-defined arrangement was already in place. The museum program would emphasize mammalian paleontology, Osborn's specific field of scientific interest. Its mission included not only publishing and developing displays on fossil vertebrates, but also annual expeditions. At that point the museum had sponsored only one expedition, in 1889; but expeditions were crucial for obtaining fossil vertebrates. Because Osborn did not actively participate in fieldwork, collectors and expeditions were necessary to the kind of department he sought to organize. The program in mammalian paleontology had strong financial support. In April 1891 Osborn submitted a proposal to Jesup in which he asked for the museum to contribute $3,500 annually to the department, an amount second only to the appropriation for the well-established Department of Mammalogy and Ornithology. On his part Osborn would take no salary for running the department and would contribute $1,500 annually to its expenses.[71] Within a few years he was paying out much more. For example, in the year 1900 alone, Osborn donated over $2,500 for expenses associated with fieldwork and paid the salaries for the departmental photographer and several preparators and artists.[72]

But Osborn, unlike Cope and Marsh, was not prepared to spend all of his or his family's money searching for fossils. At the museum, as at Columbia, he relied heavily on wealthy associates in positions of authority to help finance his program. Family friends George T. Gould, president of the Missouri Pacific Railroad, and J. W. Jeffrey, president of the Denver and Rio Grande Western Railroad, provided free passage for Osborn's collectors and reduced rates for specimen shipments. Railroad and mining work often resulted in the uncovering of fossils and those men informed their staffs to keep Osborn and the museum apprised of any finds. In contrast to Cope and Marsh, who had to pay large fees to transport fossils from the western states and territories, Osborn was able to minimize costs pertaining to some of the more expensive aspects of work in vertebrate paleontology.[73]

J. P. Morgan was one of the biggest contributors to Osborn's program. Morgan was an influential figure in the early history of the museum. During the 1880s he served as museum treasurer and subscribed annually to make up the institution's deficit. He was famous for his donation of a magnificent collection of gems to the museum, but Morgan also provided financial support for the acquisition of paleontological rarities. He contributed to the purchase of Cope's collections of fossil vertebrates in 1895 and again in 1899. For several years he provided free shipment for the transportation to New York of the gigantic remains of *Apatosaurus* and *Diplodocus* from quarries in Wyoming.[74] In addition to his well-publicized donation of $30,000 for the purchase and remounting of the Warren Mastodon, Morgan commissioned and purchased many studies of prehistoric life painted by Charles R. Knight. He privately established a large research fund specifically designated for Osborn's use. That fund, which Morgan ostensibly created in 1906–7 to keep Osborn at the museum after he was offered the secretaryship of the Smithsonian Institution, provided hundreds of thousands of dollars for work in vertebrate paleontology. Osborn channeled much of that money into the Department of Vertebrate Paleontology (DVP), but he also employed it for his own study of the Proboscidea and other projects. As Jesup noted in 1897, Morgan was one of Osborn's most powerful and committed "friends."[75]

Jesup was equally important in advancing Osborn and his department. In 1895 he gave money toward the purchase of the Cope mammal collection. A few years later, when other trustees combined to buy the Cope collection of Pampean mammals, Jesup bought and presented to the museum Cope's collection of reptiles and batrachians.[76] When he died in 1908, Jesup willed $1,000,000 to the museum. After the death of his wife in 1913, the Jesup estate donated another $5,000,000 to the institution. Osborn used several thousand dollars from that fund for his program in vertebrate paleontology.[77]

Jesup also provided institutional support for Osborn. As Osborn's goals and ambitions increased, so too did the museum appropriation for the Department of Vertebrate Paleontology. By the turn of the century that department, with an annual budget of over $10,000, was definitely one of the favored programs of the Jesup administration.[78] He also aided Osborn personally. In 1894, after Osborn began negotiations for the purchase of the Cope collection, Jesup took the unusual step of inviting Osborn to present his annual report to the board of trustees in person. Osborn called for the purchase of the Cope collection of fossil mammals, a request that represented a major commitment on the part of the museum. That purchase, along with requests from the Department of Anthropology, entailed expanding the museum's holdings and making additions to the building, staff, and facilities. Jesup wholeheartedly supported the endeavor and, after obtaining support from the museum's board, took charge of negotiating for the Cope collection.

In 1895, after referring to the annual report from Osborn's department "as the most important for the information of the trustees," Jesup was instrumental in establishing a hall for the display of fossil mammals.[79] Three years later, following the discovery of dinosaurs at Como Bluff, Wyoming, Jesup again singled out Osborn's program for special praise. "In speaking of the report of the Department of Vertebrate Palaeontology," he stated, "I feel that every trustee should read the entire document; it possesses so many items appealing to popular interest that I desire to incorporate a more than usual reference thereto in the Annual Report."[80] No other department or individual received such attention or support. Osborn, in contrast to other curators, maintained his own preparation staff and ran his department with no interference even after the appointment of a museum director. Certainly the presentation of a silver loving cup to Osborn in 1898, as a token of Jesup's and the board's appreciation of his work, had no parallel.[81]

Jesup played a central part in bringing Osborn into the museum administration. In 1900 Jesup appointed Osborn his special assistant. In that position Osborn had responsibility for making a number of important administrative decisions. He and Jesup created the new position of museum director and Osborn, after turning down the job, had a hand in appointing Brown University biologist Hermon Carey Bumpus to the position. Osborn, along with Jesup and Bumpus, launched the *American Museum Journal* (predecessor to *Natural History*) and the museum guide leaflet and handbook series of publications.[82] In 1901 Jesup, aware of the important department that Osborn had created and of the financial contributions he had made to that program, nominated Osborn to be a museum trustee. Following Osborn's election, Jesup appointed him as the museum's second vice president.[83]

Jesup also had a hand in selecting Osborn as his successor as museum president. In 1906 Morgan may have promised Osborn the presidency if he declined the Smithsonian offer, but Jesup had indicated several months before that he wanted Osborn as his successor.[84] Both men were impressed by Osborn's research and his abilities in having organized and directed a program in vertebrate paleontology. They also supported him for who he was. Because of Osborn's background and status, Jesup and Morgan had confidence in and great personal regard for him.

In later years, after Jesup and Morgan had died, other wealthy New Yorkers supported Osborn and his interests. When he was appointed president in 1908, Osborn told Percy Pyne, son of his Princeton friend Moses Taylor Pyne, that he wanted to clear out the deadwood from the board of trustees.[85] Two years later, after Bumpus accused Osborn of improprieties and unsuccessfully sought to have him removed as president, Osborn was careful to appoint close personal friends and supporters to the museum board. Seth Low, Madison Grant, and Theodore Roosevelt were among the appointees whom Osborn knew would back him and his interests. Childs Frick, the son of the steel magnate Henry Clay Frick and himself a vertebrate paleontologist, was a valued friend who donated liberally to that field of research. J. P. Morgan, Jr., Morgan's son and Osborn's cousin, followed in his father's footsteps and provided thousands of dollars of support for expeditions and displays associated with the work in vertebrate paleontology. Madison Grant contributed to work on North American mammals and served as one of Osborn's confidants in administering the board and the museum.[86]

While those individuals and others provided him with tremendous financial and political support, it is important to emphasize that Osborn played an active role in promoting himself and his program. At the museum, as at Columbia and the New York Zoological Society, Osborn effectively took advantage of his opportunities. He had well defined ideas for programs in academic as well as public biology. By delineating his plans, coordinating them with the ideas of institutional leaders, and drawing on a large network of associates for support, Osborn was able to institute many of his scientific and administrative objectives. That was true of the biology program he established at Columbia; it would also be the case with the program in vertebrate paleontology that he developed at the museum.

The study of extinct animals was his field of specialization. He knew the good specimen deposits, the kinds of questions he wanted to tackle, and the kind of economic support and personnel necessary to advance his interests. Osborn took the initiative in suggesting that the museum acquire the Cope collections. And it was Osborn who launched the effort to add work on fossil reptiles, especially dinosaurs, to the original emphasis on fossil mammals. He knew the kind of program he wanted to organize and how to adapt it to the ethos at the American Museum.

Osborn's status and connections were influential in getting him appointed to positions at Columbia and the American Museum and in enabling him to lay the foundations for scientific programs at those institutions. But Osborn was also a highly ambitious man, and he would employ those resources to create the kinds of programs that met his and his supporter's objectives. As an organizer, a promoter, and an administrator, he would use the support his friends provided him to shape a program in vertebrate paleontology.

Osborn and Vertebrate Paleontology at the American Museum

4

The American Museum offered Osborn great opportunities in his chosen field of science. With the advent of Cope and Marsh, vertebrate paleontology became a subject that one did not take up independently, at least not if one wanted to compete effectively with those figures. Osborn had such ambitions. He realized that his close affiliation with many of the museum trustees provided financial and political support that was much greater than anything available at Princeton or Columbia. Such backing would enable him to develop expeditions, collections, and displays that could equal or surpass Cope's or Marsh's efforts. Through his ties to influential associates, he also saw the chance to become a dominant figure institutionally and intellectually in American vertebrate paleontology.

Osborn took advantage of those opportunities through the program in vertebrate paleontology that he created. Help from his friends ensured that the DVP was established under "exceptionally favorable circumstances," and Osborn used such support to create a hierarchical program that he directed. That arrangement enabled him to supervise the department and at the same time to engage in administrative activities at Columbia, the Zoological Society, and a host of other organizations. Osborn continued to pursue scientific research, but now with the aid of a large group of assistants.

As the department's supervisor Osborn advanced himself and his program in a variety of capacities: by negotiating with wealthy associates for financial support; by convincing other administrators, scientists, and publishers to assist with departmental projects; and by promoting the department's achievements to the trustees, the scientific community, and the public. In developing his department in vertebrate paleontology Osborn functioned not only as a scientist but also as an administrator and a promoter. As a result he developed a program that embodied his scientific objectives as well as the ideas and values that he shared with the trustees and other patrons.

Organizing the DVP

Osborn created a Department of Vertebrate Paleontology that enabled him to maximize his administrative and scientific interests. In a letter to Jesup in 1891 he outlined an ambitious agenda of "exhibition, research, and publication" in mammalian paleontology. It was a program in which Osborn would operate by "supervising the work" of a large, diversified staff.[1] Osborn required assistants who would do the labor and would not present the problems that, as he knew so well, had plagued Marsh. Traditionally vertebrate paleontologists, including Leidy and Marsh, had used paid collectors or bone dealers to provide them with specimens. Many museums also relied on outside preparators, particularly Henry A. Ward and his natural history establishment at Rochester, New York, for mounted specimens or synoptic series of specimens. Osborn and the museum administration negotiated for the purchase of specimens and on occasion employed outside collectors. For the most part, however, he used the financial resources at his disposal to develop a centralized department, one whose members were directly responsible to the museum or to him personally.[2]

He first set out to hire a staff of collectors. In 1891, having failed to lure Hatcher away from Marsh, Osborn hired Jacob L. Wortman, previously one of Cope's collectors, as his principal assistant. He also hired O. A. Peterson, and from 1891 to 1895 Peterson and Wortman conducted a series of annual and profitable collecting expeditions in the western states and territories. Following Wortman's first season in the Big Horn Mountains of Wyoming, he and Peterson collected in Tertiary deposits throughout Wyoming, Utah, South Dakota, and New Mexico. In those first years Osborn also hired western field hands, men such as Albert Thomson and James W. Gidley, to assist with the collecting. Their work, along with the purchase of Cope's specimens, laid the foundation for the department's fine collection of fossil mammals.[3]

Osborn hired others to work in the museum. While Wortman and Peterson spent the winter months preparing the specimens they had collected, Osborn needed assistance with other tasks. He hired Charles

Earle, who had worked at the Academy of Natural Sciences and had assisted Osborn at Princeton, to catalogue the incoming materials. Osborn enthusiastically adopted the museum's emphasis on public education and exhibition and to that end hired Adam Hermann as his chief preparator. Hermann, who was later assisted by a large preparation staff, carried out Osborn's mandate to develop innovative techniques for displaying fossil vertebrates in active, lifelike poses. In addition, Osborn required artistic assistance. He brought with him to New York Rudolph Weber, the German artist he had employed at Princeton. Weber was to do line drawings of specimens for articles by Osborn, Wortman, and others. Osborn also set Weber to the task of painting watercolor reproductions of prehistoric life, and in later years employed Charles R. Knight, Erwin S. Christman, Lindsay Morris Sterling, and other artists to do that work.[4]

The program that Osborn created was hierarchical. Wortman, Peterson, Hermann, and Earle were responsible for the day-to-day work of the department, which Osborn directed and coordinated. He rarely participated in fieldwork, for example, but set the agenda for the department's expeditions. He defined the sites for exploration, the specimens of primary importance, and the reports required. It was Osborn who sent Peterson and Wortman to Lower Eocene deposits in Wyoming in early 1892, much as it was Osborn who sent Peterson to the Uintah Basin in 1893 and Barnum Brown to the dinosaur quarries at Como Bluff, Wyoming, in 1897.[5]

Osborn participated in some of those projects, but only to a limited extent. In 1897 he did some collecting at Huerfano basin in southern Colorado and examined other Eocene deposits in Wyoming and Colorado. In 1906 he studied specimens and deposits at Bitter Creek and Agate Springs, Nebraska. But for the most part his excursions to the field were to oversee department operations or to report on particularly important discoveries. When Barnum Brown found dinosaur remains at Como Bluff in 1897, Osborn visited the site. On his 1907 expedition for fossil elephants in the Fayûm Desert of Egypt, Osborn spent about two weeks touring the area, visited the pyramids and other sites with his family, and left department collector Walter Granger to spend the next several months doing fieldwork. In 1923 he joined the museum's Central Asiatic Expedition in Mongolia following the discovery of dinosaur eggs. As the DVP administrator, and later the museum president, he shared in the excitement of those finds and recognized the chance to draw public attention to his paleontological activities. When he went into the field it was usually for a brief reconnaissance, in formal attire, and often with his wife and one or two of his children in tow.[6]

Osborn also played an administrative role in the department's artistic and preparation work. In addition to assigning Hermann to develop new techniques for mounting extinct animals, he defined what kinds of exhibits the department developed and what form those exhibits took. Much the same was true of the artistic work. Osborn employed Knight and other artists and directed them to work on particular projects. Although Knight was an independent artist hired on commission, Osborn sought to direct Knight's work in ways that met his own demands, scientific as well as artistic, and embodied his interpretations.[7]

Osborn's assistants handled departmental operations. When William King Gregory became an assistant in 1900, one of his chief duties was organizing the Osborn Library, a major resource of published works on vertebrate paleontology that not only provided valuable reference material but added to Osborn's and the department's prominence in the science. As he became more involved in administrative activities at the museum and elsewhere, Osborn relied on senior staff members to oversee the work of others. By the early 1900s Hermann was in charge of the preparation staff and W. D. Matthew was responsible for departmental fieldwork and research. Gregory, in addition to duties in the library and on the new *American Museum Journal,* supervised the artwork of Christman, Sterling, and others.[8] In 1909 Osborn appointed Matthew curator of the department and made him responsible for daily operations and long-term plans. But his decisions were always subject to Osborn's approval. As museum president Osborn had the final say on all financial, personnel, and business matters pertaining to the DVP. He retained the position of curator emeritus and continued to oversee department activities. Although Osborn was an active administrator, he relied heavily on the work of his assistants. That arrangement freed him from the labor and day-to-day aspects of departmental operations and enabled him to pursue administrative ambitions and to publish on vertebrate paleontology and other subjects.[9]

The department contributed indirectly to much of Osborn's work in vertebrate paleontology. While Osborn examined specimens and constructed classifications and phylogenies for many families of fossil vertebrates, staff members did the "dirty work" of the science. Wortman, Peterson, Brown, and in later years Albert Thomson and Peter Kaisen collected, cleaned, and prepared specimens that were the basis for Osborn's descriptive and taxonomic studies. Other members of the staff were frequently called on to aid in the production of Osborn's publications. Matthew was generally the middleman in that arrangement.

As the assistant curator and later curator of the DVP, Matthew was the one through whom Osborn requested assistance with references, photographs, and drawings. Osborn frequently demanded that the department have certain specimens out and ready for his examination, as well as specific personnel ready to assist him in that work. Matthew, Gregory, Charles C. Mook, and Edwin H. Colbert, all of whom were noted vertebrate paleontologists in their own right, measured specimens and provided morphological or stratigraphic information for Osborn's work. In terms of his publications alone, the entire department was at Osborn's beck and call, even after he became museum president.[10]

Members of the department's scientific staff also helped to produce portions of Osborn's publications. Matthew researched and wrote most of the geological and morphological sections in Osborn's 1917 monograph on fossil horses.[11] Gregory, who was listed as the author of two chapters of Osborn's monograph on the titanotheres, also compiled much of the morphological data that went into several other chapters of that work.[12] In his early years in the department, Gregory assisted Osborn on the study of sauropods, and when Gregory took on other responsibilities, Charles C. Mook, another DVP scientist, completed the work for Osborn's monograph on the subject.[13] Those men and others within the department and without contributed a great deal to Osborn's study of the Proboscidea and his work on paleoanthropology.[14]

Osborn maintained a personal staff that contributed to his publications in various ways. A group of secretaries and editorial assistants prepared bibliographies and indices, coordinated photographs and drawings, and abstracted relevant literature for Osborn's books *Men of the Old Stone Age* (1915), *The Origin and Evolution of Life* (1917), and *Cope: Master Naturalist* (1930). Artists whom he hired produced the line drawings and other technical details for his publications. Osborn did contribute to those works. For paleontological studies he examined and described specimens and analyzed problems of stratigraphy, synonymy, and classification. He wrote the sections on variation, evolution, and inheritance that appeared in his articles and books. Osborn explicitly expressed his views in *Impressions of Great Naturalists* (1921), *The Earth Speaks to Bryan* (1923), and *Man Rises to Parnassus* (1927). But as he pursued a wide range of administrative and scientfic activities, Osborn employed departmental and personal staff to do much of the detailed work for his publications.[15]

Osborn reaped the rewards of such an arrangement. With the aid of his large group of assistants, he was able to publish hundreds of articles in vertebrate paleontology. Although he did not study fossil fish, amphibia, or birds, he wrote on many of the principal families of fossil reptiles and mammals. He examined a variety of problems in biology, geology, and anthropology. In addition, he wrote dozens of books and articles on science education, science and religion, and important scientists. His massive bibliography was not solely a testimony to his own industry, however; it indicated the efforts of an ambitious and wealthy administrator who put dozens of employees to work on projects that captured his interest.

The arrangement of his department enabled Osborn to profit in other ways. On occasion, Osborn's name appeared on articles largely written by others. An 1892 piece on fossil mammals from the Wasatch and Wind River Beds listed Osborn and Wortman as coauthors, however, Wortman had done the collecting and much of the research and writing. An 1895 article on fossils from the Puerco formation listed Osborn and Earle as coauthors, though the latter was responsible for much of the descriptive and taxonomic work that went into that piece. Matthew, Gregory, and others contributed a great deal of technical data to *The Age of Mammals* (1910), *The Titanotheres of Ancient Wyoming* (1929), and other publications. Osborn acknowledged their efforts, but it was his name that appeared as the sole author of such works.[16]

Osborn's name also figured prominently in many of the department's major achievements, particularly work that would be seen or read by the public. Specimens mounted by department preparators and murals painted by Charles R. Knight frequently included the statement: "done under the supervision of Henry Fairfield Osborn." He was on the scene when dinosaurs were discovered at Como Bluff in 1897 and when Cretaceous mammal teeth were uncovered in the Gobi Desert of Mongolia in 1923. Photographs of Osborn figure prominently at those events, and he claimed responsibility for some of the department's most significant discoveries. He also authored many of the major articles, popular as well as scientific, pertaining to those findings. In the case of discoveries made by the Central Asiatic Expeditions, Osborn sent telegrams, news stories, and other communications covering the explorations.[17] Not surprisingly, the public associated the department and its achievements with Osborn. He had participated in those activities by visiting field sites, examining specimens, and discussing questions of stratigraphy and classification. Still, Osborn did not engage in departmental operations on a consistent, full-time basis, and he definitely capitalized on work done in large part by his assistants.[18]

The credit that Osborn received for such work was not entirely out of the ordinary. Hierarchies were commonplace in science and many leading figures took credit for work done in conjunction with assistants.[19] At the American Museum such an arrangement also fit the circumstances. Osborn had created the department and he organized and supervised its work. He was responsible for obtaining the financial support necessary for vertebrate paleontology. Part of the money came from his own pocket. More frequently it came through solicitations from patrons, but in either case Osborn took credit for his efforts.

In addition to financial support from the trustees, Osborn had a wide network of influential friends through which he benefited. Prominent scientists such as C. O. Whitman and Charles Doolittle Walcott provided Osborn with research opportunities for himself and his assistants. His ties to publishers Robert Underwood Johnson *(Century Magazine)*, James McKeen Cattell *(Science)*, and John H. Finley *(New York Times)* enabled Osborn to promote his achievements through the popular press.[20] Because of his status as a wealthy and well-connected New Yorker, and because he created, supervised, and financed the program, Osborn was able to run his own show. Osborn's use of his power and position to capitalize on and in some instances interfere with departmental activities created difficulties with members of the DVP. So too did his personal and professional pretensions that engendered ridicule, contempt, and some bitterness within the department.

In promoting himself and his department Osborn functioned as an aristocrat. In addition to being a scientist he was a financier, manager, and salesman for the DVP. Osborn counted heavily on personal connections and persuasive influence to advance himself and his program. Moving from Princeton to the American Museum he went from being H. F. or Henry F. Osborn, to the more formal Henry Fairfield Osborn. To all except a few old friends like Scott or social equals like the Morgans, the Fricks, and the Dodges, he was always Professor Osborn.

Such distinctions extended to departmental activities. Trips by Osborn's secretaries and editorial assistants to his palatial home at Castle Rock had the appearance of a retinue of scientific servants. Carrying mountains of material by train from New York to Garrison, they worked and ate in the outer buildings on the estate, rarely in the main house with Osborn and his family. Departmental social gatherings were stratified affairs; scientific assistants dined with Osborn and his family, while secretaries, preparators, and others ate in a separate room.[21]

Osborn often flaunted his status. He let it be known when he was arriving at the museum, the zoo, or scientific meetings. Taking little notice of the matters that preoccupied his employees, he often called on them to drop everything to assist him. He offered criticisms on the personal lives of his assistants, suggesting that Matthew abandon smoking and coffee and expounding on the rewards of a daily walk or horseback ride.[22] Osborn was a wealthy man who was fully convinced of his own self-importance and often treated others in the museum, including scientists, in a condescending manner.

Osborn held his own scientific work in high regard. As indicated, he took virtually no part in the mundane aspects of vertebrate paleontology; others did the collecting, cleaning, and preparing of fossil specimens. He published on fossil systematics, but what particularly fascinated Osborn were the "philosophical questions" concerning evolution, inheritance, and biogeography. The study of those problems, he believed, was truly the basis of "creative work."[23]

Osborn also became convinced of the truth and great value of his work. As a young man starting out in the 1880s he was cognizant of his limitations, especially in experimental biology. Over the years, however, he lost all critical perspective on the character of his work. Although Osborn asked for and received trenchant criticism from his colleagues, especially Matthew, he never wavered from the belief that his interpretations were absolutely correct. He spoke of his own work in the same breath as the researches of Darwin, Huxley, or other towering figures in biology. He frequently referred to his training with Huxley and Balfour and his chance meeting with Darwin in Huxley's laboratory in 1879. Osborn came to view himself as the inheritor of their scientific mantle. He considered his own life and work exemplary, a model for making important scientific discoveries and achieving social and scientific prominence. His autobiographical sketches, notably *Fifty-Two Years of Research*, were didactic, egotistical works designed to portray his life as a lesson for aspiring young naturalists. In his own mind Osborn was a great man, and he did not hesitate to make that opinion known or to employ it to his advantage.[24]

Given his power and pretensions, it is not surprising that Osborn demanded personal and professional respect. On questions of scientific interpretation such as his ideas on evolutionary theory, Osborn accepted criticism and differing interpretations from Matthew and Gregory. But on matters of museum policy, particularly displays, he was an insistent and frequently an overbearing taskmaster. On mundane questions about a system for arranging Knight's paintings or lighting for a display of fossils from the La Brea tarpits, he demanded again and again that it be done his way. He kept close tabs on Knight's paintings and more than once demanded that wholesale changes be made in murals for the Hall of Fossil Mammals or the Hall of the Age of Man. When it came to matters of museum priorities or public education, Osborn often laid down the law to Matthew, Knight, or Hermon C. Bumpus and later Frederic A. Lucas, the museum directors.[25]

Osborn's attitudes and actions provoked some bitterness within the DVP. In 1894 Wortman, although claiming that he was not referring to Osborn, complained of the situation in vertebrate paleontology that promoted individuals on the basis of status, not merit.[26] He was further upset in 1897–98 when Osborn gave Barnum Brown, whom Wortman disliked, increasing responsibility for fieldwork. Wortman had worked for Osborn since 1891, but it was Brown who discovered dinosaurs at Como Bluff and whom Osborn dispatched on an expedition to Patagonia, a project in which Wortman had originally expressed interest. Wortman quit the American Museum for the new Carnegie Museum of Pittsburgh in late 1898. The following year he became more resentful when he was convinced that Osborn had failed to recommend him for Marsh's recently vacated position at Yale. For the rest of his life Wortman remained contemptuous of Osborn and everyone associated with the program at the American Museum.[27]

Serious problems also arose between Osborn and Oliver P. Hay. Osborn hired Hay in 1900 to work on fossil reptiles. Two years later, when Hay obtained a Carnegie Institution grant to work on fossil turtles and a bibliography of vertebrate paleontology, he participated in departmental projects only on a part-time basis. Problems, however, arose over his position, salary, and the amount of departmental assistance he would receive. Hay had ambitions beyond his work on fossil turtles or even fossil reptiles. In 1903 he was upset when Bashford Dean, Osborn's colleague in the Zoology Department at Columbia and a man of great wealth, was made curator of the Newberry Collection of fossil fishes and a new museum program devoted to that subject.[28]

Difficulties also developed over dinosaurs. Hay was at the museum when work on dinosaurs was flourishing and commanded greater priority than Hay's work on fossil turtles. Hay questioned some of Osborn's ideas on dinosaurs. He challenged Osborn's creation of the new genus *Tyrannosaurus* rather than incorporating new specimens into the existing *Deinodontus*. He disputed Osborn's, Matthew's, and Gregory's interpretation of the mounting of *Apatosaurus*. In contrast to their view, Hay maintained that *Apatosaurus*, rather than walking upright on all fours as elephants and other graviportal mammals do, may have had a sprawling pose like modern lizards. With his help some of the DVP preparators made a small restoration of the dinosaur in that manner.[29]

By 1906, when he had completed his work on fossil turtles, Hay asked to be placed in charge of the new hall of fossil reptiles. He was turned down. He was equally upset by Osborn's refusal to forward for publication a paper of his on fossil mammals. Although Osborn promised Hay the opportunity to work on fossil crocodiles, in June 1907 he claimed that the department did not have the money for such research, and Hay quit. He castigated the class system that dominated the museum, and in future years he and Osborn would continue to quarrel over interpretations and opportunities to pursue scientific research.[30]

Matthew, a leading member of the department for over thirty years, also had problems with Osborn. Although his reasons for leaving the museum for the University of California at Berkeley in 1927 are not entirely clear, Matthew had become more and more impatient with Osborn. For one thing he became critical of Osborn's scientific work. For years the two had planned to author a joint study of fossil horses, but in the mid 1910s Matthew abandoned the project. Matthew had done most of the fieldwork as well as the morphologic and stratigraphic analysis for the study. He also developed theoretical and methodological views that were significantly different from Osborn's. When Osborn proposed to write a work that focused on only a few type specimens, Matthew, well aware of the thousands of specimens in the museum's collection and the wide range of variation that Osborn was not considering, was unwilling to participate. In 1920 he wrote a critical review of Osborn's monograph, and by the end of the decade he was attacking interpretations of the pattern and process of evolution very similar to Osborn's.[31]

Matthew and Osborn also disagreed over the delegation of museum responsibilities. Since 1909 Matthew had been curator of the DVP. Although never entirely free from Osborn's interference, he had responsibility for running departmental affairs. Few problems arose until the early 1920s, when Osborn expanded the department and Matthew's responsibilities.

The issue concerned the Department of Geology. That department was directed by Edmund O. Hovey and housed the museum's invertebrate fossils. Following Hovey's death in 1924, Osborn made Matthew acting curator of the Department of Invertebrate Paleontology and Geology. He also appointed Matthew curator of a new Division of Mineralogy, Geology, and Geography, giving him responsibility for four departments. Osborn viewed the new position as an excellent administrative opportunity and a means for freeing Matthew from routine departmental work. As he told Matthew: "I consider the development of the Department of Geology and its extension through the Astronomic Gallery into two or three exhibition halls . . . as one of the great opportunities of your life."[32] Matthew, however, had always valued research more than administration and was not enthusiastic about the change. George H. Sherwood, the museum director, was probably correct when he suggested that the new responsibilities might be Osborn's way of "edging you [Matthew] out."[33]

By 1925 Matthew's personal as well as professional relationship with Osborn had deteriorated. Osborn had recently stated that he was "extremely displeased" over Matthew's decision concerning a system for cataloging Knight's paintings. He became upset over the handling of DVP affairs and demanded that Matthew institute monthly staff meetings. He also criticized one of Matthew's recent papers on correlation: "It does not seem to mark as much advance in our knowledge as is justified by the facts at hand."[34] Those issues, coupled with Matthew's increasingly critical attitude toward Osborn's work, undoubtedly influenced his decision to leave the museum.

Osborn and his work did not command respect from all who remained in the department. His interpretation of evolution and inheritance was, particularly by the 1920s, out of touch with much of the most important work being done in biology. Osborn's views on human evolution, which are discussed in Chapter 9, were influenced by his social and religious values and seriously flawed even in the eyes of his contemporaries. To assistants like Matthew, William King Gregory, and J. H. McGregor, Osborn was far from the epitome of an objective scientist. And the excessive importance he accorded himself and his scientific and social interpretations made Osborn an object of caricature and ridicule even among some of his closest associates. After he had left the museum, Matthew mockingly referred to the hyperbolic language Osborn used. Gregory too became increasingly critical of Osborn. He "is a terrific problem for all of us," Gregory noted in 1934. On several occasions he had to stand up for DVP scientists Edwin H. Colbert and Horace Wood who had opposed Osborn's views on the evolution of mammals. Gregory was faithful to Osborn, though he pointed out that he had lots of practice in "smiling hypocrisy."[35]

Nevertheless Osborn, unlike Marsh, was able to maintain a large and flourishing program in vertebrate paleontology. At Yale, Marsh's program had broken down as a result of dissatisfaction among his assistants, continued problems from Cope and Osborn, and political and economic troubles associated with the Geological Survey. Osborn's program never experienced such problems. In part that was true because of the vast financial and political resources at Osborn's disposal. Through his connections and ability to gain support from a network of influential and wealthy patrons, Osborn was able almost continuously to expand the size and scope of his program. Only during the Depression did the DVP experience monetary shortages.[36] As a result, the museum was able to offer good salaries.

Osborn was also able to offer his assistants good educational opportunities in biology and vertebrate paleontology. The department sponsored annual expeditions, possessed outstanding specimen collections, and maintained an excellent library for vertebrate paleontology. The museum offered access to other scientists and through its *Bulletin, Journal*, and guide leaflets provided ready outlets for publication. Osborn had also established cooperative arrangements with Columbia, the Marine Biological Laboratory, and the Bronx Zoo. His role in negotiating government contracts, in obtaining permission for DVP staff to visit and study at other collections, and in gaining access to important fossiliferous deposits provided opportunities in fieldwork and laboratory work that were unequalled.

Osborn was solicitous of the interests and needs of his staff. During his years as curator of the DVP, Osborn lobbied hard on behalf on his assistants. In annual reports he emphasized their contributions and requested better salaries, improved working conditions, and new projects. On occasion Osborn went out of the way to praise the work of his principal assistants. In 1896 he described the department's work with typical overstatement: "Thanks to Providence, Dr. Wortman and the staff, and the generous support of President Jesup, and other Museum friends and patrons, we have been able to more than fulfill the promise made in 1891." In 1909 and again in 1915 Osborn heaped high praise on Matthew's studies in paleontology and biogeography. He negotiated to have Gregory appointed as his successor at Columbia, and in letters to university and Zoology Department leaders he pressed for the promotion of his former student.[37]

Osborn even took an interest in the less senior members of his staff. James W. Gidley, a collector and preparator who worked for the DVP in the 1890s before moving on to the United States National Museum, made that point. Writing to Matthew in 1905, Gidley noted that his new supervisor, George P. Merrill "has been away most of the time since I came so I hardly know yet how I am going to like him, but he is no such man to work for as Professor Osborn. I expect I will wish many times I had not left my 'happy home' with the Horses in the American Museum." O. A. Peterson, who in 1899 joined the staff of the Carnegie Museum in Pittsburgh, sought to return to the American Museum on more than one occasion. Gidley and Peterson, to be sure, were interested in returning because of the excellent collections and the research and financial opportunities available at the museum. Yet they also had a commitment to Osborn and the environment that he had created.[38]

Within the DVP, Osborn gave his assistants some independence and in many cases the opportunity to structure their own careers. In 1890 when he tried to hire Marsh's assistant John Bell Hatcher for his new department, Osborn told him: "You will rank on the Museum staff and I will co-operate in keeping you ahead in every way. I want to see you successful and getting full credit for your work."[39] Although Hatcher did not join the staff and he and Osborn had a serious falling out, Osborn still built some degree of autonomy into the program. Wortman had a good deal of freedom in pursuing fieldwork and in his years on the departmental staff published many papers on fossil vertebrates. So too did Earle, Gidley, Brown, and Granger. Matthew and Gregory published prolifically on a wide range of subjects in vertebrate paleontology, and both became highly respected figures whose scientific reputations soon eclipsed Osborn's. Eventually they produced work that Osborn did not fully understand or appreciate and that contradicted his own interpretations. Nevertheless he promoted them and their work.[40]

Other department members, too, acquired reputations for their work. Barnum Brown's discoveries of dinosaurs gained him autonomy for his explorations. Throughout the early 1900s, Osborn dispatched Brown to South Dakota, Montana, and Alberta, Canada, to collect dinosaurs. But Brown also convinced Osborn to allow him to do fieldwork in Mexico, Greece, and later India. By the early twentieth century he had acquired an international and somewhat notorious reputation as one of the world's leading fossil collectors.[41] Adam Hermann, the chief preparator, although subject to Osborn's direction and criticism, effectively had a free hand in the departmental laboratory. He and Albert Thomson, Charlie Lang, and Otto Falkenbach were instrumental in developing technical innovations for the preparation and exhibition of fossil specimens. Hermann later published, at Osborn's urging, descriptions of his work in the *American Naturalist* and the *Bulletin of the American Museum*.[42] Charles R. Knight, although an independent artist who was not a member of the department staff or a museum employee, became famous for his paintings and sculptures. Drawing on the department's discoveries and Osborn's and Morgan's patronage, Knight became the world's foremost painter of prehistoric life.[43]

Osborn did not provide all members of the staff with equal opportunities for advancement. Always conscious of social distinctions, he carefully differentiated between educated, experienced assistants and others. While Osborn encouraged a Wortman or a Matthew to publish, he did not permit O. A. Peterson, whom he claimed lacked a facility for writing, to do so. While Hermann or Samuel Harmsted Chubb possessed the ability to produce outstanding displays that reflected favorably on Osborn and the department, most of the collectors, preparators, and illustrators were hired hands expected to follow instructions and do a job. Even principal staff members such as Matthew and O. P. Hay were criticized by Osborn for their work. In Osborn's program opportunities were available only to some, and even then not entirely free from Osborn's interference.[44]

Osborn established a program that worked to his benefit, disproportionately so, and his efforts on behalf of his staff and assistants were self-serving. The work of his assistants facilitated Osborn's researches, and their achievements benefited his reputation as much as their own. Yet he also developed a program that, with few exceptions, worked well. The financial and political support provided by the museum, the city, and individual trustees was the underpinning for that success. In addition, Osborn sought to establish a structure, working environment, and personal relationship with the members of his staff which, although class-dominated, would persist. For over thirty years the scientists Matthew and Gregory, the collectors Brown, Granger, Peter Kaisen, and Albert Thomson, and the preparators and artists Samuel Harmsted Chubb, Charles Christman, Lindsay Sterling, Otto Falkenbach, and Charlie Lang remained with and worked for Osborn. Adam Hermann, Erwin Christman, and George Olsen, all of whom predeceased Osborn, each spent over twenty years working in the DVP.[45]

Establishing Institutional Dominance

With administrative support and departmental resources at his command, Osborn was able to direct the program that he had created in ways that would fulfill personal as well as scientific objectives. In establishing the new department, one of his first goals was to undermine the program run by O. C. Marsh. The Yale paleontologist was still the most powerful figure in the field and was a major antagonist of Osborn's as well as Cope's. Although Osborn and Marsh had been on relatively good terms in the mid 1880s, by the end of that decade they were bitter enemies. Marsh knew that Osborn had supported Cope and Marsh's disgruntled assistants in 1885. In addition, Marsh and Osborn quarreled over research on Mesozoic mammals. When Osborn began research on that subject in 1886, he consulted with Marsh and on at least one occasion examined specimens in the Peabody Museum collection. However, after Marsh refused Osborn additional opportunities to study the specimens, Osborn severely criticized Marsh's classification of Mesozoic mammals.[46] Additional polemics followed, and by 1891 the two were engaged in a heated controversy over the subject. Personal attacks on both sides led to admonitions from other scientists and the rejection of papers for publication.[47] The rivalry took on institutional overtones as Osborn prepared to develop his department of mammalian paleontology at the museum.

In the summer of 1890, while he was still at Princeton, Osborn attempted to hire John Bell Hatcher for the DVP. Arguably the leading collector in the country, Hatcher was also a disgruntled Marsh employee. Although Osborn offered Hatcher new research opportunities that Marsh had not, he was unsuccessful in hiring Hatcher. But Osborn sought out and hired other Marsh employees: O. A. Peterson, who was Hatcher's brother-in-law, Adam Hermann, and for a time the collector W. H. Utterback were among Osborn's first employees.[48]

Osborn also confronted Marsh by challenging his collecting operations in the field. In early 1892 Osborn sent Peterson and Wortman to Lower Eocene deposits in southeastern Wyoming. Osborn was interested in collecting Eocene mammals for his new department. He also knew that Hatcher was working in the area for Marsh. Osborn still hoped to gain Hatcher's services and to acquire some of the important specimens that Hatcher was finding in that locality.[49] By hiring some of Marsh's men and initiating fieldwork in locations being worked by Marsh's staff, Osborn was directly challenging Marsh. Those developments resulted in a controversy over claims to important fossil deposits.

As the government paleontologist conducting fieldwork on public lands, Marsh had long maintained that he could prohibit outside investigators from working important localities. On a number of occasions he had used that tactic to limit Cope's fieldwork. Now in 1891–92 he tried to employ the same argument to stop Osborn. Marsh threatened Osborn and the museum with legal action if Wortman and Peterson made collections from the Lower Eocene beds of Wyoming. Osborn, however, turned the argument around and maintained that public lands could not be restricted for personal use.[50]

Osborn appealed to the museum trustees to negotiate the dispute. Osborn first suggested that he and Marsh present the issue to the Peabody Museum trustees, a proposition that Marsh declined. When Marsh sought to have Jesup limit Osborn's work, the museum president quickly came to Osborn's defense. "As I informed you personally," Jesup wrote to Marsh in February 1892, "Prof. Osborn has the entire charge of his department; the Trustees have taken this course, believing that they can repose confidence in him as a gentleman, a man of scientific attainments, and as the possessor of wise judgment in the control and management of his work. . . . The Board agrees with him, that we cannot promise to confine our explorations to any particular localities. We want to make the collections as representative as possible; therein rests their value to science."[51]

When Marsh persisted Jesup went further. Indicating to the museum secretary that he "wished him [Osborn] aided in every way possible," Jesup asked Osborn to prepare a complete statement of the affair, invited him to address the trustees on the matter, and helped to pass a resolution that condemned Marsh and supported the museum's actions. Eventually, when Jesup threatened to bring the issue to arbitration, Marsh backed down.[52] On a matter of interpretation and a test of political strength Osborn had initiated a series of controversial actions and had won.

In 1893–94 Osborn again used his influential connections to extend his department's work and to gain ground against Marsh. In 1893 Osborn sent Peterson to the Uintah Basin, an area in eastern Utah Territory known for mammalian remains. The prime fossil deposits lay on the reservation lands of the Uncompahgre Ute Indians. Yale and Princeton parties had recently gained access to those locations, but the tribal council confined Peterson to the barren, outlying beds. Peterson assumed that the Indian agent, Colonel Randall, had an interest in the mineral deposits on reservation lands and had engineered his exclusion.[53] Osborn, however, had other suspicions, particularly since both Yale and Princeton had had no difficulty doing fieldwork on the reservation.

Turning to Jesup and William C. Whitney, a trustee and the former Secretary of the Interior, Osborn sought access to the reservation lands for his department. Osborn, Jesup, and Whitney sent letters to Hoke Smith, the current Secretary of the Interior, and defined the problems such restrictions posed for the museum. Jesup noted that the situation threatened a setback in the museum's plans and would "create a great gap in our exhibits for the public." Further inquiry established that Marsh had played a part in limiting Peterson's access to the Uintah beds. By July 1894, with help from Osborn's influential friends, the reservation was opened to American Museum collecting parties.[54]

In 1892 Osborn worked to subvert Marsh by contributing to the attack on the U.S. Geological Survey. Under its director, John Wesley Powell, the survey had become a large government agency that pursued a multitude of projects and made many enemies. In addition to employing dozens of scientists on geological, paleontological, and hydrological studies, Powell sponsored a large and expensive project on a national map. He had also created an Irrigation Survey designed to regulate water use and land settlement in the West. Leaders from that area were outraged by Powell's reclamation efforts. When a recession hit in the early 1890s, politicians interested in cutting costs took aim at Powell's empire.[55]

Part of the attack focused on Marsh's work in vertebrate paleontology, and Osborn lent his voice to the chorus of critics. Writing to Iowa Senator William B. Allison, a family friend and opponent of Powell, Osborn argued that Marsh was doing a poor job of running the government program in vertebrate paleontology. He supported Cope's old claim that Marsh kept government specimens under private lock and key, even though Osborn had been allowed to examine fossils at the Peabody Museum in the 1880s. Osborn stated that under Marsh's control vertebrate paleontology was not a profitable investment and the government would fare better by supporting work in invertebrate paleontology.[56] Osborn, of course, had nothing against the study of fossil vertebrates. Rather, as Marsh told Powell, "the whole matter is with him [Osborn] a personal one." Osborn's aim was to undermine Marsh, and he succeeded. Marsh's large annual appropriation was revoked and soon after the congressional investigation he had to release Hatcher and Hermann, two of his prized assistants. Although Marsh remained on a nominal government salary and continued to publish, his program in the laboratory and the field was irreparably damaged.[57]

Osborn profited from Marsh's loss. He hired Hermann and contributed money that enabled William Berryman Scott to hire Hatcher for Princeton.[58] Later, Osborn succeeded in taking over Marsh's former position as government vertebrate paleontologist. In 1900, within a year of Marsh's death, Osborn wrote to the director of the Geological Survey, Charles Doolittle Walcott, and suggested that the government support the completion of monographs that Marsh had left unfinished. Marsh's successor at Yale, Charles Emerson Beecher, wanted that institution to maintain control of the projects. Walcott, however, realized that Osborn was negotiating from a much stronger position. In 1900 Osborn had accepted the post of honorary vertebrate paleontologist of the Canadian Geological Survey, a position that added to his scientific and administrative prestige. At the American Museum he had the financial support that would enable the government to produce the monographs at minimal expense to itself. The sizable staff of the DVP would enable Osborn to complete the projects expeditiously. With the support of Walcott and the secretary of the interior, Osborn added the position of government vertebrate paleontologist to his many other administrative roles.[59]

That appointment gave Osborn control over additional work in American vertebrate paleontology. He took responsibility for the completion of two of Marsh's unfinished studies: a monograph on sauropods and another on the brontotheres, an extinct family of fossil mammals that Marsh had named and that Osborn redesignated titanotheres. Under Osborn's direction those became major projects for the DVP. In his position as government vertebrate paleontologist Osborn arranged for assistance from other scientists. Hatcher, who had collected most of Marsh's specimens in the 1880s and 1890s, was employed to provide data on the locations, stratigraphy, and systematics of the titanotheres. So too were government geologists W. T. Lee, David White, and T. W. Stanton. Nelson H. Darton, a government scientist with expertise on the geology and underground water resources of the Rocky Mountains and Great Plains, provided Osborn with geological data as well as section maps of the Arikaree, Rosebud, and Big Horn formations that no one in the DVP was capable of producing.[60]

Osborn delegated Hatcher, who had collected Marsh's ceratopsian dinosaur specimens, to write the monograph on that suborder. Frederic Augustus Lucas, a paleontologist and comparative anatomist at the United States National Museum, was asked to complete the study of the Stegosauria. Both men were acknowledged students of fossil reptiles and were well acquainted with the Yale collections. But by assigning them those projects Osborn extended his authority over work done in American vertebrate paleontology.[61]

In his position as government paleontologist Osborn not only superseded Marsh, he developed additional opportunities for himself and his assistants. The fossil vertebrate collections at Yale, which had been off limits to all but Marsh and his staff since the late 1880s, were crucial for the work on the government monographs for which Osborn was responsible. Through negotiations with Yale officials, Osborn gained access to the Peabody Museum collections not only for Hatcher and Lucas but also for W. D. Matthew, Walter Granger, and other DVP assistants who were working on Osborn's titanothere project. The Peabody Museum collections provided material for Hermann's work on mounting the American Museum's *Apatosaurus* specimen. Marsh's collection was also important for Hay's work on fossil turtles that was indirectly related to Geological Survey research.[62]

Access to the Peabody Museum materials was not due entirely to Osborn's efforts. Beecher was reluctant to allow Osborn's staff and others the opportunity to examine those materials, but his successor, Charles Schuchert, was willing to foster good relations. As he stated, "What I'm trying to do is to make friends between all of us, and we have at Yale much to live down."[63] Still, Osborn had initiated the overtures, and in negotiations with Beecher and administrators like Edward S. Dana he sought to establish a normalized working relationship with Yale.

Osborn used his authority to extend his influence and promote his department in other ways. The Carnegie Museum of Pittsburgh, like the Peabody Museum at Yale, possessed specimens that were important for the government studies. Through arrangements Osborn made with director W. J. Holland, DVP scientists were allowed to examine fossils at that institution. In later years the department exchanged specimens with paleontologists at the University of Nebraska and the University of California at Berkeley.[64] Osborn maintained that his efforts were responsible for establishing good working relationships among American vertebrate paleontologists, and to some extent his claim was accurate. In the late 1890s he opened the American Museum collections to scientists from other institutions. In 1898 the DVP published a list of casts and duplicates for sale. Osborn also permitted outside investigators including Richard Swann Lull of the Massachusetts State Agricultural College, Frederick B. Loomis of Amherst College, and Elmer S. Riggs of Princeton to participate in DVP expeditions. Through those efforts Osborn helped to normalize relations in a field still affected by the hatred and distrust stemming from the Cope-Marsh feud.[65]

Yet despite Osborn's rhetoric, such efforts served primarily to advance him and his department. Through Osborn's negotiations his assistants obtained new research projects or the opportunity to pursue fieldwork in rich fossil deposits such as those at Agate Springs, Nebraska. Exchanges of fossils or copies of Knight's paintings promoted Osborn and the museum and enabled them to obtain casts of *Ichthyosaurus* and other European specimens. Exchanges with E. H. Barbour at Nebraska provided the American Museum with ready access to his outstanding collection of extinct proboscideans. Similar negotiations with the University of California gave the American Museum duplicates of important specimens being unearthed in the La Brea tar pits.[66] Through Osborn's ability to cultivate resources and to negotiate successfully with a wide network of scientists, politicians, and philanthropists, the DVP became the largest and leading department in vertebrate paleontology in the country.[67]

Osborn benefited from those developments. Because he did not engage in fieldwork or spend time studying collections at other institutions, he required good working relationships with other scientists and institutions. Those cooperative arrangements would aid his assistants, on whose work he relied. On those bases he could and did lay claim to major scientific and institutional achievements. He also sought to establish a dominant administrative role in the science. In addition to his positions in the DVP and the Geological Survey, he became a founder of the Society of American Vertebrate Paleontologists in 1902 and its successor the Paleontological Society in 1909. Osborn became a leading figure in his field

FIGURE 2. Henry Fairfield Osborn (neg. no. 36106)

and on many occasions used his power and prominence to dictate to other scientists. For example, in 1913, when W. J. Holland claimed that the DVP had mounted the wrong skull on *Apatosaurus*, Osborn publicly challenged Holland to prove his point. Holland backed down, though many years later he was proved correct.[68] In 1922, when O. P. Hay privately published a paper on fossil proboscideans, Osborn tried to have the Paleontological Society condemn him for violating standards of publication and distribution.[69] In that instance few geologists or paleontologists supported Osborn's position. To many in those fields he was a pompous aristocrat who had gained prominence on the basis of his wealth and connections, not his intellect or abilities. Charles Schuchert, an invertebrate paleontologist at Yale, was highly critical of Osborn, his ambitions, and his efforts to dominate work in paleontology.[70] Nevertheless, Osborn gained control over important financial and institutional resources for doing work in the subject and employed the power associated with those positions to establish a dominant role for himself and his department.

Establishing Scientific Dominance

Osborn directed the department in ways that reflected his own enthusiasms. In a literal sense his interests became the department's priorities and dominated the work of the DVP from the early 1890s to the mid 1930s. The subjects that he considered important, from paleomammalogy to paleoanthropology, were the basis for projects that the department took up. As his ambitions expanded from the study of North American fossils and formations to vertebrate paleontology on an international scale, departmental expeditions and undertakings grew accordingly. Taxonomically and geographically Osborn was able to meet his ever-growing desire to encompass the whole domain of vertebrate paleontology. His influence in the department reached to lower levels of resolution. Scientific questions that he deemed significant were the problems that Matthew and Gregory pursued. His views on the posture and habitat of *Apatosaurus*, the nature of the evolutionary process, or human evolution were the interpretations represented in the department's public displays.

Osborn also embraced and appealed to the objectives of the trustees. At Princeton, Osborn had worked exclusively in academe; his work in biology and vertebrate paleontology focused on study, publication, and the development of a program of graduate education and research. The American Museum, however, was a large, public institution whose patrons saw the evidence of vertebrate paleontology as embodying a number of their objectives. To the wealthy philanthropists who donated to the museum and dominated its board, fossil vertebrates were rare, large, and obvious facts whose display would increase the status of the museum and its benefactors. Such objects implied the possession of knowledge, further enhancing the proprietary interests of the trustees. Fossil vertebrates also had sheer entertainment value and could contribute to public education. As the documentary evidence for evolution, fossil vertebrates could convey to the public the importance of nature and nature's laws. Osborn quickly and enthusiastically embraced those objectives. While developing a program that included collecting specimens and pursuing research, Osborn also promoted projects that appealed to the educational and proprietary interests of Jesup and the museum leaders.

Paleomammalogy

The program that Osborn created in 1891 focused on paleomammalogy, his field of scientific interest and expertise. While his early work concentrated on the study of the odd-toed perissodactyls, Osborn's emphasis on North American remains meshed with the trustees' interest in developing good representative collections of North American specimens. The trustees, particularly Jesup, were also impressed by Osborn's efforts in another respect: the rapid development of a program for exhibiting fossil vertebrates.

From the outset Osborn placed a high priority on the public dimension of paleontology. He made it clear that Wortman, Peterson, and other collectors should attempt to find representative specimens that were capable of being mounted. In 1892 Osborn and Wortman emphasized the need to obtain a "good exhibition collection [of Cretaceous mammals] out of the Laramie." Osborn directed Peterson, then working in the Uintah Basin, to concentrate on mammals and to obtain complete specimens of *Protoceras, Hyopotamus,* and *Artionyx.*[71] The Cope collection, which included many mountable specimens as well as specimen fragments that complemented material already possessed by the DVP, also provided the opportunity for developing displays.

Osborn's interest in the public dimension of paleontology is evident in other respects as well. Earle's work focused on preparing specimens and cataloging the department's growing collection, but when W. D. Matthew took over that job in 1895 he had additional obligations. His task was to reexamine Cope's descriptions and classifications of the specimens in that collection. Matthew was also delegated to develop specimen labels for public displays. He later noted that during the department's early years Osborn considered almost every specimen worthy of being put on display. Thus, much of Matthew's time and effort was devoted to writing descriptions to aid the visiting public.[72]

Osborn and the museum capitalized on the abilities of Charles R. Knight. Originally employed as a commercial artist, Knight had an interest in animal painting. A frequent visitor to the museum, he also had a personal connection at the institution: Knight's father was the private secretary of J. P. Morgan.[73] In 1894 Knight did some work on extinct peccaries for Wortman that brought him to the attention of Osborn and Morgan. In 1896 Osborn employed Knight to paint fossil mammals and the environments in which they lived to accompany his paper for the *Century Magazine*. Two years later Knight worked on commission for Osborn and Morgan and produced large murals as well as bronze miniatures of extinct animals. Through Osborn's efforts the museum copyrighted Knight's work and sold reproductions of his paintings and sculpted miniatures to other institutions and individuals. Knight's work quickly gained international acclaim and added a new and dramatic dimension to Osborn's and the trustees' interest in presenting the evidence of prehistoric life to the public.[74]

Osborn also promoted the museum's objectives through the development of mounted displays of fossil vertebrates. Other museums had long used mounted displays of specimens as a means to attract and educate the public. The mastodon at Charles Willson Peale's Philadelphia Museum captured much attention in the early 1800s. So too did the first American dinosaur display, the *Hadrosaurus foulkii* that Cope, Joseph Leidy, and Benjamin Waterhouse Hawkins mounted at Philadelphia's Academy of Natural Sciences in 1868. Henry A. Ward of Rochester sold mounted displays of *Megatherium* and other fossil vertebrates to college museums and other institutions. The exhibits at Princeton's E. M. Museum, which included some of Ward's mounts and a cast of Hawkins's *Hadrosaurus*,[75] contributed to Osborn's interest in vertebrate paleontology. But it was only at the American Museum that he promoted the development of a major series of exhibits designed to educate the public.

Hermann took the lead in that effort. Hermann had worked for Marsh for sixteen years but had never mounted fossil vertebrates for display. Marsh was opposed to or at least skeptical about such work, and he only agreed to have mounts of his fossils made in 1893, after Hermann had left his employ.[76] Hermann, by all accounts, was a stodgy individual who had little interest in developing exhibition techniques, but Osborn prevailed upon him to do so. After examining fossil vertebrates on display at the British Museum, the Muséum d'histoire naturelle in Paris, and elsewhere, Osborn pushed and prodded Hermann to develop the means for mounting extinct animals in active, lifelike poses. By 1894 Hermann had developed four different techniques: mountings on bronzed uprights, relief mountings on backgrounds of imitation stone, panel mountings, and complete skeletal mountings with concealed iron work.[77]

At the time, the museum had no exhibit hall for fossil vertebrates and Hermann and the staff put together the specimens in the department's confined quarters in the basement. But Osborn brought their efforts to the attention of the trustees. He described the work in the departmental report for 1894 and included photographs of several specimens in the museum's *Annual Reports*.[78] The mounts impressed Jesup, and with his enthusiastic support the museum opened an entire hall for the exhibition of fossil mammals in November 1895. The displays were innovative, showing skeletons of an extinct creodont feeding or an ancient horse running (figure 3). According to Samuel Harmsted Chubb, who later joined the museum staff, there were some technical inaccuracies in the displays. George Brown Goode, the director of the National Museum, dismissed such work as art not science. But in general the displays captured public interest and put the American Museum at the forefront of exhibition work in vertebrate paleontology.[79]

Osborn drew upon such success to expand the size and scope of his program, and in ways that appealed to the trustees. He promoted additional projects in paleomammalogy. Osborn used the purchase of the Cope collection to justify the hiring of William Diller Matthew. He appealed to the trustees for $10,000 for a project on horses.[80] Cope's collection included many fossil horse specimens. In addition, the history of the horse family provided one of the most important documentary records for evolution.

A number of European biologists and paleontologists had examined morphological change among horses, but Marsh's work provided the most complete information on the evolutionary history of the family. Marsh and students on the Yale College expeditions discovered several new genera that indicated growth in overall body size, change in the structure of the molar teeth, and a reduction in the number of foot bones. Marsh and most scientists of the day interpreted those changes in orthogenetic terms, as a series of linear and progressive modifications from the small, five-toed animal of the Eocene to the large three-toed *Equus* of today. Marsh's work also demonstrated that North America, not Europe, was the principal center of horse evolution. Marsh, however, had worked on horses strictly within a scientific context. The specimens remained disarticulated and housed in his laboratory at Yale, and he con-

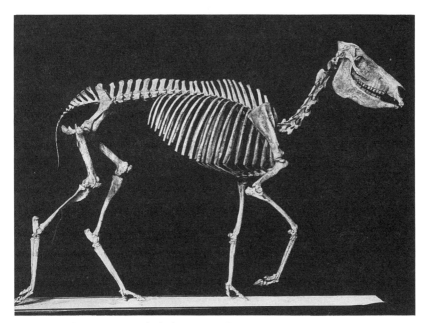

FIGURE 3. Reconstructed skeleton *Neohipparion whitneyi*
(neg. no. 334198)

fined his discussion of the evolution of the horse to brief, technical papers in scientific journals.[81]

To Osborn a project on horses presented great opportunities. It would enable him to surpass Marsh. Osborn hoped to obtain a wealth of scientific information and to distribute it to the public on a grand scale. A project on horses also provided an excellent means for fulfilling the interests of the trustees. The history of the horse family provided a means for readily conveying nature's great law of evolution. The subject illustrated the importance of American fauna. Horses were also a subject of personal interest to many of the trustees. Osborn and his family owned and rode horses, and trustees Percy Pyne, William C. Whitney, and Cornelius Vanderbilt were avid horse owners and fanciers.[82]

Osborn's first appeal did not gain support, but in 1897 Whitney gave $15,000 that enabled Osborn to develop a project on horses that entailed collection, research, and display. With that money Osborn hired James W. Gidley, then a student at Princeton, to conduct a series of expeditions in Texas and South Dakota. Matthew, Walter Granger, and Albert Thomson were also directed to search for fossil horses throughout Colorado,

South Dakota, and Texas. Those efforts added hundreds of specimens to the department's collections, and both Gidley and Matthew published notable articles on fossil horses. Osborn instructed his preparators to develop a series of mountings demonstrating the evolutionary change in the horse family. He also hired Samuel Harmsted Chubb to develop an exhibit of recent horses and a study of horses in motion.[83]

Osborn became personally involved in promoting the project. He joined horse clubs, subscribed to horsemen's publications, and lectured to horsemen's associations. Through those efforts he solicited support for the department's work from W. W. Kean, Frank Sturgis, and members of the New York Farmers' Association. Those individuals provided not only money but also specimens of recent horses for Chubb's osteological research.[84] Osborn also promoted the study of horses through publication. He and Matthew authored brief papers for the trade magazine *Horse and Driver*. Osborn wrote a popular piece on horses for the *Century Magazine* and an introduction to a book on the Arabian horse by Spencer Borden. When Osborn was invited to deliver the Harris Lectures at Northwestern University in 1906, he used the occasion to present a series of popular talks on the history of horses. He successfully promoted the work of the DVP by developing a project that had scientific significance as well as personal appeal to his wealthy friends.[85]

Other projects on fossil mammals also occupied Osborn's interest. Osborn's early work on perissodactyls had led him to study rhinoceroses and titanotheres, and his U.S. Geological Survey position allowed him to complete Marsh's unfinished work on the latter family. Departmental work on the titanotheres lasted from 1902 to 1922, occupied dozens of workers, and cost thousands of dollars. While Gregory studied morphology and musculature, Matthew and Granger provided the geologic and stratigraphic information on the basis of which Osborn determined titanothere life zones. Departmental artists and preparators contributed in other ways. Indeed a 1920 letter from Gregory to Osborn specifying the staff members who had participated in the project ran to over nine pages.[86] In addition to the government work on titanotheres, J. P. Morgan financed an expedition to Alaska for proboscideans and paid $30,000 for the purchase and remounting of the Warren mastodon. Later in the 1910s J. P. Morgan, Jr., and others contributed to the purchase of specimens and the development of displays of saber-toothed cats and other animals from the La Brea tar pits. All of those were large, striking specimens that documented evolution and attracted public attention.[87]

Osborn was eager to expand beyond paleomammalogy and research in North America. Claiming in 1895 that he had fulfilled the original contract with Jesup to create an important program in North American mammalian paleontology, he made a special plea for money for an American Museum expedition to Patagonia.[88] In the 1890s the Argentine scientist Florentino Ameghino touched off an international controversy by claiming that Patagonia was home to the oldest mammals and the center for vertebrate evolution and distribution. Ameghino's work challenged the standard interpretation that Europe and North America were the centers for the origin and geographical distribution of all major vertebrate groups. Nor was Ameghino alone in his views. A number of late nineteenth-century scientists maintained that South America was a major center of animal distribution. Many postulated that extended land bridges, or in some instances an ancient continent, had once connected South America with Australia or South Africa. A knowledge of South American and South African fauna and horizons was thus important to problems of biostratigraphy and biogeography.[89]

Osborn had other reasons for wanting to promote an expedition to Patagonia. Ameghino's radical interpretation had led American and European paleontologists to examine South American specimens and horizons, and Osborn did not want his program to be left out of a paleontological cause célèbre. As he told the trustees, "the great submerged Antarctica, a continent which undoubtedly connected South America with Australia, New Zealand, and South Africa at one point in the world's history, is now rapidly becoming a subject of the deepest scientific interest all over the world, and expeditions are being sent to obtain evidence as to the existence and limits of this continent—three start next year from England alone."[90]

Osborn was always on the lookout for new projects that would expand the department's efforts and move it to the forefront of vertebrate paleontology. His predecessors Cope, Leidy, and Marsh had confined their studies to North American horizons, and Osborn realized that research in South America and South Africa provided a means for augmenting the department's work and reputation. Osborn's interest in a South American expedition was also influenced by the ideas and activities of his close associates. In the 1890s J. P. Morgan, Cleveland Dodge, and other businessmen were expanding their markets. Theodore Roosevelt was vigorously asserting America's expansionist rights in Hawaii, Latin America, and the Philippines. Political and economic imperialism did not lead directly to Osborn's plans for a Patagonian expedition, but contemporary circumstances lent plausibility and momentum to such an endeavor.[91]

Osborn was not successful in obtaining the support he requested, but the department's objectives did expand. Although he received no financial backing for an American Museum expedition to South America, he helped persuade J. P. Morgan to sponsor a three-year Princeton University expedition and the publication of a multivolume work on the flora, fauna, and geography of South America. Osborn negotiated with Scott and Hatcher to allow Barnum Brown to accompany the Princeton expedition on its last journey in 1898–99. He also paid Brown's expenses.[92] In 1907 Osborn was able to convince Jesup to sponsor an expedition to the Fayûm of Egypt. According to Osborn, Africa was another major center of adaptive radiation and therefore important for his work on the evolution and geographical distribution of mammals. His promise to bring back new and unique specimens of large African animals, particularly extinct elephants, spurred support for his efforts to expand the size and scope of his department's activities.[93]

Dinosaurs

Osborn received greater support for expanding the department in another direction: adding work on fossil reptiles to the existing emphasis on fossil mammals. Osborn's decision to enlarge the department in that way was somewhat fortuitous. In 1897 Osborn wrote to Barnum Brown, a student of Samuel Wendell Williston's at the University of Kansas, and offered him a position at the museum collecting Mesozoic mammals. Osborn had an interest in those small, prehistoric animals and Brown had experience collecting in secondary formations.[94]

But Osborn instructed Brown to look for early mammals in well-known dinosaur quarries in Colorado and Wyoming, and it is likely that he had dinosaurs as well as fossil mammals on the agenda. Indeed in November 1895, right after the opening of the Hall of Fossil Mammals, Osborn had requested that the department's program be expanded to include all fields of vertebrate paleontology, a move the trustees approved.[95] In his first response to Osborn, Brown referred to the prospects of working at Como Bluff, precisely the place where Marsh's collectors had discovered immense dinosaur bones in the 1870s. Noting that he had previously worked the area with William H. Reed, one of Marsh's former collectors, Brown stated that "as to the reptiles, I think we can obtain any amount of material." Osborn was well aware of the popular appeal and scientific significance of dinosaurs. He also saw another opportunity to "break down Marsh's work as far as possible."[96]

Brown did discover dinosaur remains at Como Bluff in May 1897, and his findings had a powerful impact on the DVP. Osborn, who was hopeful but also somewhat skeptical about finding dinosaurs in those beds, immediately made that subject a top priority. By 1897 the DVP had enough support to outfit more than one expedition annually, and following Brown's discovery Osborn directed Wortman in Colorado, Walter Granger in South Dakota, and Matthew and Handel T. Martin in Kansas to proceed to Wyoming. The discovery was so significant that Osborn visited the Como Bluff site himself, a relatively rare appearance by the curator who supervised departmental activities from New York. With the discovery of large bone fragments of the gigantic sauropods *Diplodocus* and *Apatosaurus*, Como Bluff became a department work site for the next several years.[97]

The exciting discoveries at Como Bluff also prompted much additional activity. Besides maintaining a crew at Como Bluff through 1899, Osborn instructed department members to examine the surrounding countryside for additional dinosaur remains. Investigating an area some thirteen miles away, Walter Granger found a shepherd's cabin built out of dinosaur bones. Subsequent work unearthed a deposit richer than even the Como Bluff site. Bone Cabin Quarry, as it was called, became a major site for DVP fieldwork from 1898 to 1905. So too did the nearby sites at Nine Mile Quarry and Six Mile Gulch. Fieldwork by Granger, Albert Thomson, Peter C. Kaisen, and others produced important discoveries of *Stegosaurus*, *Camptosaurus*, and *Ornitholestes* that contributed substantially to the DVP's collection of dinosaurs.[98]

Osborn sponsored additional fieldwork and research. In 1900 he hired George R. Wieland, a paleobotanist at the Peabody Museum and an expert on fossil plants found in association with dinosaurs, to undertake a reconnaissance of Jurassic and Cretaceous formations in South Dakota.[99] Osborn also sent Brown, recently returned from Patagonia, and Granger and Albert Thomson to South Dakota. In 1902, following up a lead from William T. Hornaday that there were dinosaur remains in northern Montana, Brown began investigations in the Hell Creek formation. His work resulted in the discovery of the first fragments of the carnivorous dinosaur *Tyrannosaurus rex*, a find that created tremendous excitement at the museum. Brown later uncovered additional vertebrae and an almost complete *Tyrannosaurus* skull, and by 1906 the DVP had a unique and valuable treasure in its possession. In the Hell Creek and Lance formations Brown also discovered the remains of the dinosaurs *Anatosaurus* and *Triceratops*. In the 1910s Brown and other collectors found valuable specimens of *Ornithomimus*, *Corythosaurus*, and ceratopsian dinosaurs near the Red Deer River in Alberta, Canada. Through that work the American Museum developed the world's leading collection of dinosaurs.[100]

In response to the discoveries of dinosaurs, Osborn made a number of changes in the department. Realizing that the fieldwork in secondary horizons constituted a major new undertaking, he suggested that the department be organized into two divisions, one for fossil mammals, the other for fossil reptiles. Although that division was formalized only many years later, a de facto recognition of that separation existed at the end of the century. Matthew and Granger focused their attention on fossil mammals. Brown's work concentrated on dinosaurs, and Osborn took advantage of Brown's exciting discoveries to name, describe, and classify several new dinosaur genera. In 1900 Osborn hired Oliver P. Hay and William King Gregory to assist with the department's expanded objectives. Neither man worked primarily on dinosaurs: Hay was a specialist on fossil turtles and Gregory, then a beginning graduate student at Columbia, had responsibility for the Osborn library, the editorship of the *American Museum Journal*, and research on Osborn's titanothere monograph. Both men, however, had a knowledge of fossil reptiles and both contributed to the research and reconstruction work on dinosaurs that preoccupied the department in the first decade of the twentieth century.[101]

Osborn drew upon the discovery of dinosaurs to appeal for additional museum support. Claiming that the American Museum could become the world's leading center for fossil reptiles, Osborn impressed upon the trustees the need for major new developments. He called for the creation of a Hall of Fossil Reptiles to complement the department's Hall of Fossil Mammals. He even offered to pay for any expansion of the mammal hall if a patron could be found to finance the fossil reptile and amphibian hall. He suggested that the purchase of Cope's collection of North American fossil reptiles and batrachians offered an additional means for promoting the new dimension of the department's work.[102]

The trustees readily met those requests. Beginning in 1897 and extending over the next several years, Morgan provided free transportation of dinosaur fragments from Wyoming and Montana to New York. In 1899 E. H. Harriman sponsored a major expedition to the dinosaur fields. The trustees purchased the second Cope collection in 1899 and by 1905 had contributed enough money to construct the fossil reptile hall, just in time to accommodate the recently completed *Apatosaurus* mount. Through Osborn's prompting and salesmanship, friends and trustees were convinced that dinosaurs could significantly enhance the museum's popular appeal and worldwide reputation.[103]

Osborn pushed those efforts because he realized the great possibilities at hand. Although dinosaurs were interesting, his predecessors had not been very successful in bringing those creatures to the attention of the public. The mounting of the *Hadrosaurus* at the Academy of Natural Sciences originally generated tremendous enthusiasm, and Hawkins later mounted casts of the dinosaur at Princeton and the Smithsonian Institution. But by the turn of the century those specimens were in disrepair and attracting little attention. Marsh had not capitalized on his discoveries of dinosaurs. His collectors found hundreds of specimens of sauropodous, ceratopsian, and armored dinosaurs, and Marsh made important contributions to the understanding of dinosaur morphology and systematics. But none of his discoveries was mounted or made available to the public during his lifetime. By placing dinosaurs on display, Osborn had an opportunity to push forward his program and a dramatic means for meeting the trustees' objectives.[104]

Osborn also sponsored those efforts because he knew that other institutions were competing for dinosaurs. By the end of the century Marsh was no longer a threat, but the new Field Columbian Museum in Chicago had launched an expedition to Wyoming for dinosaurs.[105] More serious competition came from the new Carnegie Museum of Pittsburgh. Carnegie, the wealthy steel magnate, was fascinated by the accounts of the recent discoveries and made the museum's top priority the acquisition of a dinosaur "as big as a barn." In 1898 the Carnegie hired Wortman, who had directed the American Museum parties at Como Bluff the previous year. By the next summer Wortman and two other collectors had discovered a fine *Diplodocus* specimen in Wyoming. Over the next few years there was somewhat of a race between the Carnegie and American museums to mount the first sauropod. The Carnegie won, putting up its *Diplodocus* in July 1904, but the competition had spurred the DVP to increase its staff and activities.[106]

Given his objectives and his concern over the achievements of his competitors, Osborn spent thousands of dollars and added more manpower for the preparation and mounting of dinosaurs. While Hermann had had the aid of only a few assistants in the department's early years, there was now a need to expand the laboratory staff to keep pace with the tons of material coming into the museum. By 1900 the DVP had between ten and fifteen preparators on its staff, most of whom worked on dinosaurs and were paid personally by Osborn, not the museum. He hired casters, machinists, and others to aid in laboratory and preparation work.[107] The mounting of *Apatosaurus*, a matter of particular importance to Osborn, was an all-out effort that involved collectors and preparators, scientific staff members such as Matthew and Gregory, and the artists Knight and Christman. Other projects, such as the free mountings of *Allosaurus*

(1907), *Anatosaurus* (1907), and *Tyrannosaurus rex* (1910–11), and the panel mountings of *Ornitholestes* (1902) and *Camptosaurus* (1908) were also major undertakings. Each entailed scientific analysis, the study of technical and artistic questions, and the coordination of many specialized workers at great expense.[108]

The discovery of dinosaurs was, of course, also the basis for scientific research and publication. Osborn wrote many articles on the subject, including technical studies of *Diplodocus, Tryannosaurus,* and *Albertosaurus.* In later years he published on other specimens from the United States, Canada, and Mongolia. In most instances those specimens were found by Brown and other DVP staff members, though generally Osborn had the privilege of writing the first descriptions and conferring the name on the organisms.[109] Brown also wrote dozens of papers on dinosaurs. Charles C. Mook, a reptile paleontologist, wrote on *Camarasaurus* and other sauropods discovered by Cope, and Matthew wrote the museum's popular handbook on dinosaurs.[110]

Osborn made sure the public knew of the department's achievements. An article in the *New York World* in November 1898, while exaggerating the characteristics and habits of *Diplodocus,* made known the department's work at Bone Cabin quarry. In later years Osborn, Matthew, and Brown published popular articles on *Apatosaurus, Tyrannosaurus rex, Ornitholestes,* and other dinosaurs in the museum's journal and in museum guide booklets. They kept readers apprised of their work through articles and interviews in the *Independent* and *Outlook.*[111] With the completion of the mounting of *Apatosaurus* and the opening of the dinosaur hall in early 1905, the *New York Times* and *Scientific American* featured the museum's paleontological activities on a fairly regular basis.

Scientific American particularly became a vehicle for promoting the department's dinosaur work. On several occasions the magazine displayed reproductions of Knight's paintings on its cover. Articles by staff writers and museum scientists emphasized the department's rare and valuable discoveries, the importance of new restorations, and the dramatic features associated with the habits and appearance of the dinosaurs. Writers usually noted the efforts of departmental scientists and preparators, but Osborn was often acknowledged for the achievements. The statement by writer Walter L. Beasley that Osborn had "scored a two-fold paleontological triumph" by developing an exhibit that showed the carnivorous dinosaur *Allosaurus* feeding on *Apatosaurus* was not uncommon. Osborn readily gave interviews and provided information to the press.[112]

Osborn also promoted artistic reproductions of dinosaurs. In the spring of 1897, when Osborn began to sponsor work on dinosaurs, he sent Knight to work with Cope to bring his ideas on extinct vertebrates to life. Knight's depiction of Cope's *Drypotsaurus*, along with his paintings of other extinct reptiles in articles published that year by Osborn and William H. Ballou, marked the beginning of their efforts to make dinosaurs generally well known. By the early 1900s Osborn was commissioning Knight to paint watercolor reproductions of *Apatosaurus*, *Allosaurus*, *Tyrannosaursus rex*, and the other dinosaurs that the department was discovering and reconstructing. Knight's work depicted dinosaurs in active, dramatic situations of combat and struggle for survival. His paintings also embodied Osborn's emphasis on the power of nature and depicted his interpretation of the environment, structure, and habits of dinosaurs. For over two generations Knight's paintings played an important part in defining the public's conception of those animals.[113] The discoveries of dinosaurs were more than an important scientific development; they were also a means for expanding the department's efforts in fieldwork, displays, and artistic and photographic reproductions.

Paleoanthropology

Dinosaurs and fossil mammals remained central to the department's work, but Osborn also directed the DVP into yet another field of inquiry: paleoanthropology, or the study of human paleontology and evolution. Osborn's interest in that subject began around 1908 and was in part a consequence of contemporary scientific developments. In 1901 the discovery of two caves near Les Eyzies in southern France provided convincing evidence in favor of a long-disputed hypothesis: that Upper Paleolithic people had produced art. The Abbé Breuil, a young French clergyman, claimed that animal drawings in those caves were authentic and his work opened the door to new interpretations of prehistory.[114] In 1908–9 the French paleontologist Marcellin Boule examined a recently discovered Neanderthal skeleton from La Chapelle-aux-Saints. Neanderthal remains had been discovered throughout the late nineteenth century, but Boule's specimen was the most complete. In addition to Boule's find, the study of human evolution was spurred by the discovery of the famous Piltdown specimens. In 1911 the amateur archeologist Charles Dawson unearthed the first remains near Sussex, England. The discovery of additional fragments three years later led many to proclaim that Piltdown, or *Eoanthropus dawsoni*, was the true ancestor of *Homo sapiens*.[115] Osborn was well aware of those exciting developments, and having already worked on fossil reptiles and mammals he was eager to expand his interests into still another area of paleontology.

Osborn considered questions in paleoanthropology as early as 1907 but did not devote himself to the subject until some years later. In 1912 he toured the major paleolithic sites of Europe, particularly those in France and Spain. Through that research he became "intensely interested" in human evolution and made paleoanthropology his top priority. With the aid of museum assistants he published a popular text, *Men of the Old Stone Age* (1915). His associates also took up the subject. Matthew and Granger, who had recently launched a study of the fauna of the Wasatch and Wind River formations, paid close attention to extinct primates. Gregory, whose previous work had focused on the study of lower vertebrates, shifted his research emphasis to primates in the mid 1910s. Because of Osborn's enthusiasm for the subject, as well as the considerable power and influence that he wielded, questions of human paleontology and evolution became a major topic of investigation in the DVP.[116]

Osborn's interest in the subject influenced another former student and associate, Roy Chapman Andrews. Andrews, a member of the museum's Department of Mammalogy who had worked on whales, had been a student in Osborn's last class at Columbia and was well aware of Osborn's theory of the "Asiatic origin of mammalian life." Andrews became committed to proving that hypothesis by undertaking research in Central Asia. In 1912 he approached Osborn on the subject and the museum president quickly gave his approval. Andrews organized and headed two preliminary expeditions to Asia in 1916–17 and 1919 and then organized the much larger Central Asiatic Expedition.[117]

Osborn backed Andrews's scheme for a number of reasons. He was very much interested in promoting explorations for scientific as well as social reasons. He also took a personal interest in Andrews. For Osborn paleoanthropology opened new opportunities; his predecessors Leidy, Cope, and Marsh had published little on the subject and none had pursued research outside the United States. Osborn viewed the Asiatic expeditions as a means of confirming his evolutionary and biogeographical ideas. He also realized that the search for human origins was a topic of great popular and scientific appeal. Human remains, while not large, obvious facts like mastodon or dinosaur bones, were rare and highly valued objects. Discovering the birthplace of mankind had significant scientific and religious consequences. Andrews conceived of the Central Asiatic Expeditions as a project "to reconstruct its [Asia's] past climate, vegetation, and general physical conditions." But he and Osborn identified the project with the search for the "missing link" and thereby created "an enormous public interest which otherwise certainly would have been lacking."[118]

Osborn played an important role in promoting the project. He took up the project with "tremendous enthusiasm" and solicited dozens of patrons to contribute to an unequaled opportunity to discover the birthplace of humanity. As museum president he created a new department headed by Andrews and endowed it with an annual budget of $5,000. He arranged for the Field Museum to support the project in exchange for receiving the first set of duplicate specimens. He also obtained the political and diplomatic support necessary for an expedition to China.[119]

As curator emeritus of the DVP Osborn also delegated the department's resources to the Central Asiatic Expeditions. On the first expedition, in 1922, Walter Granger was the only DVP member who participated. The following year, when Andrews pointed out the vast range of paleontological and geological questions that confronted the undertaking, Osborn saw to it that more DVP collectors were added to the staff. When fieldwork in Mongolia in 1923 resulted in the discovery of new fossil mammals, dinosaurs, and most dramatically the first dinosaur eggs, he made that project the department's top priority. Osborn and his wife traveled to Mongolia that year and he rapidly released dozens of telegrams, newspaper reports, radio dispatches, and articles about the discoveries. Eventually he published thirteen scientific articles and over a dozen popular pieces on the expeditions and their work. New specimens from the Gobi Desert also dominated the research of DVP members in the late 1920s. Matthew, in association with Granger, published fourteen articles on fossil vertebrate specimens from China. Charles C. Mook and George Gaylord Simpson published two and four papers respectively, and eight more in conjunction with Gregory.[120]

Osborn directed the department's artists and preparators to devote their attention to the material coming out of Asia. In 1922 Osborn commissioned Knight to paint a mural of *Baluchitherium*, the recently discovered ancestor of the rhinoceros that was described as the largest land mammal that ever lived. Gregory, Granger, and others were instructed to complete a mount of the specimen. The celebrated dinosaur discoveries commanded even more attention. Under Osborn's instructions Elizabeth Fulda's painting of a newly discovered *Protoceratops* and a mount of the specimen were completed in 1925. In that same year paintings and a display of the expedition's dinosaur eggs and embryos were placed on exhibit with great fanfare and publicity.[121]

Osborn and Andrews worked together to promote the project on a grand scale. Osborn, who had been highly successful in selling his projects in vertebrate paleontology, found a model promoter in Andrews. He, like Osborn, kept the public well informed of "this momentous undertaking." Taking on the role of the intrepid explorer, he

delivered hundreds of lectures to dramatize and raise money for the expeditions. He wrote several popular books about his explorations, most
notably *On the Trail of Ancient Man* (1926) and *To The Ends of the Earth*
(1937). With Osborn's guidance and assistance, he took advantage of the
large network of wealthy patrons associated with the museum. At Osborn's urging he approached J. P. Morgan, Jr., and obtained $50,000 for
the project. A number of Osborn's other contacts including Arthur Cur-
tiss James, Cleveland H. Dodge, Childs Frick, and the daughter of
William C. Whitney contributed. So too did John D. Rockefeller, Jr., and
the American Asiatic Association.[122]

To obtain such support, Andrews, like Osborn, appealed to the romance of exploration. He claimed that businessmen were "adventurer[s]
at heart" and described the project as a bold, path-breaking endeavor of
"courage and endurance." He asserted: "We stand on the threshold of a
new era of scientific exploration, which is just as romantic, just as allur-
ing and just as adventurous as that of Peary and Amundsen, of Stanley
and Hedin. In almost every country of the earth there lie vast regions
which are potentially unknown. Some of them are mapped poorly if at
all, and many hold undreamed-of treasures in the realm of science. To
study these little-known areas, to reveal the history of their making and
interpret that history to the world to-day, to learn what they can give in
education, culture, and for human welfare—that is the exploration of the
future!"[123] Employing hyperbole and appeals to adventure, cherished values,
and human salvation, Andrews succeeded in raising over $600,000 for the
Central Asiatic Expeditions.

Despite the delegation of such resources, and despite some notable
discoveries, the Central Asiatic Expeditions did not meet its proclaimed
objective: the discovery of the birthplace of mankind. Scientists on the
staff made important new contributions concerning the geology of Central Asia. In addition to the *Baluchitherium*, paleontologists found remains
of new titanotheres, proboscideans, and dinosaurs as well as several specimens of rare Cretaceous mammals. The expeditions also made some
contributions to paleoanthropology. The members of the 1925 expedition found remains of a Paleolithic culture. In 1929–30 Davidson Black,
an anatomist at Peking Union Medical College who was not associated
with the museum's expedition, discovered two skulls of *Sinanthropus pe-
kinensis*, or "Peking Man." Andrews stated that that discovery "confirms
the soundness of the theory of the Central Asiatic origin of primates and
man."[124] However, evidence found in a different part of the world seriously challenged Osborn's and Andrews's view. In 1924, when the museum was spending tens of thousands of dollars searching for the oldest

human remains in Mongolia, Raymond Dart, a South African anatomist, discovered a specimen of *Australopithecus africanus* that defined Africa, not Asia, as the source of human evolution.[125]

Dart's discovery would eventually undermine Osborn's theory and the whole rationale for the Central Asiatic Expeditions, but it did not dampen contemporary support for that project. In the 1920s Dart's interpretation was controversial and not widely accepted. More importantly, Osborn's interests and enthusiasms continued to generate great support at the museum. As the president of the institution he wielded enough power to give top priority to his own projects. His reputation and status, although suspect among scientists, carried a great deal of weight with the trustees and other wealthy New Yorkers. In addition, his projects appealed to their business objectives and, in many instances, their interest in big game hunting. That was as true of the Central Asiatic Expeditions as it was of his work on dinosaurs and fossil mammals.

For Osborn, the Central Asiatic Expeditions offered the opportunity to expand and take control of an important domain of human knowledge. The expedition provided the means to possess the factual evidence pertaining to mankind's birthright. In addition, Mongolia was a vast uncharted world that was there for the taking in a scientific sense. "Roughly summarizing the results," Andrews stated, "we realized that the work had resulted in an almost overwhelming amount of new information in geology, paleontology, and geography. In spite of the pessimistic predictions before our start, we had opened a new world to science." The expeditions provided more than new data and materials. They gave the museum's scientists the means to interpret those data and to construct Mongolia's history.[126]

Imperial objectives were an integral part of the expeditions. By the early twentieth century the United States had not only gained economic and political power in much of Latin America, but had also made inroads into Asia. The annexation of the Philippines and the establishment of the Open Door policy in China in 1899 provided new opportunities. Osborn's friends and associates the Morgans, the Fricks, and others were the entrepreneurs who fueled such expansion. For them Asia was fertile ground for economic development and exploitation. Projects such as the Central Asiatic Expeditions not only followed up the openings made by political and economic expansion but embodied the same attitudes and objectives.

To Andrews Mongolia was "a land of mystery, of paradox, and promise" that had unlimited potential. His writings not only described explorations but frequently included endorsements for the Dodge cars and

Corona typewriters that the expeditions employed.[127] Andrews effectively followed the lead of Osborn who, as a man of large ambitions and vision, had planned paleontological explorations that encompassed North and South America, Europe, Asia, and Africa. Osborn appealed to his associates not only as businessmen but as trustees who recognized such explorations as the means for the museum and themselves to claim dominion over large expanses of the globe.

Central to the expeditions was another belief: that Americans possessed far greater knowledge than the Chinese or Mongolians and thus could and should take possession of such lands and scientific data. Although Andrews rarely denounced Mongolian culture and customs outright, racial assumptions were implicit in the entire undertaking. In 1928 two Chinese organizations mandated that in all future expeditions half the members be Chinese and that all scientific materials, including duplicates of fossil vertebrates, remain in China. Andrews, Osborn, and the museum contemptuously refused. The title of Andrew's introductory volume to the expeditions' publications, *The New Conquest of Central Asia* (1932), embodied the sense of priority, superiority, and the right to take control of knowledge that characterized the expeditions. Explorations to "the ends of the earth" were the means for Osborn, Andrews, and the museum to establish scientific hegemony over natural and cultural objects from throughout the world.[128]

Those explorations were also the means for Americans, especially white Anglo-Saxon Protestant Americans, to establish their presence throughout the world. Osborn frequently touted Andrews not only for the discoveries associated with the Central Asiatic Expeditions but also for his vision, courage, and commitment in undertaking such a project. To Osborn, Andrews was an intrepid explorer who served as a model of individual achievement and racial fulfillment. Such beliefs were a reflection of Osborn's commitment to another objective that permeated the museum and influenced his work: the preservation of nature. Jesup and many of the museum's leading scientists were committed to preserving America's rapidly vanishing flora and fauna. For Osborn preservation became an ideology that extended from wildlife to include racial heritage and social class. He would promote that objective through his own scientific work and through the program that he dominated at the American Museum.

The Museum, the Zoo, and the Preservation of Nature

5

By the 1920s Osborn was describing projects like the Central Asiatic Expeditions and almost all work in vertebrate paleontology as part of the "romance of natural history." Such language was promotional, designed to suggest that fieldwork and exploration were filled with a sense of spirit and adventure. On those grounds Osborn sought to gain much-needed financial support from the Morgans, Pynes, and Vernays of New York City. Such language also reflected Osborn's commitment to a particular kind of research. He employed the terms natural history and naturalist, rather than science and scientist, to distinguish the fieldwork, discovery, and description associated with exploration from the methods of the laboratory biologist who concentrated on experimentation.

Osborn's emphasis on the importance of the naturalist and the study of nature, which pertained primarily to the study of organisms in their native habitats, was partially a product of his developing ideas on scientific method and education. At Princeton, Osborn had considered himself a biologist and concentrated on pursuing research in embryology, neuroanatomy, and paleontology. His interest in developing educational resources for the new discipline was confined to establishing academic programs, biological research centers, and specialized journals. Insofar as he addressed questions about scientific method, Osborn, at least in his embryological and neuroanatomical researches, had extolled the work of the laboratory scientist. By the time he had moved to New York in the early 1890s, however, Osborn had begun to develop a philosophy that emphasized the importance of nature study. As an administrator at Columbia he took a serious interest in pedagogical questions and developed ideas similar to a number of nineteenth-century educators and philosophers.

Osborn's emphasis on nature study and outdoor science also reflected the influence of individuals with whom he was becoming closely associated at the American Museum and the New York Zoological Society. At the museum Jesup had become interested in saving rapidly vanishing flora and fauna. Together with the leaders of the museum's scientific departments, he promoted a number of projects devoted to preservation. Osborn's associates at the Boone and Crockett Club and the Zoological Society had similar objectives. Theodore Roosevelt, for example, was an outspoken advocate of the need for modern man to confront nature and participate in rugged, outdoor activities. Osborn's views bear a marked similarity to his.

The leaders of the museum and the zoo were interested in obtaining and displaying wildlife specimens for educational reasons, but their commitment carried additional connotations. Their concern for nature and its preservation was part of a reaction to modernization in late nineteenth-century America. For them the preservation of topography, flora, and fauna was part of a larger concern for preserving traditional ideals and values about race, class, and society.[1] Osborn, through his association and close working relationship with those individuals, came to view natural history as a traditional means of pursuing research and thus preserving an older way of life. That emphasis would influence not only his views on scientific method and education but also his interpretation of evolution and his emphasis on the importance of vertebrate paleontology.

Osborn first articulated his views on the importance of nature study and the naturalist in his writings on scientific method and education. Because of the new administrative and educational responsibilities he had taken on at Columbia and the American Museum in the 1890s, Osborn was often called upon to discuss science education. Although he never systematically examined methodological issues, Osborn adopted an inductivist philosophy of science that stressed the importance of the first-hand study of nature. "There can be no question," he stated in an 1892 address to the Schoolmasters Association of New York, "that the new method of direct observation of nature and the constant consideration of causes and relations of various facts observed gives to modern biological teaching its chief educational value."[2] According to Osborn, "observation and induction from nature" were the means for discovering scientific laws and constructing scientific theories.[3] But his was no naive Baconianism. It was not the details of a specimen or its characters that was important but rather a knowledge of "the relations of these characters, the history and causes of their development as regards internal structure." Students needed not only to be provided the opportunity to examine flora and fauna in their natural surroundings but also to be trained in observation, visual acuity, and creative thinking.[4]

The work of great scientists, individuals whom Osborn explicitly referred to as naturalists, most fully illustrated the importance of observation and induction as the means for doing good scientific work. He maintained that Charles Darwin's and Alfred Russel Wallace's discovery of the law governing evolution was "one of those discharges of generalization which come so unexpectedly out of the vast accumulation of facts."[5] He described others, including Cope, T. H. Huxley, and Theodore Roosevelt, as figures whose achievements rested on the direct study of nature and the ability to generalize from details. Those figures had concentrated on fieldwork and the study of organisms in their native habitats. Through observation, induction, and creative insight that yielded new generalizations, each of those "naturalists" had made notable contributions to zoology. The inductivist approach, based on careful observation and the development of generalizations derived from those observations, not the hypothetico-deductive method of the experimental laboratory scientist, was for Osborn the sine qua non of significant work.[6]

In the early 1890s Osborn applied those ideas to science education at Columbia, where he played a role in developing the foundations for specialized graduate education in the sciences. But before the end of the decade he was emphasizing the primacy of nature study. In an 1897 report on the Department of Zoology at Columbia, Osborn noted the specialized courses, research projects, and publications that he and others had developed. But he emphasized that the program sought to cultivate the "rare qualities of the *naturalist*." Osborn asserted that even "so far as specialists are concerned, the highest type is the broadest type, and that the well-trained naturalist, familiar with animals and plants in their living forms and natural surroundings is the peer of the worker with an exclusively laboratory education."[7] Although Osborn was instrumental in establishing Columbia's research tables at the Marine Biological Laboratory (MBL) and the Naples Zoological Station, he maintained that "these stations, however, valuable as they are, lack the inspiration of the free study of nature in an unknown region, which has played the most important part in the training of the world's great naturalists, such as Darwin, Huxley, and Cope, and has proved superior in its effects to the training afforded in these finely equipped summer laboratories. Such study cultivates independence of resources; a worker is thrown upon his own inventive capacity to overcome difficulties of various kinds in the discovery and collection of new and rare objects; and he becomes intimately familiar with the appearances and habits of living creatures. To supply this need the summer expeditions were instituted."[8] The Zoology Department at Columbia, much like departments at Johns Hopkins and the University of Chicago, was an academic program that emphasized experimentation, laboratory research, and specialized disciplinary development.[9] Osborn, however, was praising the traditional work of the naturalist and propounding the importance of nature study.

Osborn was not alone in his views either among scientists or educators. Scientists had traditionally described induction as the basis for doing good research. In the late nineteenth century a number of biologists, most notably Charles Otis Whitman and William Keith Brooks, began to emphasize the importance of the naturalist and the study of nature. Osborn was closely associated with those men, particularly Whitman, and it is possible that his views were a reflection of Whitman's ideas.[10]

Osborn was probably also influenced by his study of others who had examined the educational system. In the nineteenth century a number of educators and philosophers attacked the pedagogical system and called for a process of learning that emphasized the study of nature, learning by doing, and the value of the experiences of the learner. The views of Johann Heinrich Pestalozzi (1747–1827), a Swiss philosopher who had advocated an "education of the heart, the hand, and the mind," were popular in the late nineteenth century.[11] Osborn was well acquainted with the works of educators Maria Montessori (1870–1952) and Friedrich Froebel (1782–1852). It is likely that he also knew the work of John Dewey, the American educator and philosopher whose study *School and Society* (1899) advocated a return to "the close and intimate acquaintance . . . with nature at first hand, with real things and materials, with the actual processes of their manipulation, and the knowledge of their social necessities and uses."[12] Osborn's emphasis on the importance of observation, the experience of the learner, and nature study bears similarities to the views of those scholars. Yet Osborn noted that he had begun to work out his ideas before he had studied such works,[13] and his ideas on nature and nature study closely resembled the views advocated at the museum and the zoo.

By the late 1890s Osborn was devoting more attention to the museum and the zoological society than to Columbia. As he indicated in a note to his wife in 1898, he spent five days of his six-day work week doing research and administrative duties associated with those public institutions.[14] Osborn's friends at the museum provided him with much greater support and opportunity than he could ever obtain at Columbia. Osborn also realized that the museum and the zoo offered more opportunity for the firsthand study of nature. At Columbia he was able to develop some outdoor projects such as student summer courses at the MBL or the biological expeditions to Port Townsend, Washington. But those activities were secondary to formal coursework in lecture halls and laboratories. It was only through the museum and the zoo that he could help to retard the educational trends toward "premature specialization," the "extreme laboratory system," and the futile effort "to attempt to educate exclusively through research."[15]

The museum provided the opportunity for a more meaningful education through outdoor activities, particularly exploration. By the late 1880s Jesup had emerged as a strong supporter of exploration. He offered the museum's official sanction, though not money, for fieldwork in anthropology, most notably Adolph Bandelier's researches among the ancient and the living Pueblo Indians of New Mexico. Jesup personally donated thousands of dollars to Robert Peary's expeditions to the North Pole. He enthusiastically supported the museum's first expedition: Joel Allen's trip to obtain specimens of North American mammals in 1889. Two years later he readily agreed to Osborn's proposal that his new program include salaries for collectors and annual trips to the western states and territories to obtain fossils.[16]

The museum and the zoo provided another influential vehicle for nature study: the development of exhibitions. For years colleges and scientific organizations had included specimen exhibits, but a large, well-financed public institution like the American Museum furnished much greater support and justification for those endeavors. At Columbia there were personal collections in the School of Mines and the College of Physicians and Surgeons. But the university could not promote exhibits on the scale that the trustees of the museum were willing to do.[17]

By the late 1880s Jesup, Bickmore, and Allen were developing innovative displays and offering educational programs in nature study. Jesup pointed out that the exhibits were particularly important for the "indoor naturalist," the person who could not participate in explorations but could vicariously experience such outdoor activity through the museum's displays.

To their [the collections'] value must be added their ameliorating power, their educational force, and the scope they afford the higher faculties of man to apprehend the wonderful phenomena of nature, and to master and utilize her great forces.

To the multitude shut up in stone walls, to whom are afforded an acquaintance with the beauty of natural objects, or to study them in their usual aspects and conditions, the advantage of your Museum is that it affords opportunity; and out of a great number who look only vaguely and experience only the healthful excitement of a natural curiosity, one here and there may be found with special aptitudes and tastes. Perhaps some child of genius whose susceptibilities and faculties, once aroused and quickened, will repay in the field of discovery and science, through the force of some new law in its manifold applications or relations, all your expenditures. . . . The highest results of character and life offer something which cannot be weighed in the balances of the merchant.[18]

To Jesup the museum's displays offered more than information; they provided the opportunity for a transforming personal experience.

Jesup's statement suggested something more. He was calling attention to the importance of nature and nature's laws at a time when American society was becoming increasingly urban and technological. Indeed Jesup claimed that the values associated with experiencing and understanding nature were more important than the values associated with commerce and a rapidly expanding civilization. In much the same way as the landscape architect Frederick Law Olmsted envisioned Central Park as an escape from the social tensions and antagonisms of city life, Jesup suggested that the museum could be a place where people could experience nature. By emphasizing the importance of preserving and exhibiting the evidences of nature, Jesup hoped to develop the museum as a respite from civilization that, implicitly at least, educated the public about the threats posed by advancing civilization.[19]

Such objectives might appear incongruous since many of the museum's leaders had gained prominence through modern commercial and technological developments. Jesup, Vanderbilt, and Harriman had made their fortunes through the development of the railroad and its subsidiary industries. Other trustees had gained economic and social status as a result of the commercial growth associated with the late nineteenth-century industrial revolution. But it was members of an urban middle and upper middle class who were in the vanguard of the reaction against urbanization and industrialization. In the late nineteenth century an array of writers, publishers, landscape architects, scientists, and others expressed dismay and concern that modernization was isolating mankind from contact with nature. They called for a return to nature, and promoted programs of nature study, camping out, and the development of organizations like the YMCA or the Boy Scouts of America that were designed to inculcate an appreciation for the outdoors and to build character.[20] Those individuals also spearheaded the emerging preservation movement of the 1870s and 1880s. They sought to protect wildlife and forests from advancing technological innovations and increasing economic exploitation of game, timber, and mineral resources.[21]

For Jesup and some of the trustees, descendants of a New England stock who wielded economic, social, and political power, the preservation of natural resources was part of a larger agenda: it was a bulwark against the changes affecting life in the post–Civil War period. The economic, demographic, and technological changes affecting the country, and New York in particular, were a threat to the established order. By emphasizing the importance of preservation, Jesup was hoping to convey to the public a message about the significance of natural resources and traditional lifestyles. Although such a program reached its zenith in Osborn's work and administration, Jesup expanded on the museum's earlier objective of merely acquiring collections and setting out specimens and promoted projects that, in a generalized sense at least, emphasized the importance and value of nature.[22]

The Museum and the Preservation of Nature

Jesup promoted that objective through his involvement in an effort to collect and to conserve woods. In 1880 when the government was taking the tenth census, Jesup participated in one aspect of the project designed to determine the distribution and economic value of the trees of North America. The study, which entailed scientific analysis, preparation, and exhibition of trees, resulted in the development of the Jesup Collection of North American Woods.[23] Through the project Jesup became acquainted with a number of the country's leading botanists, notably Harvard's Charles Sprague Sargent. Those individuals provided Jesup with some knowledge of forestry and informed him that the expansion of railroad, timber, and mining industries posed a threat to the country's forests.[24] Jesup became convinced of the magnitude of the problem, particularly when it posed potential commercial difficulties.

In 1883, when a drought and overlogging presented possibilities of fire in the Adirondack Mountains, Jesup, as president of the New York Chamber of Commerce, lobbied the legislature for the preservation of New York woodlands. Claiming that the railroads' path through the wilderness would result in the destruction of forests, the reduction of navigable waterways, and fires, he called for the legislature to seize four million acres to "insure abundant water to the Hudson and the [Erie] Canal." After a protracted debate, the legislature created the state forest commission and the Adirondack Forest Reserve in 1885. Jesup later retreated from the political battle over the Adirondacks, but he did not abandon his interest in the preservation of woodlands or wildlife.[25]

At the American Museum, Jesup developed a collection of woods designed to present the public with interesting scientific information and to suggest the importance of preservation by exhibiting the specimens of a rapidly diminishing flora. Jesup hoped that the creation of a large collection of woods and stones would "aid in the development of our native arts and skills."[26] Jesup had a utilitarian objective, but he had additional concerns. Through the conservation of woods and stones he wanted people to recognize the importance of natural resources and of preurban lifestyles and cultures that were organized around those resources.

The interest in preservationist objectives is more evident in the work of some of the museum's first curators. Joel Allen, while noted for his scientific work, held many of the same views as Jesup. Allen, in addition to establishing cataloging systems and developing accurate and attractive displays for the benefit of the public and researchers, was keenly interested in the preservation of birds and animals. In many of his scientific studies he brought to the attention of readers the evidence of rapidly vanishing fauna. In a study of North American pinnipeds, a suborder that includes walruses, sea lions, and seals, Allen described the activities of seafaring industries that were brutally killing those animals.[27] In 1876 he published a monograph on the American bison that combined scientific research with advocacy for preservation. Allen later became a leader in forming the American Bison Society. He also helped to create both the American Ornithologists' Union and the National Audubon Society, organizations devoted in part to developing legislation for the protection of birds.[28]

Through Allen's and Jesup's efforts the American Museum became a meeting place for the American Ornithologists' Union and the headquarters for the New York chapter of the Audubon Society, which they organized. Museum expeditions and the Hall of North American Mammals that Allen initiated in the late 1880s were designed to preserve the evidence of the rapidly vanishing fauna of the continent. Allen was first and foremost a scientist who emphasized investigation and publication, but he also shared with Jesup a commitment to develop exhibits that would educate and in subtle ways influence the public about the mounting threats to organisms and their habitats.[29]

Frank Chapman, Allen's assistant who was hired in 1887, was even more devoted to the preservationist cause. Though lacking Allen's scholarly background and credentials, Chapman was an avid student of birds and soon became a productive researcher. Following his appointment, he conducted expeditions for birds and had the task of describing and classifying the increasing number of specimen collections coming into the museum. Like Allen, he was interested in questions of bird migration and coloration and published many papers on the subject. For Chapman, however, educational work was even more compelling than research: "That science which is sufficient unto itself has no excuse for its existence. If our studies of birds have no bearing on the progress and welfare of mankind they are futile; that they have such a bearing and in an exceptional degree, we know to be undeniable; it is obviously, therefore, the function of the museum to demonstrate this connection in such a manner as to render apparent the bird's place in nature and its relation to man."[30]

Chapman, influenced by Allen, Jesup, and Bickmore, wanted to develop the museum as a nature experience that had direct meaning for people. Through the creation of habitat groups, displays that exhibited birds in their natural environment, Chapman hoped "to bring the student into direct contact with Nature, show him her infinite resources and establish between him and the outdoor world an intimacy thru [*sic*] which he will derive not only pleasure, but also physical, mental, and spiritual strength." His portrayals of the feeding, nesting, and mating patterns of birds, as well as the depiction of their intimate relationship to specific physical and biotic environments, were iconographic representations of a complex and valued way of life. Chapman's displays were based on scientific study of birds and their environments. But the habitat groups served primarily as exemplars to mankind of the subtleties, beauty, and integrity of nature. By implication they represented the importance of protecting and preserving nature's creations.[31]

Chapman presented the argument for preservation more explicitly in the popular guide leaflets that he wrote to accompany such habitat groups. Chapman's booklet *The Bird Rock Group*, the first in the museum's guide leaflet series, was a popular exposition for the public that described the birds of a small island off the coast of Newfoundland. Chapman peppered his description with details of the impending destruction of those birds. Noting how the island had once served as a haven for the birds, Chapman portrayed its later history in terms of the havoc wreaked by "the bird's worst enemy—man." Fishermen and egg collectors, he argued, posed a serious threat to the continued existence of many species on Bird Rock Island. The habitat group was designed "to make, therefore, a permanent record of this characteristic phase of island life" and to preserve for posterity an understanding and appreciation of this fauna before it was destroyed by man.[32]

In the late 1880s and 1890s other museum exhibits and popular publications reflected preservationist objectives. Jesup's concern for preserving American woods and stones led to the acquisition of an endangered Sequoia specimen for the Hall of North American Woods and the publication of a guide leaflet on the subject.[33] The expanding Department of Anthropology had similar interests. In the 1890s Franz Boas, the head of the department who had spent years investigating the Indians of the Pacific Northwest, wrote to Jesup and outlined a major project for salvaging ethnographic data:

> The wonderful development of American civilization and its rapid spread over the whole area of our continent is working deep changes even in those parts of the country which until recently were uninfluenced by the culture of the white man. It is a question only of a few years, when every thing reminding us of America as it was at the time of its discovery will have perished.
>
> This fact is one that ought to stimulate us to exert ourselves to the utmost to save whatever can be saved of the knowledge of pre–Columbian America. Day by day the material on which we can base such knowledge is passing away. If we do not apply ourselves to the work of collecting information on this subject diligently and without delay, no future regrets will avail. It would seem to me that it is a duty that we owe, not only to our own country, but to all future generations, to save this knowledge. Previous generations were not able to do so, because the difficulties in the way were great, and because the scientific methods of study were not well developed. Now we have good methods, and our generation is the last that will be able to collect the data which will form the basis of the early history of America. If we do not do this, this knowledge will be lost forever.[34]

Boas was interested in the customs, history, and culture of Northwest Indians from a scientific point of view. But he did not hesitate to point out that the emphasis on preservation would appeal to Jesup and the trustees. Jesup decided to sponsor the project himself, and work by Boas and others associated with the Jesup North Pacific Expedition resulted in the collection of a mass of ethnographic material and the publication of several important studies.[35]

Other trustees sponsored similar projects. In 1899 E. H. Harriman, the president of the Union Pacific Railroad and a museum trustee, sponsored one expedition to search for dinosaur remains in Wyoming and another to obtain a wide array of scientific material in Alaska. The following year J. P. Morgan underwrote Edward S. Curtis's project to photograph the Indian tribes of North America.[36] Although preservation became a specific museum policy only during Osborn's presidency,[37] that emphasis shaped much of the work done in the late 1880s and 1890s. The interest in preservation had an impact on Osborn who in coming to New York City was eager to take advantage of the resources and emphases at the American Museum and to establish himself quickly as a leader in his field.

Roosevelt, the Boone and Crockett Club, and the Preservation of Nature

At the same time that he was gaining a foothold at the American Museum, Osborn became involved with a different public institution devoted to the preservation of nature's creations: the New York Zoological Society. That society was an outgrowth of another organization, the Boone and Crockett Club.

Established in 1887, the Boone and Crockett Club was a group of wealthy New Yorkers who, while devoted to "manly sport with the rifle," dedicated themselves to the study of animal habits and natural history and the preservation of wildlife.[38] Such objectives might appear contradictory, but the members of the organization were committed to a particular kind of hunting associated with what John F. Reiger has defined as the traditional "code of the sportsman." In that context, hunting was embodied in "the true spirit, the dash, the handsome way of doing what is to be done, and above all in the unalterable *love of fair play*."[39] Hunting was a gentlemanly activity based on the confrontation between man and animal, and the members of the Boone and Crockett Club protested against the killing and selling of animals, which had become big business in the late nineteenth century. The Boone and Crockett was one of the early organizations involved in the preservation movement, a club designed to protect wildlife and a traditional form of sport. Those objectives were most fully embodied in the work of its founders and leading members, George Bird Grinnell and Theodore Roosevelt.

Grinnell, like most members of the club, came from a prominent New York family. A graduate of Yale, he had participated in O. C. Marsh's first Yale College expedition for fossils in 1870 and in later years was a member of other western explorations. These experiences acquainted Grinnell with the lives and customs of the Plains Indians, and he became concerned that the country's expansion threatened to extinguish the Indian, the bison, and much of western wildlife. As an advocate for preservation, he took over the editorship of *Forest and Stream* in 1880 and made the magazine a platform for that cause.[40] In 1884–85, he, along with Jesup, became involved in the effort to establish the Adirondack Forest Reserve. In the following year he joined Allen and four others in founding the first chapter of the Audubon Society. At the same time he met

Roosevelt, another avid sportsman-naturalist who had spent time in the West, and Grinnell made Roosevelt aware of preservation issues. "Under Grinnell's tutelage, Roosevelt's love of big game hunting soon developed into a concern for the future of big game as he became increasingly aware of the speed with which it was disappearing."[41] Together they founded the Boone and Crockett Club. Grinnell played a leading role in organizing the club and calling for the protection of endangered cultures and species, but Roosevelt most fully embodied and popularized the concern with preservation.

Roosevelt, like Grinnell, was devoted to the pursuit of outdoor activities. As a child he became interested in natural history and throughout the late 1860s and early 1870s avidly pursued such studies, often in the company of Osborn's younger brother Frederick. Entering Harvard College in 1876, he considered a career in science, but soon became dissatisfied with the contemporary emphases in biology. He complained that the colleges "treated biology as a science of the laboratory and the microscope, a science whose adherents were to spend their time in the study of minute forms of life, or else in section-cutting and the study of the tissues of the higher organisms under the microscope."[42] Roosevelt longed for grander challenges, for work on large animals in the great outdoors, and not merely for the sake of study. In addition to his love of natural history as an intellectual pursuit, Roosevelt was an avid hunter, and throughout the 1880s he hunted and ranched in Montana and Wyoming. For him, as for other naturalists of the time, research and hunting went hand in hand.[43]

The study of nature and outdoor activities had additional significance for Roosevelt. Frail and sickly as a child, he maintained that it was through his active participation in hunting and ranching that he had conquered his weaknesses. In autobiographical works he claimed that the confrontation with nature, the struggle for existence, had enabled him to attain manhood. Describing his life as a triumph over childhood trials and tribulations, Roosevelt elevated the personal confrontation with nature to the level of ideology.[44] He became an advocate of "the strenuous life," of the need to confront nature head-on as the means for achieving fulfillment. He also believed the strenuous life was vitally important for the destiny of the nation. In dozens of speeches and addresses he claimed that "it is only through strife, through hard and dangerous endeavor, that we shall ultimately win the goal of true national greatness." While such pronouncements were little more than banalities in praise of hard work and individualism, they nevertheless reflected his anxiety about preserving nature as the means for maintaining traditional values.[45] Roosevelt was very much concerned about the impact that increasing urbanization, industrialization, and commercialization were having on American life and on the character of the American people.

Roosevelt saw the confrontation with nature as the means for retaining traditional values and institutions that he and others believed were threatened by modernization. He claimed that "overcivilization" was a threat not only to the achievement of physical vigor and manhood but also to the power and prestige of the upper class. In later years he became seriously concerned that overcivilization threatened "race suicide," that the increasing numbers of southern and eastern European immigrants entering the United States would dilute and eventually extinguish the old New England stock that had traditionally dominated American life. Roosevelt's advocacy of the strenuous life and the preservation of nature was an appeal to preserve social class and ethnic heritage in the face of the manifold changes occurring in a burgeoning urban, industrial, and pluralistic society.[46]

Roosevelt advanced such views just at the time that Osborn was becoming closely associated with members of the Boone and Crockett Club. Although Osborn had met Roosevelt as his brother's companion in the 1870s, he became better acquainted with Roosevelt, Grinnell, and other members of the club after taking positions at Columbia and the American Museum in 1891. Osborn belonged to the same clubs and moved in the same social circles as those men. Osborn no doubt was aware that members of the Boone and Crockett Club had ties to the museum. Several members of the Boone and Crockett Club provided financial support for Allen's expeditions and the Hall of North American Mammals that he developed. Osborn was not a hunter, but he became an honorary member of the club and in 1904 delivered an address on the preservation of North American wildlife.[47] He and others were also involved in a related program that emerged out of the club: the establishment of the New York Zoological Park.

As one of the leaders in the New York Zoological Society, Osborn was fully committed to the preservationist motives that inspired the creation of a zoological park. The park, as distinct from a zoological garden such as the one in Central Park, would preserve animals in their native habitats. In his welcoming address at the opening of the park in November 1899, Osborn expressed the need for preserving and protecting the park's wonders for the public.

The Ice Sheet left behind the famous "Rocking Stone," as a memorial of its visit, and there followed the forest of oak and beech, whose noble offspring are the glory of the Park. Then wandered in the Mastodon, Buffalo, the Elk, Moose, Deer, and Beaver, the Indian and finally our Dutch and English ancestors as the enemies and exterminators of all. We have to thank the former owners of this tract that the forest was preserved. The Mastodon is beyond recall, but before long his collateral descendant, the elephant, will be here; and this afternoon, as you wander through the ranges, you will see restored to their old haunts all the other noble aborigines of Manhattan. Later we shall find a place upon the Buffalo Range for the Indian and his tepee.

Yes, Nature has given the City this Park and has given us the motive for its treatment. Every natural beauty has been carefully protected and preserved, hardly a tree has been cut down. And when our general scheme of planting and enclosure is completed, all the animals of North America and many of the Old World will be seen just as they live in the woods—happier perhaps because safe from the rifle of the hunter, free from the keen struggle for existence, generously quartered and fed.[48]

Osborn was thus defining the ideology of preservation: the emphasis on the beauty and value of flora, fauna, and the physical environment and the need to preserve the evidences of nature for the welfare of the animals and the edification of mankind.

For Osborn and several members of the zoological society, the preservation of nature and wildlife was associated with the preservation of traditional social values, namely, rugged individualism, participation in outdoor activities, and keeping power in the hands of those whose ancestors had originally settled the New World. According to Madison Grant, a Wall Street lawyer and a board member of the zoological society and the museum, the Boone and Crockett Club and the society had "a mission and opportunity . . . in its efforts to preserve the game and the forests; in short to preserve to future generations some remnant of the heritage which was our fathers'."[49] In later years he expressed his views more explicitly as one of the leading advocates for race preservation. In *The Passing of the Great Race* (1916) and *The Conquest of a Continent* (1933), he claimed that the massive influx of Asian and southern and eastern European immigrants threatened the existence of the Nordic race that had founded this country. He was a strong proponent of immigration restriction. William Temple Hornaday, the zoo's director, also lashed out at the threats, including immigration, that so-called civilization posed to the native life of North America.[50] Grant and Hornaday, like Roosevelt, were anxious and upset about the changes affecting early twentieth-century New York.

Osborn became closely associated with those individuals and institutions and embraced their views. He had already developed ideas about the importance of field study and the work of the naturalist; he now began to incorporate the preservationist concern into his writings. Increasingly, his analyses of education became strident condemnations of the contemporary pedagogical system. Beginning with a number of addresses in the mid 1890s and extending over the next forty years, Osborn argued that the American educational system, while producing larger numbers of students, was not producing better thinkers. Rather, it was promoting mediocrity because the emphasis on disseminating factual information was turning students into "passive receptacles" of data instead of active, creative participants in the educational process.

Osborn decried "the prevailing system of overfeeding which stuffs, crams in and spoon-feeds, and then, as a sort of deathbed repentence, institutes creative work after graduation."[51] Modern education, he claimed, embodied a passiveness and imitative quality because "we have taken out of education the struggle to get it; we have taken away from our boys and girls the stern element of the struggle with the forces of Nature; we have, as a final step in the emasculation, substituted the woman for the man teacher."[52] For Osborn, modern education no longer embodied traditional values or even traditional role models. Removed from contact with nature and nature's laws, modern education had become domesticated and effeminate, characteristics that Osborn, as part of an elite male power structure, considered degenerate.

By the 1920s Osborn had expanded his condemnation of modern education to encompass modern society in general. In *Creative Education* (1927) he developed that argument by contrasting modern education and behaviorial patterns with those of paleolithic people. Children in the Stone Age, he claimed, were in daily contact with the outdoor environment and engaged in a constant struggle for existence. In order to survive those people had to observe their surroundings and employ creative thought and imagination. Modern life, by contrast, entailed little direct contact with nature and little need to employ observation or imagination. Modern men were imitators, slaves to convention who thought, wrote, and acted with almost no creative insight. Osborn's comparison was not scientifically sophisticated or accurate; indeed it was contrived. But it served the purpose of his argument: having lost contact with nature, mankind was degenerating.[53] The rebuilding of character and survival of the species could not be accomplished through formal education or training. On the contrary, fulfillment required an escape from the structures and systems of contemporary urban life. Outdoor activities, or their indoor vicarious equivalents, provided the means for stimulating creative thought and achieving individual as well as social salvation.

For Osborn, the museum and the zoo became the loci for educational opportunity and social and spiritual regeneration. Osborn, like Jesup, believed that the museum's exhibits served as a vicarious experience in the outdoors that could effect a personal transformation among the "indoor naturalists."

> The great function of the American Museum is to bring back to life these two masters; to restore the vision and inspiration of nature, as well as the compelling force of the struggle for existence in education. This is our antitoxin for most of the educational poisons of our day. On restoration of the privileges enjoyed by the cave boy and on coming for the first time into direct vision of the wonders and beauties of nature, not only boys and girls, but men and women, young and old, feel a thrill which they may never have experienced before. This thrill inspires them to go further to examine the objects more closely, to see all they can themselves and perhaps to go home and read what others have observed. Thus, they discover in themselves latent faculties of which they had not the least knowledge before, latent predispositions and tastes which gradually come to the surface of consciousness, new ambitions to enter the struggle for existence in science, in literature or in art. . . .
>
> In these few words we have set forth the whole theory and practice of American Museum education, namely, to restore to the human mind the direct vision and inspiration of nature as it exists in all parts of the world and as it is becoming known through all the sciences, thus to discover and encourage predispositions and tastes, thus to arouse ambitions to overcome all resistance, and to return to books and learning as the handmaids and not the masters of education.[54]

Exhibits provided a means for making contact with nature. As such they could furnish an understanding of nature and nature's laws that surpassed what the student could learn in a formal educational environment. More importantly, they enabled people to experience nature and overcome the deplorable features of a modern society characterized by ethnic pluralism, expanding opportunities for women, and increasing urbanization.

Explorations also held great psychological and social importance for Osborn. As he stated in the 1897 report on Columbia's Zoology Department, the firsthand study of nature placed students in unfamiliar surroundings and forced them to pursue research independently. Such circumstances were, of course, important for scientific work. But for Osborn the immersion in nature was a personal confrontation that led to self-fulfillment.[55] Osborn, perhaps influenced by the views of his good friend Roosevelt, glorified the outdoor study of nature as a transforming experience that could bring social and spiritual redemption.

Osborn extolled the power of nature, particularly exploration, in a number of biographical studies. Roosevelt, who had claimed that his life was transformed by years spent in the rugged, outdoor wilderness of Montana and North Dakota, was one of Osborn's favorite themes. In many articles and addresses Osborn portrayed Roosevelt as the quintessential naturalist whose experiences in nature gave meaning to his life and shaped his career. Osborn believed that the life of Howard Crosby Butler, a Princeton student, was transformed as a result of his explorations in the Middle East.[56]

Osborn made the same claim for himself. In an autobiographical statement he asserted that "except for a few early statistics, my biography actually begins with the first call to biology and geology." For Osborn, the Princeton Scientific Expeditions were an experience in nature that gave meaning and direction to his life. In later years he described the search for dinosaurs or the explorations of the Central Asiatic Expeditions in similar, inspirational terms.[57] Romanticizing the hardships and glories of fieldwork, Osborn hoped to inspire others about the possibilities and opportunities of nature study. He presented his own life and work as a testament to the significance of the transforming power of nature. His popular scientific works and his autobiography-bibliography, *Fifty-Two Years of Research*, were didactic, egotistical pieces in which Osborn explained how exploration and fieldwork had given him special insights into nature's laws that he sought to pass on to others.[58] The study of nature and exploration were opportunities for individual and racial fulfillment that were vitally important in the face of the problems that Osborn and his colleagues associated with modern life.

As John M. Kennedy and Donna Haraway have indicated, Osborn's belief in the ameliorative power of nature study was the basis for major developments at the museum. During his presidency, Osborn drew upon the enthusiasms and anxieties associated with the preservation of nature and nature study to develop explorations to the ends of the earth. Roy Chapman Andrews's journey to the Gobi Desert of Mongolia was but one of many expeditions promoted on the basis that exploration and nature study could regenerate the race. Osborn was the principal figure behind the creation of the immense Theodore Roosevelt Memorial, an encomium to the preservation of nature and the racial and sociopolitical connotations associated with it.[59]

Osborn's emphasis on nature was awash with romance and was little more than rhetoric. Although he claimed that the lives of Roy Chapman Andrews, Howard Crosby Butler, and James Terry epitomized the power inherent in museum displays or explorations, their endeavors were not so much a result of any spiritual awakening or personal transformation as they were a consequence of important connections to Osborn and the power structure in the museum and in New York City. Osborn himself rarely participated in fieldwork and the outdoor life associated with paleontology or other fields of natural history. His trips to the field were often family tours or highly publicized reconnaissances of important sites. His paleontological studies were based on specimens collected and prepared by the members of his departmental staff. His insights into evolution, which he maintained were the result of direct observation and induction, were not only derived from the study of fossil specimens but shaped by philosophical, social, and political influences. Osborn's advocacy for the study of nature and the glorification of outdoor life constituted a reactionary response to a modern urban society that he believed threatened traditional values, lifestyles, and institutions.[60]

In the 1890s, as Osborn began to give priority to the museum and the zoo over the university, his ideas echoed the views of those with whom he became closely associated. In much the same way as Roosevelt and the members of the Boone and Crockett Club had called for a return to the traditional methods and objectives of hunting, so too did Osborn advocate the importance of traditional methods of biological research that were threatened by new methodological, conceptual, and institutional developments. His emphasis on the study of nature evoked a return to traditional ways of living, thinking, and structuring society to maintain an order that placed power and prestige in the hands of the established elite to which he and the leaders of the museum and zoo belonged.

This is not to suggest that his association with the museum and the zoo *caused* him to adopt a preservationist stance. As a teacher he was well aware that other educators were emphasizing the value of the active involvement of the student and the importance of nature study in the educational process. As a well-connected member of an upper-class urban elite, he knew that many writers, architects, and sportsmen were supporting a return to nature and advocating nature study. He was also raised in an environment that emphasized maintaining and contributing to the existing social structure. However, Osborn shaped his already existing commitments and ideas in ways that reflected his changing career priorities and encompassed his associates' values and interests. Those emphases, which influenced Osborn's views on science and science education, also had an impact on his study of evolutionary theory and vertebrate paleontology.

Osborn, Nature, and Evolution   **6**

After moving to New York City in 1891, Osborn continued his study of evolution. At Princeton he and William Berryman Scott had relied on Cope's neo-Lamarckian interpretation to explain the evolution of fossil mammals. Now, however, Osborn sought to develop a new theory. That effort derived in part from scientific questions and concerns: the need to incorporate new work on inheritance and evolution into his interpretation of the fossil record. In addition, Osborn sensed new opportunities. The museum, with its resources and commitment to vertebrate paleontology, would, he told his father, enable him to "discover some of the laws" governing evolution.[1] With the data supplied by his assistants, Osborn was optimistic about developing a theory that he could apply to a whole range of problems. In the early twentieth century he defined a series of "laws" governing evolution, classification, and geographical distribution. Osborn eagerly took advantage of opportunities at the museum to establish a commanding presence in vertebrate paleontology and evolutionary biology.

Osborn was also eager to develop a theory that had meaning within the museum context. For Jesup and Osborn, the discovery of the laws of nature had more than scientific value and importance. Jesup was a religious man and committed to developing an institution in which displays conveyed moral lessons. Osborn was similarly motivated. At Princeton he had developed an interpretation of evolution that reinforced his religious beliefs. In New York his interpretation would also encompass the preservation of class and class values. Certainly Osborn's work was based on the study of thousands of fossil vertebrate specimens, and his orthogenetic interpretation was not much different from theories advanced by other biologists and paleontologists of the day.[2] His theory expanded upon ideas that Scott had already put forth. Yet Osborn also defined his theory in terms of the commitment to nature and in opposition to social and scientific developments that he deplored.

Osborn's Theory of Evolution

Osborn's study of evolution and the fossil record fit squarely in the morphological tradition of the late nineteenth century. He, like other paleontologists, comparative anatomists, and embryologists, relied on the analysis of specimens to define homological relationships and to document organic change. In the 1880s he had accepted Cope's explanation that evolution resulted from the mechanical use and disuse of parts and the transmission of those acquired changes to subsequent generations. But by the early 1890s Osborn no longer believed in the inheritance of acquired characteristics and instead embraced a new interpretation of heredity put forth by August Weismann.

A German zoologist, Weismann had recently challenged traditional biological assumptions by claiming that characters developed during the lifetime of an individual were not passed on to that individual's offspring. Distinguishing between the soma plasm, or body cells, and the germ plasm, or sex cells that are isolated from environmental effects, Weismann maintained that only changes in the germ cells are inherited. He denied the validity of the neo-Lamarckian doctrine of the inheritance of acquired characteristics. Osborn adopted Weismann's thesis of the continuity of the germ plasm to explain inheritance.[3]

Although Osborn accepted Weismann's interpretation of heredity, he could not accept the latter's explanation of evolution. Weismann was a neo-Darwinian who defined evolution in terms of the natural selection of fortuitous variations that arise through the mingling of germ plasms, or sex cells. Osborn rejected that idea on the grounds that the fossil record demonstrated that "variations follow definite lines from their incipient stages." To Osborn, such evidence indicated some relationship between germ plasm and soma plasm, though it was several years before he came up with an explanation.[4]

Weismann's neo-Darwinian interpretation also offended Osborn's philosophical and social views. Having developed his evolutionary ideas under the tutelage of McCosh and in the religious environment at Princeton College, Osborn could not accept an interpretation of the history of life based on a purely naturalistic mechanism that selected chance variations. Neither could he accept an interpretation that had unsettling social consequences. Osborn was upset that Weismann's new interpretation touched off a vociferous debate between the neo-Lamarckians and the neo-Darwinians in the late 1880s and early 1890s.[5] He also questioned the impact that Weismann's theory would "have upon the conduct of life. If the Weismann idea triumphs, it will be in a sense a triumph of fatalism; for, according to it, while we may definitely improve the forces of our education and surroundings, and thus civilizing nurture will improve the individuals of each generation, its actual effects will not be cumulative as regards the race itself, but only as regards the environment of the race; each new generation must start *de novo*, receiving no increment of the moral and intellectual advance made during the lifetime of its predecessors. It would follow that one deep, almost instinctive motive for a higher life would be removed if the race were only superficially benefited by its nurture, and the only possible channel of actual improvement were in the selection of the fittest chains of the race plasm."[6] For Osborn a theory of evolution had to do more than fit the facts. It had to be socially and philosophically reinforcing.

During the 1890s Osborn attempted to work out such an interpretation. He hoped to develop a theory that would chart a middle course and mediate between the two camps debating over inheritance. He was ambitious enough to try to construct a theory that was different and comprehensive. Osborn read widely in cytology, development, inheritance, and evolution, and he sought to incorporate recent work in those fields into his interpretation. He required a theory that could account for the regular pattern of change that he discerned in the fossil record, and he relied primarily on work done in paleontology to support his interpretation.

Osborn had previously maintained that the study of the fossils showed no occurrence of random variation, but beginning in the early 1890s he expanded that argument and claimed that the fossil record demonstrated widespread evidence of very similar changes among different organisms. In an 1892 essay written with his DVP assistant Jacob L. Wortman, Osborn claimed that specimens collected by an American Museum expedition demonstrated that among lower Eocene mammals "essentially similar types are evolved independently over and over again, and that in [the] course of what Schlosser has well termed 'modernization' we find such diverse orders as Primates, Ungulates, Insectivores, Marsupials, Rodents all exhibiting the same laws of dental modification and the same or similar 'secondary' cusps, crests, and peripheral styles." The evolution of the dental structure among several families of fossil mammals showed "an uninterrupted march in one direction."[7]

Rejecting the idea that the natural selection of fortuitous variations could account for such directed change, Osborn argued in favor of a lawlike principle that controlled the evolutionary process: "The point is that a certain trend of development is taken leading to an adaptive or inadaptive final issue—but extinction or survival of the fittest seems to exert little influence *en route*. The changes *en route* lead us to believe either in predestination—a kind of internal perfecting tendency, or in kinetogenesis. For the trend of evolution is not the happy resultant of many trials, but is heralded in structures of the same form all the world over and in age after age, by similar minute changes advancing irresistibly from inutility to utility. It is an absolutely definite and lawful progression. The infinite number of contemporary developing, degenerating, stationary characters preclude the possibility of fortuity. There is some law introducing and regulating each of these variations, as in the variations of individual growth."[8] Osborn maintained that characters such as mammalian molar teeth or titanothere horns became useful only over time; thus, neither the neo-Lamarckian nor the neo-Darwinian theory could explain the evidence found by paleontologists. According to Osborn, only a regulatory law or guiding principle could account for the widespread parallelism in the evolutionary record.

Osborn developed a teleological interpretation of evolution that rested upon a distinction made by Wilhelm Waagen and William Berryman Scott. Like those men, Osborn defined two different kinds of variations: ontogenetic variations and phylogenetic variations. The former were fluctuations that occurred in the course of an individual lifetime, namely, changes in the size, shape, or proportion of existing characters. Those variations had little long-term evolutionary significance, although they did have taxonomic importance. The differences in the size, shape, or proportion of characters served to distinguish organisms and allowed Osborn to place them into separate lines of descent. Ontogenetic variations were the result of factors that earlier theorists, the Comte de Buffon, Lamarck, Étienne Geoffroy St. Hilaire, and Darwin, had each identified as being exclusively responsible for evolution: changes in development, environment, or selection pressure.[9] For Osborn no one of those factors could explain variation, and they could only indirectly explain the origin of phylogenetic variations.

Osborn maintained that phylogenetic variations were caused by a fourth factor, the germ plasm, which he termed the hereditary factor, or ancestral potential. In his view, "while the environment and activity of the organism may supply the stimuli in some manner unknown to us, definite tendencies of variation spring from certain very remote ancestral causes: for example, in the middle Miocene the molar teeth of the horse and the rhinoceros began to exhibit similar variations; when these are traced back to the embryonic and also to the ancestral stages of tooth development of an early geological period, we discover that the six cusps of the Eocene crown, repeated today in the embryonic development of the jaw, were also the centers of phylogenetic variation; these centers seem to have predetermined at what points certain new structures would appear after these two lines of ungulates had been separated by an immense interval of time. In other words, upper Miocene variation was conditioned by the structure of a lower Eocene ancestral type."[10] Phylogenetic variations were in some sense predetermined. According to Osborn, they were latent in the germ plasm of an ancient ancestor, in this case the ancestor of the Perissodactyla. The effects of the environment and habit would produce changes in ontogeny that would stimulate the hereditary potential and produce gradual and linear evolutionary modifications.

Throughout the early 1890s Osborn sought to establish some connection between ontogenetic and phylogenetic variations, but one that was not based on the Lamarckian principle of the inheritance of acquired characteristics. In 1896 he defined that relationship in terms of a newly discovered principle of organic selection. Ontogenetic variations could arise that "may extend over an enormously long period of time . . . and predetermine the course of evolution. They set a groove, as it were, along which evolution must take its course." That interpretation explained evolution in terms of coincidence; changes in individual behavior and development set out a path that phylogenetic variations would eventually follow.[11]

Osborn's ideas were not entirely original, but they provided an explanatory means for overcoming an impasse. Just prior to Osborn's announcement of having discovered what he claimed was a new evolutionary factor, two other scientists, Conwy Lloyd Morgan and James Mark Baldwin, defined the principle of organic selection. For both men, organic selection answered difficult problems and supported the neo-Darwinian interpretation of evolution.[12] Osborn defined organic selection differently. For him the principle allowed for the reconciliation of neo-Darwinism and neo-Lamarckism. It provided the basis for suggesting that ontogenetic changes could affect the germ plasm, but without relying strictly on the inheritance of acquired characters.[13]

Osborn did not gain much recognition for his views on organic selection. Both Morgan and Baldwin announced the idea a few months before he did, and eventually Baldwin outmaneuvered Morgan and the principle was termed the "Baldwin effect."[14] In addition, Osborn incorporated organic selection within a larger theoretical construct. Lamarckism (ontogeny) and Darwinism (selection) were only two of the factors that explained evolution. The roles of the environment and heredity also had to be taken into account. Organic selection was only part of a four-part tetraplastic theory of evolution that Osborn developed.[15]

Osborn's tetraplastic, later tetrakinetic theory, served a number of purposes. It enabled him to develop an interpretation that was distinct from all others. It was an explanation that integrated the several biological processes and interpretations that he considered significant. It enabled him to explain the lawlike character of evolution found in the fossil record and to do so in a way that did not rely on neo-Lamarckian or neo-Darwinian interpretations.

Osborn's theory also bolstered his philosophical and social beliefs. The theory substantiated the philosophical idealism that had characterized his views since the 1880s. Influenced by Cope, McCosh, and Scott, Osborn could not accept the idea that evolution resulted from the randomized variation or selection of material phenomena. His theory defined evolution as the actualization of a nonmaterial potential that lay latent in the germ plasm of organisms. The actualization of that potential produced a gradual, cumulative unfolding of characters along regular lines, a lawlike process very similar to individual development. That process was not dictated by utilitarian demands but proceeded independently from the influence of the surrounding environment. Osborn often claimed that his theory was not vitalistic or deterministic, and he was correct. The original triggering of the hereditary potential depended on external factors. How, when, and why that occurred was not predetermined, and the final outcome of the evolutionary process was not fully known. Osborn could never fully explain the process, but he presented a teleological interpretation that a certain principle or law guided evolution along progressive paths. That theory left room for nonmaterial causal factors and described evolution as a process that demonstrated plan and purpose.[16]

Osborn had developed his theory by 1897, and he modified it only slightly over the next thirty-eight years. What he originally called mutations or phylogenetic variations, he later referred to as rectigradations. By the 1930s he had adopted the term aristogenes for the factors that controlled evolution, and he termed the process aristogenesis. He employed the language of physics and chemistry to explain evolution and related processes. But despite those modifications Osborn remained committed to the belief in mutations as originally defined by Waagen, and he never substantially altered his interpretation of the process and pattern of evolution.[17]

He applied that interpretation to ever-increasing amounts of fossil data uncovered by his assistants and other paleontologists. Beginning in the late 1890s he used the distinction between ontogenetic and phylogenetic variations to interpret the evolution of horses, rhinoceroses, titanotheres, and other mammals. Distinguishing between what he defined as fluctuations in existing characters and the origin of new characters, Osborn maintained that among rhinoceroses and titanotheres the evolution of molar teeth and horns was characterized by a series of small, continuous changes in a definite direction. Among horses, the foot bones, molar teeth, and body size offered similar evidence of continuous, regular change.[18] In later years he would define the evolution of elephants and primates in similar terms.

Osborn held that the study of the fossil record indicated that the evolution of all families of vertebrates constituted a series of separate, parallel phyla, or lines of descent. Relying on the distinction between ontogenetic and phylogenetic variations, Osborn used morphological distinctions to separate related organisms into distinct lines of descent. He described the evolution of almost every family of vertebrates in terms of bushlike phylogenies rather than a branching, diverging tree of life.[19]

Osborn took polyphyleticism to an extreme. Committed to the idea that only a vertical system of classification could define true evolutionary relationships, he ignored contemporary relationships and arranged organisms in terms of their ancestor-descendant affiliations. Osborn's understanding of mutations reinforced the tendency toward extreme splitting. According to Osborn, mutations, once actualized, produced cumulative, irreversible changes. On that basis, he maintained that recent organisms that lacked a character possessed by earlier forms had to be placed in a separate line of descent. In the case of the elephant family (Proboscidea), Osborn defined thirty-nine different lines of descent in which no modern form was descended from any known earlier form, but rather traced its heritage back to an unknown, hypothetical ancestor.[20]

Osborn also applied his evolutionary ideas to classification. Originally he accepted the Linnaean system of classification, but in the 1920s Osborn tried to introduce a new non-Linnaean system based on his concept of mutations. Having divided virtually all families of mammals into series of separate phyla, he examined the tempo of evolution by comparing rates of mutations in those lines of descent. Eventually he claimed that taxonomic categories could be defined on the basis of mutation rates.

Osborn's ideas were not accepted, but the attempt reflects his belief that the definition of species and other features of classification should be based on historical, phylogenetic foundations and on his understanding of evolution.[21]

Osborn's evolutionary views had a bearing on his interpretation of the geographical distribution of organisms as well. In the late 1890s Osborn took up questions on biogeography and published several studies on the subject. He also advanced a new concept: the law of adaptive radiation. Osborn maintained that distinguishing features, variations in the size and proportion of existing characters, emerged as the result of responses to environmental stimuli. In the effort to obtain food, space, and other necessary resources, organisms had adapted to local conditions and produced an evolutionary divergence or adaptive radiation:

> Now it is a well-known principle of zoological evolution that an isolated region, if large and sufficiently varied in its topography, soil, climate, and vegetation, will give rise to a diversified fauna according to the *law of adaptive radiation* from primitive and central types. Branches will spring off in all directions to take advantage of every possible opportunity of securing food. The modifications which animals undergo in this adaptive radiation are largely of a mechanical nature; they are limited in number and kind by hereditary stirp, or germinal influence, and thus result in the independent evolution of similar types in widely-separated regions under the *law of parallelism or homoplasy*.
>
> This law causes the independent origin not only of similar genera but of similar families and even of our similar orders. Nature thus repeats herself upon a vast scale, but the similarity is never complete and exact.[22]

Osborn realized that adaptive radiation was an extension of the Darwinian principle of divergence, but he explained it in accordance with his own ideas. The hereditary factor produced similar, linear patterns of descent throughout the world.

Osborn, Evolution, and Natural Law

Osborn defined the insights derived from his work in terms of a number of evolutionary laws. His tetraplastic theory of evolution became the "law of the four inseparable factors of evolution." He defined his claim that organisms evolve through separate, multiple lines of descent as the "law of polyphyleticism." His interpretation of divergence and geographical distribution became the "law of adaptive radiation." Osborn elevated to the status of a natural law virtually every generalization he made about evolution.[23]

Osborn was not alone in claiming that the study of evolution yielded such laws. In *Origin of Species* Darwin defined laws concerning the correlation of parts, variation, sterility, and many other phenomena.[24] Vertebrate paleontologists of the day were the architects of a number of evolutionary "laws." Louis Dollo, the Belgian paleontologist, defined the law of evolutionary irreversibility, although he interpreted it in terms of a series of unique, unrepeatable events.[25] Cope maintained that the increase in body size that he discerned in phyletic sequences constituted a law, while Samuel Wendell Williston held that the reduction of large numbers of similar parts or elements to specialized units was also a law of evolution. Cope's and Williston's laws were descriptive generalizations designed "to order phylogenetic events into regularities sufficiently pervasive to be termed laws."[26] For Osborn, as for many other scientists of the nineteenth century, those laws had a different ontological status. In his view "the facts [of evolution] are immutable," and the laws of evolution were more than just descriptive generalizations; they were inviolable rules of nature, equivalent to "the gravitation law of Newton."[27]

Convinced that the evolutionary laws he had discovered were unimpeachable, Osborn had no question that evolution was anything other than a continuous, directed process. Although there were significant gaps in the fossil record, Osborn claimed that the evolutionary series of horses, camels, and other families were complete and demonstrated "absolute continuity."[28] Rectigradations, the changes that gave rise to new characters, were small, gradual, and continuous changes, smaller even than the individual differences that according to Darwin were the grist for the mill of natural selection. Evolution was cumulative, irreversible, and predictable. On several occasions Osborn stated that new characters evolved precisely when and where needed and "in a certain series of extinct mammals we can predict where a new cusp will arise before its actual occurrence."[29]

Osborn interpreted his theory and its subsidiary laws as having redeeming social and moral values. The discovery of such laws substantiated his claim for the significance of the work of the naturalist, in this case the paleontologist. He also maintained that the discovery of such laws furnished an insight into the "marvellous [*sic*] order which we call Natural Law pervading all Nature." Nature was "the visible expression of the divine order of things" and evolution the lawlike orderly process that "begins and ends the purposes of God."[30]

Since his days at Princeton, Osborn had endowed scientific work with religious meaning, and his evolutionary theory fully reflected that. Osborn based his theory on the study of fossil data and explained it in terms of the specific biological processes. But he required a role for the creator as causal agent and guiding principle, and philosophical and religious influences had a bearing on the theory he constructed. Osborn endowed the study of nature with sanctity, and his theory of evolution upheld the traditional convergence of science and religion. For him the laws of evolution demonstrated the presence and handiwork of the creator every bit as much as the Bible did. On those grounds he steadfastly opposed William Jennings Bryan and the Fundamentalists who claimed that evolution undermined religion.[31]

Osborn also used his theory of evolution to condemn certain contemporary trends in the biological sciences, particularly work in genetics. Osborn was by no means alone in attacking the methods and interpretations of twentieth-century geneticists. Nor was he alone in developing an orthogenetic theory that embodied a commitment to the role of plan and purpose in the universe. However, Osborn was a prominent figure and a prolific writer, and he became one of the most outspoken critics of genetics of his time. He would employ the evolutionary theory that he had developed as a bulwark against what he considered deplorable scientific and social developments.

Osborn and the New Biology

The late nineteenth century witnessed the rise of experimental biology, a new approach that seriously challenged the methodological and theoretical foundations of traditional biological research, including Osborn's work. Osborn's scientific studies reflected the morphologist's interest in obtaining evidence to document evolution and to construct evolutionary interpretations. In developing umbrella theories that accounted for variation, development, and inheritance, Osborn and other morphologists employed traditional means of investigation: the observation and description of organic form.[32]

Experimental biology represented a different approach to the study of life. In contrast to the field naturalists and many morphologists, experimental biologists worked primarily in laboratories often in urban, academic environments. Drawing on models and methods employed in physiology and in some instances physics and engineering, they asked questions and used techniques distinct from those previously employed. Osborn and other morphologists relied on the study of structure and some form of historical explanation, that is evolution or the relationship between evolution and development, as the basis for explaining a wide range of problems.

Experimental biologists focused on specific questions and employed manipulative techniques to answer those questions. Work in descriptive embryology of the mid-nineteenth century traced the development of germ layers. In contrast, the German scientist Wilhelm Roux punctured cells at different stages of development in order to understand the factors that caused and directed that process.[33] Roux held that the analysis of development had significance for understanding inheritance, but by the 1910s biologists were differentiating development and inheritance into discrete sets of problems and employing more sophisticated, invasive techniques to answer their questions. The American biologists Ross Granville Harrison and Thomas Hunt Morgan adopted experimental techniques as the means for addressing specific questions about development, growth, and regeneration.[34] Others applied experimental techniques to the study of inheritance, and with the rediscovery of Mendel's laws in 1900, genetics emerged as an expanding field of research.

Early twentieth-century biologists called attention to notable breakthroughs in embryology, cytology, and genetics. They also touted the hypothetico-deductive method and experimental techniques on which such insights were based. Recent historical studies have suggested that experimental biology did not constitute the discontinuous, revolutionary break that its practitioners maintained. Nevertheless, the development of experimental biology had significant consequences. It offered new, exciting means for examining biological processes. It also provided specific ways for testing particular questions and solving particular problems. Consequently, work in experimental biology expanded quickly and on a number of fronts.[35]

The materials and methods employed by experimental biologists were significantly different from those used by Osborn, though he did not oppose all work in experimental biology. He was a strong supporter of the Marine Biological Laboratory at Woods Hole, for example. That institution, established by Charles Otis Whitman in 1888, originally emphasized descriptive work in embryology. But later, when its research expanded to include cytology, physiology, and biochemistry, Osborn remained a supporter. He delivered lectures at the MBL in the 1890s, served as president of its board of trustees from 1896 to 1902, and throughout his career encouraged biology students to take courses there.[36] He was closely associated with E. B. Wilson, one of the premier cytologists and embryologists of the early twentieth century. Osborn hired Wilson for the new biology department at Columbia in 1891 and remained an advocate of Wilson's work over the next thirty years. He also supported some of the work being done in genetics, notably, Francis B. Sumner's research on the deer mouse *Peromyscus*.[37]

Osborn's support of such work was based on more than just personal considerations. Although he had a close personal and professional relationship with Wilson and Whitman, and Sumner obtained his Ph.D. degree at Columbia, each of those men, and the MBL as an institution, combined morphological and experimental approaches in their biological research. Wilson, who was interested in when and how the individual becomes differentiated, did some manipulating of organisms but relied primarily on observation and comparative analysis of nuclear and cellular stages of development. Sumner, interested in the extent to which characteristics that distinguished geographic races were inherited, undertook field research, measurement, and hybridization experiments of *Peromyscus*.[38] What Osborn could not accept was work in experimental biology that challenged his interpretations and the whole thrust of work in morphology and natural history. He was most threatened by research that sought to define genetics as the sole means for explaining evolution, an interpretation embodied particularly in the work of William Bateson, Hugo de Vries, and T. H. Morgan.

The work of Bateson and de Vries, while different in many respects, promoted new approaches to and interpretations of evolution. Bateson, an Englishman whose earliest research had focused on the impact of the environment on organisms, was one of the first scientists to undertake an experimental study of evolution. In the 1890s he focused his attention on variation and in a major work, *Materials for the Study of Variation* (1894), claimed that only large, discontinuous variations had evolutionary significance. Bateson argued that internal hereditary factors, not external conditions, were responsible for such changes. His interpretation with its emphasis on random discontinuous changes as the basis for evolution stood in contrast to Osborn's, not to mention Darwin's.[39]

Bateson's views were reinforced by the studies of the Dutch botanist de Vries. Around the same time that Bateson was formulating his interpretation of evolution, de Vries's experiments on plants demonstrated the significance of large-scale changes—saltations—for variation and evolution. De Vries, like Bateson, asserted that random, discontinuous changes, which he termed mutations, were the basis for evolution. His *Mutation Theory* (1901–3) received much support from American biologists who embraced the new emphasis on experimentation.[40]

Bateson's and de Vries's studies took on added significance after 1900 when de Vries, Carl Correns, and Erich von Tschermak independently rediscovered the work of Gregor Mendel. In the 1850s and 1860s Mendel, a monk who lived in what is today Czechoslovakia, had conducted experiments on the inheritance of height, color, and seed shape in plants.

Mendel's researches demonstrated that those characters were inherited according to the laws of probability, and he hypothesized that such patterns of inheritance could only be explained by assuming that every organism possessed two factors for each inherited character: one factor inherited from the male parent, the other from the female parent. Mendel's hypothesis offered an explanation for heredity as due to elements within organisms and left little room for the neo-Lamarckian interpretation that stressed the influence of external conditions. His experiments also indicated that characters were inherited in discrete, particulate packages, and he described the inheritance of those variations in predictable, mathematical terms.[41]

De Vries and Bateson quickly adopted Mendel's laws of the segregation and independent assortment of factors (genes) as the means for explaining the results of their own researches. They became two of the chief promoters of Mendelism in Europe and America. Bateson and de Vries interpreted Mendel's work in terms of their own emphases; hence, the early Mendelians explained evolution on the basis of relatively large, discontinuous changes.[42]

T. H. Morgan's work was a particularly serious challenge to Osborn. Morgan, who originally approached the study of heredity with embryological questions in mind, became one of the foremost geneticists of the twentieth century. In the years between 1910 and 1915 he gathered together a group of Columbia graduate students whose research concentrated on genetics. Their work, most fully summed up in *The Mechanism of Mendelian Heredity* (1915), laid the foundation for the classical interpretation of transmission genetics. In subsequent years Morgan elaborated on that theory and sought to establish genetics as a specific scientific discipline. He also sought to make genetics the foundation for explaining development and evolution.[43]

In defining genetics as the basis for understanding evolution, Morgan accorded little significance to the traditional descriptive work of morphologists. Paleontologists and field biologists could accumulate new data about evolution, but Morgan maintained that descriptive biology could add nothing new to explaining the mechanisms and patterns of evolution. Indeed, descriptive work could lead to serious misinterpretations. "My good friend the paleontologist," he claimed, "is in greater danger than he realizes when he leaves description and attempts explanation. He has no way to check up his speculations and it is notorious that the human mind without control has a bad habit of wandering."[44] Morgan explicitly dismissed Osborn's work as speculative and wrong headed. He ridiculed Osborn's understanding of the evolutionary process. "I am sorry to hear," Morgan once told Osborn, "that the mammals have not evolved by mutation. It would be too bad to leave them out of the general scheme, . . . and I cannot but hope that you will relent some day and let us have the mammals back." He also dismissed Osborn's imprecise use of language, especially neologisms and speculative explanations that emphasized nonmaterial causal factors. Experimental research based on the hypothetico-deductive method and a commitment to mechanistic materialism that explained phenomena in atomistic terms were central to Morgan's views.[45]

Osborn and Morgan also clashed for personal reasons. Just as Osborn was a leading figure in paleontology, Morgan was an aggressive proponent for experimental biology and genetics. He maintained that genetics and experimental research alone could solve questions about the process and pattern of evolution. He called into question the raison d'être of Osborn's entire research program. He questioned the tremendous sums the museum trustees allocated to a field of research he considered inconsequential.[46] Osborn was not used to such treatment. As a rich and powerful figure, he expected respect and deference, even from his scientific colleagues. As a scientist, he was used to criticism of his views, but not outright condemnation or neglect of his program of research. He believed that he was ill treated by Morgan, and he was both personally and professionally offended by Morgan's attitude and behavior.

Developments in biology at Columbia offered another forum for disagreement between Osborn and Morgan. Osborn had helped bring Morgan to Columbia in 1904, but their different fields, methods, and philosophies translated into different objectives for the Zoology Department. Osborn had established a program along broad morphological lines. He hoped to maintain that orientation and to continue the department's close connection to the College of Physicians and Surgeons. But the Zoology Department became famous for work in cytology and genetics, and Morgan's successes led him to emphasize quite different priorities. He had little interest in tying the department's efforts to medicine. And he saw little need to promote paleontology, comparative anatomy, or other fields of morphology. In 1909 Osborn had some difficulty getting William King Gregory appointed as his successor, and in later years Morgan was an obstacle to Gregory's advancement and his development of a research program in vertebrate morphology.[47] In the early 1920s, following the death of George S. Huntington, the professor of anatomy in the College of Physicians and Surgeons, Osborn and Morgan clashed over whether Huntington's position should be filled by an anatomist or an experimentalist.[48]

But beyond such personal problems Osborn attacked the empirical and methodological bases of the work of those who relied exclusively on genetics. While Morgan, Bateson, and Wilhelm Johannsen ignored the researches of Osborn and other morphologists, Osborn held that only an integration of research on problems of inheritance, development, and variation could provide insights into evolution. The experimentalists explained evolution as the result of random, discontinuous variations. Osborn contended that interpretations of evolution based on genetics were empirically inaccurate since the evidence of nature did not demonstrate random, discontinuous variation. In a 1912 lecture before the Harvey Society, for example, he turned to the evidence of the paleontological record to refute the interpretations of de Vries, Morgan, and W. E. Castle. "Is it not demonstrated," he asked, "by this comparison of results obtained in such widely different families as the Bovidae, Hominidae, Titanotheriidae, and Equidae that *discontinuity in heredity affords no evidence whatever of discontinuity of origin?*"[49] In that paper and others, Osborn relied on the researches of his associate William Diller Matthew and the work of mammalogists Gerrit S. Miller and Wilfred H. Osgood to argue that the evidence from paleontology and comparative anatomy demonstrated gradual, continuous variations.

Osborn was not alone in his opposition to genetics. In the early twentieth century many field naturalists and systematists opposed the interpretations of variation, evolution, and inheritance that were emerging from the zoological and botanical laboratories. He was, however, one of the most vocal critics who railed against Bateson and Morgan for ignoring the researches of the paleontologist and the field naturalist.[50]

Beyond his contention that the researches of experimentalists were empirically inaccurate, Osborn claimed that their interpretations were of little consequence for understanding evolution. In his view, Bateson and others had "without discrimination based upon variations, which may be largely or wholly ontogenetic and temporary, the important principles of 'Fortuitous Variation' of Darwin and 'Discontinuous Variation' of Bateson, whereas it is only the laws of phylogenetic variation which are of real bearing upon the problem of evolution."[51] The random, discontinuous variations emphasized by geneticists pertained only to changes in existing parts, not the origin of new characters, and according to Osborn's interpretation such changes had little to do with evolution. To him the limitations of the experimentalist were obvious. "First, he is not always in a fair position to judge which characters are important and which are unimportant. This, for instance, is the chief difficulty with Bateson's great work, 'Materials for the Study of Variation.' Second, the zoologist and experimentalist is too short lived to observe and measure those changes, if such exist, which are so extremely slow as to be invisible and immeasurable by his mortal eye, and he is most naturally led to the conclusion that visible, observable and measurable changes, viz., *saltations, discontinuities* or *mutations* (of de Vries) are the most important if not the only changes."[52]

To Osborn the studies of the experimental zoologists and botanists were limited in scope and perspective. Consequently, those scientists were "more prone to fall into the error of 'exclusive hypotheses.'" Experimental biology was a specialized study that did not take into account research in other fields, particularly the important researches of the naturalist and the paleontologist. Only the latter had the perspective to understand which variations would have evolutionary significance.[53]

On one level Osborn responded to the rapid and wide-spread development of experimental biology by claiming significance and legitimacy for paleontology. Confronted by the conceptual and methodological threat of genetics and other experimental studies, to say nothing of their expanding institutional dominance,[54] Osborn argued strenuously on behalf of his field of research. In terms of what we today define as macroevolution and microevolution, Osborn emphasized the all-importance of the former and claimed that the microevolutionary studies of the geneticist had no relevance for the interpretation of evolutionary trends as observed by paleontologists. In the face of the challenge of a new approach, Osborn tried to make a case for the uniqueness of the paleontologist as the only scientist capable of understanding the process and pattern of evolution.

Osborn opposed experimental biology on methodological and philosophical grounds as well. An advocate for an inductivist philosophy of science, he attacked the hypothetico-deductive method touted by experimental biologists. The method of posing and subsequently testing hypotheses by experimentation, with little or no reliance on the study of nature, was to Osborn both artificial and wrong headed.[55]

Osborn struck out against the philosophical assumptions that he claimed underlay the interpretations of the geneticists. He was inherently opposed to the idea that evolution resulted from any form of random or discontinuous variation. As early as 1894 he criticized Bateson's claim that evolution was the result of such variations, and throughout his career he steadfastly opposed Mendelian genetics on those grounds. By the 1920s many geneticists had abandoned de Vries's emphasis on saltations and were interpreting mutations as relatively small changes. Osborn, however, conflated and attacked all such interpretations. Not only was random change denied by the empirical data from the fossil record, but the very possibility of explaining evolution as the result of random "accidents" was unacceptable. Any random, discontinuous change, indeed any change that was not fully predictable, was equivalent to chance or accident, events that occurred without reason, plan, or purpose. Such phenomena could have no place in Osborn's interpretation of evolution or in his conception of nature, where everything operated strictly according to law and under the guidance of God.[56]

He opposed an interpretation that evolution or any natural phenomenon was the result of material causes. Darwin's theory that variations were selected on utilitarian grounds by a naturalistic agent was a mechanistic explanation that Osborn would not abide. Neither could he accept the basic premise of Mendelian genetics: that inheritance was the result of the independent assortment and segregation of material particles, or, as it was later defined, the breakage and recombination of chromosomes that carried those particles. Evolution and inheritance were explained by nonmaterial factors. An interaction of factors triggered a potential in an organism's germ plasm that, once actualized, produced evolutionary changes independent of environment, adapation, and usefulness.

In *The Origin and Evolution of Life* (1917), Osborn explained those processes in terms of the interaction of energies. He invoked the language of physics and chemistry, but as his critics Morgan and the physiologist Jacques Loeb noted, Osborn was still explaining evolution on the basis of nonmaterial factors, that is, energies. For Osborn the interaction of energies was not reducible to physicochemical explanation or mathematical description, and neither was evolution. By the 1920s Osborn was pointing to "the failure of materialism and of pure mechanism to give an interpretation of creative evolution that satisfies our reason."[57]

Osborn's reaction to the work of those experimentalists was neither scientifically nor philosophically sophisticated. He conflated differing ideas about genetics, particularly different conceptions about the size of mutations. He also combined differing philosophical positions. He failed to distinguish between materialism and mechanism. As many studies have indicated, those are distinct philosophical ideas and one does not necessarily entail the other. A number of scientists and philosophers adhered to one, or the other, or varying combinations of both. A commitment to Darwinian evolutionary theory or Mendelian genetics did not necessitate an adherence to mechanistic explanations or philosophical materialism. Osborn, however, lumped all those together and condemned them as a whole.[58]

He did so for a number of reasons. His conflation of different scientific interpretations and philosophical beliefs was in part a rhetorical device. Rather than fully exploring the differences between particular explanations, he found it easier and more expeditious to dismiss them as a whole. His position reflected his failure to keep abreast of some of the work on inheritance and evolution. Although Osborn showed an acquaintance with the literature, he did not examine the studies of geneticists or the wide range of works on evolution closely enough to appreciate fully the spectrum of interpretations. His own work was not based on experimentation, and Osborn's preoccupation with administrative duties did not enable him to keep up with current research in biology. Religious and philosophical beliefs further influenced his views. He was committed to an interpretation of evolution that provided for plan and purpose. He often referred to his theory as a form of natural theology that defined evolution in terms of secondary laws under the control of the creator. He refused to accept any form of discontinuous change or any material factor as the causal agent of evolution. Darwinism, neo-Darwinism, de Vries's mutation theory, and the chromosomal theory of inheritance—Osborn rejected them all.[59]

His values also had a bearing on his interpretations. Osborn opposed any ideas or activities that threatened his religious views or social position. His association with the American Museum reinforced those commitments. Jesup was one of those "enthusiasts" who "shared an optimistic belief in their duty to approximate the Kingdom of God on earth through converting the ungodly, suppressing the vicious, and relieving the miserable."[60] He envisioned the museum as an institution that would employ the evidences of natural history, including evolutionary studies, to convey spiritual and social ideals. Osborn shared that commitment in his scientific studies and his museum work. Nature not only demonstrated God's handiwork, it also "was to teach respect for law and property."[61]

Those values influenced Osborn's reaction to the work of Bateson and Morgan. On a number of occasions Osborn contrasted the social and psychological consequences of his and Bateson's work on evolutionary theory. In 1915 Osborn lashed out when Bateson claimed that after sixty years scientists still had little understanding of evolution. According to Osborn, "While twenty years of observation of the normal and natural aspects of nature have brought the zoologist and paleontologist somewhat nearer to a conception of the modes of evolution, twenty years of continuous observation of the abnormal and unnatural have landed one of the leading experimentalists, William Bateson, in the state of skepticism and agnosticism expressed in his recent work."[62] To Osborn experimental biology had resulted in an intellectual dead end. He linked experimental biology with the development of unhealthy, agnostic ideas.

In later years, particularly after World War I, Osborn associated the new biology with social and political developments that he disliked. He did not directly attribute German militarism to Ernst Haeckel's or August Weismann's biology, at least not in the way that biologists David Starr Jordan or Vernon Kellogg did. But he defined World War I as the ultimate "horror of mechanism and materialism." He denounced the materialist philosophy that underlay the Russian Revolution and the rise of the Soviet Union. He further claimed that "experimentalism is partly an intruder from our material atmosphere, partly an offspring of the general revolt from authority."[63] Osborn was conflating a bewildering variety of ideas and developments, including economic materialism, philosophical materialism, and the dialectical materialism of Marxism-Leninism. They all menaced Osborn and the power structure to which he belonged. From his perspective those developments threatened to unravel the very fabric of society, and he called for "a new emphasis upon the spiritual basis of conduct rather than upon the mechanistic."[64]

Osborn advanced his evolutionary theory as that new alternative. He portrayed his work in optimistic terms as leading to important discoveries about evolution and providing spiritual inspiration and regeneration. In contrast to Bateson, whose skepticism he deplored, Osborn was supremely confident in his interpretation of evolution. He had no hesitation in stating that paleontology provided the "absolutely concrete and irrefutable evidence of the actual modes of the origin of new characters in species."[65] Throughout the 1920s and early 1930s, Osborn claimed that his work resulted in the discovery of more and more new laws. The eighteen principles of evolution that he eventually defined in 1934 constituted not only new insights into that process but also a form of social meliorism not provided by experimental biology.[66]

Even an increasing skepticism about fully understanding the causes of evolution reinforced his commitments. Osborn believed in the truth of the evolutionary laws he had discovered, but he pointed out that he had only defined the modes of evolution. The causes of evolution remained "totally unexplainable and mysterious."[67] That was not, however, a reason for despair. On the contrary, by indicating the limits of science and human understanding the study of nature was a testimony to the role of the creator in the universe. The study of organisms in their habitats resulted in the realization that science and human reason could not fully comprehend nature or the workings of the creator. As he stated in 1927,

"Every day during my forty-eight years' observation and philosophy of Nature and the biology of man, I become more of a *naturalist*, less of a scientist, still less of a rationalist. What has been the fate of the rationalism of 1876 or of the materialism of that day or of the other 'isms' which were held up to our tender student minds as bogies?"[68]

Osborn's theory of evolution, by denying pessimism, skepticism, and agnosticism, provided a positive support for religion. Rejecting the materialism and rationalism that he associated with much of modern biology, he advanced a theory of evolution that he claimed was based on the study of nature. It also met the objectives of a public-oriented institution that emphasized the elaboration and portrayal of natural laws that were socially and morally uplifting.

Osborn rejected some work in experimental biology because it represented a specialized field of study that threatened the work of the naturalist and the traditional way of doing science. In 1895 Osborn referred to the bitter debate between the neo-Darwinians and the neo-Lamarckians as "a retrograde chapter in the history of science . . . attributable largely to the unnatural divorce of the different branches of biology, to our extreme modern specialization, to our lack of eclecticism in biology."[69] In later years, his concern and criticism increased. Osborn's reaction was due in part to developments occurring in the sciences. Continued specialization in the biological sciences, which fostered a narrowing of research interests, the rise of specialized academic departments, and the formation of national disciplinary societies, helped to change the structure of scientific knowledge and academic institutions. In that process natural history was being challenged by academic biology, and in many university programs experimental laboratory research became the priority. In those institutions and in new disciplinary societies, natural historians and morphologists were being pushed to the periphery.[70] That happened to paleontology. And at Columbia and on other fronts Osborn worked to maintain the status of his field.

But the work in genetics had additional ramifications for Osborn. He claimed that experimental biology, by cutting itself off from other methods and interpretations, was symptomatic of the specialization and compartmentalization that was plaguing contemporary society. Experimental biology, as an enterprise pursued in urban centers and dependent on developments in modern technology, was an unnatural activity divorced from the firsthand study of nature, outdoor values, and the belief in the strenuous life that were vitally important to Osborn. Responding to Bateson in 1915, he argued that "if the student of genetics abandons the natural and the normal for the unnatural and the abnormal and sticks solely to his seed pan and his incubator he is in danger of observing modes of origin and behavior of characters which never have and never will occur in Nature. He may, moreover, never observe at all certain modes of origin and behavior as well as certain properties and qualities of characters which are of the most fundamental importance in relation to his particular field of heredity and hybridizing."[71] To Osborn such specialized ways of thinking and working, divorced from the firsthand study of nature, had resulted in philosophical materialism and mechanistic explanations of evolution that contradicted traditional values and ideals.

Osborn's condemnation of experimental biology and glorification of paleontology was more than an effort to legitimize his particular field of inquiry, or even his own interpretation of evolution. It reflected his commitment to the preservation of nature study and the work of the naturalist in the face of developments that were affecting not merely the biological sciences but society in general. Just as the experimental biologist worked in laboratories separate from nature and paid no attention to the methodology or the researches of the paleontologist or naturalist, so was modern man developing modes of living and thinking that had no reference to nature and nature's laws. Through the study of organisms in their habitats and traditional ways of pursuing scientific research, Osborn sought to preserve traditional ways of structuring and ordering society. By emphasizing the importance of nature and the naturalist, he hoped to maintain an older scientific order as well as an established elite whose power, prestige, and values were being challenged by the forces of change.

Osborn structured those emphases into his theory of evolution. Since the early 1890s he had sought to develop a theory that would be eclectic. In explaining variation, development, evolution, and inheritance, he drew upon the researches of contemporary biologists in several fields. He also looked to older works for inspiration. At Princeton, Osborn had showed little interest in the historical aspects of biology or evolutionary theory, but during his first years in New York he scoured the historical literature. His first book, *From the Greeks to Darwin* (1894), was an analysis of the theories of evolution that focused on the views of philosophers and scientists from antiquity to the mid-nineteenth century. The most important of those earlier interpretations, the theories of Buffon, Lamarck, Geoffroy St. Hilaire, and Darwin, not only had historical interest for Osborn but became the foundation of his own evolutionary theory. While Osborn claimed that experimental biologists were separating themselves from traditional ways of thinking and working, he was developing an interpretation of evolution based on the work of earlier theorists.[72]

In the 1920s Osborn incorporated his reaction to contemporary social developments into his theory of creative evolution, or aristogenesis. By that time Osborn was explicitly condemning what he called "the veneer of modern civilization." Modern Americans, he contended, were "slaves to convention" with few or no creative powers. Throughout the 1920s he appealed for creative work and for education that was original and imaginative. He did so by calling attention to his own accomplishments. He claimed that expeditions or museum displays could have a powerful transforming effect that was not entirely explicable in rational terms.[73] He claimed that creativity lay at the heart of the evolutionary process, thereby providing a scientific foundation for his social and educational interpretations. According to Osborn, new adaptive characters emerged without antecedent experiences; that is, they were not the direct consequences of the use and disuse of parts or of environmental influences. The emergence of such characters undermined mechanistic explanations and demonstrated that nature was a creative force. In his view "evolution is a continuous creation of life fitted to a continuously changing world."[74] By the 1920s Osborn was placing more emphasis on adaptation. But his term "creative evolution" meant little or nothing, and his theory of aristogenesis differed little, except in language, from his earlier views. His theory of creative evolution embodied his concerns about the lack of creativity that characterized modern civilization.

That theory supported the established social and political order. Osborn's insistence that evolution is a gradual, continuous process reflected his staunch opposition to any form of discontinuous change. In addition to condemning the interpretations of early twentieth-century geneticists, he rejected almost all efforts that called for social, economic, or political change. The women's movement, the graduated income tax, and the Russian Revolution were abnormal changes that denied the laws of nature and threatened the very existence of human society.[75] Osborn explained evolution as a series of slow, cumulative changes controlled by heredity, by an ancestral germ plasm that was responsible for initiating change and directing it along orderly, purposeful lines. That interpretation, which Osborn applied to the evolution of several families of fossil vertebrates, also reflected his view that the evolution of society should be under the control of those who possessed a particular ancestry, those who belonged to an elite. His concern for maintaining an older way of life and a particular hereditary germ plasm is most fully defined in his work on human evolution.

Osborn and Human Evolution

Osborn's interest in paleoanthropology was in part an extension of his earlier research. Since the 1880s he had studied fossil mammals and with the aid of his assistants had written many works on horses, titanotheres, and proboscideans. Much of that work was summed up in *The Age of Mammals* (1910), the first major text by an American vertebrate paleontologist to examine specimens and horizons in North America in relationship to those in Europe and Asia. The last chapter of that book included a discussion of the physical and cultural characteristics of ancient humans. Some of the issues and interpretations that characterized his study of fossil mammals are evident in his work in paleoanthropology. Osborn's *Men of the Old Stone Age* (1915) was in one sense a companion piece to *The Age of Mammals*.[76]

Men of the Old Stone Age, a highly successful book that went through thirteen printings in Osborn's lifetime, was a compendium of recent work in archeology and anthropology. Inspired by developments in those fields, Osborn had toured a number of prominent European archeological sites in 1912.[77] Characteristically, Osborn's fieldwork included a brief reconnaissance of the relevant locations and drew heavily on the work of others. One scholar has claimed that *Men of the Old Stone Age*, which devotes more attention to artifactual evidence than to fossil remains, was largely written by Nels C. Nelson, the principal archeologist at the American Museum.[78] Considering how Osborn relied on Matthew and Gregory for other studies, that claim rings true. But the book also bears Osborn's imprint; the interpretation of human culture and evolution was definitely his own.

Throughout the book, Osborn argued that modern humans are distinct, both physically and culturally, from people in the Paleolithic period. The oldest evidence of physical and cultural remains testified to the fact that Europe and Asia in the Paleolithic period were peopled by distinct races, possibly distinct species or even genera of humans. *Pithecanthropus* and the Heidelberg specimen, according to Osborn, probably did not belong to the genus *Homo*.[79] He also claimed "that the Piltdown race was not related at all either to the Heidelbergs or the Neanderthals, nor was it ancestral to any of the older races of the Old Stone Age, or to any of the existing species of modern man. As shown in the human family tree in Chapter VI, the Piltdown race represents a side branch of the human family which has left no descendants at all."[80] Osborn held that the Neanderthals were an evolutionary side branch not ancestral to any modern race of *Homo sapiens*. He was not alone in expelling the Neanderthals from the family tree of modern man; Marcellin Boule and Arthur Keith, two leading paleoanthropologists of the day, did so too.[81] But for Osborn that separation had particular significance.

Osborn made a special effort to distinguish the Neanderthals from another, nearly contemporary, race, the Cro-Magnon. The two groups lived almost simultaneously in southern and western Europe, but Osborn emphasized their differences and argued that there was no basis for evolutionary descent from one to the other. The Neanderthals were a heavyset, low-browed people who had developed a flint-making industry. The Cro-Magnon were a tall, erect people with high foreheads, and they possessed a demeanor and a level of intelligence little different from modern humans. A powerful, nomadic race, the Cro-Magnon had easily displaced the Neanderthals and subsequently developed a higher level of cultural achievement. The cave paintings of southern France, which Osborn praised as the birthplace of modern art and sculpture, were the work of the Cro-Magnon. Their graves and burial sites, in contrast to the tumuli of the Neanderthals, showed evidence of religious rites and a high level of spiritual awareness.

Although the Cro-Magnon, like the Neanderthals, had died out and left no modern ancestors, they represented the epitome of the Old Stone Age: a virile, progressive people whose cultural achievements were more significant than those of later Neolithic races. Indeed Osborn maintained that after the flowering of Paleolithic life among the Cro-Magnon there was a decline. The races that existed in the Neolithic period—a Mediterranean type, an Alpine type, and later a Nordic type—had emigrated into Europe from different directions. In some respects they possessed characteristics that Osborn admired: strength, courage, and strong family loyalty. But in terms of artistic and cultural achievements they ranked far below the Cro-Magnon.[82]

Osborn's *Men of the Old Stone Age*, like *The Age of Mammals*, was replete with information on geographical distribution; the races of mankind, like the families of fossil vertebrates, had originated in and migrated from Central Asia.[83] His views on evolution and classification influenced his interpretation of the biological and cultural relationships among early peoples. Just as he had emphasized morphological differences as the means for establishing distinct lines of descent among related animals, so he made sharp morphological and taxonomic distinctions among the different races of mankind. The pattern of human evolution was not a branching, diverging tree of life but a series of separate, parallel lines. Human evolution did not entail descent from one race to the other, or even the commingling of one race with another; instead it was a series of replacements. Different races were the product of different germ plasms and had separate and distinct evolutionary histories.[84]

But Osborn's interpretation of human cultural and biological evolution was more than just an extension of his previous paleontological researches. In one respect his views represented a continuation of a tradition of nineteenth-century physical anthropology that focused on racial characteristics as the means for classifying and studying mankind. Pierre Paul Broca, Paul Topinard, and William Z. Ripley were but a few of the late nineteenth-century anthropologists who constructed typologies and racial hierarchies on the basis of physical characteristics. For many of those anthropologists, racial characteristics were unchanging, and race determined the cultural as well as physical features of a people.[85] Despite the impact of evolutionary theory and Franz Boas's theory of cultural relativism, both of which challenged the emphasis on unchanging physical characteristics as the means for understanding human evolution and culture,[86] many, including, Osborn, remained committed to an interpretation based on physical anthropology.

The evidence of physical differences among peoples was the basis for Osborn's adherence to polygenesis, the doctrine that human races were separate species. He also claimed that race influenced all aspects of a people's existence. Osborn believed that racial characteristics were the embodiment of an ancestral germ plasm that, like the germ plasm that controlled animal evolution, controlled racial evolution and all aspects of a race's intellectual, cultural, and behavioral characteristics. The Neanderthal and Cro-Magnon peoples, for example, possessed different racial characteristics and therefore had different histories, physical features, and cultural achievements. As he once noted, "there is a racial soul as well as a racial mind, a racial system of morals, a racial anatomy." For Osborn race was all-important in understanding human evolution.[87]

That social and political commitments influenced Osborn's interpretation of human evolution and culture is evident in his interpretation of human history after the Paleolithic period. According to Osborn, the various human races and species of the Old Stone Age had not mixed. In addition to his claim that the Neanderthals and Cro-Magnon had remained separate, Osborn, in spite of the evidence from the Grimaldi specimens in Spain, maintained that Africans had not migrated into Europe during the Paleolithic.[88] The races of that period had remained pure and distinct. But after the extinction of the Cro-Magnon, different races had begun to mingle, in large part as a result of the onset of civilization. Increasing civilization and the domestication of life, accompanied by the abandonment of a nomadic existence and the necessity of struggling against the elements, marked the beginning of mankind's divorce from nature. The rise of civilization brought with it the potential for decline. Not all peoples in all places were adversely affected. The ancient Greeks, like the Cro-Magnon, represented the height of humanity's achievement. But for the most part man's separation from nature and the mixing of the races had brought a decline since the Paleolithic period.[89]

Osborn defined the problem associated with civilization and racial mixture as not merely affecting Neolithic peoples but also his own group: the members of New England stock from northwestern Europe. In addition to developing a theory that emphasized the importance of nature and the undesirable effects of specialization, Osborn constructed an interpretation of human evolution that supported the reaction of many upper-class Americans to contemporary social and political developments. Osborn and other members of his class stood fast against social and demographic changes, particularly the immigration that was affecting all aspects of contemporary life and culture.

In the late nineteenth century, the influx of millions of southern and eastern Europeans, many of whom entered and remained in New York City, changed the face of American society and culture. Most of these immigrants became part of a lower class that lived and worked in terrible conditions and had little political power. But their increasing numbers presented a serious threat to those Protestant, northwestern Europeans who had traditionally dominated American society, including such institutions as the American Museum.[90] Concerning his own neighborhood in the Hudson River highlands, Osborn frequently complained of the menace of Italian workers and merchants whom he called "bootleggers" and whose presence he claimed threatened his family and others in the area. The continued immigration and mixing of different races was to him morally repugnant as well as biologically and socially debilitating.[91]

Osborn's *Men of the Old Stone Age* was more than a compendium of recent research in anthropology and archeology. It was an interpretation of human culture and evolution designed to maintain the power, prestige, and purity of the elite to which he belonged. Osborn claimed that the study of nature was the basis for his conclusions, but the emphasis on nature was merely the language, or rhetoric, that he employed in the effort to preserve, in the face of change, a traditional power structure.

Osborn plied the theme of the transcendent importance of race in many publications. He wrote articles that extolled the Scandinavian race in particular, and published biographical studies that defined race as the means for explaining the life and work of prominent individuals. In *Impressions of Great Naturalists* (1921), Osborn argued that the different character of the naturalists John Muir and John Burroughs was a consequence of their Scottish and Nordic backgrounds respectively. According to Osborn, Burroughs conducted his nature studies in the eastern United States primarily because "the soul that rose with him had its setting for countless generations in the north." Biographical sketches of Cope, Roosevelt, and museum trustees emphasized family background and racial heritage.[92] Such emphases were not uncommon in biography at the time. Osborn pointed out that race alone was not entirely responsible for such developments; racial evolution was a response to particular environments. However, once a particular race developed in a particular environment, it would not change. The actualization of a racial germ plasm in a specific environment would determine both the physical and cultural characteristics of the members of that race for thousands of years.

Osborn became actively involved in political efforts designed to counteract the threat of immigration and racial mixture. In the 1910s he became a prominent figure in the eugenics movement, a popular and wide-ranging effort of differing constituencies that sought to breed better people. In the United States much of that effort focused on negative eugenics, or removing from the breeding population those that were considered unfit. Throughout the country, scientists, physicians, and political leaders, most of whom maintained that heredity was more important than environment, characterized thousands of people as "unfit" or "feebleminded."

In addition to establishing sterilization laws in over twenty states, eugenicists worked for immigration restriction. Osborn was a member of the Immigration Restriction League. He corresponded with Senator Albert Johnson, head of the congressional committee that established the Immigration Restriction Acts of 1921 and 1924, and was a powerful supporter of Charles B. Davenport and H. H. Laughlin, who lobbied hard for such laws.[93] He also aided and encouraged Madison Grant, his colleague on the boards of trustees at the Bronx Zoo and the museum whose publications emphasized the all-importance of race and called attention to the ways in which the tide of immigration was diluting and threatening the existence of the old New England stock. Grant's books, *The Passing of the Great Race* (1916) and *The Conquest of a Continent* (1934), included laudatory forewords by Osborn, and the two men were the prime movers behind the development of the Galton Society, a eugenics organization centered at the American Museum. By the early 1930s Osborn was supporting Hitler's and Mussolini's programs of racial hygiene in Germany and Italy.[94]

Osborn also promoted a program of positive eugenics that emphasized the need for greater reproduction by "the fit." Claiming that the "purest of New England stock is not holding its own," he called for a program of "birth selection" whereby the best in society would reproduce only among themselves and in greater numbers than ever before. He contrasted his program of birth selection to Margaret Sanger's program of birth control and looked to eugenics as the means for increasing the white Anglo-Saxon Protestant elite of which he was a part.[95] To Osborn the promotion of eugenics was a "patriotic duty of the first importance," an obligation to preserve and perpetuate the Nordic stock and its important racial characteristics. He identified the principal values and ideals of American life with that group; democracy, liberty, and capitalism were racial characteristics, limited to the members of the old New England stock. The "old-fashioned American values" were associated with members of his class and ethnic heritage.[96]

Osborn viewed eugenics as more than a patriotic concern; it was a vitally important biological and public health issue. The "selection, preservation, and multiplication of the best heredity" was a necessity if the Nordic race and American values were to survive.[97] Well aware of the ways in which evolution had resulted in extinction in the animal kingdom, Osborn was concerned about the possible extirpation of the human race, or at least of his own ethnic group. He maintained that contemporary life, which allowed for the mixing of races and provided the opportunity for women to move beyond their separate sphere, was in conflict with nature's laws and could result in degeneration. According to Osborn, such developments carried the potential for, but did not necessarily entail, decline. It was possible that human evolution could be redirected. By recognizing the importance of race and the power of heredity, restricting different races to their own domains of social and sexual activity, and allowing the New England stock to maintain its biological and social ascendancy, humanity and society could be preserved.[98]

In the 1910s and 1920s eugenics, nativism, and the call for immigration restriction gained a wide following in the United States. After World War I the writings of Grant, Lothrop Stoddard, and others who warned of the consequences of immigration and racial mixture captured a substantial audience. Thousands of individuals, many of them members of traditional elites, joined immigration restriction leagues in an effort to turn their ideology into law.[99] Osborn participated in those efforts and justified those actions on the basis of his scientific interpretations. Maintaining that his studies had defined important laws of nature, he applied his interpretations of evolution and inheritance to promote eugenics.

Yet Osborn's work was not merely an attempt to apply those interpretations. His ideas were an outgrowth of such social and political values. In Princeton and New York he had matured in an environment that was socially and religiously conservative. Since the early 1890s his scientific researches had been influenced by the commitment among leading figures at the museum and the zoo to preserve nature and much else from the effects of modernization. Influenced by those objectives, Osborn had adopted the preservationist program and incorporated it into his interpretations of scientific methodology and education, evolution, and inheritance. The preservation of nature and nature's laws lay at the heart of his scientific work, and he promoted a campaign to indicate how modern life was out of touch with those laws. He did so in the usual manner: through addresses, published writings, and political activities. But Osborn also disseminated his ideas and enthusiasms through policies, programs, and displays at the American Museum.

7

Representing Nature:
The Portrayal of Prehistoric Life
at the American Museum

In the years between 1908 and 1933 Osborn employed his powerful position to make the American Museum into a concrete expression of his scientific and social beliefs. As museum president he created and received support for projects that embodied his commitment to the preservation and elaboration of nature's laws. Under his direction the museum launched educational programs designed to present the values of nature study to the schoolchildren of New York City. Worldwide explorations to the ends of the earth were dramatic means for extolling the naturalist and preserving rugged, outdoor values in an industrial age. Osborn viewed the development of exhibits as serving a similar purpose. Since the 1890s museum exhibits had included preservationist concerns, but Osborn sought to promote those objectives on a grand scale. He was interested in developing displays that portrayed his evolutionary interpretations. He also employed them to put across his concern for maintaining traditional values. In 1909, soon after he became museum president, preservation became official museum policy.[1]

Osborn developed a number of exhibits and entire new halls that were designed to emphasize the preservationist theme. He inaugurated a Hall of Public Health in 1909. That project reflected current developments in public health, particularly the emphasis on bacteriology and preventive medicine. The hall was originally designed to educate the public about the etiology of tuberculosis and ways to prevent contracting the disease. But by 1913 Osborn was suggesting that the hall's director, C. E. A. Winslow, include additional exhibits designed to protect the public

152

against other threats to health. For Osborn one of those threats was unrestricted immigration.[2]

Osborn was the central figure in the creation of the Theodore Roosevelt Memorial. A monumental exhibit that required the construction of an entire new wing of the museum on Central Park West, the memorial was a glorification of Roosevelt's life, emphasizing his work as a naturalist. Osborn initiated the idea for the memorial and lobbied extensively for municipal support. As Donna Haraway has argued, the memorial's African Hall, conceived and designed by the explorer and taxidermist Carl Akeley, was an encomium to racial heritage. Similar statements are evident in a number of exhibits on the museum's ground floor: the displays of Roosevelt's expeditions and a diorama of the Pilgrims meeting the Indians.[3]

Osborn placed a high priority on developing new and dramatic means for portraying prehistoric life through the DVP. His emphases included scientific objectives. Osborn, Matthew, and Gregory were interested in producing mounts and restorations that accurately represented vertebrate morphology. They directed Knight and other department artists to portray ancient organisms in realistic biotic and physical conditions. Many of the efforts to construct mounts involved problems concerning the relationship between skeletal and muscular structure, particularly posture and the position of the bones and muscles when the animal was moving or engaged in other actions. As a result, scientific research and interpretation had an important bearing on the displays that were erected.

Osborn's interest in developing exhibits that showed prehistoric animals in lifelike poses and conditions reflected his concern for the preservation of nature. At the museum, Jesup had supported Allen's and Chapman's efforts to develop some of the first habitat groups, displays that presented animals in characteristic activities and environments. Those displays, while placing a premium on scientific accuracy and seeking to provide the public with educational information about animals, also emphasized other objectives. Chapman, in particular, sought to provide the public with a means for appreciating birds and their complex habits and adaptations. He hoped to make the public aware of the threats to birds and thereby promote the cause of wildlife protection.[4] Osborn had similar objectives. He too wanted to present the evidences of nature in such a way that the public would come to appreciate animals and their habits, mechanical adaptations, and relationship to their environment.

Beginning in the 1890s, Osborn promoted those objectives through the development of a project that included restorations and mountings of recent and fossil horses. For work on recent horses he hired Samuel

Harmsted Chubb, "a machinist by trade but a naturalist by avocation."
As a young man, Chubb had independently pursued an interest in preparing and mounting specimens. His work, accompanied by frequent
trips to the American Museum, led him to criticize some of the DVP
exhibits as incomplete and inaccurate.[5] After seeing examples of Chubb's
work, Osborn hired him with money from the Whitney Fund; when
money from that source expired he personally paid Chubb's salary.
Through his close relations with wealthy horse owners, Osborn acquired
for the museum the skeletons of two famous race horses, Sysonby and
Lee Axworthy, both of which Chubb mounted. At Osborn's request
Chubb created a mounting of a man and rearing horse that for a time was
the museum's logo.[6]

Chubb also developed new means for exhibiting horses in motion.
Recent work in photography, particularly the studies of Eadweard
Muybridge, had demonstrated that horses have all four feet off the
ground when running at a full gallop. Chubb sought to demonstrate the
phases of the horses' action in their skeletal detail. From a makeshift rig
that was attached to the roof of the museum and held him about thirty
feet off the ground, Chubb photographed horses in motion below. Using
those pictures and comparative osteological analysis, he developed striking displays of horse skeletons (figures 4 and 5). Chubb's mounts reflected his concern for creating exhibits that were anatomically accurate.
He also wanted to "express beautiful movements, animation, and even animal motions, so that not only the student and the artist but the casual
museum visitor would discover beauty in them."[7]

Chubb's work was a means to meet the museum's and Osborn's objectives. His studies provided valuable scientific data on horses and contributed to Osborn's interest in the relationship between form and function
in animals. His displays portrayed the beauty, power, and nobility of the
horse that Osborn wanted to convey. Chubb's work, both his displays
and a guide leaflet that he coauthored with Matthew, also defined the
importance of the horse for mankind. The mount of the rearing horse
depicted the animal's strength and majesty. But for Osborn the mount,
which he entitled "The Breaking of the Horse," also "expresses unwilling subjection, and the position of man—as if holding a bridle—of intelligent control."[8] The study of the horse demonstrates "his present beauty
of form and superb mechanism of limb and tooth structure." Through
such study "we recognize his [the horse's] subsequent great influence on
human civilization as well as his part in literature, in poem and in story;
we read daily more and more of his present culture and popularity, and
speculate upon his future in competition with machines of human man-

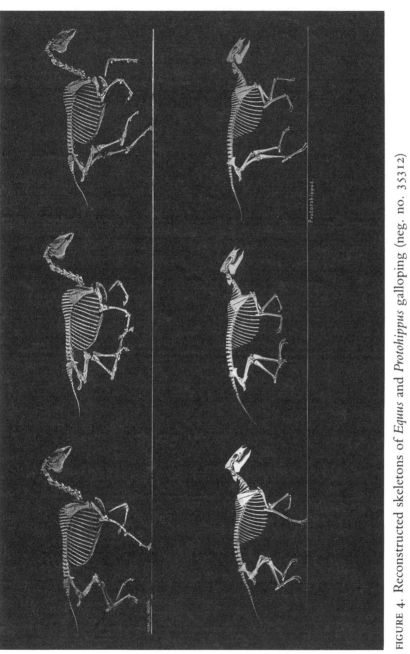

FIGURE 4. Reconstructed skeletons of *Equus* and *Protohippus* galloping (neg. no. 35312)

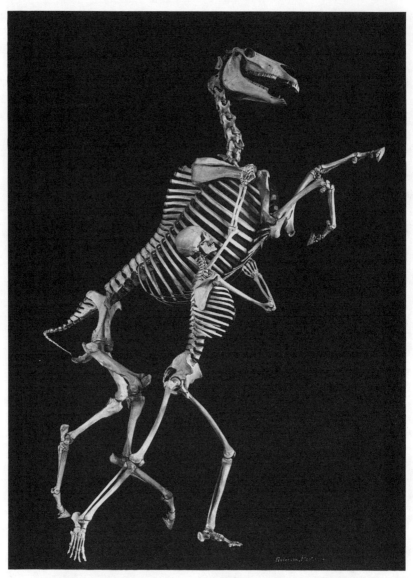

FIGURE 5. Reconstructed skeletons of Rearing Horse and Man
(neg. no. 325985)

ufacture which are rapidly increasing in efficiency."[9] Chubb's horse displays embodied Osborn's concern for alerting the public about the status of nature in the wake of advancing civilization, in this case, the automobile.

The dinosaur exhibits that Osborn and the DVP developed depicted similar themes. That work involved greater concern with scientific and technical questions because dinosaurs, more than horses, presented problems when it came to developing specimen mountings. In the mid-nineteenth century Benjamin Waterhouse Hawkins, relying on the interpretation of the British anatomist and paleontologist Richard Owen, had looked to the rhinoceros and other large mammals as the model for the dinosaur reconstructions he built in England and America.[10] The gigantic sauropod dinosaurs discovered later in the century, however, had no modern analogues and presented difficult scientific problems.

The sheer size and weight of a creature like *Apatosaurus* raised questions about its habitat, posture, and means of locomotion. Given the size and bulk of those creatures, did they crawl like modern reptiles, or did they walk upright like elephants or other large graviportal mammals? Some paleontologists, like O. P. Hay and Gustav Tornier, argued that *Apatosaurus* and *Diplodocus* had a sprawling pose and crawled like reptiles.[11] Osborn argued that those and other sauropods were primarily aquatic creatures that occasionally ventured onto land to breed and lay eggs. Studies indicated that the immense *Diplodocus* had hollowed out vertebrae and a very light skeletal structure, and according to Osborn it could rear up on its hind legs to feed off the tops of trees. *Apatosaurus* was a much heavier animal, and Osborn, Matthew, and Gregory claimed that with its imperfect skeletal structure and musculature it could only carry its massive weight by living in the water. They also maintained that it had an erect though rather bowlegged posture, and DVP staff members developed new studies to substantiate that claim.[12]

In 1904, when Hermann and the preparatory staff had finished cleaning the bones of *Apatosaurus* and were readying them for mounting, Matthew and Walter Granger undertook a study to determine the posture of the animal. At the Bronx Zoo they dissected recent reptiles and applied their findings to the dinosaur. They articulated dinosaur bones in specific positions. Then they pasted on broad sheets of paper that represented muscles running from the point of origin to the point of insertion. That provided a crude model of muscle and skeletal structure from which they inferred the pose of *Apatosaurus*.[13] The model could also be changed: bones and sheets of paper representing muscles could be manipulated to infer how the animal may have moved, then repositioned if the relationship between bone and muscle did not seem correct. A series of sketches, probably done by Erwin Christman, indicates that department members examined a number of possible positions to determine the animal's stance and motion before agreeing on one interpretation. Thus, scientific analysis, and what might be called an experiment, played a role in the mounting of the *Apatosaurus* specimen in 1904–5.[14]

The *Apatosaurus* was the first dinosaur the DVP mounted, and subsequently better techniques were developed to exhibit those creatures. Osborn and the DVP staff continued to work closely with the staff at the Bronx Zoo, particularly with Raymond Ditmars, the curator of reptiles, whose films of those creatures in action provided additional information for inferring how dinosaurs may have moved. DVP artists and preparators also created more sophisticated models. Small-scale replicas of dinosaurs in which every bone could be disarticulated became important tools for considering the problems of functional morphology and exhibition. Such models could be used to study a range of poses and the changing positions of the bones and muscles during motion. They also provided a means for studying other actions, including the bending of the head and neck in order to feed. The use of those models, combined with studies in comparative osteology and myology, enabled Osborn and Mook to make inferences about the habits of *Camarasaurus* and other sauropods.[15]

The emphasis on understanding habits and functions also reflected Osborn's desire to portray dinosaurs as once-living creatures. While DVP scientists, preparators, and artists drew upon the best contemporary knowledge pertaining to dinosaur morphology, habits, and environment for the exhibits they erected, they also depicted dinosaurs in dramatic situations. The mounts frequently showed animals in motion or combat and served as entertainment for the visiting public. The mounts were a means to portray the power and magnificence of nature's creations. In the early 1910s the DVP developed a display of two *Anatosaurs,* duck-billed herbivorous dinosaurs. One animal was shown eating foliage from the ground. The other, according to a description written by Barnum Brown, was up on its toes searching the surrounding area after being "startled by the approach of a carnivorous dinosaur, *Tyrannosaurus,* their enemy." Another mounting, completed in 1907, showed an *Allosaurus,* a carnivorous dinosaur, devouring the remains of *Apatosaurus* (figure 6). Matthew noted that the exhibit "gives to the imaginative observer a most vivid picture of a characteristic scene of that bygone age, millions of years ago, when reptiles were the lords of creation, when 'Nature red in tooth and claw' had lost none of her primitive savagery."[16]

FIGURE 6. Reconstructed skeleton of *Allosaurus* devouring *Apatosaurus* (neg. no. 35422)

The emphasis on the raw power and ferocity of nature's creations was most forcefully portrayed in the displays of *Tyrannosaurus rex*. Here too the DVP relied on scientific analysis, using birds as the analogues from which to infer the skeletal and muscular relations and posture of the dinosaur. Originally the department planned to erect a mounting of two tyrannosaurs that would show the animals attracted to the same prey. One dinosaur was displayed crouching over the prey, the second advancing at "very nearly the full height of the animal." The exhibit demonstrated a good knowledge of dinosaur morphology and preparation technique. It also conveyed the violent struggle for existence that characterized life in nature.[17]

That display was never mounted, but the individual *Tyrannosaurus* specimen put up in 1910, with jaw open and ready for combat, conveyed the ferociousness of the creature. Even the name, which Osborn coined after originally referring to the animal as *Deinodontus,* had the same connotation (figure 7). The dinosaurs, more than any other creatures, represented the awesome, terrifying power of nature. Their sheer size left the visitor dwarfed and in awe. An early plan that called for a mounting that showed a man in relationship to the tyrannosaur suggested the overwhelming disproportion in size.[18]

Osborn promoted the development of artistic representations of those organisms. His own interest in art may in part have prompted the large reproductions he sponsored. From an early age Osborn had shown an interest in painting, and he was well acquainted with the nature artist Frederic Edwin Church, a neighbor and close family friend. At Princeton, Osborn organized a sketch club and did most of the specimen drawings for his and Scott's early papers.[19] It was only in the 1890s, however, that Osborn began to promote paintings as a means of portraying prehistoric life, and again he did so largely in response to developments already being emphasized at the American Museum. Chapman's early habitat groups of birds included background paintings of appropriate environments. The Jesup Expedition to collect Northwest Indian artifacts included the production of large murals of Indian life. Paintings by the artists Will S. Taylor and F. W. Stokes emphasized the relationship of man to nature: how Indians and Eskimos relied upon fish, trees, and other products of the environment for their industries and way of life. In the paintings by Stokes and Taylor, those people were viewed as having a harmonious relationship with nature. While the Indians and Eskimos used the products of the environment for their own benefit, they were also fully integrated into nature. The need to understand one's surroundings and to maintain a close relationship with nature was also a theme in the DVP's paintings of prehistoric life.[20]

FIGURE 7. Reconstructed skeleton of *Tyrannosaurus rex* (neg. no. 36188)

Although Osborn had requested Rudolph Weber to paint a number of small watercolor reproductions in the early 1890s, it was Knight who became the principal artist of prehistoric life and depicted the themes that Osborn wanted to convey. After first employing Knight to paint the fossil mammals discussed in his 1896 paper, "Prehistoric Quadrupeds of the Rockies," Osborn sent the artist to work with Cope to bring to life some of the important fossil reptiles Cope had discovered. Although Cope died three weeks after Knight's internship, their collaboration resulted in a number of important paintings. Among those were restorations of *Hadrosaurus,* the dinosaur that Cope had helped to mount in the late 1860s, and a pair of dryptosaurs *(Laelaps),* the leaping carnivorous dinosaur Cope had discovered in the 1860s. Knight's painting captured the dryptosaurs in the midst of combat. Subsequently, Osborn commissioned Knight to paint virtually all the principal dinosaur specimens discovered by American Museum parties.[21]

Knight stuck to his own artistic standards and interpretations, but he worked closely with Osborn and other members of the DVP to show the structure, habits, and environments of prehistoric life. Knight's paintings, done in the expansive, romantic landscape style of the time, included details of the climate, plant life, and geography of the Jurassic and Cretaceous periods. Knight noted that Matthew "for years was my chief consultant and adviser on matters of pose and difficult bone structure, and what unusual forms might indicate in the living animal."[22] Osborn's influence was also evident. Knight's restoration of *Apatosaurus* painted in 1898 reflected Osborn's interpretation that the animal lived in water but also spent some time on land. His portrayal of *Diplodocus* embodied the same interpretation, as well as Osborn's ideas on the great length of the creature's tail, its ability to rise up on its rear legs, and its use of short rakelike teeth to eat water plants. His paintings of the *Allosaurus* group, the *Anatosaurus* group, and the *Tyrannosaurus* portrayed the aggressive, combative qualities of those organisms in a manner that was more imposing than the fossil mounts.[23]

Osborn and the American Museum were not alone in developing such mounts or even in displaying Knight's paintings. The discoveries of dinosaurs in the late 1890s prompted exhibits at Yale, the Carnegie Museum, the Field Museum, and the United States National Museum. At Yale, Charles Emerson Beecher directed the mounting of the back legs and pelvis of Marsh's *Apatosaurus* in 1901, but it was the crew at the Carnegie, John Bell Hatcher, W. J. Holland, and Arthur S. Coggeshall, that created the first mounting of a complete sauropod, *Diplodocus carnegiei.*[24] At the National Museum Charles W. Gilmore, head of the Division of Vertebrate Paleontology, oversaw the mounting of many dinosaurs between 1903 and 1941. Gilmore had a good understanding of dinosaur morphology and the technical details of preparation, and his mountings of *Diplodocus, Stegosaurus,* and other dinosaurs embodied important revisions. His work also depicted those creatures in motion. His mounting of *Camptosaurus* was constructed "with the intention of conveying to the observer the impression of a rapidly walking animal." For the National and Carnegie museums Knight painted dinosaur murals that rivalled his work at the American Museum.[25]

Although there was widespread interest in dinosaurs, exhibits at institutions other than the American Museum were influenced by developments occurring in New York. Coggeshall, whose technical innovations were largely responsible for the first *Diplodocus* mounting, and Thomas Horne, one of the principal preparators at the National Museum, were originally employed in the DVP preparation laboratory. Charles Schuchert, the director of Yale's Peabody Museum, was inspired by exhibits at the American Museum to promote mountings at the Peabody. Richard Swann Lull, the vertebrate paleontologist responsible for developing many of the dinosaur displays at Yale, had obtained his Ph.D. degree with Osborn and had worked closely with the DVP staff in the years 1899–1903. Knight also began his work at the American Museum, and only in later years did he offer his services to other institutions.[26]

Those early efforts fit in with existing interests and emphases at the American Museum. Osborn embraced the objectives of Allen and Chapman for preserving nature through the development of displays and paintings of birds, mammals, and Indians. He first promoted similar initiatives in 1893–94 when he instructed DVP staff members to develop mountings of extinct mammals in action. The mounts and restorations of dinosaurs were a further development along that line. Those efforts were designed to provide the public with a sense of the anatomy, physiology, habits, and environments of those extinct reptiles. But the American Museum was unique in developing mounts that portrayed dinosaurs in combat. In part that was true because the museum possessed some singular specimens: *Apatosaurus* vertebrae that showed tooth marks left by an *Allosaurus*.[27] More importantly, such displays meshed with Osborn's interest in glorifying the struggle for existence.

Displaying Evolution

Osborn devoted attention to developing displays that embodied his interpretation of evolution. Again, the evolution of horses provided one of the most significant examples. Having interpreted the history of the horse family in orthogenetic terms, Osborn drew upon the museum's resources and its commitment to public education to impress his views on the public in a manner impossible for most other scientists. Earlier exhibits had shown one or possibly two specimens together in rather artificial poses, but Osborn directed his staff to design displays that demonstrated the evolution of the horse throughout the Cenozoic era. By 1908 the Hall of the Age of Mammals included an exhibit of seven mounted specimens representing the major stages in that sequence. In addition to the exhibit, Osborn arranged for the display of Knight's paintings of extinct horses, charts documenting the evolution of the feet, teeth, and skull, and an informative guide leaflet on the subject (figure 8). All those materials, especially the mounted specimens and the charts, presented a clear and forthright message: the evolution from the small *Eohippus* of the Eocene to the modern *Equus* of today had occurred in a gradual, linear manner demonstrating the regularity of the laws of nature. It was a message that had a long-lasting influence. By the 1920s scientists, including Matthew and Gregory, were refuting orthogenetic interpretations. Nevertheless, the museum's display and message remained intact and influenced public perceptions about evolution at least into the 1950s.[28]

Osborn's study of titanotheres provided another opportunity to present the evidence of nature's laws to the public. According to Osborn, the titanotheres, like the horses, demonstrated that evolution was a cumulative series of changes that resulted in a multiplicity of linear, parallel trends. The first titanotheres, *Eotitanops*, had been small doglike animals in the Eocene epoch. Eventually some had evolved into massive creatures like the late Miocene *Brontops robustus* that was over ten feet high at the shoulder and weighed several tons. In addition to the increase in body size, specific features had evolved in a similar fashion. The teeth had evolved progressively, though at differing rates in differing lines of descent. More fascinating to Osborn was the evolution of the animal's horns. Beginning as small nodules, they achieved a size that was larger and a shape that was more bizarre than the horns of the rhinoceros or any other living mammal. Those features gave the creatures a strange, ferocious appearance even though titanotheres were herbivores.[29]

For Osborn, those structures were not the product of adaptation and the natural selection of random variations. He explained the evolution of the "biocharacters" of the titanotheres as "rectigradations [which] appear to indicate a germinal predisposition or predetermination to vary in the same direction, those predispositions being more apparent in the more closely related phyla and less apparent in remotely related phyla." His

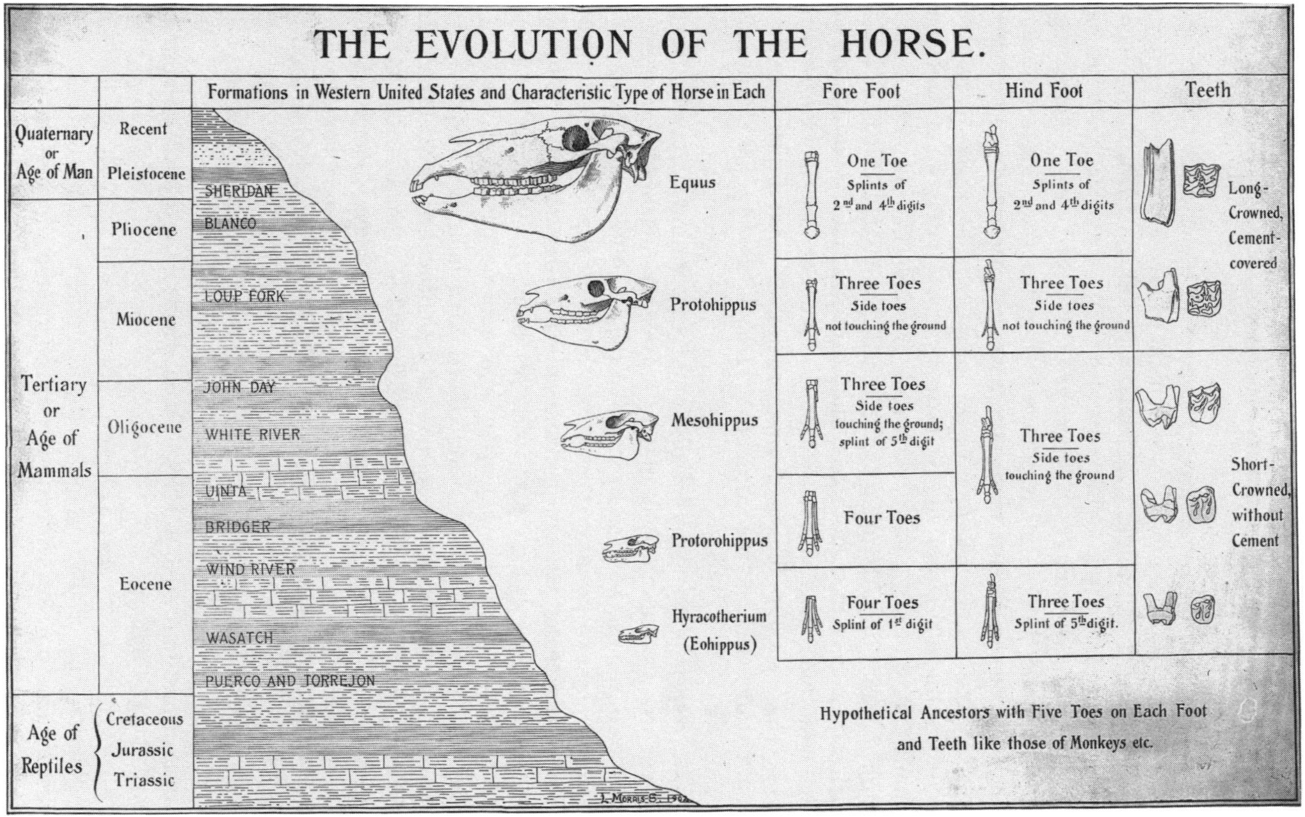

THE EVOLUTION OF THE HORSE.

Age	Formations in Western United States and Characteristic Type of Horse in Each	Fore Foot	Hind Foot	Teeth
Quaternary or Age of Man — Recent, Pleistocene	SHERIDAN, BLANCO — Equus	One Toe. Splints of 2nd and 4th digits	One Toe. Splints of 2nd and 4th digits	Long-Crowned, Cement-covered
Pliocene				
Miocene	LOUP FORK — Protohippus	Three Toes. Side toes not touching the ground	Three Toes. Side toes not touching the ground	
Tertiary or Age of Mammals — Miocene / Oligocene	JOHN DAY, WHITE RIVER — Mesohippus	Three Toes. Side toes touching the ground; splint of 5th digit	Three Toes. Side toes touching the ground	Short-Crowned, without Cement
Eocene	UINTA, BRIDGER — Protorohippus	Four Toes	Three Toes. Splint of 5th digit	
Eocene	WIND RIVER, WASATCH — Hyracotherium (Eohippus)	Four Toes. Splint of 1st digit		
	PUERCO AND TORREJON			
Age of Reptiles — Cretaceous, Jurassic, Triassic	Hypothetical Ancestors with Five Toes on Each Foot and Teeth like those of Monkeys etc.			

J. MORSE 95

FIGURE 8. Chart demonstrating the evolution of the horse (neg. no. 35522)

belief in the importance of a hereditary predisposition that yielded an irreversible pattern of evolutionary change was most fully defined in the titanothere monograph.[30]

That interpretation was also represented in the displays Osborn instructed the DVP staff to produce. Knight painted a number of pictures of titanotheres, but projects undertaken by other staff members were more imposing. In 1900 Osborn directed Gregory, his principal assistant on the titanothere project, to supervise DVP artist Erwin S. Christman in developing displays of titanotheres. Together they constructed and placed on display life-size plaster models of *Eotitanops* and a more recent gigantic species, *Brontotherium platyceras*. The *Brontotherium* alone possessed formidable power and majesty, while its contrast with the other animals illustrated the extent to which evolution had occurred in that family (figure 9). Osborn's researches had demonstrated that the most striking evidence of titanothere evolution was the increase in the size of the skull and horns. Therefore, he directed Gregory and Christman to develop a series of life-size titanothere skulls.[31] That display became a unique landmark in the museum's Hall of the Age of Mammals (figure 10).

The display of titanothere skulls combined scientific and artistic work to put across a multiplicity of messages. Gregory's detailed knowledge of the tooth, mouth, and jaw structure of the titanotheres enabled Christman and him to produce restorations that distinguished those animals from rhinoceroses and other related animals. Gregory's understanding of functional morphology, particularly his knowledge of titanothere musculature as inferred from comparison with modern tapirs and rhinoceroses, also influenced the display.[32] Furthermore, the exhibit presented Osborn's conception of evolution. The display of four titanothere skulls from four different epochs, arranged chronologically and in evolutionary sequence, demonstrated the progressive march of evolution. There, modeled in clay, was Osborn's view that evolution resulted in ever larger, more complex, and more baroque skull and horn structure.[33] The display also embodied another and perhaps more important message. Both the display and accompanying information indicated that the evolution of those large, bizarre creatures had ended abruptly in the Miocene epoch; titanotheres, unlike horses, had become extinct. Extinction was, for Osborn, a natural law that had scientific as well as social meaning.

In scientific terms alone, Osborn was fascinated with the question of extinction, and his monograph on the titanotheres included an extended discussion of the issue. Although he considered the impact of the physical environment and competition with other organisms, Osborn empha-

FIGURE 9. Reconstructed models of titanotheres *Brontotherium platyceras*, *Brontops borealis*, and *Eotitanops gregorii* (neg. no. 313463)

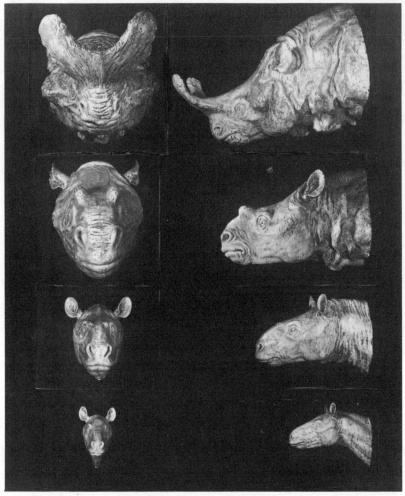

FIGURE 10. Reconstructed titanothere skulls (neg. no. 219321)

sized that the evolutionary process itself was responsible for extinction. Because he believed that evolution was an irreversible process that was not dictated by the need to adapt to environmental circumstances, a character could become overdeveloped and evolve to the point where it was harmful to an organism's survival. "An animal," he claimed, "may specialize to an extraordinary degree in a single mode of subsistence, and the food on which it subsists may be diminished or destroyed; or a race of animals may expend its energy largely in the development of certain single organs, such as horns or tusks, which become dominant and interfere with the proper development of other organs."[34]

The evolution of horns was probably not responsible for the extinction of the titanotheres. Osborn identified the evolution of specialized grinding teeth that were incapable of meeting changing environmental conditions as the most likely factor in the demise of the animals. Specialization could thus result in extinction. Osborn, like Cope and Scott, believed in a "law of the unspecialized," which favored those organisms that did not reach an evolutionary cul de sac. He applied that interpretation of evolution and extinction to the titanotheres as well as several other families of mammals.[35]

The laws of evolution and extinction were more than scientifically significant; they also had social meaning for Osborn. Just as specialization had killed the titanotheres, so too, according to Osborn, did that law have relevance for modern man and society. The forces of modernization, the increasing emphasis on specialized ways of working, thinking, and living were bureaucratizing and compartmentalizing human existence. Modernization posed a threat to knowledge and the continuation of the human species. The "law of the unspecialized" applied to mankind as well as to animals: those who participated in exploration and learned to appreciate nature's laws and understand their meaning for society would survive. The titanothere display, much like the displays of dinosaurs, instilled visitors with fear and fascination. The exhibit of those bizarre, hoofed mammals also embodied Osborn's commitment to engage the spectator in a manner that enabled him or her to understand nature and nature's laws. Through these displays humans could learn from the example of the titanotheres and prevent extreme specialization and possible extinction.

Osborn and the Hall of the Age of Man

In addition to the displays of horses, titanotheres, and dinosaurs, Osborn developed a major exhibit in line with his interests in paleoanthropology. The Hall of the Age of Man, like Osborn's other projects, was a grandiose undertaking that reflected his enthusiasms and interpretations. Begun in 1915, it was designed to complement the halls of fossil mammals and reptiles and to depict man's relationship to nature. Osborn wanted to portray ancient man in association with the ecological features of the Pleistocene period. With thousands of dollars of support from J. P. Morgan, Jr., Osborn commissioned Knight to produce paintings of the four seasons during the glacial epoch. Knight's large watercolor restorations of a glacial winter in France, spring on the Somme River in France, summer in Missouri, and autumn in New Jersey presented the environment and major faunal groups, mammoths, mastodons, reindeer, and bison, that coexisted with human races in the last period of the Ice Age. Knight also painted two other representative scenes, one portraying South American mammals of the Pleistocene, the other animals from the tarpits of Rancho La Brea, California. To accompany the murals, Matthew and the DVP staff developed displays of mounted specimens of South American ground sloths and the remains of animals from a deposit at Rancho La Brea.[36]

By far the most striking and controversial features of the hall were the exhibits pertaining to paleoanthropology. The hall was a large-scale reproduction of Osborn's interpretation of human culture and evolution as embodied in *Men of the Old Stone Age*. It included cases representing the typical features of the different races or, according to his interpretation, species of mankind. In addition to artifacts, the cases contained casts of the most important fossil hominids. There were also restorations of Paleolithic races made by J. Howard McGregor, a Columbia University professor and close associate of Osborn and Gregory. McGregor was a zoologist who possessed artistic skill, and he assisted Osborn by reconstructing the skulls and mandibles of the different races, or species, of man. In 1915 and again in 1921 Osborn arranged for McGregor to examine the original fossil hominid specimens at European institutions, and on the basis of his studies McGregor produced his own reconstructions.[37]

More prominent than the skull and teeth restorations were McGregor's full-scale sculptured busts of each race. Relying on his own research and Gregory's knowledge of the relationship between skeletal and muscular structure in primates and other vertebrates, McGregor produced busts that showed the typical pose and position of the head as well as the principal morphological characteristics of each race. In some instances McGregor added features for the benefit of the public. Speaking of the Neanderthal specimen, he noted that "as a concession to popular taste, the hair was modeled on a plaster cast of the bold plane, and a slight suggestion of the beard added." Those changes, he claimed, were "not sufficient to disguise the form of the retreating chin, an important racial feature." McGregor was creating "racial portraits" of the principal hominid groups that, more than the skeletal fragments themselves, would capture public attention.[38]

The display cases and McGregor's models also presented Osborn's interpretation of human evolution. One large case, designed to define man's relationship to the primates, had a bust of *Pithecanthropus* between the hominids and simians, a reflection of Osborn's belief that that specimen possibly did not belong to the genus *Homo*. The other specimens pointed out that the anthropoids had evolved separately from any species or race of the Hominidae. It was only in the mid-1920s that Osborn articulated his views on the relationship between men and other primates, but he made it clear in displays in the Hall of the Age of Man that anthropoid evolution had nothing to do with human evolution. The lines linking different specimens, although drawn by Gregory, reflected Osborn's interpretation that descent from a common hypothetical ancestor had yielded separate lineages for *Pithecanthropus,* Piltdown, Neanderthal, Cro-Magnon, and modern man. That point was reinforced by a series of separate flat cases, each of which included the artifacts, fossil fragments, and McGregor's reconstructions and busts of a particular group (figures 11, 12).[39]

In line with Osborn's interpretation, the various races were represented as distinctly human, and as showing no affinity to the apes: "In these models, and in all the restorations of men by Charles R. Knight under my direction, the controlling principle has been to make the restoration as *human* as the anatomical evidence will admit. . . . No doubt, our ancestors of the early Stone Age were brutal in many respects, but the representations which have been made chiefly by French and German artists of men with strong gorilla or chimpanzee characteristics are, I believe, unwarranted by the anatomical remains and are contrary to the conception which we must form of beings in the scale of rapidly ascending intelligence."[40] On the basis of Osborn's views, McGregor reconstructed Neanderthal as a heavy-browed, dull-witted creature that stood in marked contrast to the restoration of Cro-Magnon as an intelligent, high-browed being.

Equally imposing were Knight's murals of early man, also supervised by Osborn. In addition to the paintings of Pleistocene mammals, Osborn commissioned Knight to paint three murals that represented three distinct stages of human culture and evolution. Knight was not fully convinced of the accuracy of such representations. But Osborn was, and he spared no effort or expense to have Knight produce paintings that he believed would indelibly imprint his interpretation of human history on the minds of museum goers.

The first mural, which was completed in 1915 and served as the frontispiece to *Men of the Old Stone Age,* was entitled "The Neanderthal Flint Workers." Knight's painting portrays the members of a Neanderthal family in what Osborn defined as a typical setting. In addition to a mother and child, the painting shows three generations of males engaged in activities

FIGURE 11. Case with reconstructed bust, skeletal fragments, and descriptive information on Neanderthal race (neg. no. 310881)

FIGURE 12. Case with reconstructed bust, skeletal fragments, and descriptive information on Cro–Magnon race (neg. no. 310882)

associated with their crude flint-making industry: a grandfather working the flint against stones, a father equipped with a flint-tipped spear, and a son carrying up flint from the lowlands. The family is posed in front of a cave similar to some of the celebrated Paleolithic sites found in southern France. In line with Osborn's demands, there is no evidence of any building structures or other features that could suggest an advanced stage of cultural evolution. In the painting, the family's flint-making activities have been interrupted by the sighting of woolly rhinoceroses, and the father is poised, with spear raised, ready for action. Following Osborn's instructions, Knight presented the Neanderthal family "in a pose natural to wild men." The mural emphasized what became the classical view of the Neanderthal: a slouching, slow-moving unintelligent race with brutish physical features (figure 13).[41]

Quite different was a second mural portraying the Cro-Magnon race in all its glory. In the center of the painting a Cro-Magnon man is drawing the figure of a mammoth on a cave wall. The artist, shown naked from the waist up, is a tall erect figure whose anatomy presents a marked contrast to the Neanderthal figures. Here the emphasis is not on muscular individuals with low foreheads and protruding chins. Instead, the mural portrays alert, graceful figures with distinctly modern physical features. The mural indicates that the Cro-Magnon, like the Neanderthals, were dependent on their physical and biotic environment: the woolly mammoth on the cave wall was their source of sustenance as well as artistic inspiration; the artist's palette is the shoulder blade of a reindeer; and the principal artist wears a necklace made of animal teeth. Yet Knight's painting also reflects the mental and cultural superiority that Osborn ascribed to the Cro-Magnon. The artists are engaged in the creative activity of painting, and two other figures hold lamps in hollowed-out stones, products of Cro-Magnon handiwork. A third figure is engaged in making paints by mixing earth with tallow. The artist's earring suggests the concern with religion that characterized the Cro-Magnon (figure 14).[42]

The third mural, entitled "Neolithic Stag Hunters," was an encomium to nature that also represented Osborn's views on human evolution. The mural depicts a northern European tribe of half-clad men shown at the end of a hunt. Having vanquished a deer, they surround their prey in a clear portrayal of power and strength. The muscular anatomy of the chieftain and the wild look of the Nordic youth holding a wolf radiate the robustness and beauty of natural man in combat with the elements. As Osborn noted: "This race was courageous, warlike, hearty. . . . [Living] in a rigorous northern climate, it was chiefly concerned with the struggle for existence, in which the qualities of endurance, tribal loyalty, and the

FIGURE 13. Mural of Neanderthal Flint Workers by Charles R. Knight (neg. no. 39441A)

FIGURE 14. Mural of Cro-Magnon Artists by Charles R. Knight (neg. no. 322602)

rudiments of family life were being cultivated." In one respect, the Neolithic stag hunters embodied all that Osborn valued: the strength, power, and noble features of humans in direct confrontation with nature. The Stag Hunters possessed modern physical attributes and represented mankind in the first phases of civilization. Yet despite those qualities the Neolithic people were "of a lower intelligence and less artistic skill than the Cro-Magnons."[43] Although they possessed physical strength, the Stag Hunters did not engage in artistic or intellectual activities. Their weapons, bowls, and ornamental pieces do not equal the achievements of the Cro-Magnon.

The Neolithic Stag Hunters do not represent decline, but in comparison to their predecessors they at least suggest it. Osborn employed the representations of both the Cro-Magnon and the Neolithic people to serve as a message for modern man. Through Knight's paintings he was praising the qualities associated with life in direct contact with the environment and pointing to the possibility of mankind's decline from a high point achieved by the Cro-Magnon at the end of the Paleolithic period (figure 15).

The Hall of the Age of Man was a powerful statement, a personal interpretation that Osborn sought to establish as public belief. The fossil specimens, reconstructions, and murals, which he pushed to have completed in time for the International Eugenics Congress held at the museum in 1921, were a striking manifestation of his social and political concerns. *Men of the Old Stone Age* and the Hall of the Age of Man represented his appeal to the strength and power of earlier races that lived in the wild, followed the hunt, and maintained a nomadic existence. Those were the characteristics of the Cro-Magnon and the Nordic race of Neolithic times. They were the qualities, values, and even the lifestyle that, as Osborn argued in *Creative Education*, modern man should emulate.[44] For Osborn, what was natural was also pure. The earliest races had not mixed with others; the unnatural mixing of races was a degenerative feature brought on by increasing divorce from life in the wild. The Hall of the Age of Man was more than an exhibit of paleoanthropological materials. It reflected Osborn's belief that only by preserving nature and racial purity, particularly the purity of the English, Scots, and Scandinavians most closely related to the Nordic tribes of Neolithic times, could mankind halt the rapidly accelerating decline toward racial suicide and extinction.

Conclusion

Osborn's interpretation of human evolution aroused controversy among scientists. A number of anthropologists, principally Robert Lowie, Clark Wissler, and Margaret Mead, were outraged by his views on race and evolution. They also resented Osborn's power, which enabled him to transform personal prejudices into museum policy. Franz Boas, who developed a very different understanding of culture and evolution, staunchly opposed Osborn's ideas on race and immigration restriction. To many biologists Osborn's views of evolution and inheritance were speculative and untenable; they also rejected his efforts to apply those interpretations to human biology and contemporary political affairs. T. H. Morgan and Herbert Spencer Jennings, for example, refused to participate in the 1921 International Eugenics Congress because of its political overtones.[45]

Osborn's views also provoked criticism at the museum. One of the trustees, Felix Warburg, disliked the racial overtones of the Hall of the Age of Man. None of the scientists who worked on the hall fully accepted Osborn's views on human evolution or contemporary issues of race relations and immigration. Matthew, Gregory, and McGregor believed in taxonomic hierarchies and shared the common racial prejudices of the day. Matthew maintained that Europeans and Americans were superior to nonwestern peoples, and in examining races he employed some of the typological categories that Osborn did. Gregory, whose work on paleoanthropology is examined in Chapter 9, held many of the same views.

However, Matthew, Gregory, and McGregor did not accept Osborn's interpretation of human evolution. Matthew and Gregory believed that humans had evolved from primates, specifically an arboreal ancestor. They also did not share Osborn's interest in applying their ideas on human evolution to contemporary social and political problems. Matthew, Gregory, and McGregor belonged to the Galton Society, but even Gregory, the long-time secretary of the organization, did not play an active role in promoting immigration restriction or other policies based on eugenic principles. Their participation in the activities of that organization indicated their belief that the study of race was a legitimate topic of scientific investigation. It also reflected the power structure at the museum. Matthew, Gregory, and McGregor had all been Osborn's students; they were also his assistants. That meant they worked for him and on the projects that he defined as important. Throughout the 1910s and early 1920s they all participated actively in the construction of the Hall of the

FIGURE 15. Mural of the Neolithic Stag Hunters by Charles R. Knight (neg. no. 37952)

Age of Man, but without embracing Osborn's interpretations or his political program.[46]

Additional contradications and ironies are inherent in the edifice that
Osborn constructed. He went to great efforts to publicize the museum's
work, particularly its explorations and exhibit halls. By the 1920s the
museum was attracting over 100,000 visitors annually,[47] but it is likely
that the vast majority neither understood nor accepted the moral messages that Osborn was trying to convey. Many museum goers have
claimed that the displays of fossil horses provided them with an understanding of evolution that they equated with progress. Even in such
cases, however, the public response could be quite different from what
Osborn intended. Two youngsters inspired by the horse display, H. J.
Muller and Stephen Jay Gould, developed evolutionary interpretations
and political philosophies diametrically opposed to Osborn's.[48]

Most of the other exhibits carried messages that were even less explicit.
The vast majority of visitors had no idea of Osborn's views on race,
society, or the preservation of nature and thus no sense of the message
being conveyed in the murals in the Hall of the Age of Man. For most,
the museum served as a source of entertainment where people could also
acquire some empirical knowledge. In the later 1930s the museum developed new and different means for conveying the scientists' views to
the public. G. K. Noble, an ethologist and curator of the Hall of Animal
Behavior, created displays using mechanical contrivances to put across
specific messages. An exhibit in that hall depicting a typical barnyard
scene with hens and rooster was transformed when the visitor moved
closer and tripped an electric eye. The display then showed the setting
from a hen's point of view, and a recording described the social order in
the barnyard.[49] The lessons in the DVP and the Hall of the Age of Man
were not as technologically sophisticated or clearly defined. Osborn and
some of the principal scientists who knew his interpretations realized that
the displays reflected Osborn's ideas on nature, class, and race. But for
those who visited the museum it was a form of theater, a pleasure palace
filled with dinosaurs, titanotheres, and other entertaining features.

Irony is also inherent in the message that Osborn tried to convey. In
the halls of the museum and in his own work, Osborn expressed anxiety
over specialization in science and society. Yet he created a highly specialized institution. Under his direction the entire museum was oriented
toward a program of preservation. The museum added several science
departments, in many instances departments that were as specialized as
programs in the universities. The DVP itself was one of the few specialized programs in vertebrate paleontology in the country. In addition

to working in the public sphere, Osborn and his assistants pursued technical research on the classification, evolution, and distribution of extinct vertebrates.

At the same time that he was calling attention to the problems of specialization associated with a modern society, Osborn was building a specialized scientific department. Osborn did not reconcile, probably did not even recognize, such contradictions. Nor did such contradictions undermine his program. On the contrary, Osborn promoted massive public education efforts to put across his interpretations and was influential in developing a program of scientific research in vertebrate paleontology that he and his associates pursued. That was another dimension of his agenda for antiquity.

8

Organisms in Space and Time: William Diller Matthew and Vertebrate Paleontology at the American Museum

The contradictory character of Osborn's influence is evident in his impact on scientific work in vertebrate paleontology. In one respect his position, interests, and interpretations had a retarding effect on the subject even in his lifetime. Few shared his ideas on classification, inheritance, and the causes of evolution. By the 1920s many scientists were distancing themselves from his preoccupations with eugenics and immigration restriction. Because of his power and pretensions, many, including vertebrate paleontologists of a younger generation, had little respect for Osborn personally or professionally. That vertebrate paleontology did not attract the same interest and attention as experimental research in genetics, cytology, and biochemistry was not, of course, Osborn's responsibility. But his antagonistic relationship to T. H. Morgan and Morgan's program in genetics at Columbia reinforced the theoretical, methodological, and institutional separation of vertebrate paleontology from much of the rest of early twentieth-century biology.

In other ways, however, Osborn did influence vertebrate paleontology at the American Museum and, through the museum, the field more generally. By the early twentieth century the museum was the country's leading center for the study of vertebrate paleontology. Osborn played a central role in creating an institutional framework that helped develop a major public education center and encouraged the pursuit of scientific research in the laboratory and the field. Through his administrative and promotional efforts he helped create a program that sponsored numerous expeditions, possessed the nation's premier collection of fossil vertebrate

182

specimens, and included a large and diversified staff of scientists, collectors, and preparators who assembled an impressive array of mountings and murals.

Osborn also established an intellectual context for pursuing research problems in vertebrate paleontology. He had an interest in a wide range of biological, geological, and anthropological questions, and although his interpretations reinforced social and political values, Osborn was genuinely interested in the scientific study of those subjects. He published dozens of descriptive, systematic papers on fossil vertebrates. His ambition to examine what he defined as the most important and interesting issues led him to develop a theory of evolution in the mid 1890s and then to pursue research on a number of related topics. In addition to studies of variation and inheritance, questions of geographical distribution, biostratigraphy, and correlation captured his attention.

The analysis of evolutionary questions had been central to vertebrate paleontology throughout the nineteenth century. Georges Cuvier, Richard Owen, and others had considered problems of evolution and functional morphology.[1] Cope had addressed a broad spectrum of subjects including variation, development, and inheritance. Paleontologists in the early twentieth century also took up those issues. Although scholars often define museum scientists as systematists preoccupied with questions of synonymy, description, and classification, the vertebrate paleontologists E. C. Case and John C. Merriam wrote on evolution and development. Questions of geographical distribution, functional morphology, and biostratigraphy were also relevant to vertebrate paleontology.[2]

But scientists at the DVP examined those questions more fully than their contemporaries, and in no small part because of Osborn. Osborn's status and influence enabled him to make topics that he found "intensely interesting" the subject of departmental investigations. Several of his assistants, notably William Diller Matthew and William King Gregory, had learned vertebrate paleontology from Osborn at Columbia. At the museum, as at Princeton, Osborn put students to work on projects relevant to his interests. When Matthew became his principal assistant in the late 1890s, Osborn was interested in questions of biostratigraphy and geographical distribution. He also recognized the importance of functional, evolutionary, and paleoanthropological questions. Osborn did not examine those questions in detail, but he delegated his assistants to pursue those topics. He also encouraged them to address the theoretical questions pertaining to those subjects. Many of Osborn's assistants, including Matthew, came to dislike him personally. Matthew and Gregory rejected Osborn's interpretations and eventually developed their own views on problems in evolutionary biology. But given Osborn's interests, power, and manner of operating, he had an important influence on the research problems that his assistants pursued.

Biostratigraphy and Correlation

Osborn relied heavily on Matthew because he demonstrated an ability for doing sound work in geology and systematics. Prior to his work with Osborn, Matthew's primary interest was in geology and invertebrate paleontology. The son of George Frederic Matthew, a Canadian geologist well known for his studies of the Paleozoic invertebrates around St. John, New Brunswick, Matthew had participated in his father's research and decided to pursue a career in geology. Enrolling in the School of Mines at Columbia College, he completed the undergraduate program and earned a Ph.D. degree in geology in 1895. It was only in his last year of graduate school that Matthew took Osborn's courses in mammalian morphology and vertebrate evolution. He joined the DVP and embarked on a career in vertebrate paleontology with a strong background in geology.[3]

Matthew's earliest work illustrated the influence that his knowledge of geology and stratigraphy would have on vertebrate paleontology. One of his first assignments from Osborn was to catalogue the department's collection of specimens, including the recent purchase of the Cope collection of fossil mammals. The task entailed recataloging and reclassifying many specimens. Matthew's study, accompanied by stratigraphic information provided by Cope and Wortman, resulted in a notable contribution to vertebrate paleontology: that Cope's Puerco Formation was composed of two units, the Puerco and the Torrejon, which did not share any species in common.[4] That study was based on laboratory analyses of specimens, but when Matthew began fieldwork in the western states in 1897, he filled his field notebooks with detailed stratigraphic and geologic information on the localities he examined.

Such research led Matthew to revise the taxonomy of Tertiary vertebrates. His study of sediments and mammal specimens also led him to oppose the standard interpretation that Tertiary deposits were the remnants of freshwater lakes. He maintained that the deposits of the White River Miocene were lacustrine formations produced by wind-blown loess on broad flood plains. Matthew helped to overturn an interpretation that had dominated American geology and vertebrate paleontology for over two decades.[5]

Matthew's abilities were important to Osborn when the latter became preoccupied with questions of biostratigraphy and correlation in the late

1890s. Since the mid-nineteenth century scientists had defined the age of geological strata on the basis of their fossil contents. Paleontology was therefore important in working out both the absolute and relative ages of the earth. Determination of the age of and stratigraphic relationship among organisms was also significant for understanding evolution. Any attempt to define the evolution of a species or to work out a phylogeny required an understanding of the law of superposition, the principle that fossils in higher strata were more recent than those in lower strata; an understanding of faunal succession; and a good knowledge of the relative age of fossils. To understand the evolution of organisms also required establishing the time equivalence, what is called correlation, among stratigraphic units in different parts of the world. Traditionally, scientists relied on invertebrate fossils for defining stratigraphy and correlation, but Osborn was a strong advocate of the use of fossil vertebrates.[6]

Osborn's interest in those problems was spurred by his belief that other vertebrate paleontologists were far ahead of the DVP in their work on stratigraphy and correlation. The French paleontologist Charles Depéret was making notable contributions to stratigraphy; so too were William Berryman Scott and John Bell Hatcher at Princeton. In contrast to Leidy, Cope, and Marsh, Scott paid close attention to the stratigraphic and lithologic conditions of the deposits he worked. Hatcher's descriptions of the geology and stratigraphy of fossil vertebrate horizons surpassed the work of other contemporary American vertebrate paleontologists.[7] The uproar over Florentino Ameghino's claim that South American fauna and horizons antedated those in other parts of the world offered Scott and Hatcher an additional opportunity to make their mark in biostratigraphy. Osborn was eager to have his program catch up.

Questions about biostratigraphy and correlation had a bearing on Osborn's work in evolution. After developing a theory of evolution in the mid 1890s, Osborn had some difficulty applying it to the fossil record. In an 1897 study Osborn argued that the understanding of the evolution of rhinoceroses was mired in confusion because of the lack of a definite time scale for fossils from different parts of the world. In order to make sense of the phylogeny of rhinoceroses, indeed to make sense of the evolution and geographical distribution of any fauna, "a more exact correlation of European and American horizons appeared to be an essential."[8]

Osborn embraced correlation as a priority and in the next few years published several papers on the subject. Characteristically, he became an advocate, publicist, and organizer who enlisted the help of others in promoting an international vanguard for reform. Submitting trial charts to vertebrate paleontologists in Europe and America, he solicited information and suggestions for correlating Tertiary fauna and horizons world-wide.[9] He also began to rely on Matthew and other assistants to obtain stratigraphic information for the study of North American fauna and horizons.

In 1900, when Osborn became vertebrate paleontologist of the Geological Survey, he expressed an interest in preparing accurate geological sections for his monograph on the titanotheres. Osborn hired Hatcher, Nelson H. Darton, and Frederick B. Loomis, investigators associated with institutions other than the American Museum, to undertake field-work for that study. In 1903 Hatcher and T. W. Stanton, an invertebrate paleontologist who worked for the Geological Survey, studied the titanotherium beds. Darton, who was an expert on the geology and underground water resources of the Great Plains, did reconnaissance work. He used sectioning and other techniques that provided important information on the contents and thickness of Oligocene and Miocene formations. In addition, his geological maps were invaluable since no one in the DVP was capable of doing that work.[10]

Equally important was the work done by Matthew and Granger. In 1902 Osborn assigned those men to do a stratigraphic and paleontological study of the Bridger Basin in connection with the titanothere monograph. They were instructed to make precise stratigraphic records of all specimens they obtained. Matthew and Granger divided the Bridger Basin Formation into five units, including subdivisions within those units. Through the use of columnar sections they provided data on the location, thickness, and geological features of each unit. Thus, they were able to define the stratigraphic level and distribution of hundreds of vertebrate species and genera.[11] On the basis of the research of Darton and Matthew and Granger, Osborn in 1909 published "Cenozoic Mammal Horizons of Western North America." That work provided detailed faunal information and correlations for every major Cenozoic horizon and was a distinct improvement over the earlier studies of Cope and Marsh.[12]

The work by Matthew and Granger also brought recognition for Matthew. For Osborn's study, Matthew had compiled a list of Tertiary mammals that defined the range of virtually all genera and species of fossil mammals through every major stratigraphic unit. The work that Matthew did in connection with Osborn's monograph was the basis for one of Matthew's most significant studies, "The Carnivora and Insectivora of the Bridger Basin." A model stratigraphic analysis of an individual formation, that work surpassed almost anything previously done in American vertebrate paleontology. As Matthew's colleague William King

Gregory pointed out many years later, the monograph on the Bridger Basin included major phylogenetic revisions of several families and orders of fossil mammals.[13]

Matthew also examined questions about the correlation of fauna and horizons. His work contributed to the correlations in Osborn's 1909 paper and later in Osborn's titanothere monograph. Those studies resulted in some controversy. In the mid-1910s, when Matthew, Granger, and Gregory had completed much of the geologic and stratigraphic work on the titanothere monograph, Osborn submitted portions to T. W. Stanton, chief of the Section of Paleontology and Stratigraphy of the Geological Survey. In their research Matthew and Granger had defined stratigraphic units on the basis of faunal contents or life zones rather than following the Geological Survey tradition of employing geographic terms that referred to formations or mappable units. The different practices created difficulties between Osborn and his associates and the Geological Survey, though the latter eventually allowed Osborn to publish his monograph using the life zone designations.[14]

Less easily resolved was another controversy, one in which Matthew played an important role: the debate over the Cretaceous-Tertiary boundary. The dividing line between the Cretaceous and Tertiary periods was an important topic to geologists and paleontologists. The periods help to define the demarcation between two of the major geological eras: the Mesozoic, or so-called age of reptiles, and the Cenozoic, or so-called age of mammals. Consequently, the designation of the boundary had geological and evolutionary implications. The determination of that boundary was the subject of some controversy.

Traditionally, vertebrate paleontologists had divided the Cretaceous and Tertiary periods on the basis of the presence or absence of certain organisms: dinosaurs had lived in the Cretaceous, but not in the Tertiary; placental mammals appeared only in the Tertiary. Although that interpretation had been challenged by the paleobotanist Leo Lesquereux in the 1870s, most vertebrate paleontologists continued to rely on that designation and on the primary importance of fossil vertebrates for distinguishing between the two periods. Matthew not only upheld that distinction but refined it by drawing the boundary between the Lance, a Cretaceous formation, and the Puerco, a Tertiary formation.[15]

In the 1910s the standard interpretation was challenged by some geologists and paleontologists, most notably F. H. Knowlton. A paleobotanist employed by the Geological Survey, Knowlton maintained that the fossil plant record did not demonstrate a break between the Upper Cretaceous and the Paleocene. Instead, the break, a major unconformity, occurred much earlier, as indicated by evidence from the Belly River Formation. On the basis of that determination, Knowlton maintained that the Fort Union Formation and the Lance Formation, which included horizons that contained dinosaurs, belonged to the Tertiary period.[16]

Matthew rejected Knowlton's interpretation on several grounds. In terms of geological phenomena, he claimed there was no evidence of a major diastrophic break between the Cretaceous and Tertiary. There were instead local environmental changes and faunal migrations. He used the occasion of the dispute with Knowlton to argue for the importance of using fossil vertebrates to define strata and to determine relative age. Because of their complex internal skeletal structure, fossil vertebrates indicated adaptive responses to environmental effects and provided "a more precise, exact measure of time" than did invertebrate fossils or fossil plants.[17]

In 1914 Matthew, together with Osborn, Barnum Brown, and W. J. Sinclair, a Princeton vertebrate paleontologist who worked on many American Museum expeditions, debated Knowlton on the Cretaceous-Tertiary boundary issue at a session of the Geological Society of America. Osborn did little more than coordinate and introduce the session; the real task of combating Knowlton was undertaken by Matthew and the others. The issue was not resolved at that session, and in later years paleontologists and geologists redefined the problem by offering a new interpretation of the Cretaceous-Tertiary boundary. But the meeting did provide a public forum for the vertebrate paleontologists, led by Matthew, to present a united front for the kind of research they did, the data they employed, and the interpretation they espoused.[18]

Matthew played a central role in promoting Osborn's interest in reforming correlation on an international scale. Following his submission of trial charts to European and American paleontologists, Osborn obtained financial support for a project on correlation. In 1908 the Bache Fund of the National Academy of Sciences provided him with a grant to coordinate international research on biostratigraphy and correlation. With Osborn directing the project, Matthew went to work soliciting data from vertebrate paleontologists from throughout the world. He asked for information on geological and geographical conditions and on the abundance, age, range, and distribution of species and genera.[19] Osborn incorporated much of those data into *The Age of Mammals*, the first work by an American vertebrate paleontologist to integrate information on the evolution, migration, and distribution of fossil vertebrates from Europe, Asia, and North America. Matthew also translated and published studies by Louis Dollo, a Belgian paleontologist, and Santiago Roth, a South

American paleontologist. Through his study of Roth's work, Matthew contributed to a debate over the biostratigraphy and correlation of South American fossils and horizons.[20]

European and North American paleontologists had long defined South American fauna as the descendants of northern fauna. However, in the late nineteenth century the Argentine scientists Florentino and Carlos Ameghino and Santiago Roth interpreted the succession, evolution, and distribution of fossil vertebrates in very different terms. Ever since Darwin's discovery of an odd toxodont in 1833, scientists had recognized the peculiarity of South American fossil mammals. Subsequent discoveries of edentates and bizarre slothlike creatures accentuated the differences between the mammals of South America and elsewhere. Using those data, Florentino Ameghino claimed that South America, specifically Patagonia, was the center of vertebrate evolution. In addition, Ameghino maintained that the mammalian horizons and fauna of that region antedated those in other parts of the world. Based on his argument that most mammals, including man, had originated in Argentina, Ameghino "considered nearly all of his pre-Recent faunas as older than they really were."[21]

Ameghino's theory was reinforced by the fieldwork of his brother Carlos. In 1887 Carlos discovered remains of fossil mammals at the Barrancas Blancas in Patagonia. Those specimens, lying just above the marine beds in the region, were much older than anything found in the Pampas or described in Florentino's *Fossil Mammals of South America* (1880). In later years Carlos found older fossils, including the South American perissodactyl *Pyrotherium*, in the Santa Cruz region. On the basis of that work he claimed that the Santa Cruz formation included two separate units, the older of which he called "Notostylops as that is the most characteristic and abundant genus, [and] is indisputably Cretaceous since it is perfectly conformable with the Guarantic terrane."[22]

Florentino employed those discoveries to reinforce his theory of the South American origin of vertebrates. Noting that the Notostylops and Pyrotherium fauna were older than the Patagonian marine fauna, Florentino insisted that the mammals were from the Cretaceous period. He identified the older Notostylops fauna as belonging to the Lower Cretaceous. The Pyrotherium fossils, he claimed, were found in association with dinosaurs and therefore belonged to the Upper Cretaceous. Associating large, highly specialized mammals with dinosaurs, Ameghino attributed to the Santacrucian mammals a much older age than mammals anywhere else in the world. Such evidence substantiated his theory that Argentina was the source of vertebrate evolution and migration. But his interpretation contradicted the views of other vertebrate paleontologists.[23]

The claims of the Ameghinos and Roth produced a worldwide reaction. The French paleontologists Albert Gaudry and André Tournouër traveled to South America to inspect the Ameghinos's collections. So too did Richard Lydekker of the British Museum and W. B. Scott of Princeton. In 1897 Scott, with financial backing from J. P. Morgan, launched the Princeton Patagonian Expeditions and sent John Bell Hatcher to study South American formations and specimens. Hatcher, a proponent of the need to establish precise stratigraphic records, explored Patagonia on three expeditions and collected enough fossil and recent specimens to keep Scott and other scientists occupied for the next thirty years.[24]

Hatcher's work also threw serious doubts on Ameghino's interpretations. Finding no mammalian remains associated with dinosaurs, he was led to "seriously question the stratigraphic position of the Pyrotherium beds as determined by the brothers Ameghino." Based on his analysis of vertebrate specimens and the horizons in which they were found, he claimed that "there is absolutely no ground . . . for presuming that the mammalia of this region were any more advanced in early Tertiary times than were the mammals of the northern hemisphere." The evidence from fossil invertebrates was equally damaging, and Hatcher, never one to suppress his personal opinions, described Florentino Ameghino's work as thoughtless and inaccurate.[25]

Matthew did not visit Patagonia, but he criticized the interpretations of the South American paleontologists. Matthew knew of Hatcher's criticisms and was well aware of efforts by Gaudry and Max Schlosser to reinterpret Ameghino's geology and paleontology. Matthew drew upon those studies and his own knowledge of North American and European fossil vertebrates to challenge the interpretations of the Argentines. His translation of Roth's paper, as part of the National Academy of Science project on correlation, included a highly critical review of Roth's correlations. Throughout the piece Matthew argued that because Roth had failed to compare South American fauna with similar North American and European fauna his work was seriously flawed.[26]

A few years later, in his most famous study, "Climate and Evolution" (1915), Matthew refuted Ameghino's interpretations and correlations. Matthew maintained that Ameghino, in his effort to substantiate the argument that vertebrate families had originated in Argentina, had constructed impossible phylogenies. For example, Ameghino's interpretation of the evolution and distribution of the horse was, according to Matthew, completely untenable. Relying on his knowledge of the evolution and systematics of almost all families of extinct mammals, Matthew redefined the entire sequence of Argentine fauna as interpreted by Ameghino. He defined the Notostylops unit, which according to Ameghino was a Lower Cretaceous formation that included dinosaurs and early mammals, as Eocene. He systematically correlated each of Ameghino's South American units with Tertiary units of more recent age.[27] Matthew's redefinition of those South American fauna rested not only on his knowledge of systematics, stratigraphy, and correlation but on his conviction that the "correlation of widely distant formations is so intimately bound up with problems of geographical distribution and migration, that the two series of problems must be studied and solved together."[28] For Matthew, a proper interpretation of correlation rested on a knowledge of the origin and geographical distribution of vertebrates, a topic that he also took up in association with Osborn's interests.

Paleobiogeography

In the late 1890s Osborn's interest in evolution and correlation led him to examine the geographical distribution of animals. Again it was his study of the evolution of rhinoceroses, which demonstrated the occurrence of similar animals as far apart as southern France and Colorado, that prompted Osborn to pursue questions concerning the origin and migration of vertebrates. While he read and published much on the subject, Osborn also relied on the researches of other scientists. He adopted the views of Philip Sclater and Richard Lydekker, two British scientists, and divided the world into three geographical realms and nine regions. He argued for the northern origin of most families of mammals.[29]

Osborn also maintained that other realms and regions had served as centers for the adaptive radiation of some families and genera. He was enthusiastic about the work of the British paleontologist C. W. Andrews and became convinced that Africa had been a major center of mammalian evolution and radiation. Earlier scientists had argued that Africa had been populated by faunal invasions from Europe and Asia, but Osborn suggested that successive northern migrations from southern Africa were the source of most of the continent's animals. Ruminants, mastodons, dinotheres, and later edentates, perissodactyls, and hyracoides had all migrated out of Africa to the northern regions, he maintained. Osborn overstated the importance of that hypothesis, but his exaggerations and enthusiasm resulted in a museum expedition to the Fayûm of Egypt in 1907.[30]

More exciting to Osborn was the possibility of another major source of evolution and migration: Antarctica. The concept of an extended southern land mass had received support from the British botanist Joseph Dalton Hooker and a number of nineteenth-century biologists and geographers. On the basis of their studies Osborn was convinced that there had existed "an Antarctic continent at various times connecting South America, South Africa, Australia and New Zealand."[31] A connected southern land mass could unravel some of the most perplexing problems of biogeography: the distribution of the marsupials, the distribution of sirenia in Africa and South America, and the presence of edentates and proboscideans in Africa. In the early 1900s, Osborn instructed DVP scientists and artists to develop map restorations of Antarctica to demonstrate its connections to Africa, Australia, and New Zealand.[32]

But within ten years Osborn's views about southern land connections had changed. In his book the *Age of Mammals* (1910) Osborn recapitulated his ideas on Africa and Antarctica as major regions of adaptive radiation and faunal migration. However, in the same text he made an abrupt reversal and argued that "the greater part of the animals and plants of the southern continents are of northern origin, and that the evidence advanced for Antarctic connections is probably explainable through distribution from the North."[33] The change in Osborn's views probably resulted from the work of Matthew, who had become very interested in questions of biogeography.

Matthew's earliest studies of biogeography embodied a number of Osborn's ideas. Matthew's first work, like Osborn's, included DVP maps that defined changes in land mass, ocean basins, and animal migration and described the hypothetical outlines of the continents in earlier epochs. He followed Osborn's suggestion that some mammals, such as the creodonts, had originated in Antarctica. He also adopted Osborn's idea that Antarctica, though a source of distribution, had no connection to southern Africa.[34] But while Osborn offered intriguing ideas and was interested in a range of questions concerning biostratigraphy, correlation, and geographical distribution, it was Matthew who did firsthand research and delved much further into the study of those subjects.

For Matthew, the study of geographical distribution entailed not only a knowledge of Cenozoic fauna and formations but also an understanding of structural geology and geological dynamics. His views were influenced by the work of the American geologist T. C. Chamberlin.

In the 1890s Chamberlin attacked the nebular hypothesis, the doctrine that had long dominated the understanding of earth history. According to that doctrine, the earth had begun as a hot, molten mass and uniformly became cooler.[35] Chamberlin's studies of the Ice Age challenged that view, and in 1897 he argued that there had been periodic shifts in the earth's climate and the relative elevation of the sea and land. The amount of carbon dioxide in the atmosphere played a central part in this argument. According to Chamberlin, extensive erosion of the land produced shallow seas that provided excellent breeding grounds for coral and other lime-secreting organisms. The release of carbonic acid gas by those organisms yielded an increased amount of carbon dioxide, which increased the temperature and produced a warmer, moister atmosphere. Eventually, erosion and the build up of sediment in the oceans resulted in an imbalance in the earth's pressure system. Uplifting occurred, and the rising of the land and corresponding deepening of the sea basins left a smaller area for lime-secreting organisms and lessened the amount of carbon dioxide in the atmosphere. That phenomenon, coupled with increased erosion and the development of coal formations, reduced the amount of carbon dioxide and created periods of colder, more arid climate. Chamberlin thus advanced a theory of earth history based on alternating conditions: submergence of the land and extension of shallow seas that produced a warm, moist climate, followed by cold, arid climates that coincided with land elevation.[36]

Chamberlin applied his theory to the evolution of invertebrates,[37] and Matthew extended it to the study of vertebrate life. In an address to the Linnaean Society of London in 1902, Matthew argued that periods of erosion and continental depression produced an overflowing of shallow seas, which isolated land masses and fauna. During a time of warm, moist conditions, arboreal and amphibious organisms evolved and, being isolated from other organisms, became distinct. Conversely, "the period of cold and arid climate will be a period of great land extension and connection between continents. The varied climate will induce a great variety of forms of animal life, and the communication between continents will favor the worldwide spread of the more advanced types of animals, and the displacements by them of provincial faunas in all parts of the world."[38] Drawing on Chamberlin's concept of alternating climatic and geological conditions, Matthew in 1902 and again in 1906 described the geographical conditions and fauna that had evolved in the late Cretaceous and Tertiary periods.

Matthew's adherence to Chamberlin's theory had additional implications for his understanding of paleobiogeography. The doctrine of alternating conditions suggested that geological and geographical changes had occurred within a relatively stable framework. In discussing Chamberlin's views, Matthew noted that "the conclusion appears unavoidable that in a broad way the present distribution of land and shallow water on the one hand, of deep water on the other, has been substantially unchanged."[39] In other words, existing continental land masses and ocean basins were permanent. That argument was not only implicit in Chamberlin's work, it also characterized the interpretations of Charles Darwin and Alfred Russel Wallace whose writings on biogeography influenced Matthew.

The similarities and differences among organisms in different areas of the world was a subject that Darwin sought to explain in terms of his theory of evolution by natural selection. In *Origin of Species* (1859) he claimed that the geographical and biological relationships among organisms were not adequately explained by the hypothesis that each species was created at several separate points on the earth. Rather, each species "had been produced in one area alone" and had subsequently migrated and evolved. Darwin, who accepted the uniformitarian principle that geological phenomena and processes were basically similar in the present and the past, did not believe that such migrations had occurred across extended land bridges that once existed. He claimed that "we may infer that where our oceans now extend, oceans have extended from the remotest period of which we have any record; and on the other hand, that where continents now exist, large tracts of land have existed, subjected no doubt to great oscillations of level, since the earliest silurian period."[40] Having rejected the occurrence of extended land bridges, Darwin accumulated data and conducted experiments to demonstrate that plants, birds, and insects were capable of migrating long distances.[41]

Wallace, the codiscoverer of the theory of evolution by natural selection, further developed those arguments. His *Geographical Distribution of Animals* (1876), a detailed description of the vertebrates in the several regions and subregions of the world, was grounded on the idea that minor changes in physical geography could account for the geographical distribution of organisms. Wallace was attracted to the hypothesis of land bridges at an early age, but he later emerged as a leading opponent of that doctrine. He developed an understanding of biogeography based on migrations that had occurred over geological and geographical features similar to those of today.[42]

Drawing on contemporary ideas about the depth and extent of the earth's waters, Wallace argued that while great expanses of land may have been submerged at one time in the past, the total amount of land surface could not have exceeded that which now exists. Additional information demonstrated that the shallowest areas of water, hence those areas where land elevation would most likely occur, were near land masses. According to Wallace, changes in the "distribution of land and sea must have taken place more frequently by additions to, or modifications of pre-existing land, than by the upheaval of entirely new continents in mid-ocean." Eschewing hypotheses of ancient continents and extended land bridges, Wallace held that new land masses arose close to or in connection with previously existing lands. For Wallace, minor changes in physical geography and known means of animal migration were sufficient to explain the geographical distribution of organisms.[43]

Equally influential were Darwin's and Wallace's arguments for the northern origin and distribution of organisms. Darwin, defending that interpretation in a discussion of the Ice Age, explained it in terms of the greater land mass, greater number of organisms, and the more advanced evolutionary state of organisms in the northern regions of the world.[44] Wallace elaborated on that point. In his view

all the chief types of animal life appear to have originated in the great north temperate or northern continents; while the southern continents—now represented by South America, Australia, and South Africa with Madagascar—have been more or less completely isolated, during long periods, both from the northern continent and from each other. These latter countries have, however, been subject to more or less immigration from the north during rare epochs of approximation to, or partial union with it. In the northern, more extensive, and probably more ancient land, the process of development has been more rapid, and has resulted in more varied and higher types; while the southern lands, for the most part, seem to have produced numerous diverging modifications of the lower grades of organization, the original types of which they derived either from the north, or from some of the ancient continents in Mesozoic or Palaeozoic times.[45]

Wallace applied that interpretation to the mammals of Europe, North America, and South America. He was the first biogeographer to make extensive use of vertebrate paleontology, and he pointed out that Europe possessed many more fossil genera and families than the other continents. He also claimed that among organisms common to the three continents, the European remains were the oldest. From Wallace's perspective most mammals had originated on the European continent and had spread to North and subsequently South America in the Eocene and Miocene periods.[46]

Matthew accepted much of Wallace's interpretation, although for a time he had some reservations about the Holarctic theory. In 1906 he maintained that the origin of the Condylarthra, primitive mammals of the late Cretaceous, was best explained in terms of migration by way of an extensive Antarctic continent. His interpretation of the continents in the early Tertiary included a map showing the connections of the Antarctic with South America and Australia, the same map that Osborn had employed.[47] But within a few years Matthew had rejected the hypothesis of an extended southern land mass and fully accepted Wallace's interpretations of physical geography and geographical distribution. His study, "Climate and Evolution" (1915), was an extended argument for the northern origin and dispersal of vertebrate life and the permanence of the continents and ocean basins. Matthew's views hardened as he became more knowledgeable about the fossil record and increasingly opposed to differing interpretations of structural geology and biogeography.

In his 1906 essay Matthew accepted the Asiatic, or Holarctic, origin of a number of mammalian families. His studies demonstrated that carnivores, artiodactyls, and perissodactyls had migrated from a northern center of origin.[48] Later research on the deer family reinforced his views, and by 1915 Matthew had explained most families of mammals on the basis of that interpretation. Research on fossil rodents demonstrated that the Ischyromyidae were of a North American—European origin, and he claimed that "all other rodents may be derived from this group by divergent, parallel, and in some respects convergent evolution."[49]

One of the most difficult problems Matthew faced was how to explain the distribution of marsupials on the basis of the Holarctic theory. He argued against the hypothesis of an Antarctic connection between Australia and South America during the Tertiary by relying on studies by Pauline Dederer and Robert Broom that suggested that diprotodont marsupials were not present in South America. He denied that the resemblance between modern Australian marsupials and Tertiary marsupials of South America was the result of an Antarctic connection between the continents. Instead, he claimed that the "resemblance is not closer than between parallel adaptations in distinct families of the true Carnivora, whose genealogy has been more or less completely traced back through independent lines of descent from unspecialized common ancestors." For Matthew, the similarities that characterized those organisms and distinguished them from others were a result of independent "adaptation to predaceous terrestrial life and have been so assumed in numerous independent parallel adaptations of the same sort among placental Carnivora."[50]

Matthew could not bring all mammalian families into the fold. Edentates, particularly the anteaters and tree sloths, and hystricomorph rodents suggested possible South American origins. Yet "a careful consideration of these supposed exceptions shows that, if due allowance be made for parallelism and for the imperfection of the record, each one can be more satisfactorily interpreted in accordance with the general law."[51] That general law was the northern origin and distribution of vertebrates by known means of migration.

Matthew's commitment to the Holarctic theory was also influenced by his reaction to other interpretations of the earth's geological and biological history. In the early twentieth century, the theory of northern origins and stable ocean basins and land masses met with several serious challenges. Sunken continents and extended land bridges became standard in the work of paleogeographers, particularly those scientists whose studies focused on invertebrates and plants. Though Matthew had little knowledge of those organisms, such interpretations went directly against his geological and biological views. Theories of land bridges and drifting continents violated his understanding of geological processes based on the principle that current means and rates of action explained past geological developments. They also violated his interpretation of the history and distribution of organisms. In "Climate and Evolution" Matthew was doing more than arguing for the northern origin of vertebrate life. He was also attempting to refute what had become a popular interpretation of the geological and biological history of the southern hemisphere.

Studies by late nineteenth-century scientists indicated similarities among flora and fauna as far apart as Patagonia and New Zealand. In *Origin* Darwin described such similarities but attributed them to migration across long distances. But by the 1890s scientists were invoking extended land bridges to account for such phenomena. Arnold Ortmann, an invertebrate paleontologist, claimed that with the exception of Wallace's theory "all explanations of this zoogeographical fact have started from the fundamental idea that there must formerly have existed a connection between the respective parts by a land bridge, and opinions differ only as to the location and probable extent of it."[52]

Others, including the Swiss paleontologist Ludwig Rütimeyer, and the British geographers H. O. Forbes and Charles Hedley, explained such similarities in terms of former land connections via Antarctica. Forbes referred to a large continent that embraced Australia, New Zealand, South Africa, and South America. Hedley held that narrow strips joined those land masses to the known Antarctic continent.[53] Those scientists relied on both land and freshwater animals and on plants to substantiate their views. Ortmann, who examined the invertebrates brought back by the Princeton Patagonian Expedition, argued that the marine fossil fauna of Patagonia "are to be regarded as an additional proof of the for-

mer connection of South America with Australia and New Zealand."
Ortmann, like Hedley, suggested that in the late Cretaceous and early
Tertiary periods those connections were not necessarily continuous. He
also held that connections between Antarctica and Austral lands did not
necessarily coexist with the connection between Antarctica and South
America. But Ortmann fully supported the hypothesis that former land
bridges to Antarctica accounted for the similarities among marine fossils
in Patagonia, Australia and New Zealand.[54]

Ortmann found little evidence to indicate a connection between Antarctica and South Africa, but he invoked another popular hypothesis to
explain resemblances between the marine fossil fauna of Patagonia and
other tropical regions: Hermann von Ihering's theory of Archiplata and
Archhelensis. Von Ihering, a Swiss biologist, claimed that the South
American continent was composed of two distinct faunal areas. A southern part called Archiplata included what is now Chile, Argentina, Uru-
guay, and southern Brazil. The connection of Archiplata to Antarctica
was, for von Ihering, the means for explaining the close biogeographical
relations between South America and Australia and New Zealand. The
northern area he termed Archhelensis, a land mass that included northern
Brazil and the Caribbean. Archhelensis was connected to West Africa by
way of the island of St. Helena. For von Ihering that connection explained "the intimate relations between the fresh-water faunas of Africa
and Brazil."[55] Ortmann believed that the existence of Archiplata could
account for the similarities between the Patagonian fauna and animals of
the West Indies and Europe. Carl Eigenmann, an ichthyologist from Indiana University who examined the freshwater fishes from the Princeton
Expedition, also accepted von Ihering's ideas.[56]

Matthew adamantly opposed the theories of land bridges and drifting
continents. He pointed to the "enormous geological and geophyscial difficulties which these continental bridges would have to explain." In response to the land bridge proposed by Ortmann, as well as Wegner's
continental drift theory, Matthew claimed it was necessary to provide a
vera causa to demonstrate that continents have a tendency to drift and that
such a tendency can detach continental masses from their anchorage.
Matthew, like Wallace, argued that the deep ocean basins, and the iso-
static balance that maintained them, had been permanent and not subject
to radical changes in structure. Matthew also pointed to the absence of
abyssal deposits in the sedimentary successions in continental regions to
bolster, on geological grounds, his opposition to the land bridge hypotheses.[57]

The evidence from the fossil record played an even more important role in Matthew's stance. Matthew rejected land bridge hypotheses for the southern hemisphere on the grounds that the use of paleontological evidence to support such hypotheses was incorrect. In response to the continental drift hypothesis, he claimed that Wegner's interpretation of the relations of land fauna "is quite impossibly wrong." He pointed to egregious errors in the bridge-building hypotheses advanced by Hans Gadow and R. F. Scharff. Gadow's factual errors concerning the evolution of creodonts and horses were just so much grist for Matthew's mill.[58] Matthew also took exception to what he considered a naive and incorrect interpretation of the fossil record. Matthew, in contrast to Osborn and other paleontologists, was well aware of the imperfection of the fossil record and cautious in his interpretation of evolution. On many occasions he stated that phylogenies constructed by paleontologists, himself included, were only approximate. That same cautious attitude characterized his interpretation of the fossil record for the purposes of understanding geographical distribution.

Matthew attacked the bridge builders for the partisan use of negative evidence. A number of bridge builders argued that because fossil remains had not been found in particular horizons, the organisms must not have existed in those areas at that time. Gadow claimed that because no marsupials had been found in the Tertiary of Asia, they must have reached Australia via Antarctica from South America. For Matthew such an argument was specious since no marsupials had been found in Antarctica. In addition, even though marsupial remains had not been discovered in Asia, that did not mean they did not exist there at that time. On the contrary, "the presence of marsupials in the early Tertiary of Europe on one side of Holarctica and of North America on the other side raises a strong presumption of their presence in the intervening region of Asia from which no fossils are known. They are not found in the later Tertiary of Europe and America, so that we should not expect to find them in the later Tertiary of Asia."[59]

Matthew rebuked the supporters of land bridge hypotheses for uncritically accepting the data of the fossil record. For von Ihering, Scharff, and others the presence of Tertiary marine deposits in the interior of South America suggested that South America first became a single continent at that time. For Matthew such evidence was not presumptive; it reflected instead the periodic alterations in the earth's surface. South America, like North America and the other continents, was a land mass of great antiquity.[60] The evidence of the fossil record, whether new deposits, discontinuous distributions, or the lack of remains, could not be taken at face value.

Matthew drew upon his background in paleontology to criticize the bridge builders in another respect: their failure to understand the intricacies of correlation. Land bridge hypotheses rested on establishing similarities among disjunctively distributed organisms. But according to Matthew, many paleogeographers did not properly distinguish between two important but different concepts: synchronism, the phenomenon that organisms in different regions existed at the same time, and homotaxis, the phenomenon that faunas from different regions have similar taxa but may be of different ages.[61] The failure to distinguish properly between synchronism and homotaxis could create problems by leading scientists to misinterpret the evolutionary and chronological relationships among organisms from different regions. Matthew argued that that kind of misunderstanding characterized Eigenmann's interpretation of the freshwater fishes of Patagonia.

According to Eigenmann, none of the modern freshwater fishes of South America were descended from North American fishes. Matthew, though not a student of fossil fishes, had no trouble in pointing out that several South American genera were typical of the Green River Eocene of Wyoming. Catfish and characins, primitive and waning in North America, were an important element of the South American fauna. Eigenmann's error, in Matthew's view, lay in his failure to recognize that the fossil fish of South America were merely modern examples of northern genera from an earlier time. Eigenmann did not properly understand homotaxis, and that resulted in confusion in his interpretation of the evolution and the geographical distribution of freshwater fishes.[62] For Matthew, Eigenmann's misinterpretation was also symptomatic of a deeper problem: the failure to understand the basics of geological correlation. Such misunderstandings, he maintained, had resulted in the creation of unwarranted and unnecessary land bridges and posed problems for understanding the evolution and the geographical distribution of fossil vertebrates.

Matthew argued that Ameghino's work also misintepreted homotaxial relations. Ameghino had turned the origin and geographical distribution of animals on its head; consequently, he had created a series of improbable phylogenies and inaccurately defined the evolutionary, chronological, and distributional relationships among the families of fossil mammals. Ameghino's theory had also led him to interpret homotaxial relations in such a manner as to give priority and older age to South American fauna and horizons. According to Matthew, "If we believe, as does Dr. Ameghino, that the principal theatre of evolution of the mammals lay in the temperate regions of South America, and that the mammal population of the North was derived by migration from that center (by way of Africa across a tropical landbridge not now existing), it will be equally obvious that the southern formations will be more ancient than their homotaxis, impartially considered, would lead us to believe. The result will be to assign to the Cretaceous period those southern faunae which are homotaxial with the early Eocene of the North; to the Eocene those faunae that are homotaxial with the Middle Tertiary of the North, and so on."[63] It was not only the evidence of the fossil record but a misunderstanding of basic principles that undermined Ameghino's interpretation. A proper knowledge of biostratigraphy and correlation, of homotaxis and synchronism, and a commitment to uniformitarianism, specifically the principle of actualism that defined known agents and processes operating at known rates and forces as the means for explaining past geological events, substantiated the theory of the northern origin and distribution of fossil vertebrates.

Not all contemporary scientists accepted Matthew's interpretation. Some geologists and invertebrate paleontologists like Charles Schuchert criticized his reliance on Chamberlin's theory. Schuchert claimed that Matthew's interpretation of vertebrate distribution in the Cenozoic had little application to invertebrate life in that or earlier ages. Thomas Barbour, an ichthyologist and the director of Harvard's Museum of Comparative Zoology, questioned Matthew's theory as it applied to island fauna.[64]

Yet the detail and scope of his work had a powerful impact on Osborn's views. Osborn's *Age of Mammals* was a treatise on geographical distribution and correlation that depended heavily on Matthew's contributions. His comprehension and application of the principles of biostratigraphy and correlation, his detailed knowledge of Tertiary geology and stratigraphy, and his understanding of the origin, distribution, and evolution of most families of fossil vertebrates influenced Osborn's work. It is likely that Matthew's knowledge and interpretation of geographical distribution led Osborn in 1910 to abandon his belief in a great southern land mass and to explain the several distinct "faunal phases" of the Cenozoic Era in terms of changing physiographic and faunal relations between North America and the northern Eurasian land mass Holarctica.[65]

Matthew's views as defined in "Climate and Evolution" influenced a generation of vertebrate biologists and paleontologists. His argument for geological permanentism and the Holarctic theory of geographical distribution provided an interpretive framework for additional research in vertebrate biogeography. According to the herpetologist Karl Schmidt, "The publication of Matthew's *Climate and Evolution* in 1915 was an event of primary importance in the field of animal geography. . . . A considerable number of subsequent distributional studies by students or disciples of Matthew have been based on Matthewsian principles; and the modern period of zoogeography must be dated from 1915."[66] Biologists including P. J. Darlington, George S. Myers, and others accepted Matthew's commitment to permanent ocean basins and land masses, his understanding of distributional patterns, and his belief in the impact of the environment on animal distribution. They extended his interpretation of the evolution and distribution of mammals to freshwater fishes, amphibians, and reptiles.[67]

Matthew also influenced the biogeographical work of his young colleague in vertebrate paleontology, George Gaylord Simpson. In an early paper on the subject, Simpson noted that "the general type of geographic history assumed by Matthew to be typical for mammals is . . . here more explicitly supported." Eventually, Simpson went beyond Matthew and developed a more comprehensive interpretation of geographical distribution that received much support from American zoogeographers. Nevertheless, Matthew had stimulated the younger man's interest in the subject and had advanced an interpretation of vertebrate evolution and distribution that Simpson later built upon.[68]

Through the work of Matthew and later Simpson the DVP gained a reputation as a leading center for research in biogeography. From the 1910s to the 1960s paleontologists at that institution produced studies that had an important bearing on the understanding of vertebrate evolution and distribution. Their work and influence rested upon the institutional and intellectual foundation established by Osborn. He contributed little in the way of new or original interpretations. However, he generated an enthusiasm for the study of biostratigraphy and geographical distribution that created the financial and institutional opportunities for research in that field. The subjects that captured Osborn's interest and attention became departmental projects, and it was as an assistant and contributor to Osborn's work that Matthew first became involved in and fascinated by paleobiogeography. Matthew put forth an influential interpretation in paleobiogeography, though that work was stimulated, supported, and made a departmental priority by Osborn.

Evolution

Osborn's interests and influence had an impact on the evolutionary studies pursued in the DVP. Osborn's views on evolution were at odds with the work of many contemporary biologists, but he emphasized the

FIGURE 16. William Diller Matthew (neg. no. 116557)

unique contribution that paleontologists could make to the study of variation, evolution, and inheritance. His views influenced his associates Matthew and William King Gregory. In his courses at Columbia, Osborn, like McCosh at Princeton, pointed out to his students the importance of examining causal questions. At the museum he not only directed his assistants to compile data, but discussed and debated with them interpretations of how and why vertebrates had evolved. He also encouraged them to develop their own evolutionary interpretations.[69] By the 1920s Matthew and Gregory had rejected Osborn's ideas and were putting forth quite different interpretations of evolution. That development was per-

haps a consequence not only of their own research but of their reactions
to Osborn's work. But Osborn's emphasis on the need to address theoretical problems pertaining to fossil vertebrates promoted ongoing debate and research among his DVP associates. In contrast to vertebrate
paleontologists at other institutions who devoted little attention to questions of variation, evolution, and inheritance, the principal scientists at
the DVP examined those problems, and in the cases of Matthew and
Gregory put forth new interpretations.

Matthew's interest in evolutionary questions had its basis in paleobiogeography. Directed in the late 1890s to provide the stratigraphic and
taxonomic information for Osborn's studies on correlation and geographical distribution, Matthew examined the impact that migration,
distribution, and changing environmental conditions could have on the
evolution of vertebrates. Matthew, more than Osborn, realized that a
theory of evolution depended upon a knowledge of the patterns of animal
migration and the factors responsible for it. In contrast to Osborn, who
believed that an organism's hereditary makeup controlled the process and
pattern of evolution, Matthew emphasized the role that migration and
changes in external conditions played in evolution.

Matthew's emphasis on biogeography led him to express some skepticism about the fossil record and what it could reveal about evolution.
Realizing that a knowledge of the fossil record required an understanding
of the migrations and geographical distribution of ancient organisms,
Matthew was not confident that the data of the geological past could
easily or readily answer questions about the nature of the evolutionary
process. This is evident in the manner in which he addressed the question
of whether evolution was a result of continuous or discontinuous variations.

The debate over the nature of variations created controversy among
many early twentieth-century scientists, but Osborn answered the question with supreme confidence. He held that the fossil record clearly demonstrated that evolution was a result of continuous "mutations." To the
end of his days he repudiated experimental biologists who defined discontinuous variations and genetic mutations as the grist for the mill of
evolution.[70]

Matthew agreed with Osborn that variations were infinitesimal and
evolution a continuous process. But he maintained that only by knowing
the origins and considering the geographical distribution of organisms
could the study of the fossil record help to solve such a problem. In any
region distant from a center of dispersal, the geological record would
appear to be discontinuous. In other instances, such as the camel family

that had originated in North America, there existed a continuous fossil record close to their center of dispersal.

The point at present to be considered is that in series as the camels, oreodonts, peccaries, we do have a sufficiently close approach to a continuous series to warrant our believing that the true process of their evolution in the center of their dispersal was a gradual one. . . . But the later, larger and more complete the series of specimens studied, the more perfect the record in successive strata and the nearer the hypothetic center of dispersal of the race, the closer do we come to a phyletic series whose intergrading stages are well within the limits of observed individual variation in the race. The known facts of vertebrate paleontology are, in my opinion, utterly inadequate to prove whether the development of races was or was not wholly continuous. But I think that the evidence, considered in relation to the imperfection of our knowledge, goes to show that the gaps were not normally wide.[71]

For Matthew, the fossil record could offer insights into the nature of evolution only when the migrations of ancient organisms were taken into account. Even then paleontology provided only an approximate answer.

Matthew maintained that migration and the factors that induced migration were the causal mechanisms that explained the evolutionary process. In some of his earliest comments on evolution, he argued that migration, more than mutation, played a primary role in evolution. In the evolutionary series for the horse "it appears probable that each 'stage' represents in most cases a migration rather than a mutation of the species." According to Matthew, "most of the changes in fauna in a locality were due to successive waves of migration, setting out from the region in which the new climatic conditions first appeared."[72] Matthew understood that migrations could account for problems in the fossil record that had long troubled advocates of evolution: gaps in the record and the sudden appearance of new groups, such as the new orders of mammals that appeared in the basal Eocene. He emphasized that migration and the factors that cause migration, namely, changes in external, environmental conditions, were central to the evolutionary process. His was no naive environmentalism; he interpreted evolution in terms of the dynamic, changing relationship between animals and their environment. For Matthew, evolution was a process of adaptation in which organic change occurred in relation to changes in the surrounding physical and biological conditions.

Matthew's recognition of the importance of environmental factors for evolution led him to advance an interpretation that, for an American vertebrate paleontologist of the time, was distinctive. In contrast to Cope and Osborn, who looked to some factor internal to the organism to explain evolution, Matthew understood descent with modification in relationship to changes in the climate and elevation of the earth's surface. Drawing on Chamberlin's theory of alternating conditions, Matthew claimed that periods of land elevation, which were associated with reduced amounts of carbon dioxide and a cold, arid climate, resulted in extensive animal migration and evolution. The evolution of the grassy plains and open steppe lands of the interior of North America and Eurasia, for example, had provided the conditions for successive waves of migration and the rapid evolution of the horse, camel, and other mammals. Concluding a 1902 address to the Linnaean Society of London, he stated that the "main trend of [mammalian] evolution was not a predeterminate one, carried out on certain lines inherent in the organism, but was an adaptation to changing external conditions. As the climate changed and with it the conditions of their habitat, the animals changed correspondingly, and those races which were best fitted for the new conditions, either because of natural adaptability or because in their original habitat the new conditions were earlier reached than elsewhere and they thus had a handicap over their competitors, these races spread widely and became dominant."[73]

Matthew explained evolution in terms of the adaptation of organism to environment and rejected deterministic, orthogenetic theories, including Osborn's. Cope and Osborn had understood adaptation. However, they based their interpretations on internal biological mechanisms by means of which organisms responded to external conditions. Osborn held that external factors initially triggered the ancestral germ plasm and subsequent evolutionary change was the result of an internal mechanism that produced mutations regardless of outside conditions. Matthew did not concern himself with the intricacies of how organisms responded biologically to changing circumstances. Instead, he realized that environmental factors were the key to adaptation and evolutionary modification, though he did not delve into a detailed analysis of the dynamics of that process. Despite his close association and even collaboration with Osborn, Matthew ignored Osborn's concern with internal biological mechanisms, rejected his deterministic theory, and accepted the Darwinian interpretation that evolution "is due to the pressure of the environment, acting through selection upon individual variations."[74]

Matthew's commitment to a Darwinian interpretation of evolution is evident in a number of his studies on the families of fossil mammals. Among the earliest and most important of those was his examination of the evolution of the saber-toothed cats. First discovered in the late nine-teenth century, the machaerodonts were the subject of much analysis and speculation. Several vertebrate paleontologists, including the Americans William Berryman Scott and Frederick B. Loomis, interpreted the evolution and extinction of those animals as a result of irreversible evolutionary trends and overspecialization. According to those interpretations, evolution followed predetermined paths that, once begun, could not be re-versed and that took on an increased momentum often leading to extinction. Some claimed that the canine teeth of the saber-toothed cats had evolved in that manner and eventually reached such a stage of over-specialization that the animals could not open their jaws wide enough to eat. Scott did not accept that interpretation, but he explained evolution as an irreversible process that often resulted in the overspecialization of parts and extinction.[75]

Matthew refused to accept any such interpretation and denounced the idea that the overspecialization of canine teeth had resulted in the extinc-tion of saber-toothed cats. For him, the evolution of the tooth structure of the machaerodonts and the extinction of those animals were a product of their adaptation to changing biotic conditions. In a 1901 paper and again in a classic 1909 study of the evolution of the Felidae, he argued that primitive cats were well adapted to prey upon large ungulates. As the ungulates became larger, thicker-skinned, and more powerful, the saber-toothed cats also "became progressively larger, more powerful and de-veloped longer and heavier weapons to cope with and destroy them."[76] The extinction of the machaerodonts resulted, in his view, from several factors, the most important of which was the growing scarcity and lim-ited geographic range of the pachyderms. He denied any role for evolu-tionary irreversibility or momentum and claimed that the idea "that a race can continue specializing in some particular direction beyond the point where the specialization is of use, and so far as to cause the actual extinction of the entire race, the environment remaining unchanged, ap-pears to me utterly impossible."[77] The utilitarian value of any character was the principal determinant of its evolution, and "the moment the harmfulness of a character . . . outbalanced its usefulness" natural selec-tion would ensure its elimination. Organisms existed in a delicate bal-ance, subject to the pressure of changing environmental factors and conditions. They had to adapt to such circumstances or face extinction, and for Matthew natural selection was responsible for promoting adapta-tion or eliminating organisms.[78]

Matthew's study of the horse most fully represents his view that changes in environmental factors resulted in a process of evolution based on the natural selection of random variations. Matthew first defined his interpretation of the evolution of the horse in a series of popular pamphlets. As assistant curator and later curator of fossil vertebrates at the museum, Matthew's duties included writing guides to the department's important collections. One of those guides provided information about fossil horses and the evolution of the horse family. As he noted in the introduction to the 1913 edition of that guide, "the history of the evolution of the horse . . . affords the best known illustration of the doctrine of evolution by means of natural selection and the adaptation of a race of animals to its environment."[79] Matthew described a number of well-known evolutionary changes that had occurred among horses: the disappearance of the side toes; the increase of the length of the leg and foot; and the development of short-crowned, from high-crowned, molar teeth. Osborn explained those changes in terms of irreversible trends first initiated in a hypothetical ancestral organism of the early Eocene. Matthew defined the modifications as a result of adaptations to changing conditions: "All these changes in the evolution of the horse are adaptations to a life in the region of the level, smooth grassy plains which are now its natural habitat. At first the race was better fitted for a forest life, but it has become more and more completely adapted to live and compete with its enemies or rivals under the conditions which prevail in the high dry plains of the interior of the great continents."[80]

Matthew claimed that the evolution of the horse went hand in hand with the evolution of the plains environment itself. The morphological changes among horses were the result of the "natural selection, acting as it does in nature on innumerable individuals. . . . [That agent] is perfectly competent to produce the results observed in the time calculated under the pressure of known and inferred changes in climate, physical and geographic conditions, and associated fauna."[81]

The study of fossil horses led Matthew to offer insights on another evolutionary problem: the nature of variations and the species concept. Here again Matthew's views differed from those of his colleagues. Most vertebrate paleontologists of the early twentieth century were typologists and generally neglected the distribution or range of variations of the specimens they studied.

Individual differences among specimens were of little consequence to those scientists for a number of reasons. For the purposes of description and classification, the first order of business for the paleontologist, such variations were of little moment. To the museum scientist who prepared specimens for analysis or public display, individual variations among specimens were relatively insignificant. For some scientists, such as Osborn, theoretical assumptions led to the neglect of the wide range of variations and the study of only type specimens, the individual or composite forms that most fully represented and defined the characteristics of a species or genus. Most vertebrate paleontologists therefore did not examine the range or distribution of individual differences within a species.[82] According to standard historical interpretations, it was not until the 1930s, when a new systematics emerged, that individual and geographic variations became important to evolutionary biologists.[83] Yet by the mid-1920s Matthew, while not defining species in terms employed by the later systematists and population geneticists, began to break away from a typological concept of species and to argue for the importance of individual differences among fossil specimens.

Matthew's rejection of the traditional typological species concept may have stemmed in part from his theoretical commitment to Darwinism, which disposed him to recognize the importance of individual variations for evolution. Despite his hesitation about the completeness and accuracy of the fossil record, Matthew maintained that natural selection operated on continuous variations, and in that context individual differences among specimens took on meaning.

It is also likely that the extensive amount of fossil material at his disposal led Matthew to adopt his distinctive interpretation. By virtue of his position at the American Museum, Matthew had access to a collection of fossil vertebrate specimens, including a collection of fossil horses, that was unparalleled. The opportunity to participate in fieldwork, which he did almost annually from 1895 to 1927, also contributed to his interpretation. Matthew, through his fieldwork and the chance to examine the more than 25,000 specimens in the DVP, became increasingly aware of the wide range of variation found among specimens from single deposits or specific formations.[84]

Matthew's recognition of the range and significance of variations first became evident in the 1910s when he and Walter Granger authored a series of papers on the vertebrate fauna of the Wasatch and Wind River formations of the Lower Eocene. As Matthew noted in the introduction to that series, research projects made possible by several American Museum expeditions yielded "exact records of level and locality of every specimen, [and] have made it possible to correlate the faunas and trace the evolution of the various races much more precisely and certainly."[85] Based on that work, Matthew and Granger made new determinations of the stratigraphy and evolutionary relationships among Lower Eocene mammals. That work also brought to light the extensive amount of variation among those animals. In his description of fossil creodonts, for example, Matthew frequently referred to the large number of specimens at his disposal. In one respect the wide range of variations among specimens posed problems for Matthew; a continuous lament of the difficulty of determining specific or generic differences runs throughout the study. But such evidence also led him to recognize that an attempt to define taxonomic relationships on the basis of any individual specimen was "wholly untrustworthy."[86]

Even more important was Matthew's research on the deposits from the Snake Creek fauna of western Nebraska. In 1916 the initial work done in those beds by Matthew and Harold J. Cook, another vertebrate paleontologist, indicated such extensive variation among mammals that Matthew suggested that "the greater numbers of individuals afford a much surer basis for distinguishing species than is usually the case in vertebrate paleontology." He defined species to "include a rather wide range of variation" and not "the fine splitting that is customary among modern systematic zoologists."[87]

Continued excavations at the Snake Creek beds resulted in the discovery of thousands of fossil horse specimens and provided Matthew with the opportunity to put forth a new interpretation of variation and the species concept. After determining that the vast amount of fossil material indicated the existence of four distinct zones of Tertiary Equidae, he claimed that the Snake Creek fauna included

many thousands of individuals, no two of them exactly alike in the complex details of tooth construction. If the standards of species distinction that have been accepted by most American students of fossil Equidae were applied conscientiously to this great collection, the result would be to place upon record scores if not hundreds of "new species" from this one locality. But the thousands of isolated teeth or other fragmentary specimens would clearly show that there are no really constant and uniformly associated distinctions between such "species." They are merely individual differences and it is the scanty or fragmentary character of the material or a failure to make a thorough and impartial study of all the materials available for comparison, the natural tendency to compare only the types or best preserved specimens, or to use drawings in place of the originals, that have been responsible for maintaining many of these species as distinct.[88]

Matthew's work on the Snake Creek fauna points to the importance of the opportunities made available to him at the American Museum. Matthew, more than vertebrate paleontologists at any other institution, had the means to undertake a thorough, comparative study of fossil horse material. The American Museum provided the money and the manpower for the exploration of the Snake Creek deposits for several years. The excellent collection in the DVP provided the opportunity to compare specimens from those beds with other material. Such resources and data led Matthew to question typological interpretations and to alter the traditional understanding of variation and the species concept. As a result, in 1918 he objected to Osborn's continued emphasis on the study of just type specimens and broke off plans for their collaborative study on fossil horses.[89] Matthew also brought his understanding of variation and the species concept into line with the latest researches in other fields of biology, including genetics.

Throughout the 1920s Matthew sought to make paleontologists more aware of the significance of individual variations and to clarify the species concept. Writing in 1925 to Francis B. Sumner, Matthew claimed that it was not practical for paleontologists to define species in a narrow sense. For Matthew, a species was "defined by a group of associated fixed (hence inherited) characters, and including many interbreeding strains with a tinge of hybridism all around the contacts of its distribution range with that of other related species."[90] Drawing upon his knowledge of the Snake Creek fauna and his later work on the fossil vertebrates of the Tertiary beds of Texas, Matthew came to "appreciate the real scope of species as it exists in nature, constituted of a large number of interbreeding strains, of more or less differing heredity. The interbreeding ranges all the way from continuous to occasional; its results are seen in characters of individual variation, sometimes intergrading, often intermingling though not intergrading. It is not reasonably probable that a large number of nearly related individuals living in the same locality, watering at the same pool, similar so far as we have any indications, in habits and environment would fail to interbreed. . . . And so long as they habitually or frequently interbreed, directly or indirectly, they are not distinct species."[91]

Matthew sought to replace a typological understanding with a view that defined species in terms of large numbers of interbreeding individuals that varied in all but certain fixed characteristics. He also called on other paleontologists to take into account the wide range of individual variations. Advocating the need to base the understanding of fossil species on the known range of modern species, Matthew attempted to define rules and regulations for defining species that would end a lamentable species mongering and would enable paleontologists to recognize reasonable ranges and limitations for fossil species.[92]

Matthew's analysis of the species concept led him to examine contemporary research in genetics. That too constituted a break from the ordinary. Many early twentieth-century vertebrate paleontologists adhered to either neo-Lamarckian or orthogenetic theories that denied the significance of genetics. Naturalists and experimentalists differed markedly in their interpretations of inheritance, variation, and mutation. They also used different biological materials, methodologies, and language.[93] Osborn had little use or regard for genetics, but even his status and the force of his arguments did not keep Matthew from studying experimental biology and bringing the findings of genetics to bear on the evidence of the fossil record.

In 1925 Matthew wrote to the geneticists T. H. Morgan and Francis B. Sumner and outlined his views on variation, the species concept, and evolution. To both men Matthew emphasized that research in experimental biology is "essential to the understanding of the problems I am working on," and he sought to open a dialogue through which "different viewpoints [can be] competently and fairly presented." He defined his views "as to the inheritance and non-inheritance of variations" and hoped to obtain the reactions of leading experimental biologists. As he told Sumner, he fully accepted the distinction between congenital and environmental variations and recognized that "congenital variations are due to differences in the germ-cells, and obey the laws of Mendelian inheritance, including the various linkages, sex-restrictions, recessive features, etc." Matthew, who believed that variations were continuous and evolution a gradual process, also told Sumner that "the same laws that apply to the abnormalities that have been principally studied [by geneticists] would apply equally to the minute heritable variations which selection could preserve and ultimately accumulate."[94]

By 1930 Matthew was convinced of the similarity between the genetic mutations examined by experimental biologists in the laboratory and the continuous variations he found in the field. As he stated in a paper of that year, "The nature of these variations is much better understood than it was in Darwin's time, thanks especially to the researches of T. H. Morgan and his school. Some of them are inherited according to certain definite laws. They are 'mutations' of the same nature as the larger more conspicuous and more occasional mutations which geneticists have studied in detail. Others are the non-heritable differences between individuals, due to slight or considerable differences in their environment and growth history."[95]

Matthew accepted the findings of classical genetics. Admittedly, he never systematically applied genetics to the fossil record, and he did not develop a comprehensive theory of evolution. He did, however, attempt to bridge the gap between naturalists and experimentalists and to reconcile research in paleontology with genetics and experimental studies of

evolution. Recognizing the extent and importance of individual variations and the distinction between phenotype and genotype, Matthew
employed his understanding of variation to develop an interpretation
that, for a vertebrate paleontologist of the time, was new and different.

Matthew's views on variation and evolution led him to challenge the
traditional understanding of the pattern of evolutionary change. Matthew was always skeptical of reading too much into the fossil record, and
by the 1920s he no longer hesitated to criticize claims, including Osborn's, that the fossil record demonstrated irreversible evolutionary
trends. On the basis of his understanding of the causes of evolution and
his detailed knowledge of the stratigraphic and systematic relationships
among fossil mammals, Matthew condemned vertical systems of classification, orthogenetic interpretations, and bushlike phylogenies. Work
on the carnivores from the Snake Creek beds, as well as his last studies on
the fossil horses and rhinoceroses of the Pliocene of Texas, led Matthew
to argue that each family represented an individual line of descent, not
separate, parallel lineages.

In contrast to Osborn and Scott, Matthew downplayed the importance
of evolutionary parallelism. He defined evolution as a divergent process
that resulted from continuing "environmental pressure, bringing about
selection, change of geographic range, creation of new 'mutations,'
[and] elimination of old ones."[96] Natural selection, operating on individual heritable variations, controlled both the process and pattern of evolution and produced divergent modification within monophyletic lines of
descent.

Conclusion

Matthew's views on evolution and related questions, like his interpretation of geographical distribution, influenced the work of Simpson.
Matthew had some personal association with Simpson. In 1924, when
Simpson was still a graduate student at Yale, the two spent a month
doing fieldwork in Texas. When Simpson came to the American Museum in 1927, it was to replace Matthew who had left for the University
of California at Berkeley. The two men kept up an active correspondence, and Simpson was impressed by Matthew's "remarkable insight
and his fine philosophy of science and of life." Even more important than
their personal relationship was the impact that Matthew's writings had
on Simpson. The latter testified that "I absorbed every word he spoke,
and . . . read every word he had written."[97]

Matthew never fully incorporated genetics into his work, nor did he apply statistical analysis to the distribution of variation among fossil populations. It was Simpson who would do so; his *Tempo and Mode in Evolution* (1944) drew upon the findings of population genetics to fashion a new interpretation of the fossil record. But Matthew's work provided a means for interpreting the fossil record in accordance with selection theory, for realizing the important bearing of genetics on the fossil record, and for understanding and examining variations among fossil specimens that would have important consequences for systematics. Matthew's work provided a foundation upon which Simpson would build.[98]

In developing an interpretation of evolution and related questions that influenced Simpson, Matthew had rejected Osborn's views. Based on his research in biogeography, Matthew looked to the environment as the principal agent of organic change. Accepting the theory that natural selection was the mechanism of evolution, Matthew repudiated Osborn's understanding of both the process and pattern of evolution. By paying close attention to stratigraphy, systematics, and distribution, Matthew recognized the significance and extent of individual differences and rejected Osborn's understanding of variation and inheritance. In the study of evolution, unlike biogeography, there was little common ground between the two men.[99]

It is possible to construe Matthew's interpretations as a reaction against Osborn's views. Matthew spent much of his career concentrating on fossil systematics and biogeography, and it was only in the late 1910s and 1920s that he began to elaborate his views on inheritance and the pattern and process of evolution. By that time, he had thousands of specimens at his disposal, had established his reputation, and, given his intimate acquaintance with Osborn's work, may have felt the need to express his views as a means of counteracting Osborn's. It was in the 1920s that Matthew left the museum because of disagreements with Osborn, and that too may have influenced him to elaborate on his ideas.

Yet Matthew's views reflected Osborn's influence. Such a claim may seem problematic since Matthew's mature interpretations of evolution, inheritance, classification, and the species concept were very different from Osborn's. However, Matthew first expressed his views on evolution in the early years of the first decade of the century. At the time he and Osborn were not at odds. Osborn had assigned Matthew to do research on biostratigraphy and correlation, and that work eventually was the basis for Matthew's evolutionary ideas.

Matthew pursued his investigations within the institutional and intellectual context that Osborn had created. The DVP provided the facilities, the opportunities, and a well-established infrastructure that enabled Matthew to devote his career to research in the laboratory and the field. The impetus to go beyond description and classification, to examine problems pertaining to evolution, variation, and inheritance, derived in no small part from Osborn's interests and concerns. Osborn had developed a theory of evolution and applied it to a wide range of geological and biological questions. He impressed upon his staff the need to deal with causal questions in their work. Matthew did so. He developed insights and interpretations of the fossil record that contradicted Osborn's, but Matthew's work also constituted a response to the issues that Osborn had considered important. Matthew's work was a manifestation of the topics and program of research that had interested Osborn and that he had institutionalized in the Department of Vertebrate Paleontology.

9 Fossils and Function: William King Gregory and Vertebrate Paleontology at the American Museum

Osborn's administrative dominance and his enthusiasm for the analysis of biological problems, which had initiated the museum work on paleobiogeography and evolutionary theory, also promoted work in another field of investigation: the study of the functional morphology of fossil vertebrates. Earlier paleontologists, notably Georges Cuvier, Vladimir Kovalevsky, and Louis Dollo, had emphasized the importance of functional questions. So too did others such as the British paleontologist D. M. S. Watson, who sought to understand pose and motion among primitive reptiles.[1] But only at the American Museum did the study of questions pertaining to animal habits, function, and adaptation become the basis for a well-defined program of research.

The specific combination of factors at the American Museum enabled such a program to flourish. Theoretical questions considered and partially pursued by Osborn provided the impetus for DVP scientists to integrate the study of form with function. He also promoted the study of those questions within the context of the museum's educational emphasis and his concern for employing displays to convey moral lessons. Matthew took the lead in examining functional questions and applying new techniques to the study of fossil vertebrates. But another of Osborn's students and long-time associates, William King Gregory (1876–1970), became the premier figure in that area of investigation. Drawing on the facilities, opportunities, and emphasis on biological questions that existed at the DVP, Gregory developed a program of research on the functional morphology of fossil vertebrates.

216

Because of the intellectual and institutional context in which he operated, Gregory's research on problems of function and adaptation had significant consequences for vertebrate paleontology at the American Museum and elsewhere. In 1920, by virtue of close personal and professional ties to Osborn, Gregory became the head of the new Department of Comparative Anatomy at the American Museum. That opportunity, coupled with his ties to the DVP and his position as professor of vertebrate paleontology in the Zoology Department at Columbia, enabled Gregory to influence two generations of students in vertebrate paleontology and comparative anatomy. Through his positions at the American Museum and Columbia, he directed and contributed to a program of study that expanded the domain of questions, techniques, and understanding within vertebrate paleontology.

In addition to refining the understanding of the adaptation and evolution of fishes, reptiles, and amphibians, Gregory studied primates. Emphasizing the role played by habit, function, and change of function in the evolution of primates, Gregory put forth an influential interpretation of primate phylogeny in the 1920s. His ideas challenged Osborn's understanding of the relationship between humans and anthropoids. Gregory, like Matthew, attacked Osborn's theories and advanced a different interpretation of variation, evolution, and inheritance that had a bearing on George Gaylord Simpson's seminal work in the 1930s and 1940s.

Yet despite their different views, Gregory and Osborn developed the American Museum as a center for the study of fossil and recent primates. Osborn's interest in paleoanthropology was the impetus for Gregory's original investigations, and in spite of the divergence in their interpretations, Osborn encouraged Gregory's work. The two also maintained close personal and professional relations. As museum president Osborn provided resources that enabled Gregory to pursue such study and led others interested in paleoanthropology to become associated with the museum. Gregory's investigations were pursued within a context that linked him and his students to Osborn and Osborn's interests.

Background

Throughout his career, Gregory profited from his close ties to Osborn. Gregory began his undergraduate education at Columbia in 1897 and originally worked with Bashford Dean on the study of fishes. He took Osborn's courses in vertebrate morphology and evolution, and by 1900 he had shifted his emphasis to vertebrate paleontology. He was soon employed as one of Osborn's assistants in the DVP and helped with a number of administrative tasks as well as scientific work on Osborn's research projects. Osborn placed Gregory in charge of his library of vertebrate paleontology and made him editorial assistant for the new *American Museum Journal*. Gregory also worked on Osborn's monographs on sauropods and titanotheres.[2]

In contrast to Matthew, who was skilled in fieldwork and knowledgeable in geology and stratigraphy, Gregory was primarily a morphologist. As a student who acquired a fine knowledge of comparative vertebrate anatomy, and one who was willing to assist his mentor, he became a valued asset to Osborn. In his early years Gregory, in addition to working on Osborn's monographs, edited Osborn's *Evolution of the Mammalian Molar Teeth To and From the Tritubercular Type* (1907). He also assisted with Osborn's classes at Columbia. In 1909, when Osborn retired from teaching, he had Gregory appointed as his successor. Gregory, more than Matthew, had a loyalty to and close personal relationship with Osborn, though never as equals. Osborn was always *facile princeps* (clever master); Gregory, *fides achates* (faithful servant). Nevertheless, intellectual and personal ties bound Gregory and Osborn even when Gregory developed interpretations that challenged Osborn's work.[3]

Osborn's interest in problems of form and function fostered Gregory's work on problems of functional morphology. In his courses at Columbia, Osborn exposed Gregory and other students to those questions. In part, Osborn had developed an interest in functional questions from Cope, whose work suggested the importance of animal habits and motions in relation to adaptation. Probably more influential were the studies of the Russian paleontologist Vladimir Kovalevsky. In an 1892 address Osborn pointed to the educational value of Kovalevsky's approach to the study of fossil specimens: "If a student asks me how to study paleontology, I can do no better than to direct him to the 'Versuch einer natürlichen classification der fossilen Hufthiere,' out of date in its facts, thoroughly modern in its approach to ancient nature. This work is a model union of the detailed study of form and function with theory and the working hypothesis. It regards the fossil not as a petrified skeleton, but as moving and feeding; every joint and facet has meaning, each cusp a certain signficance."[4]

On occasion Osborn examined questions relating function to structure in his work. In a paper published in 1900 he claimed that among heavy mammals like elephants and uintatheres: "The straightening of the limb is an adaptation designed to transmit the increasing weight through a vertical shaft. Correlated with it are the shifting of the facets into the direct line of pressure and the alteration of their planes from an oblique to a right or horizontal angle with relation to the vertical shaft."[5] In his monograph on the titanotheres Osborn examined similar questions,[6] and he, Gregory, and Matthew held many discussions concerning the mechanics of how particular organs had operated and evolved.

Osborn also directed his associates to pursue investigations on problems of functional morphology. Although social and educational concerns underscored his interest, the problems of mounting fossil vertebrates as once-living organisms also posed scientific and technical questions. The mountings of *Apatosaurus, Diplodocus,* and other large vertebrates raised questions about animal pose and motion. As a result, DVP scientists, preparators, and artists began to concern themselves not merely with the study of skeletal hard parts but also with the analysis of the muscle and nervous systems of extinct vertebrates.

Matthew, then Osborn's principal assistant, played a leading role in that work. Writing to Osborn in January 1904, Matthew indicated that he, Charles Knight, Walter Granger, and others from the DVP were dissecting recent reptiles at the Bronx Zoo in order to understand the muscular system and locomotor apparatus of those organisms.[7] Years later, in an obituary article on Matthew, Gregory described that work more fully:

> During the years before 1905, while the skeleton of the huge *Brontosaurus* [*Apatosaurus*] was being removed from the matrix and restored and mounted by Adam Hermann and his assistants, Doctor Matthew studied the problems involved in the reconstruction and mounting. Before the limbs and girdles were mounted, he and Walter Granger dissected an alligator, marked the areas of origin and insertion of the limb muscles on the girdles and limb bones, and then identified as far as possible the corresponding areas on the bones of the *Brontosaurus*; finally, by means of scale drawings and paper strips representing the muscles, they endeavored to determine the course and direction of the principal muscle masses in so far as they would influence the posture of the limbs and girdles, especially the angulation of the elbows and knees. This was apparently the first application of the data of comparative myology to the mounting of an extinct animal and the studies that Matthew and Granger made at this time led eventually to further developments of those subjects of comparative myology and osteology by other workers in the Museum and elsewhere.[8]

Matthew's myological and osteological studies led him to analyze the structure, habits, and habitat of *Apatosaurus*. He defined it as an amphibious reptile whose massive limb and body weight required water as a buoying mechanism but whose long neck enabled it to wade to considerable depths and to forage for food among water plants or tree tops.[9]

Matthew's study of habits, pose, and motion among extinct vertebrates appeared primarily in popular articles that described exhibits.[10] Nevertheless, he employed comparative myology to examine functional questions and developed an approach that, as the quotation suggests, influenced Gregory.

Gregory, though not a part of the crew that dissected reptiles at the zoo, took up similar questions on *Apatosaurus* early in his career. Among his administrative and scientific duties in the DVP, Gregory supervised department artists who were working on Osborn's government monographs. The production of line drawings of specimens and reconstruction work fell within his purview. Traditionally, reconstruction involved determining the appearance and structure of organisms and developing appropriate illustrations. But for Osborn and the DVP it also meant making reconstructions out of plaster casts and clay models that served as prototypes for mounted skeletons.[11] Gregory directed DVP artist Erwin S. Christman's work along those lines. Much of Christman's and Gregory's work pertained to creating plaster reconstructions of titanotheres, but it also included reconstructions of sauropod dinosaurs.

As participants in the DVP effort to mount *Apatosaurus*, Gregory and Christman examined questions concerning the animal's pose, locomotion, and musculature. In 1901–2 Christman, under Gregory's direction, made a series of drawings depicting how the dinosaur might have walked. Illustrations from different perspectives indicated a concern for understanding the structure of the dinosaur limbs and shoulder girdle, how such structures could accommodate motion and the shifting of body weight, and the muscles involved in such functions.[12] Working closely with an artist and other scientists and preparators on that problem, Gregory recognized the importance of studying muscle systems, the relationship of muscles to skeletal structure, and the role that both muscle systems and skeletal structure played in animal locomotion. He addressed those questions in one of his first publications, a paper on the weight of *Apatosaurus*.[13]

Gregory and Functional Morphology

Gregory's interest in functional morphology led him to ask new questions and to employ new approaches. Seeking to understand how structures operated and why they varied among different organisms, Gregory at times drew upon interpretations from mechanics. In a 1912 paper on the principle of animal locomotion he claimed "that the limbs of quadrupeds are compound levers and that the relative lengths of the upper, middle and lower segments are adapted to specific loads, muscular powers, and speeds."[14]

Functional morphology also played a role in his efforts to classify and to reconstruct the phylogenies of vertebrate families. Gregory, like other morphologists of the late nineteenth and early twentieth centuries, sought to establish evolutionary relationships among organisms. But he maintained that an understanding of the adaptive purpose of characters was necessary in order to determine their phylogenetic or taxonomic value. The construction of phylogenies required not only a careful comparative examination of morphological characters but also an understanding of function and change of function. In his Ph.D. dissertation, "The Orders of Mammals" (1910), Gregory pointed to changes in habit as the means for explaining the taxonomic differences that separated marsupials and monotremes. He applied that to several other families of mammals as well.[15]

In order to understand adaptation and evolution, Gregory studied the impact of pose and motion on an organism's skeletal and muscular systems. In "The Orders of Mammals" he pointed to change of function as a means for explaining adaptations and divergent evolutionary trends. The *Cynodont*, an early marsupial, had diverged from monotremes because "owing to the assumption of semi-arboreal habits it lost the Monotreme characters of the shoulder girdle. . . . Improved climbing powers resulted from the atrophy of the episterium and procoracoid, the reduction of the coracoid, the pulling outward of the glenoid away from the middle line and the development of the prespinous fossa and its muscles."[16] Changes in habit and function that affected the organs of motion had resulted in changes in morphology and musculature. Gregory recognized that on the basis of myological analysis he could determine the evolution of particular structures, such as how the paired limbs of lower vertebrates had evolved from the lobate paired fins of primitive fish.[17] The analysis of how muscles and structural hard parts operated to affect the use, adaptation, and evolution of the locomotor apparatus became the hallmark of Gregory's work in comparative anatomy and vertebrate paleontology. It also became the basis for a research program in comparative myology and osteology that he directed at Columbia University and the American Museum.

A Program of Scientific Research

Valuable institutional resources contributed to Gregory's program of research on fossil and living vertebrates. In the 1890s Osborn had established cooperative relations among the American Museum, Columbia University, and the Bronx Zoo. Graduate students at Columbia had access to collections at the museum, and scientists and students working at the museum could study animals from the zoo.[18] Osborn had several graduate students who took advantage of those facilities, but such resources had particular significance for Gregory. His interest in determining homologies, reconstructing extinct organisms, and explaining the habits, functions, and adaptations of those organisms required the study of recent as well as fossil vertebrates. Gregory and his students, more than other vertebrate paleontologists, needed collections and laboratory facilities for dissecting recent organisms. Because the DVP and the zoo filled those needs only in part, Gregory looked to Osborn for additional support. In 1920 Osborn created a Department of Comparative Anatomy, designed for Gregory's researches and with Gregory as its head. It was a small department that included Gregory, S. H. Chubb, Harry Raven, Miles Conrad, and J. Dudley Morton. But it soon possessed its own collections and became a center of research on the functional morphology of fossil vertebrates.[19]

In contrast to Osborn, who pursued a multitude of administrative and scientific endeavors, Gregory devoted his attention to teaching and training students in vertebrate morphology and paleontology. Although he and his students made use of the DVP collections and personnel, they also pursued investigations that reflected the questions and methods Gregory considered important. Gregory and his students combined the paleontologist's emphasis on the study of skeletal hard parts with research in comparative vertebrate myology. Based on his earlier work, which suggested that an understanding of form and function would throw light on adaptation and evolution, Gregory realized that a systematic examination of how and why muscle activity influenced skeletal structure offered important research opportunities. Such study would explain the structure and use of parts among extinct vertebrates, advance the understanding of the evolution of specific muscular and skeletal systems, and provide new insights into evolutionary relationships and transformations.

In 1915 Gregory and his student L. A. Adams claimed that "the probable steps in the transformation of the reptilian into the mammalian condition could be obtained by a study of the muscles of the pterygoid region in existing reptiles and mammals." In addition, the transformation of reptilian jaw muscles into the ear muscles of mammals "might . . . be further elucidated by a careful reconstruction of the jaw muscles of *Cynognathus* and by a study of the muscles of the middle ear in mammals."[20] Research on vertebrate myology and osteology thus offered a means for determining homologies and reconstructing extinct organisms, though in a way that differed from the traditional approach of the paleontologist. Fossils generally included no remnants of musculature, but by studying the myology and osteology of analogous living organisms and establishing homologies with fossil vertebrates, scientists could make inferences about the muscular structure of extinct organisms. That became the backbone of Gregory's program of research.[21]

Much of the work done by Gregory and his students focused on the examination of transitional specimens. A 1918 study by Gregory and Charles L. Camp concentrated on reconstructing the primitive therapsid *Cynognathus* "because its girdles and limbs, while fundamentally reptilian, exhibit certain well marked modifications in the direction of the mammalian, and especially of the monotreme, type; so that it is fair to assume that the musculature of these parts was equally progressive toward the mammalian type."[22] The determination of homologies and the reconstruction of such a primitive organism could shed light on the structure and evolutionary divergence of early reptiles and mammals.

Gregory's students Alfred Sherwood Romer and Roy W. Miner examined transitional organisms that represented important stages in vertebrate evolution. Romer's work, which compared the skeletal structure of large series of fossil reptiles to living reptiles and mammals, refined the means for determining homologies and inferring muscular structure among extinct vertebrates. His work offered insights into the changes in myology and osteology necessary for the evolution of the locomotor apparatus in reptiles and early mammals. It also traced the evolution of mammalian muscle systems from earlier reptilian forms.[23] Miner's work on *Eryops* established the combined amphibian-reptilian structure of that specimen and provided the "key to the fundamental tetrapod musculature, and may be taken as a starting point for interpreting that of higher forms."[24] Integrating the study of osteology and myology, Gregory and his students went beyond earlier efforts to reconstruct both the musculature and skeletal systems of primitive vertebrates.

Gregory, and in later years Romer, drew upon studies in comparative myology and osteology to address questions of functional morphology.[25] The 1918 paper by Gregory and Camp, which had as its primary objective the reconstruction of *Cynognathus,* was also a study of the relationship between structure and function in a large number of vertebrates. Following a description of the muscle systems of vertebrates, Gregory and Camp offered a myological explanation for the differences in animal motion and pose. They noted that among small animals that do not raise the body high off the ground, the lifting of the foot or leg is produced by muscles running from the backbone to the knee and other muscles running from the pelvic region to the femur. But among quadrupeds and other large animals whose bodies are above the ground, the "muscles are reinforced by the greatly expanded gluteal mass," and require an expansion of the pelvic bone to support the gluteal muscles. More highly advanced organisms had functional needs and requirements that differed from those of other organisms and had developed different muscles and skeletal structures for controlling motion. The study of functional morphology could provide, as Gregory concluded, "an adaptational reason both for the reduction of the ilia and loosening of the sacrum in fully aquatic types, and for the opposite expansion of the ilium and extension of the sacrum in animals that hold the body well above the ground."[26]

Gregory also employed osteological and myological studies to investigate evolutionary questions. Based on the study of the locomotor apparatus, Gregory noted important structural differences among primitive reptiles and mammals. Among Permian reptiles the locomotor structure prevented the pelvis from moving too far to the left and presented an obstruction that affected pose and motion. Primitive mammals, however, had evolved a different pelvic structure in which the ilium was in front of the acetabulum and the pubis and ischium were behind and below it. According to Gregory, that arrangement served "to twist the pelvis and to prevent collapse when one limb is lifted." The change in pelvic structure also related to a forward turning of the femur that brought the animal's knees in toward the limbs and the feet close to the midline of the body. That arrangement allowed for the transmission of weight more directly through limbs in line with the knee joint. It also provided for a shift and expansion of the ilium. As Gregory noted, "the expanded gluteal and iliac muscles function as much to overcome the tendency to collapse when one foot is raised from the ground as to move the femur of the advancing limb."[27] Here Gregory not only explained the relationship of muscle and skeletal structure and function to animal motion but also defined a transformation of the reptilian pelvis to the mammalian pelvis. That change, which accounted for differences in the manner of pose and motion between early reptiles and more recent vertebrates, also pointed to a major evolutionary modification.

Gregory and the Study of Primates

Studies of fossil and recent vertebrates offered insights into evolution, but it was Gregory's research on primates that led him to investigate questions on the nature of the evolutionary process. Those studies, like his work on amphibians and reptiles, combined comparative examination of skeletal and myological systems with a concern for problems of functional morphology and evolution. Here too Gregory focused on animal habit and function, particularly motion. Gregory's research on primates, which occupied much of his attention after 1913, led him to develop a particular theory concerning the evolutionary relationship between men and anthropoids. That work, which established his reputation as a leading authority on paleoanthropology, also led him in the 1920s to oppose Osborn's understanding of evolution.

Gregory's work on primates reflected important influences occurring in paleoanthropology at the time. Most intriguing was the recent discovery of Piltdown, the complex of a fossilized human skull and ape-like canine teeth discovered in England in 1912. Gregory, along with Osborn, Matthew, and other leading scientists, discussed the validity of the specimen and its bearing on the evolutionary relationship between humans and apes.[28]

Developments within the DVP were perhaps even more influential in turning Gregory's attention to the study of primates. Osborn took up the study of paleoanthropology in the early 1910s, and it became a topic of priority for members of the DVP. Osborn probably suggested that Gregory write his first paper in paleoanthropology, a popular piece on Piltdown for the *American Museum Journal* in 1913. Around the same time, Gregory and McGregor became involved in the development of the Hall of the Age of Man. In addition, Granger and Matthew discovered fragments of the primitive lemur *Notharctus* in 1912 and turned to Gregory for assistance in describing the specimen. Provided with the opportunity to examine *Notharctus*, Gregory applied the same methods that he, Romer, and Miner had used in their analyses of fossil reptiles. He provided a detailed analysis of the myological and osteological structure of that organism and determined its classification and phylogeny.[29] Gregory's initial study classified *Notharctus* only in relationship to other early primates: lemurs, lorises, and tarsiers. But his interest in primates soon expanded, and in 1916 he published an analysis of the evolutionary relationship of humans, fossil hominids, and anthropoids.[30]

Gregory relied in part on comparative analysis of mammalian dentition to determine those evolutionary relationships. He argued that the tooth structure of several extinct anthropoids, particularly members of the genus *Dryopithecus*, had an important bearing on primate phylogeny. According to Gregory, the tooth structure of *Dryopithecus* demonstrated patterns found in the earliest anthropoids of the Lower Oligocene epoch. It was also "the fundamental ancestral pattern in the Orang, Gorilla, Chimpanzee and even Man, but it is more or less masked in each of these by secondary modifications." He concluded his 1916 study by claiming that different species of *Dryopithecus* had given rise to gorillas, chimpanzees, and possibly the fossil hominid *Pithecanthropus*. *Dryopithecus* was the stem form for the family Simiidae, while the genus *Sivapithecus* had an analogous position for the Hominidae. "Man and the anthropoids," Gregory maintained, "have been derived from a primitive anthropoid stock and . . . man's nearest existing relatives are the chimpanzee and gorilla."[31]

In developing the thesis of the anthropoid ape ancestry of humans, Gregory became a leading proponent of the brachiationist position: the doctrine that humans and anthropoids had evolved from a primitive arboreal ancestor. Based on his own research, as well as studies by the British scientists Sir Arthur Keith and Grafton Eliot Smith, Gregory claimed that "all the palaeontologic, zoologic and embryologic evidence supports the conclusion that from their first appearance the Primates as an order were thoroughly arboreal and that the terrestrial habits of the baboons and man are a later acquisiton."[32] He defined the gibbons as the primitive brachiators that, having developed a bipedal, erect posture, gave rise to man and the anthropoids. Without claiming that humans had descended from any living form of great ape, he held that because of the common heritage of brachiation an animal of ape-like morphology was the immediate ancestor to man.[33] Gregory was one of the first among American anthropologists or paleontologists to accept Raymond Dart's interpretation that *Australopithecus* provided documentary evidence demonstrating the evolutionary connection between humans and apes.[34]

Not everyone accepted Gregory's interpretation. Gerrit Miller, a prominent American mammalogist, maintained that although man and the apes shared a common ancestry, the human line of descent had branched off from a generalized primate stock.[35] Two other American scientists, Dudley J. Morton and Adolph Schultz, argued that the great apes were far too specialized to give rise to humans. They maintained that the Simiidae and Hominidae had evolved independently from a more primitive gibbonlike ancestor.[36] Nevertheless, Gregory's theory enjoyed some support in the 1920s and 1930s. That interpretation also highlighted his concern with functional morphology, specifically his emphasis that function and change of function are crucial for evolution.

Gregory's thesis rested on the concepts of habitus and heritage that he put forth to explain present day differences among related organisms. Heritage, according to Gregory, was the sum of an organism's characters that have persisted from earlier times. Heritage corresponded to the homologies that define an organism's evolutionary relationship to earlier forms. Habitus referred to the totality of characters that adapt it to any mode of life. Because changes in an organism's environment or habits could produce adaptations or secondary modifications, a habitus might mask its heritage. But a knowledge of form and function, along with a recognition of the difference between habitus and heritage, would throw light on major evolutionary transformations. Using the principles of heritage and habitus, Gregory defended his theory of man's ape ancestry.[37]

One of the most difficult problems for Gregory's interpretation concerned the differences in foot structure between humans and anthropoids. It was well known that anthropoids, unlike humans, possess an opposable hallux that enables them to grasp objects with the foot. Gregory had to account for that difference in order to establish a common heritage. Employing the evidence of myology and osteology, he argued that the human foot possesses "indelible traces of remote arboreal origin" and intimate morphological similarities to the anthropoid foot. Gregory also analyzed the weight distribution in the human and anthropoid foot. Among quadrupeds the main axis of weight distribution passes through the third or middle digit of the hind foot. In anthropoids and humans the axis of weight has shifted inward and passes between the great toe and the final digit.[38] Embryological evidence offered additional support. Adolph Schultz, an embryologist at Johns Hopkins University, claimed that the whole fetal foot recalls the anthropoid condition and differs widely from the adult foot.[39] Gregory thus brought together information from several lines of research to document the heritage of man and anthropoids.

Most important for Gregory was the argument from habitus. There were relatively few structural changes involved in the evolution of the gorilloid foot to the human foot, but Gregory contended that modifications in habits, function, and way of life had produced a major transformation. The transformation of a gorilloid form of foot into the human type was the result of differing conditions "namely the transformation of erectly sitting, brachiating quadrumana into erectly walking, plantigrade bipeds. When the Miocene ancestors of the Hominidae began to spend more time on the ground and less time in the trees it was perfectly natural that their powerful hallux should have been utilized as the main axis of the foot, instead of the weaker digits II, III, IV; because on rough forest ground the strongly grasping hallux with its powerful flexors and adductors would be almost as useful in maintaining the balance in the upright pose as it would be in the trees."[40]

The change from an arboreal to a terrestrial way of life did not immediately produce extensive morphological change. Gregory was describing the change that made a gorilloid foot with opposable hallux serviceable on the ground. But over time additional changes associated with a terrestrial existence occurred. Bipedal locomotion and changes in the ways of obtaining food produced structural modifications in the legs, feet, and arms that "resulted in a fully bipedal, cursorial type capable of invading the plains."[41] Keith, Morton, and others defined the skeletal and muscular changes that had occurred. Gregory used their studies to advance an argument that defined changes in habit, locomotion, and structure as the means for transforming an ape-like animal into a forerunner of man.

Changes in habit and use were also the factors that resulted in the evolution of man's upright posture. The habit of sitting upright, according to Gregory, conditioned the loss of the tail and produced structural changes in the backbone, thorax, and pelvis. It also freed the hands for prehensile uses and led to the evolution of brachiation. Gregory maintained that brachiation, or motion accomplished by swinging beneath the tree branches with the arms held above the head, "very probably took rise in the earliest anthropoids and has been carried to an extreme specialization in the excessively long-armed gibbon."[42]

Brachiation involved more than the development of a new means of locomotion. Gregory, drawing on the work of Keith, claimed that the evolution of brachiation also trained the arms in supination; improved the brain, eyes, and balancing mechanism; and led to the evolution of the human arrangement of the viscera.[43] Changes in habit and function, specifically motion, had led ape-like animals on the path to evolving structural characteristics that are essentially human. According to Gregory, only through a study of function and structure that combined myological and osteological analysis and emphasized the importance of habits and adaptations could scientists establish accurate phylogenies and develop a meaningful understanding of primate evolution.

Functional Morphology and the Evolution of Primates: Gregory vs. Osborn

Gregory's recognition of the importance of changes in habit and function influenced his views on the pattern and process of evolution. The study of the evolution of primates indicated marked changes, occasionally even

FIGURE 17. William King Gregory (neg. no. 411647)

reversals, in evolutionary trends. Gregory pointed out that because other scientists often overlooked or misunderstood such changes, discrepancies existed in the interpretation and reconstruction of the course of primate evolution. He noted as an example that, according to his interpretation, the evolution from *Propliopithecus* to *Pliopithecus* to gibbons entailed a reduction in the size of the third lower molar. But Guy Pilgrim, an English paleontologist who defined evolution in linear terms, refused to accept the idea that such a reduction could occur among organisms in the same line of descent. He, therefore, excluded specimens with a short third molar from the phylogeny of those with a long third molar.

To Gregory that was orthogenesis at its worst, and in 1916 he attacked Pilgrim's views:

Perhaps the majority of paleontologists of the present time who believe in orthogenesis, the irreversibility of evolution and the polyphyletic origin of families will assume that a short molar must keep on getting shorter, that it can never get longer and then again grow relatively shorter, and therefore that *Propliopithecus* with its extremely short third molar and *Dryopithecus* with its long m_3 are alike excluded from the ancestry of the Gorilla, in which there is a slight retrogression in length of m_3. After many years of reflection and constant study of the evolution of the vertebrates, however, I must conclude that "orthogenesis" should never mean solely that structures and races evolve in a certain direction, or toward a certain goal, only until the direction of evolution shifts toward some other goal. I believe that "irreversibility of evolution" means only that past changes irreversibly limit and condition future possibilities, and that, as a matter of experience, if an organ is once lost the same (homogenous) organ can never be regained, although nature is fertile in substituting imitations. But this does not mean, in my judgment, that if one tooth is smaller than its fellows it will in all cases continue to grow smaller.[44]

Gregory could not accept Pilgrim's deterministic understanding of evolution, which did not even allow for changes in the size of characters. Neither could he accept Pilgrim's phylogenetic interpretation: the idea that gorillas and chimpanzees were not descended from any species of *Dryopithecus* "but trace their origin on separate parallel lines to unknown proto-anthropoid stock that lived somewhere far back in the Lower Miocene."[45] Gregory defined *Dryopithecus* or a similar organism as the ancestor for several primate families, including the Simiidae and Hominidae. Unlike Pilgrim, Gregory emphasized the resemblances between humans and anthropoids and explained differences in terms of changes of habit and function. Such changes produced transformations among organisms in a single line of descent, and Gregory wholeheartedly embraced the idea of evolution as a divergent process.

While Gregory at first contrasted his views to those of Pilgrim and another British scientist, Frederick Wood Jones,[46] eventually he also criticized Osborn's work. Osborn had emphasized morphological and taxonomic differences in all his studies, including his work on the evolution of primates. Writing on the relationship between the modern races of mankind, Osborn had expressed the views of a typologist and polygenist, one who maintained that human races were separate species and the product of separate lines of evolutionary descent.[47] Those ideas reflected Osborn's polyphyletic understanding of mammalian evolution. They also fit well with his support of eugenics and immigration restriction.

Gregory experienced some frustration because he realized that Osborn's evolutionary ideas were in part a manifestation of social and political beliefs. During Osborn's lifetime Gregory helped to maintain the American Museum as the center for the Galton Society, a eugenics organization, and as the meeting place for the 1921 and 1932 international conferences on eugenics. But Gregory, unlike Osborn and Madison Grant, perceived the Galton Society as a center for the discussion of scientific questions pertaining to race, not as an organization for promoting a political and social agenda. In 1930, after pointing out that he did not share Osborn's and Grant's "generous impulse to labor for the protection of this country against the invasion of 'barbarians,'" he resigned as secretary of the organization. In 1935 he quit the society entirely because of its overt racial and political objectives.[48]

In his own work Gregory did not use science to address social and political problems directly. He did subscribe to taxonomic hierarchies, and in popular works, such as *Our Face from Fish to Man*, he gave a privileged position to the branch of the evolutionary tree leading to humans. He also developed in the museum a Hall of the Natural History of Man, which in its mural, "Man Among the Primates," depicted the white race as the furthest removed in evolutionary terms from anthropoids and early hominids (figure 18).[49] Yet that hall and its wall painting on the museum's second floor conveyed a message different from Osborn's Hall of the Age of Man on the fourth floor. According to Gregory the human species had evolved from primates, and all races belonged to the species *Homo sapiens*. From his perspective, attempting to establish permanent differences between races on the basis of physical, behavioral, or cultural characteristics presented difficulties.[50] Gregory believed in racial differences as a legitimate topic of scientific investigation and his views reinforced existing prejudices. But he did not directly employ science to promote social and political objectives.

Osborn's views, according to Gregory, also reflected his religious beliefs. Osborn's work in the 1910s and early 1920s distinguished between modern races and denied a close evolutionary relationship between humans and fossil hominids. Beginning around 1925 Osborn explicitly sought to undermine the theory of man's ape ancestry. In such works as *Man Rises to Parnassus* (1927) he maintained that archaeological evidence

FIGURE 18. Wall Painting of Man Among the Primates
(neg. no. 315595)

from the Red Crag deposit in southwestern England suggested the presence of intelligent human life as early as the Pliocene. On that basis Osborn argued that humans had evolved from a hypothetical "Dawn Man" ancestor of the Eocene epoch, which was distinctly separate from the simian line of evolution.[51]

But, as Gregory realized, social and religious considerations influenced Osborn's interpretation. Following World War I Osborn became distressed over the advance of materialism and the demise of old-time religion and old-time Americanism. In the 1920s Osborn opposed William Jennings Bryan's fundamentalist attack on evolution, largely because he had spent a lifetime trying to reconcile science with religion. In 1923 Osborn, along with many other prominent scientists, signed a statement maintaining that scientific research supported religion.[52] Osborn's evolutionary theory could be reconciled with religion because he maintained that organic change proceeded in definite directions and embodied plan and purpose. But in the wake of the Scopes Trial and declining "civilization," Osborn wanted to make the point more directly by removing "the myth and bogey of ape-man ancestry."[53]

Gregory condemned Osborn's views. In a lengthy letter to his British colleague D. M. S. Watson, Gregory complained that Osborn's dawn man theory stemmed directly from his participation in the Fundamentalist controversy. Osborn, Gregory claimed, was simply seeking to make peace with religious believers, and the dawn man theory had no real basis in fact. Gregory placed no stock in religious explanations and was an outspoken critic of antievolutionists, whom he satirically referred to as "pithecophobiacs." Osborn's work disturbed Gregory precisely because it gave excellent ammunition to the antievolutionist cause.[54]

Gregory also pointed to scientific problems inherent in the dawn man theory. Osborn, in his evolutionary studies of horses, titanotheres, and proboscideans, had emphasized morphological differences. His commitment to a polyphyletic interpretation of evolution was based upon establishing such differences as the foundation for taxonomic splitting. He had employed that approach in *Men of the Old Stone Age*, where he differentiated hominids on the basis of physical and cultural characteristics and claimed that "the lines of descent of the races of the Old Stone Age consisted of a number of entirely separate branches."[55]

Osborn applied those distinctions with greater force to the relationship between humans and anthropoids. In a series of papers published between 1927 and 1930, Osborn defined morphological, functional, and behavioral characteristics that he claimed had long distinguished the Hominidae from the Simiidae. He argued that those differences demonstrated that humans and apes had evolved from separate families and in distinct biogeographical regions. He opposed the hypothesis of an arboreal ancestry for man on the basis that such a mode of existence and locomotion had resulted in structures that could never characterize humans. According to Osborn, a long period of brachiating had produced a lengthening of the arms and shortening of the legs that changed the foot into a handlike structure and the hand into a hook. The last point was especially significant: "The brachiating hand of the ape was used as a hook—apes do not grasp a branch with the fingers and thumb but hook the whole hand over the branch, as trapeze workers do today—and the thumb was therefore a grave danger. If man had gone through a prolonged period of brachiating in the branches of trees he would have lost his thumb."[56] Humans, however, possessed an opposable thumb that was all-important in the tool-making process, and Osborn was convinced that primate evolution could not yield such a thumb. The human foot, adapted for running, was markedly different from the foot structure of primates. In addition, differences in brain capacity and attendant psychological and behavioral characteristics most definitely separated humans from apes.

Osborn relied on environmental and cultural arguments to support his case. Human races had evolved independently from "the Hominidae, [who were] ground living, cursorial, alert, capable of tool-making, and living in a relatively open country on the high plateaus and plains of northern Asia." Apes, however, belonged to a distinct family that had lived in tropical forests and were "brachiating, sluggish, and incapable of tool-making." Osborn's commitment to typology, taxonomic splitting, and deterministic evolution, precluded the possibility that one family could ever have evolved from the other. His views on biogeography, particularly his belief in the Asiatic origin of mankind, reinforced that commitment.[57]

Osborn's views directly contradicted Gregory's, and not surprisingly Gregory struck out at the dawn man theory. For personal reasons Gregory had reservations about attacking Osborn, but the challenge to his many years of research, the glaring weaknesses in Osborn's work, and the wide dissemination of Osborn's views led him to criticize Osborn's interpretation. Gregory maintained that Osborn had no concept of the importance of change of habit and function for evolution. Osborn, he stated, had "a total inability to recognize that primitive brachiation is the entire key to the immediately prehuman habits."[58] And Osborn did not understand the crucial distinction between habitus and heritage. As a result, he had incorrectly interpreted contemporary differences between men and apes as evidence of permanent dissimilarities.

In an effort to refute Osborn's ideas, Gregory turned to the morphological evidence and functional explanations that formed the foundation for his interpretation of primate phylogeny. At meetings of the Galton Society in 1928, he and J. H. McGregor amassed evidence documenting the relationship of humans to apes and discussed the data with Osborn.[59] In scientific meetings and published papers, Gregory turned again and again to the evidence of the feet, hands, and dentition that demonstrated intimate similarities between humans and apes. He employed the arguments from functional morphology and pointed out that changes in habits had conditioned profound changes in the use and structure of parts. The debate between the two men was carried on in newspapers, journals, and even in the displays in their two different halls in the American Museum. Despite the mass of evidence that Gregory presented and the widespread support for his position within the scientific community, Osborn never altered his belief in the dawn man theory. Virtually no one else, however, accepted his interpretation.[60]

Gregory attacked not only Osborn's dawn man theory but the entire theoretical structure upon which it rested. Osborn, according to Gregory, had uncritically transferred his understanding of mammalian evolution to the evolution of primates. That had resulted in a misinterpretation about the rates of evolutionary change. Osborn, applying evidence from perissodactyl evolution to primate evolution, claimed that if it had taken over sixty million years to produce slight differences in dentition between horses and tapirs, an equal length of time was required to produce the differences between humans and chimpanzees.[61] Gregory refuted that argument. He had done a great deal of work on Osborn's titanothere monograph and on paleoanthropology, and he knew that the structural characteristics of humans and apes were more variable than those that distinguished horses and tapirs. He also knew from morphological, embryological, and physiological evidence that humans and apes were more alike than horses and tapirs. Therefore, rates of evolutionary change could not accurately be applied from one to another.[62]

Gregory used the evidence from perissodactyls and primates to criticize Osborn's interpretation of the pattern of evolutionary trends. For years Osborn had reinforced his commitment to orthogenesis with a belief in the irreversibility of evolution. Referring to the work of Louis Dollo, the Belgian paleontologist who had defined the law of irreversibility, Osborn argued that for remote ancestors to be considered part of a line of descent, they had to exhibit unmistakable signs of the characters evident in their descendants. Those that did not exhibit such characters he placed in separate lineages. Osborn employed his interpretation of Dollo's law to shore up his commitment to polyphyleticism and linear change.[63] But as Gregory pointed out, Osborn's "viewpoint is apt to lead to a sort of *emboitment* hypothesis in which the visible characters of the late forms are mentally imputed even to their very remote, undifferentiated ancestors. For reasons now to be set forth, it seems very likely that Professor Osborn has unconsciously adopted this *emboitment* hypothesis when he demands that in the very remote Eocene ancestors of man the relative lengths of the fore and hind limbs and the relative length, mobility, and opposability of the thumb must clearly approach those of modern man."[64]

Gregory claimed that Osborn had misinterpreted Dollo's principle of irreversibility and was reading the present into the past. Dollo, according to Gregory, had realized that irreversibility did not exclude changes in the size or proportions of characters or reversions in the evolution of characters. His law maintained only that an organ once lost is never regained; it did not deny changes in function or form among organisms in a line of descent.[65] For Gregory it was precisely those kinds of transformations in habit or function that explained primate evolution. Refuting Osborn's interpretation of irreversibility, Gregory also rejected the commitment to orthogenesis, extensive parallelism, polyphyleticism, and taxonomic inflation that lay at the heart of Osborn's work. Osborn's interpretation yielded bushlike phylogenies of parallel, rectilinear lines of descent. Gregory's concept of the pattern of evolution emphasized an ever-branching, diverging tree of life.[66]

Gregory also rejected Osborn's understanding of variation, inheritance, and the causes of evolution. Osborn had neglected and denied the occurrence of widespread variation in mammalian evolution. Gregory emphasized the extent and importance of variability among primates. Variation among the primates, including man, was "far more plastic" than it was among horses and tapirs. Comparing "various human races we shall find a far wider range of variability among them, while in even a small collection of orang and chimpanzee teeth the range of variability will be astonishingly wide."[67]

Environmental and geological changes operated on an unstable germ plasm to produce variation among men and the anthropoids, according to Gregory. Changing opportunities and hereditary instability provided for variation and evolution, but not in a deterministic sense. Gregory claimed instead that "my own studies on the phylogeny of fossil and recent mammals lead me to visualize evolution as follows: (a) a growing and very plastic process with occasional change or reversal in the trend of reduction or enlargement of parts; (b) with occasional change in the direction of function; (c) successive ancestors with growing or changing potentiality, opening out or restricting itself at each horizon; (d) variability irregular, sometimes very large; (e) chance universal and primordial; predetermination derived and secondary, solely a result of historical growth."[68] Osborn had denied that chance or random variation played any role in evolution. But for Gregory, as for Darwin, random variation was the grist for the mill of evolution. Orthogenesis as defined in Osborn's interpretation was merely a derived feature of little practical or theoretical significance.

Gregory, like Matthew, had some knowledge of the work being done in early twentieth-century genetics. Although he had personal difficulties with T. H. Morgan, Gregory recognized the importance of research being done in experimental biology. He understood that chance and law were not mutually exclusive concepts. As he once pointed out, "Mendel's law is assuredly associated with the Curve of Probability, and I do not see how 'chance' can be eliminated in the long run from matings, and hence from predictable probabilities of inheritance."[69] Gregory was not fully conversant with the research being done in genetics, but he understood that genetic mutations, which he identified with random, heritable variations, were central to the evolutionary process.

He also believed there could be a reconciliation between work in paleontology and genetics. Writing to the British naturalist W. P. Pycraft in 1936, Gregory noted that "the pressure of populations and other aspects of Natural Selection play an important role both in enforcing standardization and in changing standards. Assuredly the external environment sets conditions to which those who dwell in it must conform. Also, at least some of our leading geneticists (e.g., Morgan, Jennings, Conklin) have always insisted that the final results are produced by the reaction of forces in the germ plasm with those in the cytoplasm. I can not see that there is any conflict between sound work in genetics, paleontology, taxonomy, and comparative anatomy."[70] Although Gregory did not incorporate genetics into his work, his interpretation of evolution provided a foundation on which paleontologists and anatomists could build bridges to biology.

As the letter to Pycraft indicates, Gregory recognized that natural selection operated on random variations to produce descent with modification. He rarely discussed the causal mechanisms of evolution, but Gregory did adopt "the principle that the natural selection of heritable variations (mutations of the geneticists) conserves and integrates originally independent variables and tends to eliminate aberrant or 'fortuitous' variations and lethals that lie too far to one side of the curve."[71] Gregory did not regard natural selection as an all-sufficient mechanism that pro-

duced any or all combinations of evolutionary change. Habits and existing patterns that integrated structure and function, what he termed
organic designs or the basic patents in nature, conditioned or limited the
evolutionary changes that could occur.[72]

He often discussed evolution in the context of adaptation, and at times
his language smacked of teleology and obscured his commitment to Darwinism. Nevertheless, as he told the South African paleontologist Robert
Broom, natural selection produced adaptation and evolution:

"Planning" is simply the result of experience read backward and projected into
the future. To me the "purposive" action of a beehive is simply the summation
and integration of its units, and Natural Selection has put higher and higher
premiums on the most "purposeful" integration. It is the same way (to me) in the
evolution of the middle ear, the steps in the Cynodonts (clearly shown by me in
1910 and by you later in Oudenodon) make it easier to see how such a wonderful
device as the middle ear could arise without any predetermination or human-like
planning, and in fact in the good old Darwinian way, if only we admit that as the
"twig is bent the tree's inclined" and that each stage conserves the advantages of
its predecessors. . . . The simple idea that planning is only experience read backward and combined by selection in suitable or successful combinations takes the
mystery out of Nature and out of men's minds.[73]

By 1935 Gregory had defined his views on variation, evolution, and
inheritance, although not in a systematic, comprehensive manner. On the
basis of his interest in functional morphology, he looked to animal habits,
functions, and changes of function as the means for explaining the evolutionary divergence of humans and anthropoids. Changes in ways of life
and modes of locomotion, principally brachiation and later ter-
restrialism, resulted in changes in habits, functions, and structures that
characterized primate evolution. Emphasizing the importance of habit
and function Gregory repudiated Osborn's interpretation of primate
phylogeny and his entire theory of evolution. Gregory's explanation of
the pattern and process of evolution, the significance and extent of random variations, and the relevance of genetics for understanding those
phenomena offered a new interpretation to Alfred Sherwood Romer,
Edwin H. Colbert, Horace Wood, and others among the younger generation of vertebrate paleontologists and comparative anatomists whom he
taught.[74]

Gregory's work also influenced Simpson, although perhaps not as
much as Matthew's did. Simpson thought highly of Gregory's ideas on
cusp rotation and concresence in molar teeth, and he once claimed that
Gregory's work on the evolution of fish skulls was a "constant source of

inspiration."[75] In 1936 Gregory invited Simpson to contribute a paper to a symposium on supraspecific variation. Simpson later claimed that the topic was new to him and the paper hard to construct but that it resulted in one of his "door-opening" works on evolutionary theory. He also claimed that Gregory's views on evolutionary rates as defined in a 1947 paper "Monotremes and the Palimpsest Theory" were influential.[76] Gregory and Matthew, through their work in systematics as well as in their views on evolutionary questions, became important models who laid out new approaches and interpretations for the next generation of vertebrate paleontologists.

Gregory, Osborn, and Paleoanthropology at the American Museum

Although Gregory and Osborn debated and disagreed over paleoanthropology and evolutionary theory, their differences did not mar personal relations nor did they disrupt research at the American Museum. On the contrary, Osborn actively encouraged Gregory's work in those areas. Prior to a forum on paleoanthropology at the American Philosophical Society in 1927, Gregory informed Osborn he felt compelled to dissent from his mentor's views. At the top of Gregory's note Osborn wrote back: "Delighted to have you do this—see you in Philadelphia."[77] Osborn, though no doubt interested in presenting and defending his own interpretation, had also encouraged his students and associates to examine evolutionary problems. The study of those "broad philosophical questions" was the heart and soul of biology for Osborn. Gregory's interpretations differed radically from Osborn's, but his views reflected Osborn's interest in promoting scientific research on theoretical questions at the DVP. Osborn could, and did, view the work of his students and associates as redounding to his credit.

Gregory's interest in paleoanthropology and the resources at his command influenced a number of other scientists to pursue research in that field at the American Museum. Some were graduate students at Columbia. Herbert O. Elftmann and Harriet Waterman, for example, both examined pelvic structure and function in an attempt to define pose and motion among fossil and recent mammals.[78] Dudley J. Morton, a physician at Yale Medical School, joined the faculty at Columbia's College of Physicians and Surgeons soon after Gregory established his department at the museum. Morton focused his attention on the study of foot structure and function, and he differed from Gregory in his interpretation of primate phylogeny and human evolution. But as a research associate in the museum's Department of Comparative Anatomy, Morton worked closely with Gregory, and the latter's emphasis on the analysis of habit, function, and change of function influenced the methodology that Morton employed and the issues that his work addressed.[79] Gregory coauthored many papers on the study of fossil hominids and human evolution with the New York dentist Milo Hellman. In the early 1930s M. F. Ashley Montagu, another scientist interested in anatomy and paleoanthropology, took courses with Gregory and worked in association with Gregory's program at the museum.[80]

Osborn's interest reinforced Gregory's and helped make the museum a center for research on paleontological and evolutionary issues pertaining to humans and other primates. Osborn's work in paleoanthropology, as in biogeography and the study of evolution and inheritance, was based on research done by others and was condemned and criticized by many. Yet because of his power and position and his enthusiasm for the subject, Osborn was able to bring together many from within the museum and elsewhere to work on paleoanthropology.

His studies had benefited from the work of many museum scientists, most notably Nels C. Nelson who became a prominent figure in early twentieth-century anthropology and archeology.[81] Osborn also received assistance from Columbia University colleagues J. H. McGregor and Frederick W. Tilney, a faculty member in the College of Physicians and Surgeons who studied the skull and brain structure of fossil hominids. In the 1920s Osborn obtained money from a wealthy associate, James Arthur, for an annual endowed lecture on human evolution. In 1932 Osborn chose Tilney, whom he had already made a research associate of the museum, to deliver that lecture.[82] The studies by Morton, Tilney, and McGregor never commanded the international reputation of Gregory's work. Nor did the museum rival the programs in physical anthropology that Aleš Hrdlička and E. A. Hooton established at the United States National Museum and Harvard University respectively.[83] But Osborn's active interest in paleoanthropology led him to encourage and make resources available at the museum for research, education, and exhibition work in that field.

Gregory's work, important in its own right, was accomplished within a particular environment: an institution that combined economic, social, and scientific support with a well-defined set of research objectives and interests. And his work in functional morphology and primatology was in part a consequence of the institution that Osborn had done so much to create. The American Museum provided the money, the students, and the research materials that in no small part contributed to Gregory's success.

Equally important was the emphasis on the study of biological questions pertaining to vertebrate paleontology. That Gregory was led to pursue the study of functional morphology, to undertake research on fossil and living primates, and to go beyond the description and classification of specimens to address questions of evolution, variation, and inheritance reflected the intellectual influences operating within the American Museum. Osborn and Matthew initially defined the questions that Gregory addressed and the techniques he adopted. In addition, their sustained discussions, evaluations, and analyses of those problems over a period of almost thirty years had a continuing impact on Gregory's interpretations. Gregory, like Matthew, did not adopt the social and political objectives that interested Osborn, and he advanced a new and different interpretation of evolution that seriously challenged Osborn's views. But despite those differences Gregory and Osborn promoted research and public education on human evolution at the museum. They also maintained the fruitful relationship between the museum and Columbia University. Working in the context that Osborn had done so much to create, Gregory developed methods and interpretations that sustained the American Museum as a leading center for scientific research in vertebrate paleontology and related fields.

10 The Osborn Legacy: Remnants and Reversals

In the first third of the twentieth century, Henry Fairfield Osborn had a powerful impact on American vertebrate paleontology. At the American Museum, he created a flourishing program in what was a marginal field of scientific research. More than that, he developed a program that dominated American vertebrate paleontology in almost all respects. Yet Osborn's successes eventually brought problems. His program prepared the way for reversals both at the museum and in vertebrate paleontology.

At the American Museum, Osborn created a program that was ambitious and in many respects successful. In part that was due to the financial and political support he received from Jesup, Morgan, and others. In addition, Osborn was a successful organizer, administrator, and promoter. At Princeton and later at the American Museum, he demonstrated not only an ability to recognize important research problems but also to understand the social and educational objectives of the administrators of those institutions. He effectively mobilized resources and organized and directed colleagues and assistants to carry out the necessary work on the projects he deemed important. The combination of his scientific interests, social connections, and administrative abilities for envisioning and supervising work on a wide variety of projects enabled Osborn to establish a dominant institutional and intellectual position in American vertebrate paleontology. At the museum he fulfilled personal objectives including undermining Marsh and sustaining the legacy of Cope. More importantly, he established a department that, in terms of expeditions, collections, displays, or almost any other category, was the leading program of its kind in the United States, if not the world.

242

Osborn had an influence in changing the character of the science. At the museum, he provided assistants with opportunities that had not always been readily accessible. The museum offered opportunities for fieldwork and laboratory work on a large scale. Through the connections he established with Columbia and the Bronx Zoo, Osborn made additional research and educational opportunities available to his assistants. He also developed projects that provided a number of scientists, artists, and preparators with the means to gain recognition for their work and to structure their careers, although he did so largely for the purposes of promoting his own work and career. As an administrator with a multiplicity of commitments, he did not have time to do the laborious work in vertebrate paleontology, and a large, diversified corps of assistants contributed substantially to furthering his personal ambitions. Osborn's efforts were no different from what had been occurring in other fields for years. But in the United States vertebrate paleontology was different from most other fields; it was a science that depended on entrepreneurs, and as a result it was subject to their whims and wishes.[1] In contrast to Cope and Marsh, Osborn helped develop research and career opportunities for assistants as well as congenial relations among competing institutions.

Osborn expanded the domain of research for American vertebrate paleontologists. Enthusiastic backing from his wealthy and powerful friends enabled Osborn to create a program that pursued paleontological activities on an international scale. Although Princeton took the lead in developing a major expedition to South America in the late 1890s, Osborn and the American Museum eventually went much further in establishing an international presence. His interest in biogeography, biostratigraphy, and correlation spurred Osborn, hence his department, to encompass the world in a paleontological sense. As a result of his preoccupation with exploration, a function of imperialist ambition as well as upper-class anxiety, the museum undertook expeditions on a scale unmatched by any other institution. The discoveries of Cope and Marsh attracted European interest. Osborn equaled their efforts, but in addition he directed American interests outward by sending paleontologists to analyze fauna and formations throughout the world.

Osborn also helped make the construction of public displays a standard feature of vertebrate paleontology. Although fossils had been displayed in museums and public shows throughout the nineteenth century, Osborn was the first American paleontologist to promote large, lifelike exhibits on a systematic basis. He also employed a multiplicity of genres. In addition to mounted specimens of extinct animals in active poses, he directed assistants to develop interpretive charts, murals, and sculptured miniatures of extinct animals. Following the development of innovative techniques for displaying fossil mammals in the mid-1890s, the DVP produced massive displays of dinosaurs and fossil hominids. Although Osborn was not alone in putting mounted skeletons on display in the late 1890s, he helped initiate those efforts. By the early twentieth century many American natural history museums had large skeletal mounts, murals, and other means for portraying fossil vertebrates.

Osborn succeeded in institutionalizing his interest in a wide range of scientific problems related to the study of fossil vertebrates. In the early twentieth century, when questions concerning evolution became increasingly uninteresting to academic biologists, Osborn promoted the study of those problems through his own work and the work of his assistants. In part the pursuit of evolutionary questions was a result of his intellectual influence; it was also a consequence of his power and authority. By virtue of his social status, reputation, and role in the museum, Osborn instructed assistants to pursue projects that captured his interest and attention. Paleontologists at the American Museum, like their counterparts at other institutions, devoted much of their attention to fossil systematics. But it is not coincidental that in New York, Matthew, Gregory, and later George Gaylord Simpson and Edwin H. Colbert published much more on problems of inheritance, evolution, and geographical distribution than did their colleagues elsewhere.

Yet Osborn's efforts bred institutional as well as intellectual problems. The vast, multifaceted program he constructed was dependent on support provided by trustees and other wealthy friends. During his years as museum president, Osborn succeeded in tripling New York City's contribution to the museum's maintenance fund, but money for new programs, exhibits, and major expeditions came from patrons. Many among the rich and powerful who supported Osborn's programs in the 1910s and 1920s were hit hard by the Depression. In the 1930s they could not continue to contribute to Osborn's projects.[2] By relying heavily on donations from New York elites, Osborn and the museum had not obtained money from other sources. Foundations, which became major benefactors of American scientific research in the 1920s, did not support the museum's programs. John D. Rockefeller personally contributed to the Central Asiatic Expeditions, but the Rockefeller Foundation did not. In the mid-1920s the Galton Society applied to the Laura Spelman Rockefeller Memorial for funds to conduct research on Australian aborigines. But when Beardsley Ruml realized that Osborn had supported his own interests by drawing liberally on the large private research fund J. P. Morgan had created, foundation money was not forthcoming.[3]

Osborn's program was highly personalized. For forty years he relied on the support of trustees and wealthy associates, men who were close personal friends and who shared his interests. By the early 1930s, however, that support began to wane. In 1933, after twenty-five years in office, Osborn was pressured to resign the museum presidency. While he still tried to rely on personal friendships, enthusiasms, and rhetoric, Osborn had difficulty convincing the museum's leaders to provide him with money from the Morgan fund to complete his study of the Proboscidea.[4] In 1942 a management review of the museum confirmed what many had suspected for years: not only had Osborn's program received special financial and administrative favors but also Osborn had tapped into the Jesup and Morgan funds in ways that were not completely legitimate.[5] By the 1930s trustees, administrators, and scientists were interested in an institution that was well organized and efficiently run, not a museum that catered to the special interests of one individual or a small clique.

Trustees and administrators reacted against the museum's scientific and educational emphases that also reflected Osborn's personal interests and enthusiasms. The 1942 management survey written by Clark Wissler, the former curator of anthropology, pointed out that under Osborn the museum had become overcommitted to programs that emphasized preservation and evolution and to the construction of huge dioramas that attracted public attention but had no teaching value.[6] Huge sums were expended to promote expeditions to sustain ethnic vigor or to substantiate particular scientific interpretations. Displays demonstrating the evolution of horses or titanotheres and the construction of the entire Hall of the Age of Man were expensive efforts dedicated to reifying Osborn's views. While few explicitly objected to those interpretations, a number of museum leaders seriously questioned the continued allocation of resources to sustain such efforts. In 1942 the new museum president, A. E. Parr, declared that evolution was no longer a significant field of investigation and dissolved the Department of Vertebrate Paleontology. That measure was only temporary and was a reaction to the excesses of the Osborn era. When a new Department of Geology and Paleontology was established a few years later, it had less priority, less money, and a smaller staff than it had in Osborn's time.[7] The halls and displays that Osborn had constructed remained, not only because they were popular but also because the museum had little interest in allocating money or manpower to revamp them or disassemble them.

Osborn's scientific views also engendered notable reversals. Osborn emphasized the significance of theoretical problems and directed assistants to examine those issues, but few accepted his emphases or interpretations. By the 1930s his outright rejection of genetics and experimental biology was no longer viable, and many scientists had distanced themselves from the hereditarian eugenics of the 1910s and 1920s.[8] Matthew, Gregory, and McGregor realized that Osborn's dawn man theory was little more than an effort to sustain religious and social values. Gregory strongly disagreed with his mentor's interpretation, and Matthew noted that Osborn was "playing ducks and drakes with his great scientific reputation by writing this sort of drivel."[9] Those men rejected Osborn's understanding of variation, evolution, and inheritance, and they challenged the system of classification and interpretation of evolutionary trends that characterized his work. Younger paleontologists also criticized Osborn. Alfred Sherwood Romer and Glenn Jepsen attacked his theory of aristogenesis as well as his bushlike phylogenies. The English zoologist Julian Huxley dissented from Osborn's orthogenetic views and in the early 1940s advanced an explanation for the increase in size of titanothere horns based on allometry and relative growth.[10] Students of the next generation realized the need to reinterpret Osborn's scientific work and to divorce themselves from the personal and political excesses that characterized his program.

To an extent, Osborn's ideas exacerbated the scientific and institutional isolation of vertebrate paleontology in the United States. That vertebrate paleontology was a marginal field of study by the early twentieth century was not due to Osborn or any one individual but was a consequence of the changing structure of American science and new conceptual and methodological developments occurring in the biological sciences. However, Osborn's deep and long-standing differences with T. H. Morgan and other proponents of experimental biology exacerbated the problem.

In Germany, where Morgan's chromosomal theory of inheritance met with resistance, the study of evolution was not subsumed by genetics. Paleontologists continued to examine evolution, and their work was taken seriously by other scientists. German paleontologists, like Americans, were for the most part concentrated in museums, but their institutional separation was not compounded by intellectual isolation.[11] In the United States, however, Morgan and Osborn condemned each other's methods and interpretations. Morgan's personal contempt for Osborn extended to the field of vertebrate paleontology, and he discouraged his students from doing work in that subject or in anatomy. Osborn directed his students and associates to stay away from Morgan's brand of experimental biology. In the 1920s Gregory was advising prospective paleontology students to apply to Columbia through the Geology, not the Zoology, Department. Thus, they would not be subjected to Morgan and the battery of genetics courses he demanded of any zoology graduate student.[12] Because of the status of both Osborn and Morgan, that controversy had consequences beyond Columbia or New York City, and it only added to the marginal status of vertebrate paleontology.

Not until the 1940s, when George Gaylord Simpson applied the findings of population genetics to the data of the fossil record, was vertebrate paleontology integrated into modern biology. In *Tempo and Mode in Evolution* (1944), Simpson refuted the older neo-Lamarckian and orthogenetic interpretations, including Osborn's, and explained evolution in terms of the natural selection of genetic mutations within populations. He also abandoned the hostility toward genetics that had characterized Osborn's work. His work was well received by biologists, and Simpson emerged as one of the architects of the new evolutionary synthesis.[13]

Ironically, Simpson's work was fostered by the institution Osborn had created, but his interpretation helped eclipse Osborn's views on the process and pattern of evolution. Although Simpson was educated at Yale, he took up the analysis of evolution, geographical distribution, and inheritance during his years in the DVP. Simpson's interest in those questions did not stem directly from Osborn but reflected the resources and emphases that Osborn had built into his program in vertebrate paleontology. The American Museum provided good opportunities for fieldwork as well as fine collections, notably the large and varied collection of fossil horses that played an important role in Simpson's arguments in *Tempo and Mode*. The DVP, as a reflection of Osborn's interests and enthusiasms, was characterized by a concern with theoretical questions. Osborn's fascination with evolution and related issues influenced Matthew, Gregory, and later Simpson to pursue those problems. In doing so they developed approaches and interpretations that supplanted Osborn's. It is not surprising that the figure who played the most important role in transforming the understanding of the fossil record came out of the DVP. But Osborn's assistants employed his departmental resources and pursued his interests in ways that would eventually undermine his work.

Osborn's legacy is ambiguous. In certain respects it is easy to dismiss him as a pompous and rather ridiculous figure whose interpretations had little or no influence. His status and authority derived largely from his connections to wealthy and powerful New Yorkers. His scientific interpretations failed to incorporate the leading conceptual and methodological developments of the day and were influenced by social and political values. Yet he played an important role in developing early twentieth-century American vertebrate paleontology. Osborn, particularly in his later years, was a bloated, egotistical figure whose views required reinterpretation; nevertheless he established the institutional foundations and promoted the scientific research that would effect that reinterpretation.

Notes

Introduction

1. Charles Schuchert to William Diller Matthew, 27 February 1905, Charles Schuchert Correspondence, Archives, Department of Vertebrate Paleontology, American Museum of Natural History.
2. David Hammack, *Power and Society: Greater New York at the Turn of the Century* (New York: Columbia University Press, 1987).

1. Vertebrate Paleontology and American Science, 1850–1900

1. On the growth of vertebrate paleontology see Henry W. Menard, *Science: Growth and Change* (Cambridge, Mass.: Harvard University Press, 1971), 31–35. See also Martin J. S. Rudwick, *The Meaning of Fossils: Episodes in the History of Palaeontology*, 2d ed. (Chicago: University of Chicago Press, 1985); idem, *The Great Devonian Controversy: The Shaping of Scientific Knowledge Among Gentlemanly Specialists* (Chicago: University of Chicago Press, 1985); James A. Secord, *Controversy in Victorian Geology: The Cambrian-Silurian Dispute* (Princeton: Princeton University Press, 1986). On fossils and natural theology see Peter J. Bowler, *Fossils and Progress: Paleontology and the Idea of Progressive Evolution in the Nineteenth Century* (New York: Science History, 1976).
2. Rudwick, *The Great Devonian Controversy*, 17–41; Secord, *Controversy in Victorian Geology*, 14–38. On America see Sally Gregory Kohlstedt, *The Formation of the American Scientific Community: The American Association for the Advancement of Science, 1848–1860* (Urbana: University of Illinois Press, 1976), 59–65.
3. Charles Coleman Sellers, *Mr. Peale's Museum: Charles Willson Peale and the First Popular Museum of Natural Science and Art* (New York: Norton, 1980), 123–58. On Hawkins see Adrian J. Desmond, "Central Park's Fragile Dinosaurs," *Natural History*, 83 (October 1974): 65–71; *Proceedings of the Academy of Natural Sciences of Philadelphia*, 20 (1868): 202–4, 304–5; Edward J. Nolan, "History of the Academy of Natural Sciences," Manuscript Collection 463, Library, Academy of Natural Sciences of Philadelphia, 366–67, 519–43.
4. Charles Darwin, *On the Origin of Species by Means of Natural Selection, or the Preservation of Favoured Races in the Struggle for Life* (1859; reprint ed., Cambridge, Mass.: Harvard University Press, 1964), 80–130, 279–345.
5. On *Archeopteryx* see Thomas Henry Huxley, "Remarks on *Archaeopteryx lithographica*," *Proceedings of the Royal Society of London*, 16 (1868): 243–48. On ammonites see Alpheus Hyatt, "The Genesis of the Tertiary Species of Planorbis at Steinheim," *Anniversary Memoirs of the Boston Society of Natural History* (1880): 1–114. On horses see Vladimir Kovalevsky, "Monographie

der Gattung *Anthracotherium Cuv.* und Versuch einer natürlichen Classification der fossilen Hufthiere," *Palaeontographica*, 3 (1873): 131–210; 4 (1874): 211–90; 5 (1874): 291–346; Ludwig Rütimeyer, "Beitrage zur Kenntniss der fossilen Pferd und zur vergleichenden Odontographie der Hufthiere uberhaupt," *Verhandlungen der Naturforschenden Gesellschaft in Basel*, 3 (1863): 558–696.

6. Garland E. Allen, *Life Science in the Twentieth Century* (1975; reprint ed., Cambridge: Cambridge University Press, 1978); William Coleman, "Morphology Between Type Concept and Descent Theory," *Journal of the History of Medicine and Allied Sciences*, 31 (1976): 149–75. See also Ronald Rainger, "The Continuation of the Morphological Tradition: American Paleontology, 1880–1910," *Journal of the History of Biology*, 14 (1981): 129–58.

7. Patsy A. Gerstner, "The 'Philadelphia School' of Paleontology: 1820–1845" (Ph.D. dissertation, Case Western Reserve University, 1967); George Gaylord Simpson, "The Beginnings of Vertebrate Paleontology in North America," *Proceedings of the American Philosophical Society*, 86 (1942): 161–68. On college collections see Sally Gregory Kohlstedt, "Museums on Campus: A Tradition of Inquiry and Teaching," in Ronald Rainger, Keith R. Benson, and Jane Maienschein, eds., *The American Development of Biology* (Philadelphia: University of Pennsylvania Press, 1988), 15–47; idem, "Curiosities and Cabinets: Natural History Museums and Education on the Antebellum Campus," *Isis*, 79 (1988): 405–26.

8. Spencer Fullerton Baird to Joseph Leidy, 18 November 1850, 2 February 1852, 6 August 1856, 28 January 1856, 14 February 1856, Joseph Leidy Correspondence, Manuscript Collection 1, Academy of Natural Sciences. Letters from Leidy's network of collectors are in the Leidy Correspondence.

9. On Leidy's role in the museum see Nolan, "History of the Academy," 21; Minutes of the Academy of Natural Sciences, 21 September 1852, 5 October 1852, Manuscript Collection 502 B, Academy of Natural Sciences. On the *Hadrosaurus* see *Proceedings of the Academy of Natural Sciences of Philadelphia*, 10 (1858–59): 216–17; 20 (1868): 202–4, 304–5. On Leidy's assistance to others see Ferdinand V. Hayden to Leidy, 29 January 1858, 8 April 1861, 10 October 1865; Fielding Bradford Meek to Leidy, 1 June 1856, 28 February 1858, 8 May 1862, Leidy Correspondence.

10. Joseph Leidy, "The Ancient Fauna of Nebraska, Or, A Description of Remains of Extinct Mammalia and Chelonia, from the Mauvaises Terres of Nebraska," *Smithsonian Contributions to Knowledge*, 6 (1854): 19–99; idem, "Cretaceous Reptiles of the United States," *Smithsonian Contributions to Knowledge*, 14 (1865): 1–140; and idem, *The Extinct Mammalian Fauna of Dakota and Nebraska. Including an Account of Some Allied Forms from other Localities, together with a Synopsis of the Mammalian Remains of North America* (1869; reprint ed., New York: Arno, 1974).

11. Joseph Leidy to Charles Darwin, n.d. [1860] in William Shainline Middleton, "Joseph Leidy, Scientist," Joseph Leidy Papers, Archives, University of Pennsylvania, Alumni Records.

12. The quotations are from Leidy, "Ancient Fauna of Nebraska," 29; idem, *Extinct Mammalian Fauna*, viii. See also Joseph Leidy, "On the Difference between Animals of the Same Species Inhabiting Europe and America," *Proceedings of the Academy of Natural Sciences of Philadelphia*, 22 (1870): 72–73;

idem, "Remarks on Fossil Elephant Teeth," *Proceedings of the Academy of Natural Sciences of Philadelphia*, 24 (1872): 416–17.

13. Edward Drinker Cope, "The Fossil Reptiles of New Jersey," *American Naturalist*, 1 (1867): 23–30; idem, "Synopsis of the Extinct Batrachia, Reptilia, and Aves of North America," *Transactions of the American Philosophical Society*, n.s., 14 (1870). On Marsh see correspondence with Cope and Samuel P. Lockwood, O. C. Marsh Papers, microfilm edition, reels 3, 11, Manuscripts and Archives, Yale University Library; Marsh pocket notebooks, folders 1867–70, Archives, Peabody Museum of Natural History, Yale University. See also O. C. Marsh, "Notice of Some New Mosasauroid Reptiles from the Greensand of New Jersey," *American Journal of Science*, 2d ser., 48 (1869): 392–97.

14. Nathan Reingold, *Science in Nineteenth-Century America: A Documentary History* (New York: Hill and Wang, 1964), 236–50.

15. Henry Fairfield Osborn, *Cope: Master Naturalist. The Life and Writings of Edward Drinker Cope with a Bibliography of His Writings by Subject* (Princeton: Princeton University Press, 1930); Charles Schuchert and Clara Mae LeVene, *O. C. Marsh: Pioneer in Paleontology* (New Haven: Yale University Press, 1940).

16. On Hayden's ties to Philadelphia see Hayden to Leidy, 10 October 1865, 22 November 1865, 15 May 1874, 20 September 1878, Leidy Correspondence. Hayden became professor of geology at the University of Pennsylvania in 1865: Edward Potts Cheyney, *The History of the University of Pennsylvania* (Philadelphia: University of Pennsylvania Press, 1940), 272. On Marsh see Thomas G. Manning, *Government in Science: The U.S. Geological Survey, 1867–1894* (Lexington: University of Kentucky Press, 1967); William H. Goetzmann, *Exploration and Empire: The Explorer and the Scientist in the Winning of the American West* (1967; reprint ed., New York: Norton, 1978), 583–91.

17. On Cope's active role in the academy see *Proceedings of the Academy of Natural Sciences of Philadelphia*, 11–32 (1860–80). On Cope's descriptions of habits and habitats and his sketches of prehistoric animals see Cope, "Fossil Reptiles of New Jersey"; idem, "Extinct Batrachia, Reptilia, and Aves of North America," 115–16. Cope's restorations are also reproduced in Osborn, *Cope*.

18. Edward Drinker Cope, "The Laws of Organic Development," *American Naturalist*, 5 (1871): 593–605. See also Edward Drinker Cope, *On the Origin of the Fittest: Essays in Evolution* (New York: Appleton, 1887); idem, *The Primary Factors of Organic Evolution* (Chicago: Open Court, 1896).

19. Charles Darwin to Alpheus Hyatt, 4 December 1872, in Francis Edward Darwin, ed., *More Letters of Charles Darwin*, 2 vols. (New York: Appleton, 1903), 2: 341–42. See also letters to Cope from Albert Gaudry, Arnold Guyot, Richard Owen, and H. G. Seeley in Edward Drinker Cope Papers, Quaker Collection 956, Haverford College. Those individuals, like Cope, all maintained that nonmaterial factors caused organic change; see Adrian Desmond, *Archetypes and Ancestors: Palaeontology in Victorian London 1850–1875* (Chicago: University of Chicago Press, 1984).

20. Edward J. Pfeifer, "The Genesis of American Neo-Lamarckism," *Isis*, 56 (1965): 156–67; George W. Stocking, "Lamarckism in American Social Science, 1890–1915," in George W. Stocking, *Race, Culture and Evolution: Essays*

in the History of Anthropology (New York: Free Press, 1968), 234–69.
21. O. C. Marsh, "On a New Sub-Class of Fossil Birds," *American Journal of Science*, 3d ser., 5 (1873): 162; Joseph Leidy to O. C. Marsh, 31 January 1873, Leidy Correspondence.
22. Hatcher's correspondence with Marsh, 1888–92, Marsh Papers, reel 8. See also O. C. Marsh, "American Jurassic Mammals," *American Journal of Science*, 3d ser., 20 (1887): 327–48; idem, "Discovery of Cretaceous Mammalia," *American Journal of Science*, 3d ser., 43 (1892): 249–62. On the discovery of dinosaurs in Wyoming and Colorado in the late 1870s see Marsh's correspondence with Arthur Lakes, W. H. Reed, and Samuel Wendell Williston, Marsh Papers, reels 10, 13, 18. See also John H. Ostrom and John S. MacIntosh, *Marsh's Dinosaurs* (New Haven: Yale University Press, 1967).
23. Archibald Geikie, "The Toothed Birds of Kansas," *Nature*, 22 (16 September 1880): 457–58. See also O. C. Marsh, *Odontornithes: A Monograph on the Extinct Toothed Birds of North America* (Washington, D.C.: Government Printing Office, 1880); idem, *Dinocerata: A Monograph of an Extinct Order of Gigantic Mammals* (Washington, D.C.: Government Printing Office, 1885); idem, "The Dinosaurs of North America," *Annual Report of the United States Geological Survey*, 16, pt. 1 (1896): 133–244.
24. O. C. Marsh, "Fossil Horses in America," *American Naturalist*, 8 (1874): 291–92.
25. T. H. Huxley, *American Addresses, With a Lecture on Biology* (New York: Appleton, 1877), 73–90; Charles Darwin to O. C. Marsh, 31 August 1880, in Schuchert and LeVene, *Marsh*, 246–47.
26. With the exception of some support for promoting Hayden's expeditions and purchasing his specimens, Leidy to Hayden, 21 January 1857, Joseph Leidy II, "Biography of Joseph Leidy," Joseph Leidy II Papers, Manuscript Collection 167, Academy of Natural Sciences, the academy did not sponsor research or expeditions until the late 1880s: Nolan, "History of the Academy," 475–90. Until 1896 Marsh received no salary from Yale: Timothy Dwight to Marsh, 27 May 1896, Marsh Papers, reel 4. In addition, the Peabody Museum was an independent institution with its own charter, budget, and board of trustees. Administrators of Yale University officially became members of that board only after Marsh's death: Records of the Board of Trustees, Peabody Museum, 30 October 1900, 14 March 1904, Archives, Peabody Museum of Natural History.
27. On the Cope–Marsh rivalry see Reingold, *Science in Nineteenth-Century America*, 236–50; Elizabeth Noble Shor, *The Fossil Feud Between E. D. Cope and O. C. Marsh* (Hicksville, N.Y.: Exposition Press, 1974).
28. On Cope's controversies see Nolan, "History of the Academy," 330, 398–99; Minutes of the Academy, 15 April 1873, 20 January 1874, 14 April 1874. On Cope and the academy see "The Academy of Natural Sciences," *Penn Monthly* (March 1876): 173–80; editorials in *American Naturalist*, 14 (1880): 38–42, 117–20, 356–59, 793–95; 16 (1882): 663–64; 18 (1884): 510–11, 1234. See also Ronald Rainger, "The Rise and Decline of a Science: Vertebrate Paleontology at Philadelphia's Academy of Natural Sciences, 1820–1900," *Proceedings of the American Philosophical Society* (forthcoming).
29. Fred Brown to O. C. Marsh, 3 November 1886, 4 January 1889, Marsh Papers, reel 2; W. H. Reed to Marsh, 22 December 1877, 19 January 1878, 9 September 1878, Marsh Papers, reel 13.

30. Samuel Wendell Williston to Marsh, 1 June 1877, Marsh Papers, reel 18. Samuel Wendell Williston to John Wesley Powell, 15 October 1884, Marsh Papers, reel 18. See also Elizabeth Noble Shor, *Fossils and Flies: The Life of a Compleat Naturalist, Samuel Wendell Williston (1851–1918)* (Norman: University of Oklahoma Press, 1971).
    Marsh's only teaching was to substitute for Yale professors James Dwight Dana or A. E. Verrill on occasion: James Dwight Dana to Marsh, 24 April 1869, Marsh Papers, reel 4; and Dana to Marsh, 27 February 1867, Marsh File, Archives, Peabody Museum. Registers for Yale College and the Sheffield Scientific School for 1866 to 1899 record no courses taught by Marsh, and he was dropped from the Sheffield Register in 1879: Russell H. Chittenden, *History of the Sheffield Scientific School of Yale University*, 2 vols. (New Haven: Yale University Press, 1928), 1: 109. Although some of Marsh's assistants completed dissertations, none was in vertebrate paleontology: George Bird Grinnell, "The Osteology of *Geococcyx Californianicus*" (Ph.D. dissertation, Yale College, 1880); E. H. Barbour, "On the Osteology of *Heloderma*" (Ph.D. dissertation, Yale College, 1887); Charles Emerson Beecher, "Brachiospongidae: A Memoir on a Group of Silurian Sponges," *Memoirs of the Peabody Museum*, 2 (1889): 1–28. G. R. Wieland's work was on fossil plants and was published only after Marsh's death.
31. John Bell Hatcher to Marsh, 21 August 1885, 3 August 1889, 24 May 1890, Marsh Papers, reels 7 and 8. Although Marsh agreed to allow Hatcher to arrange collections and to publish, Agreement between John Bell Hatcher and O. C. Marsh, 20 December 1890, 8 January 1891, Marsh Papers, reel 8, Hatcher published only after he left Marsh's employ: Hatcher correspondence with Marsh, 1891–93. See also Ronald Rainger, "Collectors and Entrepreneurs: Hatcher, Wortman, and the Structure of American Vertebrate Paleontology circa 1900," *Earth Sciences History*, 9 (1990): 14–21. On Marsh's assistants see Shor, *Fossil Feud*.
32. Leidy's statement is in Henry Fairfield Osborn, "Joseph Leidy," *Biographical Memoirs National Academy of Sciences*, 7 (1913): 365. See also Leidy to A. G. Hamlin, 17 August 1873; Leidy to Judge Van A. Carter, 27 April 1874, Leidy Correspondence. On specimens Leidy received see John Wesley Powell to Leidy, 17 March 1885; Joseph Willcox to Leidy, 29 March 1887, 13 September 1890, Leidy Correspondence.
33. Osborn, *Cope*, 277–94, 413–46,
34. Edward Drinker Cope to Annie Pim Cope, 24 January 1884, 11 April 1884, Edward Drinker Cope Papers, Archives, Department of Vertebrate Paleontology, American Museum of Natural History. See also Joseph M. Maline, "Edward Drinker Cope (1840–1897)" (Master's thesis, University of Pennsylvania, 1974).
35. Schuchert and LeVene, *Marsh*; Manning, *Government in Science*. On dropping Marsh from the Survey see Powell to Marsh, 5 August 1892, Marsh Papers, reel 13; Charles Doolittle Walcott to Marsh, 12 August 1892, 12 October 1892, Marsh Papers, reel 18. On his later employment at $2,000 and then $1,000 salary see Walcott to Marsh, 17 July 1893, 1 July 1898, Marsh Papers, reel 18. See also Chapter 4.
36. Robert Singleton Peabody to Marsh, 24 February 1891, Marsh Papers, reel 22.
37. Dwight to Marsh, 27 May 1896. On mortgaging his home see *New Haven Union*, 9 November 1899, Marsh Papers, reel 23. On Marsh's supervision of

graduate work see his correspondence with G. R. Wieland, Marsh Papers, reel 18.

38. Colin B. Burke, "The Expansion of American Higher Education," in Konrad H. Jarausch, *The Transformation of Higher Learning 1860–1930: Expansion, Diversification, Social Opening, and Professionalization in England, Germany, Russia, and the United States* (Chicago: University of Chicago Press, 1983), 108–30. See also Diane B. Paul and Barbara A. Kimmelman, "Mendel in America: Theory and Practice, 1900–1919," in Rainger, Benson, and Maienschein, *American Biology*, 281–310; Charles E. Rosenberg, "Science, Technology and Economic Growth: The Case of the Agriculture Experiment Station Scientist," in Charles E. Rosenberg, *No Other Gods: On Science and American Social Thought* (Baltimore: Johns Hopkins University Press, 1976), 153–72; Margaret Rossiter, "The Organization of the Agricultural Sciences," in Alexandra Oleson and John Voss, eds., *The Organization of Knowledge in Modern America, 1860–1920* (Baltimore: Johns Hopkins University Press, 1979), 211–48.

39. Manning, *Government in Science*, 217–27; Charles W. Gilmore, "A History of the Division of Vertebrate Paleontology in the United States National Museum," *Proceedings of the United States National Museum*, 90 (1941): 305–77. Osborn's role as government vertebrate paleontologist is discussed in Chapter 4.

40. Kohlstedt, "Museums on Campus"; idem, "Curiosities and Cabinets"; Frederick J. H. Merrill, "Natural History Museums of the United States and Canada," *Bulletin of the New York State Museum*, 62 (1903): 1–213; Alfred G. Mayer, "The Status of Public Museums in the United States," *Science*, 17 (1903): 843–51.

   In 1894 a dispute arose over George Baur's position at the University of Chicago: T. C. Chamberlin Papers and William Rainey Harper Papers, Joseph Regenstein Library, University of Chicago; George Baur Correspondence, Archives, Museum of Comparative Zoology, Harvard University.

41. Burke, "The Expansion of American Higher Education"; Philip J. Pauly, "The Appearance of Academic Biology in Late Nineteenth-Century America," *Journal of the History of Biology*, 17 (1984): 369–97; Percy E. Raymond, "Invertebrate Paleontology," in Geological Society of America, ed., *Geology, 1888–1938: Fiftieth Anniversary Volume* (New York: Geological Society of America, 1941), 90–94.

42. Allen, *Life Science*, 21–72; Philip J. Pauly, *Controlling Life: Jacques Loeb and the Engineering Ideal in Biology* (New York: Oxford University Press, 1987); Garland E. Allen, "Naturalists and Experimentalists: The Genotype and the Phenotype," *Studies in History of Biology*, 3 (1979): 179–209; Keith R. Benson, "From Museum Research to Laboratory Research: The Transformation of Natural History into Academic Biology," in Rainger, Benson, and Maienschein, *American Biology*, 49–83.

43. "Introduction," in Rainger, Benson, and Maienschein, *American Biology*, 3–11. See also the essays in *Journal of the History of Biology*, 14 (1981): 89–191. On morphology and disciplinary societies see Toby A. Appel, "Organizing Biology: The American Society of Naturalists and its 'Affiliated Societies,' 1883–1923," in Rainger, Benson, and Maienschein, *American Biology*, 87–120.

44. Allen, *Life Science*. See also Menard, *Science: Growth and Change*, 29–83.

45. T. H. Morgan, *A Critique of the Theory of Evolution* (Princeton: Princeton University Press, 1916). See also Garland E. Allen, "T. H. Morgan and the Emergence of a New American Biology," *Quarterly Review of Biology*, 44 (1969): 168–88; Menard, *Science: Growth and Change*, 83.

46. Annual reports of the Peabody Museum of Natural History, Charles Schuchert Papers, box 40, Manuscripts and Archives, Yale University Library. See also Brian J. Skinner and Barbara L. Narendra, "Rummaging Through the Attic: Or, A Brief History of the Geological Sciences at Yale," in *Geological Society of America Centennial Special Volume 1* (Boulder, Colo.: Geological Society of America, 1985), 372. On Columbia see Henry E. Crampton, *The Department of Zoology of Columbia University, 1892–1942* (New York: Columbia University Press, 1942), 66–83. On Princeton, where only six students took Ph.D. degrees in the field in those years, see "Geological Sciences at Princeton," Geological and Geophysical Sciences File, Princeton University Archives, Seeley G. Mudd Library, Princeton University. On discouraging students from going into that field see Shor, *Fossils and Flies*, 191–93; George Gaylord Simpson to Bobb Schaeffer, 6 March 1935, George Gaylord Simpson Papers, series 1, American Philosophical Society.

47. On Yale see Charles Schuchert to Herbert E. Gregory, 18 February 1905, Yale Record Group 14 P, Accession 12/35, Manuscripts and Archives, Yale University Library; Schuchert to Richard Swann Lull, 20 December 1905, 6 January 1906; Lull to Schuchert, 3 December 1905, Schuchert Papers, boxes 3, 31. On Kansas see Shor, *Fossils and Flies*, 127–201; Clifford S. Griffin, *The University of Kansas: A History* (Lawrence: University of Kansas Press, 1974), 148, 244–45. On Nebraska see E. H. Barbour, "Report of the Progress of the Nebraska State Museum," *Bulletin of the Nebraska State Museum*, 2 (1938): 1–16. See also C. Bertrand Schultz, "Memorial to Erwin Hinckley Barbour," *Proceedings of the Geological Society of America for 1947* (1948): 109–17. On California see Chester Stock, "John Campbell Merriam," *Biographical Memoirs National Academy of Sciences*, 26 (1951): 211–12.

48. Helen J. McGinnis, *Carnegie's Dinosaurs: A Comprehensive Guide to Dinosaur Hall of the Carnegie Museum of Natural History, Carnegie Institute* (Pittsburgh: Carnegie Institute, 1982), 11–21. On the Field Museum see Alfred Sherwood Romer to Bryan Patterson, 14 March 1935, Alfred Sherwood Romer Papers, box 4, Harvard University Archives.

2. Osborn, Scott, and Paleontology at Princeton

1. "Sturges, Jonathan," *National Cyclopaedia of American Biography* (New York: James T. White, 1893), 3: 350; "Osborn, William Henry," *Dictionary of American Biography* (New York: Scribners, 1934), 14: 72–73. On William Osborn's role in railroads see Thomas Cochran, *Railroad Leaders, 1845–1890: The Business Mind in Action* (Cambridge, Mass.: Harvard University Press, 1953), 44–48. See also Carlton J. Corliss, *Mainline of Mid-America: The Story of the Illinois Central Railroad* (New York: Creative Age, 1950).

2. Virginia Reed Osborn to Henry Fairfield Osborn, 28 July 1878, Henry Fairfield Osborn Papers, box 2, New-York Historical Society. On his mother's charitable activities see Henry Fairfield Osborn, *Creative Education in School, College, University and Museum: Personal Observation and Experience of the Half-Century 1877–1927* (New York: Scribners, 1927), 284, 298–99.

3. William Osborn's interest in his son's career is referred to in William Berryman Scott, "Memoirs," box 6, notebook 4, William Berryman Scott Papers, Firestone Library, Princeton University. See also Osborn, *Creative Education*, 298.
4. Thomas Jefferson Wertenbaker, *Princeton, 1746–1896* (Princeton: Princeton University Press, 1947), 3–24.
5. James McCosh, "The Place of Religion in Colleges," *Minutes and Proceedings of the Third General Council of the Alliance of the Reformed Churches Holding the Presbyterian System* (Belfast, 1884), 466–69. See also J. David Hoeveler, Jr., *James McCosh and the Scottish Intellectual Tradition: From Glasgow to Princeton* (Princeton: Princeton University Press, 1981), 101–7, 255–56.
6. Hoeveler, *McCosh*, 101.
7. William Milligan Sloane, ed., *The Life of James McCosh: A Record Chiefly Autobiographical* (New York: Scribners, 1896), 198–204. See also James McCosh, "Academic Training in Europe," *Inauguration of James McCosh, D.D., L.L.D., as President of the College of New Jersey* (New York, 1868), 35–96. McCosh rejected Eliot's views on the role of religion and elective courses in college in *The New Departure in College Education, Being a Reply to President Eliot's Defense of it in New York* (New York, 1885). On the differences between McCosh and other college presidents see Laurence R. Veysey, *The Emergence of the American University* (Chicago: University of Chicago Press, 1965).
8. Hoeveler, *McCosh*, 238.
9. Wertenbaker, *Princeton*, 293. On educational reform at Princeton in the 1870s see Wertenbaker, *Princeton*, 298–315; and Hoeveler, *McCosh*, 241–49.
10. Willard Thorp, "The Founding of the Princeton Graduate School: An Academic Agon," *Princeton University Library Chronicle*, 32 (1970–71): 1–4.
11. Hoeveler, *McCosh*, 238.
12. John C. Green School of Science File, Princeton University Archives, Seeley G. Mudd Library, Princeton University. See also Henry B. Cornwall, "John C. Green School of Science," in *The Princeton Book: A Series of Sketches Pertaining to the History, Organization, and Present Condition of the College of New Jersey* (Boston: Houghton, Osgood, 1879), 279–89.
13. James McCosh, "Course of Study in the Academical Department," in *The Princeton Book*, 128. For McCosh's views on science education see Hoeveler, *McCosh*, 245–46, 249–60. Arnold Henry Guyot, *Creation, or the Biblical Cosmogeny in the Light of Modern Science* (New York: Scribners, 1884). See also Leonard Chester Jones, *Arnold Guyot et Princeton* (Neuchâtel: Secrétaire de l'Université de Neuchâtel, 1925); and David N. Livingstone, *Darwin's Forgotten Defenders: The Encounter Between Evangelical Theology and Evolutionary Thought* (Grand Rapids, Mich.: Erdmans, 1987), 77–80.
14. Minutes of the Trustees of the College of New Jersey, 22 June 1874, 28 June 1875, Princeton University Archives. See also Arnold Guyot, "The Museum of Geology and Archaeology," in *The Princeton Book*, 264–68.
15. William Libbey, Jr., "The Life and Scientific Work of Arnold Guyot," *Contributions of the E. M. Museum of Geology and Archaeology*, 3 (1884). See also Jones, *Guyot et Princeton*, 59, 91.
16. Guyot, "The Museum of Geology and Archaeology." See also Arnold Guyot to the Board of Trustees of the College of New Jersey, 24 June 1876, Trustee Minutes. On Hawkins's work see Adrian Desmond, "Central Park's Fragile Dinosaurs," *Natural History*, 83 (1974): 65–71; Richard C. Ryder, "America's First Dinosaur," *American Heritage*, (March 1988): 68–73.

17. S. R. Winans, "Franklin C. Hill," *Princeton College Bulletin*, 3 (1891): 2–4. See also Annual Reports, E. M. Museum of Geology and Archaeology, E. M. Museum File, Princeton University Archives; Franklin C. Hill and R. H. Rose, "Sketches and Photos of Mounted Fossils; Geological Museum at Princeton," E. M. Museum File.
18. Wertenbaker, *Princeton*, 304. The new faculty are listed in the Princeton General Catalogue, 1870–80.
19. On the Catskill Mountains expedition see William Berryman Scott, *Some Memories of a Palaeontologist* (Princeton: Princeton University Press, 1939), 48–49. Scott notes the amounts raised for the 1877 and 1878 expeditions in "Memoirs," box 5, notebook 1; and box 6, notebook 3. On the money put up by Libbey's father see Guyot, "Museum of Geology and Archaeology"; and Trustee Minutes, 17 June 1878, 20 June 1878.
20. On the museum see the E. M. Museum File; Scott, "Memoirs," box 6, notebook 7. The Trustee Minutes, 20 June 1878, refer to Libbey's wish to designate the museum as the E. M. Museum, in honor of his wife Elizabeth Marsh Libbey.
21. Scott, "Memoirs," box 5, notebook 1.
22. McCosh's frequent use of the phrase "bright young men" is noted in Hoeveler, *McCosh*, 285.
23. Scott, *Some Memories*, 84–131. On financial assistance provided by William Henry Osborn see Scott, "Memoirs," box 5, notebook 1. On McCosh's role in appointing Scott see McCosh to Scott, 12 December 1879, 15 March 1880, James McCosh Correspondence, Firestone Library, Princeton University. On Guyot's role in hiring Scott see Guyot to Scott, 11 February 1880, Charles Hodge Papers, box 27, folder 14, Firestone Library, Princeton University.
24. William King Gregory, "Henry Fairfield Osborn," *Biographical Memoirs National Academy of Sciences*, 19 (1938): 53–119. On Osborn's plans see letters to William Berryman Scott, 19 June 1880, 29 July 1880, 7 October 1880, 8 October 1880, Osborn Papers, box 2. Scott claimed that McCosh asked him to obtain Osborn for Princeton: "Memoirs," box 5, notebook 1. On Osborn's position as the first E. M. Fellow in biology see Princeton General Catalogue, 1880–83.
25. On physiological psychology see Princeton General Catalogue, 1883–86. See also Osborn and McCosh, "A Study of the Mind's Chamber of Imagery," *Princeton Review*, 13 (1884): 50–72; Henry Fairfield Osborn, "Illusions of Memory," *North American Review*, 138 (1884): 476–86; idem, "Visual Memory," *Journal of Christian Philosophy*, 3 (1884): 439–50.
26. Henry Fairfield Osborn to William Berryman Scott, 9 November 1877, Osborn Papers, box 2. See also Scott, "Memoirs," box 6, notebook 3.
27. The reprimand from Osborn's father is in Scott, "Memoirs," box 6, notebook 4. On Osborn's work in railroad administration see Osborn to Scott, 19 June 1880.
28. William Henry Osborn to Henry Fairfield Osborn, 15 May 1882, 15 June 1882, Osborn Papers, box 2.
29. Osborn's and Scott's salaries are noted in the Trustee Minutes, 8 November 1883, 13 November 1884. Osborn's appointment as professor of comparative anatomy was approved "provided the salary be raised outside the funds of the College": Trustee Minutes, 18 June 1883. In a letter to his father, 11 June 1883, Osborn Papers, box 3, Osborn complained about his status and hinted

that his father paid his salary. On Osborn's threat to resign see Osborn to McCosh, 21 October 1884, Osborn Papers, box 20.

30. The salaries of Osborn, Hill, and Weber were provided for by "a friend of the College": Trustee Minutes, 13 November 1884, 21 June 1886.

31. Osborn to Scott, 19 June 1880. Scott refers to William Osborn's emphases in "Memoirs," box 8. On William Osborn as a powerful personality and entrepreneur see Cochran, *Railroad Leaders*, 72–76.

32. A. Hunter Dupree, "Agassiz, Alexander," *Dictionary of Scientific Biography* (New York: Scribners, 1970), 1: 71–72; Elizabeth Noble Shor, "Verrill, Addison E.," *Dictionary of Scientific Biography* (New York: Scribners, 1976), 14: 1–2; "Mark, E. L.," *National Cyclopaedia of American Biography* (New York: James T. White, 1907), 9: 271–72. On Hopkins see Keith R. Benson, "American Morphology in the Late Nineteenth Century: The Biology Department at Johns Hopkins University," *Journal of the History of Biology*, 18 (1985): 163–205.

33. Henry Fairfield Osborn to William Berryman Scott, 12 April 1884, Osborn Papers, box 3; Henry Fairfield Osborn to Edward Drinker Cope, 28 July 1884, Edward Drinker Cope Papers, Archives, Department of Vertebrate Paleontology, American Museum of Natural History. See also Toby A. Appel, "Organizing American Biology: The American Society of Naturalists and its 'Affiliated Societies,' 1883–1923," in Ronald Rainger, Keith R. Benson, and Jane Maienschein, eds., *The American Development of Biology* (Philadelphia: University of Pennsylvania Press, 1988), 87–120.

34. Scott, "Memoirs," box 5, notebook 1; box 5, notebook 3; and box 6, notebook 8.

35. Henry Fairfield Osborn to E. B. Poulton, 20 March 1884, Osborn Papers, box 3. The quotation is from a flier, 5 February 1885, entitled "Plan of Organization for a Proposed Biological Journal subject to alteration by the Board of Editors when chosen."

36. E. L. Mark to Henry Fairfield Osborn, 24 March 1884, 17 May 1884, 26 May 1884, Osborn Papers, box 3. On Osborn's support for Whitman's program at the Marine Biological Laboratory see Henry Fairfield Osborn to Seth Low, 4 March 1892, 7 January 1893, 3 May 1895, Seth Low Papers, Central Record Files, Low Memorial Library, Columbia University. Osborn was the President of the Board of Trustees of the MBL from 1896 to 1902: Charles Otis Whitman Correspondence, Archives, Department of Vertebrate Paleontology, American Museum of Natural History. Osborn's students published their theses in Whitman's *Journal of Morphology*. See note 41 below.

37. Osborn's and Scott's courses are listed in the Princeton General Catalogue, 1881–91. Scott, "Memoirs," box 5, notebook 1 refers to the Wundt Club. On Osborn's and Scott's roles in the Princeton Science Club see Princeton Science Club File, Princeton University Archives. Scott, "Memoirs," box 5, notebook 1 refers to the sketch club that Osborn organized.

38. Henry Fairfield Osborn to Moses Taylor Pyne, 11 May 1886, Osborn Papers, box 4. On Scott's claim see "Memoirs," box 6, notebook 10. The Class of 1877 Biological Laboratory is described in the *Princeton College Bulletin*, 1 (1889): 4–15. Scott refers to the Pynes as supporters of his and Osborn's work: *Some Memories*, 46.

39. Garland E. Allen, *Life Science in the Twentieth Century* (1975; reprint ed., Cambridge: Cambridge University Press, 1978), 1–6; William Coleman,

"Between Type Concept and Descent Theory," *Journal of the History of Medicine and Allied Sciences*, 31 (1976): 149–75; Stephen Jay Gould, *Ontogeny and Phylogeny* (Cambridge, Mass.: Belknap, 1977), 68–206.

40. Henry Fairfield Osborn, "Observations upon the Foetal Membranes of the Opossum and other Marsupials," *Quarterly Journal of Microscopical Science*, n.s., 23 (1883): 473–84; idem, "Preliminary Observations on the Brain of Menopoma," *Proceedings of the Academy of Natural Sciences of Philadelphia*, 36 (1884): 262–74. Concerning his embryological work on marsupials and placental mammals, Osborn stated that "having once been near the fire of inferential biology, I will leave the question of the physiology of the yolk-sac placenta in the able hands of [the German physiologist Emil] Selenka": Henry Fairfield Osborn, "Foetal Membranes of the Marsupials: The Yolk-Sac Placenta in Didelphys," *Journal of Morphology*, 1 (1887): 380. See also Henry Fairfield Osborn, *Fifty-Two Years of Research, Observation and Publication, 1877–1929: A Life Adventure in Breadth and Depth* (New York: Scribners, 1930), 65.

41. Theses by Osborn's Princeton students included Henry Orr, "A Contribution to the Embryology of the Lizard," *Journal of Morphology*, 1 (1887): 311–72; Isaac Nakagawa, "The Origin of the Cerebral Cortex and the Homologies of the Optic Lobe in the Lower Vertebrates," *Journal of Morphology*, 4 (1890): 1–10; Charles F. W. McClure, "The Segmentation of the Primitive Vertebrate Brain," *Journal of Morphology*, 4 (1890): 33–56; Oliver S. Strong, "The Cranial Nerves of Amphibia," *Journal of Morphology*, 10 (1895): 101–230; Alvin Davison, "A Contribution to the Anatomy and Physiology of *Amphiuma means*," *Journal of Morphology*, 11 (1895): 375–410.

42. Henry Fairfield Osborn, "A Memoir upon *Loxolophodon* and *Uintatherium*, Two Genera of the Sub-Order Dinocerata," *Contributions of the E. M. Museum of Geology and Archaeology*, 1 (1881): 5–54; idem, "On *Achaenodon*, an Eocene Bunodont," *Contributions of the E. M. Museum of Geology and Archaeology*, 3 (1883): 23–35.

43. Henry Fairfield Osborn to William Berryman Scott, 11 July 1880, Osborn Papers, box 2.

44. Henry Fairfield Osborn to William Berryman Scott, 18 October 1885, November 1885, 30 November 1885, Osborn Papers, box 4; Henry Fairfield Osborn and William Berryman Scott, "*Orthocynodon*, an Animal related to the Rhinoceros, from the Bridger Eocene," *American Journal of Science*, 3d ser., 24 (1882): 223–25; idem, "On the Skull of the Eocene Rhinoceros, *Orthocynodon*, and the Relation of this Genus to Other Members of the Group," *Contributions of the E. M. Museum of Geology and Archaeology*, 3 (1883): 1–22.

45. Osborn to Scott, 18 October 1885, 30 November 1885, Osborn Papers, box 4.

46. Osborn referred to his father's advice in letters to William Henry Osborn, 4 June 1885, Osborn Papers, box 4; 29 November 1885, Osborn Papers, box 5. On reducing his teaching see Henry Fairfield Osborn to William H. Roberts, 11 May 1886; Roberts to Osborn, 10 July 1886; Osborn to Pyne, 11 May 1886, all in Osborn Papers, box 4. On references to Osborn's assistants see Princeton General Catalogue, 1887–91. See also Henry Fairfield Osborn to William Church Osborn, 7 November 1886, Osborn Papers, box 4.

47. On Scott's salary see Trustee Minutes, 16 June 1884, 17 June 1884, 13

November 1884. An endowment was approved and Scott became the Blair Professor of Geology. On 15 June 1885 the board indicated it could not pay Hill's salary or support the E. M. fellowship, E. M. Museum File. A resolution of 21 June 1886 stated that Hill and Osborn's artistic assistant would be paid by the same source that paid Osborn's salary: Trustee Minutes, 21 June 1886.

On hiring collectors see Edward Drinker Cope to Henry Fairfield Osborn, 13 May 1885, Cope Papers. On Osborn's line drawings in early publications see Henry Fairfield Osborn, "Memoir upon *Loxolophodon* and *Uintatherium*," plates i–iv; "Brain of Menopoma," plate 6, 280–81.

48. Although Scott, *Some Memories*, 150–88, makes no reference to Osborn on college collecting trips in the 1880s, Osborn did participate in some of those expeditions: Henry Fairfield Osborn to Lucretia Perry Osborn, 4 September 1886, Osborn Papers, box 4; Henry Fairfield Osborn to William Berryman Scott, 20 September 1887, Osborn Papers, box 4. But Osborn's letters from the field were written at the end of the expedition season, suggesting that his participation was limited. See also Chapter 4.

49. Arnold Guyot to Edward Drinker Cope, 29 July 1875, 12 December 1875, Edward Drinker Cope Papers, Quaker Collection 956, Haverford College. Guyot was one of the few scientists who supported Ferdinand V. Hayden's geological surveys: Ferdinand V. Hayden to Joseph Leidy, 12 May 1874, Joseph Leidy Papers, Collection 1, Library, Academy of Natural Sciences; Thomas G. Manning, *Government in Science: The U.S. Geological Survey, 1867–1894* (Lexington: University of Kentucky Press, 1967), 54–55. On Osborn's early contact with Cope see Henry Fairfield Osborn to Lucretia Perry Osborn, 19 May 1881, 25 May 1881, Osborn Papers, box 3.

50. Cope to Osborn, 13 May 1885.

51. Charles Schuchert and Clara Mae LeVene, *O. C. Marsh: Pioneer in Paleontology* (New Haven: Yale University Press, 1940). On Cope see Henry Fairfield Osborn, *Cope: Master Naturalist. The Life and Letters of Edward Drinker Cope with a Bibliography of His Writings Classified by Subject* (Princeton: Princeton University Press, 1930), 277–94, 413–46; Joseph M. Maline, "Edward Drinker Cope (1840–1897)" (Master's thesis, University of Pennsylvania, 1974).

52. Scott, "Memoirs," box 6, notebook 3; Henry Fairfield Osborn to William Berryman Scott, 5 November 1878, 8 December 1878, Osborn Papers, box 2; 26 June 1881, Osborn Papers, box 3.

53. On Marsh's assistants' accusations see Cope to Osborn, 26 July 1885, 27 October 1885, 28 November 1885, Cope Papers. On Scott's consultations with Marsh's assistants see "Memoirs," box 6, notebook 9; William Berryman Scott to Henry Fairfield Osborn, 1 November 1885, Osborn Papers, box 4. On Osborn's role in the Marsh affair see Osborn to Scott, November 1885, 19 November 1885, 3 January 1886, Osborn Papers, box 4. See also Osborn's diary entry, 13 November 1885, Osborn Papers, box 24.

54. Scott to Osborn, 1 November 1885; Cope to Osborn, 21 October 1886, 15 December 1886, Cope Papers.

55. Osborn to Scott, 19 November 1885; Henry Fairfield Osborn to Edward Drinker Cope, 22 November 1886, Henry Fairfield Osborn Papers, Central

Archives, Library, American Museum of Natural History. Cope asked for that letter in Edward Drinker Cope to Henry Fairfield Osborn, 21 October 1886; he thanked Osborn for his support in a letter of 15 December 1886, Cope Papers.

56. On Baur see Osborn to Scott, 10 March 1886. Agassiz and Whitman were not favorable to Osborn's and Scott's journal: Alexander Agassiz to Henry Fairfield Osborn, 21 May 1885, Osborn Papers, box 4; Scott, "Memoirs," box 5, notebook 2. But Agassiz was no friend of Marsh and in 1885 criticized the government's sponsorship of the latter's work: Manning, *Government in Science*, 131–36, 207. In 1886 he turned Samuel Garman's fossil collection in the Museum of Comparative Zoology over to the Princetonians and published their study of that collection in the museum's journal: Henry Fairfield Osborn and William Berryman Scott, "Preliminary Account of the Fossil Mammals from the White River Formation contained in the Museum of Comparative Zoology," *Bulletin of the Museum of Comparative Zoology*, 13 (1887): 151–71; idem, "Preliminary Account of the Fossil Mammals from the White River and Loup Fork Formations contained in the Museum of Comparative Zoology, Part II," *Bulletin of the Museum of Comparative Zoology*, 20 (1890): 65–100.

57. William Berryman Scott and Henry Fairfield Osborn, "The Mammalia of the Uinta Formation," *Transactions of the American Philosophical Society*, n.s., 16 (1890): 461–572.

58. Gould, *Ontogeny and Phylogeny*, 69–114; Peter J. Bowler, *The Eclipse of Darwinism: Anti-Darwinian Evolution Theories in the Decades Around 1900* (Baltimore: Johns Hopkins University Press, 1983), 68–69, 77, 82–84, 90–91, 155–76. On Balfour see Frederick B. Churchill, "Balfour, Francis Maitland," *Dictionary of Scientific Biography* (New York: Scribners, 1970), 1: 420–22.

59. James McCosh and George Dickie, *Typical Forms and Special Ends in Creation* (Edinburgh: Thomas Constable, 1856).

60. Charles Hodge, *Systematic Theology*, 3 vols. (London: Thomas Nelson, 1874), 2: 12–41; idem, *What is Darwinism?* (New York: Scribners, 1874); David N. Livingstone, "The Idea of Design: The Vicissitudes of a Key Concept in the Princeton Response to Darwin," *Scottish Journal of Theology*, 37 (1984): 329–57.

61. James McCosh, *The Religious Aspect of Evolution* (New York: Putnam, 1881), 60–61. See also James McCosh, *Christianity and Positivism: A Series of Lectures to the Times on Natural Theology and Apologetics* (New York: Robert Carter, 1871); idem, *Development: What it Can Do and What it Cannot Do* (New York: Scribners, 1883).

62. Livingstone, "The Idea of Design," 342–51; Hoeveler, *McCosh*, 275–78, 287–91.

63. On McCosh's reference to Scott's work see *The Religious Aspect of Evolution*, xii, 39–45. See also Osborn, *Fifty-Two Years of Research*, 58.

64. Cope, "On the Origin of Genera," *Proceedings of the Academy of Natural Sciences of Philadelphia*, 20 (1868): 269. On Cope's later interpretation see Edward Drinker Cope, *On the Origin of the Fittest: Essays in Evolution* (New York: Macmillan, 1887); idem, *Theology of Evolution: A Lecture* (Philadelphia: Arnold, 1887).

65. William Berryman Scott, "Some Points in the Evolution of Horses," *Science*, 7 (1886): 13; Scott and Osborn, "The Mammalia of the Uinta Formation," 478.
66. Henry Fairfield Osborn, "The Evolution of the Mammalian Molars to and from the Tritubercular Type," *American Naturalist*, 22 (1888): 1074–75.
67. Henry Fairfield Osborn, "On the Structure and Classification of the Mesozoic Mammalia," *Journal of the Academy of Natural Sciences of Philadelphia*, 2d ser., 9 (1888): 186–265; Scott and Osborn, "The Mammalia of the Uinta Formation," 531–69.
68. Osborn, "The Evolution of Mammalian Molars." Osborn criticized Cope's views in Scott and Osborn, "Mammalia of the Uinta Formation," 559–69.
69. August Weismann, *The Germ Plasm: A Theory of Heredity*, trans. W. Newton Parker and Harriet Ronfeldt (London: Scott, 1893). Henry Fairfield Osborn, "Evolution and Heredity," *Biological Lectures Delivered at the Marine Biological Laboratory at Woods Hole for 1890* (1891): 130–41; idem, "Are Acquired Variations Inherited?" *American Naturalist*, 25 (1891): 191–216; idem, "The Present Problem of Heredity," *Atlantic Monthly*, 67 (1891): 353–64.
70. William Berryman Scott, "On the Osteology of *Mesohippus* and *Leptomeryx*, with Observations on the Modes and Factors of Evolution in the Mammalia," *Journal of Morphology*, 5 (1891): 371.
71. William Berryman Scott, "On the Osteology of *Poebrotherium*: A Contribution to the Phylogeny of the Tylopoda," *Journal of Morphology*, 5 (1891): 72.
72. Scott, "*Mesohippus* and *Leptomeryx*," 393–94. See also William Berryman Scott, "On Variations and Mutations," *American Journal of Science*, 3d ser., 48 (1894): 355–74. On Waagen see Wilhelm Waagen, "Die Formenreihe des Ammonites subradiatus. Versuch einer paläontologische Monographie," *Benecke Geognostische und Paläontologische Beiträge*, 2d ser., 2 (1869): 181–256.
73. Bowler, *The Eclipse of Darwinism*, 141–81.
74. The quotations are from Guyot, *Creation*, 117; Guyot to Scott, 11 February 1880.
75. McCosh, *The Religious Aspect of Evolution*, 39–45. On Scott's collaboration with McCosh see Glen L. Jepsen, "William Berryman Scott," in Alexander Leitch, *A Princeton Companion* (Princeton: Princeton University Press, 1978), 432–33. On orthogenetic and polyphyletic interpretations see Adrian Desmond, *Archetypes and Ancestors: Palaeontology in Victorian London 1850–1875* (Chicago: University of Chicago Press, 1984), 175–203.
76. On Brooks see Benson, "Biology Department at Johns Hopkins"; idem, "H. Newell Martin, W. K. Brooks and the Reformation of American Biology," *American Zoologist*, 27 (1987): 759–71. On Whitman see Jane Maienschein, "Cell Lineage, Ancestral Reminiscence, and the Biogenetic Law," *Journal of the History of Biology*, 11 (1978): 129–58; idem, "Whitman at Chicago: Establishing a Chicago Style of Biology?" in Rainger, Benson, and Maienschein, *American Biology*, 151–82.

3. Osborn, Science, and Society in New York City

1. Henry Fairfield Osborn to William Berryman Scott, 14 August 1890, Henry Fairfield Osborn Papers, box 5, New-York Historical Society. On Hopkins see Keith R. Benson, "American Morphology in the Late Nineteenth Cen-

tury: The Biology Department at Johns Hopkins University," *Journal of the History of Biology*, 18 (1985): 163–205. On Clark see Jane Maienschein, "Whitman at Chicago: Establishing a Chicago Style of Biology?" in Ronald Rainger, Keith R. Benson, and Jane Maienschein, eds., *The American Development of Biology* (Philadelphia: University of Pennsylvania Press, 1988), 155–57. In 1890 Osborn's salary at Princeton was raised to $1,600: E. C. Craven to Henry Fairfield Osborn, Osborn Papers, box 5. By contrast, Low offered Osborn $4,000 at Columbia: "Report of the Special Committee on the Disposition of the Legacy of Chas. M. Da Costa, Recommending the Establishment of the Department of Biology," Exhibit B, Minutes of the Trustees of Columbia College, 11 (1890–91): 7, Low Memorial Library, Columbia University.

2. Henry Fairfield Osborn to Lucretia Perry Osborn, 26 February 1888, Osborn Papers, box 5, New-York Historical Society.

3. See Osborn family correspondence in the Osborn Papers, boxes 3–5, 14–15, New-York Historical Society.

4. David C. Hammack, *Power and Society: Greater New York at the Turn of the Century* (New York: Columbia University Press, 1987), 65–79. Hammack defines five elites in late nineteenth-century New York City.

5. Ibid., 33.

6. Ibid., 50.

7. Ibid., 50–51. On William E. Dodge see Richard Lowitt, *A Merchant Prince of the Nineteenth Century: William E. Dodge* (New York: Columbia University Press, 1954). See also "Sturges, Jonathan," *National Cyclopædia of American Biography* (New York: James T. White, 1893), 3: 350; "Osborn, William Henry," *Dictionary of American Biography* (New York: Scribners, 1934), 14: 72–73; "Phelps, Anson Green," *Dictionary of American Biography* (New York: Scribners, 1934), 14: 525–26.

8. Carlton J. Corliss, *Mainline of Mid-America: The Story of the Illinois Central Railroad* (New York: Creative Age, 1950); Thomas C. Cochran, *Railroad Leaders, 1845–1890: The Business Mind in Action* (Cambridge, Mass.: Harvard University Press, 1953), 44–48, 133–35, 422–27. On Harriman see Lloyd J. Mercer, *E. H. Harriman: Master Railroader* (Boston: Twayne, 1985), 24–48. On Morgan see Herbert L. Satterlee, *J. Pierpont Morgan: An Intimate Portrait* (New York: Macmillan, 1939), 95–122. See also Allan Nevins, *Abram S. Hewitt. With Some Account of Peter Cooper* (London: Harper, 1935), 158; Robert McElroy, *Levi Parsons Morton: Banker, Diplomat and Statesman* (New York: Putnam, 1930), 37. Morgan's investment firm had close relationships with Jesup's by the late 1860s: Satterlee, *Morgan*, 130, 243.

9. In addition to the Osborns, Morgan, Dodge, and William T. Blodgett lived in the Hudson River Highlands. On the family's charity work see Henry Fairfield Osborn, *Creative Education in School, College, University and Museum: Personal Observation and Experience of the Half-Century 1877–1927* (New York: Scribner's, 1927), 284, 298–99. See also articles in the *Daily Inter-Ocean*, 30 December 1887; *Christian Work and Evangelist*, 27 May 1905, Osborn Papers, box 22, New-York Historical Society.

10. Osborn's correspondence with the Reverend William Stephen Rainsford is in Henry Fairfield Osborn Papers, Central Archives, Library, American Museum of Natural History. See also Satterlee, *Morgan*, 120, 130; Nevins, *Hewitt*, 544–45.

11. Albert Bickmore, "Autobiography," 39–40, Central Archives, Library, American Museum of Natural History; Paul Russell Cutright, *Theodore Roosevelt: The Making of A Conservationist* (Urbana: University of Illinois Press, 1985), 89. Correspondence between Henry Fairfield Osborn and Roosevelt is in Osborn Papers, Central Archives.

12. Satterlee, *Morgan*, 102–16. A genealogy indicating the family's ties to the Dodges is in Osborn Papers, box 1, New-York Historical Society.

13. Thomas Bender, *New York Intellect: A History of Intellectual Life in New York City, From 1750 to the Beginnings of Our Own Time* (Baltimore: Johns Hopkins University Press, 1987), 169–205. See also Phyllis Dain, *The New York Public Library: A History of its Founding and Early Years* (New York: New York Public Library, 1972).

14. Bender, *New York Intellect*, 175.

15. Douglas Sloan, "Science in New York City, 1867–1907," *Isis*, 71 (1980): 35–76.

16. Ibid., 53. On Low see Gerald Kurland, *Seth Low: The Reformer in an Urban and Industrial Age* (New York: Twayne, 1971).

17. James Martin Keating, "Seth Low and the Development of Columbia University 1889–1901" (Ph.D. dissertation, Columbia University, 1973), abstract, 1–2. Keating also discusses the separate character of the schools at Columbia, 55–87.

18. Ibid. The quotation is from Bender, *New York Intellect*, 269. See also James Brander Matthews, et al., *A History of Columbia University 1754–1904* (New York: Columbia University Press, 1904), 234–305.

19. Seth Low, "President Low's Inaugural Address," in *Proceedings of the Installation of Seth Low L.L.D. as President of Columbia College in the City of New York, February 3, 1890* (New York: Printed for the College, 1890), 54.

20. "Low, A. A.," *Dictionary of American Biography* (New York: Scribners, 1933), 11: 444–45; "Low, Seth," *Dictionary of American Biography* (New York: Scribner's, 1933), 11: 449–50; Kurland, *Seth Low*, 11–18. Osborn to Lucretia Perry Osborn, 5 January 1890, Osborn Papers, box 5, New-York Historical Society, notes that Low visited Osborn's father who was sick at the time.

21. Henry Fairfield Osborn to Seth Low, 1 May 1890, Osborn Papers, Central Archives. It is possible that Nicholas Murray Butler, a faculty member at Columbia who in 1886 had joined the Princetonians on a fossil hunting expedition, may have influenced Low's decision to contact Osborn. Henry Fairfield Osborn to Nicholas Murray Butler, 14 February 1921, Nicholas Murray Butler Papers, Central Record Files, Low Memorial Library, Columbia University, refers to a letter from Butler of 29 April 1890 on the subject. On Butler's participation in the 1886 trip see William Berryman Scott Papers, box 5, Firestone Library, Princeton University. On Butler's role at Columbia see Matthews, *A History of Columbia*, 225–35.

22. Osborn to Low, 25 April [1890], 1 May 1890, Osborn Papers, Central Archives. Other letters that refer to plans for the new department include Osborn to Low, 21 September 1890, 24 December 1890, 28 February 1891, 25 March 1891; Low to Osborn, 30 December 1890, 19 February 1891, all in Seth Low Papers, Central Record Files, Low Memorial Library, Columbia University.

23. Philip J. Pauly, "The Appearance of Academic Biology in Late Nineteenth-Century America," *Journal of the History of Biology*, 17 (1984): 369–97. See

also several of the papers in Rainger, Benson, and Maienschein, *American Biology.*

24. "Report of the Special Committee on the Legacy of Chas. M. Da Costa," 2.

25. Ibid., 4, Exhibit A.

26. Osborn to Butler, 14 February 1921, Butler Papers.

27. Osborn's Cartwright lectures were published as "Present Problems in Heredity: The Contemporary Evolution of Man," *American Naturalist,* 26 (1892): 455–81; "Difficulties in the Heredity Theory," *American Naturalist,* 26 (1892): 537–67; "Heredity and the Germ Cells," *American Naturalist,* 26 (1892): 642–70. See also Low's report in *Columbia College Annual Report,* 1891; Low to Osborn, 4 February 1891, Low Papers. In 1878 Osborn took a course in physiology from John Call Dalton: Osborn Papers, Central Archives. Huntington interned at Bellvue Hospital where Osborn's father was a trustee: George S. Huntington to Osborn, 29 April 1891, Osborn Papers, Central Archives; Osborn to William Darrach, 24 July 1924, Butler Papers. On Lee's lectures see Henry E. Crampton, *The Department of Zoology at Columbia University, 1892–1942* (New York: Columbia University Press, 1942), 16. See also Alejandro C. Laszlo, "Physiology of the Future: Institutional Styles at Columbia and Harvard," in Gerald L. Geison, ed., *Physiology in the American Context, 1850–1940* (Bethesda, Md.: American Physiological Society, 1987), 67–96.

28. William King Gregory, "Memorial of Bashford Dean (1867–1928)," in E. W. Gudger, ed., *Bashford Dean Memorial Volume-Archaic Fishes,* 2 vols. (New York: American Museum of Natural History, 1930–42), 1: 1–4. On Northrup see John I. Northrup, *A Naturalist in the Bahamas: A Memorial Volume* (New York: Columbia University Press, 1910). Osborn organized, helped finance, and wrote the introduction to that work: Osborn to John B. Pine, 1 November 1909, Butler Papers.

29. Seth Low to Henry Fairfield Osborn, 28 March 1895, 5 March 1896, Low Papers; Osborn to Butler, 14 February 1921. On the change from the use of the term biology to zoology at Columbia and elsewhere see Pauly, "The Appearance of Academic Biology."

30. Osborn to Low, 7 June 1894, Low Papers.

31. Osborn to Low, 7 February 1896, 4 March 1896, [21 April 1896], 14 February 1898, Low Papers; Butler to Osborn, 5 February 1902, Osborn to Butler, 6 February 1902, Pine to Osborn, 20 October 1909, Butler Papers. The kind of inscription that should be provided for those contributing to the departmental library and Schermerhorn Hall is defined in Osborn to Low, 14 February 1898.

32. William E. Dodge to Henry Fairfield Osborn, 28 February 1896, Low Papers; Cleveland H. Dodge to Henry Fairfield Osborn, 4 December 1903, Osborn Papers, Central Archives.

33. The quotation is from Osborn to Low, 7 January 1893, Low Papers. Other references include Osborn to Low, 4 March 1892, 3 May 1895, Low Papers.

34. Osborn to Low, 1 March 1894, 4 March 1896, 22 April 1896, Low Papers. See also Henry Fairfield Osborn, "Zoology at Columbia," *Columbia University Bulletin,* 18 (1897): 1–10.

35. Osborn to Low, 2 May 1894, 1 June 1894, 7 November 1894, Low Papers. See also Henry Fairfield Osborn, "A Three Year Course for the Degree (Ph.D.)," (n.p. [1893]); Henry Fairfield Osborn and William A. Keener, "The

Degree of Doctor of Philosophy. Suggestions" (n.p. [1894]), in Henry Fairfield Osborn Collected Papers, Osborn Library, Department of Vertebrate Paleontology, American Museum of Natural History (DVP).

36. Osborn to Low, 7 January 1893, 1 March 1894, 7 February 1896, Low Papers; Osborn to Butler, 21 January 1909, Butler Papers. Among the works in the series that Osborn helped to arrange were Henry Fairfield Osborn, *From the Greeks to Darwin: An Outline of the Development of the Evolution Idea* (New York: Macmillan, 1894); Arthur Willey, *Amphioxus and the Ancestry of the Vertebrates* (New York: Macmillan, 1894); Bashford Dean, *Fishes Fossil and Living* (New York: Macmillan, 1896); E. B. Wilson, *The Cell in Development and Heredity* (New York: Macmillan, 1896); T. H. Morgan, *Regeneration* (New York: Macmillan, 1901).

37. Crampton, *The Department of Zoology of Columbia University*, 20–21. See also Osborn to Low, 23 November 1899, Low Papers.

38. On Osborn's membership in the Century Association see correspondence in the Osborn Papers, Central Archives. On New York social clubs see Bender, *New York Intellect*, 134–40, 213–16; Francis Gerry Fairfield, *The Clubs of New York* (New York: Henry L. Hinton, 1873). On Osborn's membership in scientific organizations see Henry Fairfield Osborn, *Fifty-Two Years of Research, Observation and Publication, 1877–1929: A Life Adventure in Breadth and Depth* (New York: Scribners, 1930), 141–42.

39. William A. Bridges, *Gathering of Animals: An Unconventional History of the New York Zoological Society* (New York: New York Zoological Society, 1974), 14–98. See also Henry Fairfield Osborn to Hermann W. Merkel, 23 May 1925, Osborn Papers, Central Archives; Henry Fairfield Osborn, Andrew H. Green, and C. Grant LaFarge, "Preliminary Plan for the Prosecution of Work of the Zoological Society Presented to the Executive Committee, 26 November 1895," *New York Zoological Society, Reports on Site of the Garden* (1895): 3–10; reports of the executive committee in *Annual Reports of the New York Zoological Society*, 1–5 (1897–1901); Henry Fairfield Osborn, "The New York Zoological Park," *Science*, 7 (1898): 759–64.

40. Albert S. Bickmore, "Autobiography." See also John Michael Kennedy, "Philanthropy and Science in New York City: The American Museum of Natural History, 1868–1968" (Ph.D. dissertation, Yale University, 1968), 12–74.

41. Lowitt, *Dodge*; "Phelps, Anson Greene." On the elder Theodore Roosevelt see Edmund Morris, *The Rise of Theodore Roosevelt* (New York: Ballantine, 1979), 32–98. A. T. Stewart, the owner of the country's largest department store by the 1860s, was not a board member or founder of the American Museum but his name was among those who organized the museum: Geoffrey Hellman, *Bankers, Bones and Beetles: The First Century of the American Museum of Natural History* (Garden City, N.Y.: Natural History Press, 1968), 18; "Stewart, Alexander Turney," *Dictionary of American Biography* (New York: Scribners, 1934), 18: 3–5. See also Frederic C. Jaher, *The Urban Establishment: Upper Strata in Boston, New York, Charleston, Chicago and Los Angeles* (Urbana: University of Illinois Press, 1982), 180–82.

42. Satterlee, *Morgan*, 93–140; William Adams Brown, *Morris Ketchum Jesup: A Character Sketch* (New York: Scribner's, 1910); Edward Sanford Martin, *The Life of Joseph Hodges Choate*, 2 vols. (New York: Scribner's, 1920), 1: 161–288.

43. Nevins, *Hewitt,* 523–24. On Dodge see Carlos Martyn, *William E. Dodge: The Christian Merchant* (New York: Funk and Wagnalls, 1890), 285.
44. Jaher, *Urban Establishment,* 208. See also Hammack, *Power and Society,* 133–39.
45. Lowitt, *Dodge,* 200; Martyn, *Dodge,* 57–80; Satterlee, *Morgan,* 122–29, 154–56; Brown, *Jesup,* 2–3, 23–25, 40–50.
46. Jaher, *Urban Establishment,* 243. See also Hammack, *Power and Society,* 101–2.
47. The quotation is from Andrew H. Green to the Trustees of the American Museum of Natural History, 13 January 1869, in Bickmore, "Autobiography." See also L. P. Gratacap, "History of the American Museum of Natural History," chap. 3, Central Archives. On museums see Lynn L. Merrill, *The Romance of Victorian Natural History* (New York: Oxford University Press, 1989), 107–37; Susan Stewart, *On Longing: Narratives of the Miniature, the Gigantic, the Souvenir, the Collection* (Baltimore: Johns Hopkins University Press, 1984).
48. The quotation is from a letter from nineteen men interested in establishing a museum to the Commissioners of Central Park, December 1868, Central Archives. On the collections of Stuart, Haines, and Dodge see Kennedy, "Philanthropy and Science," 38. On Morgan see Satterlee, *Morgan;* Andrew Sinclair, *Corsair: The Life of J. Pierpont Morgan* (Boston: Little Brown, 1981). On Henry Osborne Havemeyer see Frances Weitzenhoffer, *The Havemeyers: Impressionism Comes to America* (New York: Abrams, 1986).
49. Gratacap, "History," chap. 3, 9–23. Jesup's 1880 report is in Central Archives. See also Brown, *Jesup,* 149–51.
50. Gratacap, "History," chap. 3, 23. See also Kennedy, "Philanthropy and Science," 64–74.
51. Gratacap, "History," chap. 4, 12–33; Kennedy, "Philanthropy and Science," 80–87.
52. E. D. G. Prine to Morris K. Jesup, 29 November 1887; Morris K. Jesup to D. Ives, 1887; and in several entries in the Minutes of the American Museum Board of Trustees, 1886–87, all in Central Archives. The Archives also contain letters to Jesup pertaining to the building's expansion and Bickmore's lectures.
53. Joel Asaph Allen, "Recent Progress in the Study of North American Mammals," *Transactions of the New York Academy of Sciences,* 10 (1891): 75–76. On Allen see Frank M. Chapman, "Joel Asaph Allen," *National Academy of Sciences Memoirs,* 21 (1927): 1–20. See also Joel Asaph Allen, *Autobiographical Notes and a Bibliography of the Scientific Publications of Joel Asaph Allen* (New York: American Museum of Natural History, 1916).
54. *Annual Report of the American Museum of Natural History,* 17 (1885–86): 10–11.
55. Kennedy, "Philanthropy and Science," 100–105.
56. See, for example, Allen's papers "The West Indian Seal (Monachus tropicalis)," *Bulletin of the American Museum of Natural History,* 2 (1887): 1–34; "A Review of some of the North American Ground Squirrels of the genus Tamias," *Bulletin of the American Museum of Natural History,* 3 (1890): 45–116; "On a Collection of Birds from Chapada, Matto Grosso, Brazil, made by Mr. Herbert H. Smith. Part I. Oscines," *Bulletin of the American Museum of Natural History,* 3 (1891): 337–80; "Part II. Tyrannidae," *Bulletin of the American Museum of Natural History,* 4 (1892): 331–50; "Parts III and IV, Pipridae to

268   *Notes to Pages 59–61*

Rheidae," *Bulletin of the American Museum of Natural History,* 5 (1893): 107–58. The *Bulletin* also served as an important outlet for Osborn and members of his department.

57. The quotation is from Morris K. Jesup to Seth Low, 17 January 1891, Central Archives. Jesup commented on Allen's report in Trustee Minutes, 11 December 1885.

58. Morris K. Jesup to Henry Fairfield Osborn, 22 September 1903, Central Archives.

59. Gratacap, "History," chap. 4, 48–49; Trustee Minutes, 8 February 1889, 5 April 1889, 16 February 1891. On entomology see letters from William Beutemiller to Jesup, 1888–91. On archeology and ethnology see letters to Jesup from M. F. Savage, Herbert H. Smith, and Frederick Starr, Central Archives.

60. The quotation is from *Annual Report of the American Museum of Natural History,* 19 (1887): 11–12. On the mastodon see R. P. Whitfield to Morris K. Jesup, 24 May 1887, Central Archives; Trustee Minutes, 24 May 1887.

61. R. P. Whitfield to Morris K. Jesup, 4 February 1889, Central Archives.

62. Marsh's work was especially praised: Richard Owen to O. C. Marsh, 10 July 1877, O. C. Marsh Papers, microfilm edition, reel 13, Manuscripts and Archives, Yale University Library; Charles Darwin to O. C. Marsh, 31 August 1880, quoted in Charles Schuchert and Clara Mae LeVene, *O. C. Marsh, Pioneer in Paleontology* (New Haven: Yale University Press, 1940), 246–47; Archibald Geikie, "The Toothed Birds of Kansas," *Nature,* 22 (16 September 1880): 457–58. See also Nathan Reingold, *Science in Nineteenth-Century America: A Documentary History* (New York: Hill and Wang, 1964), 236–50.

63. Some of Allen's researches included the study of fossil specimens: Joel Asaph Allen, "The American Bisons, Living and Extinct," *Memoirs of the Museum of Comparative Zoology,* 4 (1876): 1–246. Whitfield was an invertebrate paleontologist: Clifford M. Nelson, "Whitfield, Robert Parr," *Dictionary of Scientific Biography* (New York: Scribners, 1977), 14: 312–13.

64. Jesup read a letter from Cope offering to become the curator: Trustee Minutes, 14 May 1888. See also E. H. Barbour to Morris K. Jesup, 21 February 1889, 19 March 1889, Central Archives. Baur was aware of the position: George Baur to Osborn, 12 June 1889, Baur Correspondence, Archives, Department of Vertebrate Paleontology, American Museum of Natural History.

65. Joel A. Allen to Robert Ridgway, 13 March 1891, Central Archives.

66. Kennedy, "Philanthropy and Science," 113. No record of this letter is in the Marsh Papers. See also Jesup's reference to the support that Osborn's friends would provide: Trustee Minutes, 8 May 1891.

67. Osborn to William Berryman Scott, 24 July 1890, 14 August 1890, 2 September 1890, Osborn Papers, box 5, New-York Historical Society; Osborn to John Bell Hatcher, 15 August 1890, 28 August 1890, Hatcher Correspondence, Archives, DVP. See also Ronald Rainger, "Collectors and Entrepreneurs: Hatcher, Wortman, and the Structure of American Vertebrate Paleontology circa, 1900," *Earth Sciences History,* 9 (1990): 14–21.

68. Seth Low to Morris K. Jesup, 20 August 1890, Low Papers. On Low's role in creating alliances between Columbia and other New York institutions see Frederick Paul Keppel, *Columbia* (New York: Oxford University Press, 1914), 37–38, Appendix A.

69. Osborn, "Zoology at Columbia," 3; James Howard McGregor, "The American Museum and Education in Science," *Columbia University Quarterly*, 19 (1917): 322–24.
70. Morris K. Jesup to Seth Low, 2 September 1890, Central Archives. On the resolution of the issue see Trustee Minutes, 5 December 1890. On Osborn's joining the museum staff in October 1890 see "Henry Fairfield Osborn," Personnel Files, box 1:7, Archives, DVP.
71. Henry Fairfield Osborn to Morris K. Jesup, 18 April 1891, DVP Annual Report, 1891, box 1:1, Archives, DVP. See also Trustee Minutes, 8 May 1891.
72. On Osborn's contributions to DVP operations, including subscriptions to make up deficits, see DVP Annual Reports, 1892–1910. Osborn's total contributions to the museum exceeded $80,000: Clarence Hay to Henry Fairfield Osborn, 21 February 1934, Osborn Papers, box 10, New-York Historical Society.
73. On assistance from J. W. Jeffrey see DVP Annual Reports, 1892–97; Jacob L. Wortman to Osborn, 7 June 1892, 14 May 1894, Wortman Correspondence, Archives, DVP; Henry Fairfield Osborn to W. Andrews, 21 October 1901, General Correspondence, Archives, DVP. On assistance from George Gould see DVP Annual Report, 1897; Henry Fairfield Osborn to J. H. Winser, 13 April 1899, Central Archives. In contrast see O. C. Marsh to Lloyd W. Bowers, 30 November 1898, Marsh Papers, reel 2.
74. On Morgan's assistance see DVP Annual Report, 1897; Morris K. Jesup to J. P. Morgan, 9 September 1897; Jesup to J. H. Winser, 12 September 1897; Winser to Jesup, 20 September 1897; Winser to Jacob L. Wortman, 20 September 1897; C. W. Calloway to Winser, 23 September 1898, 10 August 1899, all in Central Archives.
75. The quotation is from Jesup to Winser, 12 September 1897. On Morgan's contributions to Knight's paintings see DVP Annual Report, 1898; Osborn to Morgan, 8 February 1898, 26 March 1903, 2 March 1904, Morgan Correspondence, Archives, DVP. On the Warren Mastodon see Osborn to J. P. Morgan, Jr., 19 February 1906, 13 April 1906, Morgan Correspondence. On Morgan's support of expeditions to Alaska see the DVP Annual Reports, 1906–7.
    Clark Wissler, "Survey of the American Museum of Natural History Made at the Request of the Management Board in 1942–43," Central Archives, 391, refers to the Morgan fund and notes that Morgan's contributions to mineralogy and vertebrate paleontology totalled $450,000. See also Osborn's correspondence with George Sherwood, Roy Chapman Andrews, F. Trusbee Davison, and Fred H. Smyth on his work on the Proboscidea monograph in the 1930s, Osborn Papers, Central Archives.
76. On Jesup's negotiations for the Cope mammal collection see Trustee Minutes, 23 December 1894, 30 January 1895. Jesup contributed $2,000 to help purchase that collection. On Cope's reptile and amphibian collection see DVP Annual Report, 1899; Trustee Minutes, 19 January 1900, 16 January 1903. On the Fayûm Expedition see Jesup to Osborn, 26 December 1906, DVP Field Correspondence, box 2:3, Archives, DVP.
77. Wissler, "Survey," 50, indicates that Osborn's department received the following amounts from the Jesup Fund: 1920, $51,000; 1925, $34,000; 1930, $19,000; and 1935, $22,000. Jesup also contributed money to make up de-

partmental deficits: DVP Annual Reports, 1898–1901. On Jesup's great regard for Osborn see Jesup to Osborn, 26 December 1906.

78. DVP Annual Reports, 1891–1910. The budget climbed from $21,000 in 1905 to $87,000 in 1935. Most of that money came from special funds and disbursements. The DVP had additional money, not indicated in the department's annual reports, for exhibit and preparation expenses. In 1934 the department spent $21,000 for exhibition and preparation, and in 1935 $20,000: Wissler, "Survey," 45–60.

79. The statement is from Trustee Minutes, 11 November 1895. On Osborn's presentation to the board see Trustee Minutes, 11 November 1894, 23 November 1894. On Jesup's negotiations for the Cope collection see Trustee Minutes, 23 December 1894, 30 January 1895. Jesup also negotiated for the purchase of the Cope reptile and amphibian collection: Trustee Minutes, 21 April 1899, 19 January 1900. See also Edward Drinker Cope Correspondence, box 1, Archives, DVP.

80. Trustee Minutes, 14 February 1898.

81. Jesup initiated the idea for the cup and presented it to Osborn: Trustee Minutes, 9 November 1896, 18 December 1896, 31 December 1897. On the preparation staff see DVP Annual Reports, 1895–1910.

82. Osborn indicated that he was asked to take that position on 15 October 1899: Osborn Papers, box 24, New-York Historical Society. See also Osborn to Jesup, 26 May 1898, Central Archives; Osborn to Low, 23 November 1899, Low Papers. Osborn referred to turning down the directorship on 13 September 1900 and 10 December 1900: Osborn Papers, box 24, New-York Historical Society. See also Osborn to Jesup, 13 February 1901; Jesup to Hermon C. Bumpus, 17 December 1900, Central Archives. Osborn reported on many items, including the creation of a popular guidebook and a monthly or bimonthly magazine: Trustee Minutes, 19 January 1900.

83. Hermon C. Bumpus to Albert S. Bickmore, 14 February 1901, Central Archives. On 14 December 1900, Osborn noted that Jesup wanted to appoint him a trustee and vice president: Osborn Papers, box 24, New-York Historical Society.

84. On Morgan's role see Kennedy, "Philanthropy and Science," 160; listing of telephone call from Morgan to Osborn, 5 December 1906, Osborn Papers, Central Archives. No actual statement exists that indicates Morgan promised Osborn the museum presidency at that time. On Jesup's role see Osborn diary entries, 9 February 1906, 12 October 1907, Osborn Papers, box 24, New-York Historical Society. The first reference to Morgan's involvement is on 22 January 1908, the day Jesup died, when Morgan assured Osborn that his selection to the presidency was settled: Osborn Papers, box 24, New-York Historical Society.

85. Osborn to Percy Pyne, 9 December 1908, Osborn Papers, Central Archives.

86. On Bumpus's accusations and the controversy that led to his removal as museum director see Osborn Papers, box 20, New-York Historical Society. Madison Grant became a trustee in 1908, Theodore Roosevelt in 1918, and Childs Frick in 1919. These and other trustees contributed to dozens of projects: on the horse fund see Osborn to Percy Pyne, 19 December 1912, folder 424, Central Archives; on expeditions to Alaska for mastodons see Osborn to J. P. Morgan, Jr., 28 April 1908, Osborn Papers, Central Archives; on Charles R. Knight's paintings see Osborn to J. P. Morgan, Jr., folder 249c,

Central Archives. Osborn once told Grant that "your duty on the Board is to enlighten our trustees. They do not know—how can they know—what anthropology, archeology, early human history, palaeontology, marine zoology, ichthyology, entomology mean to the life, welfare, and intellectual progress of our people": Osborn to Grant, 28 May 1920, Osborn Papers, Central Archives.

4. Osborn and Vertebrate Paleontology at the American Museum

1. Henry Fairfield Osborn to Morris K. Jesup, 18 April 1891, Department of Vertebrate Paleontology Annual Report, 1891, box 1:1, Archives, Department of Vertebrate Paleontology, American Museum of Natural History.
2. Joseph Leidy, *The Extinct Mammalian Fauna of Dakota and Nebraska Including an Account of Some Allied Forms from Other Localities, together with a Synopsis of the Mammalian Remains of North America* (1869; reprint ed., New York: Arno, 1974); Charles Schuchert and Clara Mae LeVene, *O. C. Marsh: Pioneer in Paleontology* (New Haven: Yale University Press, 1940), 169–225. See also Sally Gregory Kohlstedt, "Henry A. Ward: The Merchant Naturalist and American Museum Development," *Journal of the Society for the Bibliography of Natural History*, 9 (1980): 647–61.
3. DVP Annual Reports, 1891–95. See also DVP Field Correspondence, box 2:3; DVP Field Diaries, box 6:2; the correspondence of Wortman, Peterson, and others, Archives, DVP.
4. On Weber see DVP Annual Reports, 1892–93; General Correspondence, Archives, DVP. On Earle, Christman, Sterling, and others see DVP personnel files, box 1:7, Archives, DVP. See also William King Gregory, "Erwin S. Christman, 1885–1921, Draughtsman, Artist, Sculptor," *Natural History*, 21 (1921): 620–25; Henry Fairfield Osborn, "Lindsay Morris Sterling," *Natural History*, 31 (1931): 563. On Knight see "Restorations by Charles R. Knight" and "Murals by Charles R. Knight," box 1:7, Archives, DVP; Sylvia Massey Czerkas and Donald F. Glut, *Dinosaurs, Mammoths and Cavemen: The Art of Charles R. Knight* (New York: Dutton, 1982).
5. Osborn to Jacob L. Wortman, [1894], Wortman Correspondence; Osborn to O. A. Peterson, 17 November 1893, 16 May 1894, DVP Field Correspondence, box 2:3; Osborn to Barnum Brown, 24 March 1897, Brown to Osborn, 30 March 1897, Brown Correspondence, Archives, DVP.
6. Osborn kept few field notebooks or diaries. Scattered notes on fieldwork are in Henry Fairfield Osborn Papers, boxes 19 and 24, New-York Historical Society. On Osborn at Como Bluff see Barnum Brown to Osborn, 28 June 1897, Brown Correspondence; DVP Field Diaries, box 6:2, folder 6. On the Fayûm expedition see DVP Field Correspondence, box 2:3. On Central Asia see Henry Fairfield Osborn Papers, Central Archives, Library, American Museum of Natural History; Chester A. Reeds, gen. ed., *The Natural History of Central Asia*, 6 vols. (New York: American Museum of Natural History, 1927–40), vol. 1: *The New Conquest of Central Asia. A Narrative of the Field Work of the Central Asiatic Expeditions in Mongolia and China, 1921–1930*, by Roy Chapman Andrews, 225–29.
7. On Osborn's correspondence with Knight see Osborn Papers, Central Archives; folders 249 and 1262, Central Archives.
8. DVP Annual Reports, 1899–1904.

9. Osborn correspondence with W. D. Matthew, Matthew Correspondence, Archives, DVP.

10. See, for example, Osborn to Matthew, 26 July 1920, 6 January 1923, 3 May 1923, 11 January 1924, Osborn Correspondence, Archives, DVP.

11. Henry Fairfield Osborn, "Equidae of the Oligocene, Miocene and Pliocene of North America: Iconographic Type Revision," *Memoirs of the American Museum of Natural History*, n.s., 2 (1918): 1–217. See also Matthew to Osborn, 7 July 1914, 30 October 1916, Henry Fairfield Osborn Papers, Archives, DVP; Osborn to Matthew, 31 May 1912, Osborn Correspondence. In a letter to Matthew, Osborn stated, "I am deeply interested in these notes on the nomenclature of the horses. I am mentally utterly unfitted for work of this kind and am extemely glad to have your cooperation and publication to guide my future work": Osborn to Matthew, 3 December 1917, Osborn Correspondence.

12. Henry Fairfield Osborn, *The Titanotheres of Ancient Wyoming, Dakota, and Nebraska*, 2 vols. (Washington, D.C.: Government Printing Office, 1929), 2: 703–25, 727–31, 828–31. On Gregory's work on the monograph see DVP Annual Reports, 1901–2, 1907; Gregory to Osborn, 2 December 1916, 19 November 1917, packages 2 and 3, and July 1916, October 1916, Osborn Papers, packages 2 and 3, Archives, DVP.

13. Henry Fairfield Osborn and Charles C. Mook, "*Camarasaurus, Amphicoelias*, and other Sauropods of Cope," *Memoirs of the American Museum of Natural History*, n.s., 3 (1921): 247–387. On Mook see Osborn-Mook correspondence and Osborn to David White, 28 January 1921, Osborn Papers, Central Archives. See also Mook Correspondence, Archives, DVP.

14. Matthew to Osborn [1915] and Matthew, "The Nomenclature of the Proboscidea: A Criticism of Some Generally Accepted Views," (1918), Osborn Papers, Central Archives. On Mook see Osborn to Matthew, 8 June 1922, 8 July 1922, Osborn Papers, Central Archives. On Edwin H. Colbert's assistance see Osborn Papers, Central Archives, and Osborn Correspondence, DVP. See also Edwin H. Colbert, *A Fossil Hunter's Notebook: My Life with Dinosaurs and Other Friends* (New York: Dutton, 1982), 67–82. Those men and Osborn's secretaries were responsible for the posthumous publication of Henry Fairfield Osborn, *Proboscidea: A Monograph of the Discovery, Evolution, Migration and Extinction of the Mastodonts and Elephants of the World*, 2 vols. (New York: American Museum Press, 1936, 1942). The assistance that Osborn received in paleoanthropology is discussed in Chapter 9.

15. Osborn Papers, packages 2, 3, 9, 10, Archives, DVP. On DVP staff as well as Osborn's personal staff see DVP personnel files, box 1:7, Archives, DVP.

16. Henry Fairfield Osborn and Jacob L. Wortman, "Fossil Mammals of the Wahsatch and Wind River Beds, Collection of 1891, "*Bulletin of the American Museum of Natural History*, 4 (1892): 81–147; Henry Fairfield Osborn and Charles Earle, "Fossil Mammals of the Puerco Beds, Collection of 1892," *Bulletin of the American Museum of Natural History*, 7 (1895): 1–70. See also Osborn, *Titanotheres*; idem, *The Age of Mammals in Europe, Asia and North America* (New York: Macmillan, 1910). When Osborn began work on a second edition of the *Age of Mammals* in the late 1920s, he assigned chapters to assistants and was going to list them as coauthors of the work: Osborn Papers, packages 7–13, Archives, DVP.

17. Osborn took credit with Brown for the discovery of a *Diplodocus* femur at Como Bluff: Henry Fairfield Osborn, "A Skeleton of *Diplodocus*," *Memoirs of the American Museum of Natural History*, 1, pt. 4 (1898): 191. A picture of him at the site is in Edwin H. Colbert, *The Great Dinosaur Hunters and Their Discoveries* (1968; reprint ed., New York: Dover, 1984), 78–79. On the Central Asiatic Expeditions see Henry Fairfield Osborn, *Fifty-Two Years of Research, Observation and Publication, 1877–1929: A Life Adventure in Breadth and Depth* (New York: Scribners, 1929), 41–45. Pictures of Osborn in the Gobi are in Andrews, *The New Conquest of Central Asia*, 222–23.
18. See, for example, Benjamin C. Gruenberg, "Henry Fairfield Osborn: America's Foremost Paleontologist," *Scientific American*, 105 (22 July 1911): 73, 79.
19. Steven Shapin, "The Invisible Technician," *American Scientist*, 77 (1989): 554–63.
20. Osborn was associated with Johnson through the Century Association. His publications for the *Century Magazine* are in Osborn, *Fifty-Two Years*, 10–24. Cattell was a member of the Psychology Department at Columbia from 1895 to 1917. Osborn wrote annual reviews of vertebrate paleontology for *Science* from 1899 to 1906. Cattell later gave prominent coverage to Osborn's publications on evolution: "Paleontology Versus Genetics," *Science*, 72 (1930): 1–3; "Aristogenesis, The Creative Principle in the Origin of Species," *American Naturalist*, 68 (1934): 193–235. Osborn also published in Cattell's periodicals *Scientific Monthly* and *School and Society*. On Osborn's more than thirty articles in the *New York Times* see Osborn, *Fifty-Two Years*, 37–54.
21. Colbert, *A Fossil Hunter's Notebook*, 71–72; idem, *Digging Up the Past: An Autobiography* (New York: Dembner, 1989).
22. Osborn to Matthew, 11 July 1922, 25 August 1925, Osborn Correspondence.
23. Osborn, *Fifty-Two Years*; Henry Fairfield Osborn, *Creative Education in School, College, University and Museum: Personal Observation and Experience of the Half-Century 1877–1927* (New York: Scribners, 1927).
24. Osborn, *Fifty-Two Years*, 55–73; Henry Fairfield Osborn, "Huxley on Education," *Science*, 32 (1910): 569–78; Henry Fairfield Osborn, *Impressions of Great Naturalists* (New York: Scribners, 1924), vii–xxvi. For insightful and amusing accounts of Osborn see Colbert, *A Fossil Hunter's Notebook*, 67–82; George Gaylord Simpson, *Concession to the Improbable: An Unconventional Autobiography* (New Haven: Yale University Press, 1978), 39–45.
25. For the "Neanderthal Flint Workers" mural for the Hall of the Age of Man Osborn insisted that Knight produce a painting showing "each . . . man in a pose natural to wild men, without chairs, who are accustomed to damp ground, and therefore squat, or kneel on a rough piece of skin": Osborn to Knight, 28 July 1919, Osborn Papers, Central Archives. See also folders 249 and 1262, Central Archives. On the La Brea tar pits issue see Matthew to Osborn, December 1919, Frederic A. Lucas Correspondence, Archives, DVP; Matthew to Osborn, 12 December 1919, and Lucas to Osborn, 12 December 1919, Osborn Correspondence.
26. Jacob L. Wortman to Osborn, 21 October 1894, Wortman Correspondence.
27. Wortman to Osborn, 8 September 1897, Wortman Correspondence; Os-

born to Walter Granger, 15 May 1899, DVP Field Correspondence, box 2:3. See also Ronald Rainger, "Collectors and Entrepreneurs: Hatcher, Wortman, and the Structure of American Vertebrate Paleontology circa 1900," *Earth Sciences History*, 9 (1990): 14–21.

28. Oliver P. Hay to Henry Fairfield Osborn, 20 July 1903, DVP Field Correspondence, box 2:3; "Conversation between Henry Fairfield Osborn and O. P. Hay, 12 February 1906," Hay Correspondence, Archives, DVP.

29. Hay to Osborn, 18 July 1905, Hay Correspondence; Holland to Osborn, 22 November 1909, Holland Correspondence, Archives, DVP. See also Oliver P. Hay, "On the Habits and Pose of Sauropodous Dinosaurs, especially of *Diplodocus*," *American Naturalist*, 42 (1908): 672–81. The mount was displayed at the 1906 meeting of the American Society of Vertebrate Paleontologists: W. J. Holland, "A Review of Some Recent Criticisms of the Restorations of Sauropod Dinosaurs Existing in the Museums of the United States, with Special Reference to that of *Diplodocus carnegiei* in the Carnegie Museum," *American Naturalist*, 44 (1910): 260–61.

30. "Conversation between Henry Fairfield Osborn and O. P. Hay"; Hay to Osborn, 19 June 1907, Hay Correspondence. Hay condemned the museum in O. P. Hay to W. D. Matthew, 23 May 1906, Matthew Correspondence.

31. Matthew to E. H. Barbour, 8 March 1916 and Matthew to Walter Granger, 8 August 1927, Matthew Correspondence; Osborn to William Berryman Scott, 5 February 1921, Osborn Papers, box 9, New-York Historical Society. See also Ronald Rainger, "Just Before Simpson: William Diller Matthew's Understanding of Evolution," *Proceedings of the American Philosophical Society*, 130 (1986): 453–74.

32. Osborn to Matthew, 25 August 1925, Osborn Correspondence; George H. Sherwood to Matthew, 8 December 1925, Matthew Correspondence.

33. Sherwood's statement is in Barnum Brown to William Diller Matthew, n.d. [1926–27], Central Archives. Brown disagreed with Sherwood's assessment.

34. On cataloging Knight's paintings see Osborn to Matthew, 8 February 1925. On DVP affairs see Osborn to Matthew, 19 February 1925. On Matthew's correlation paper see Osborn to Matthew, 9 April 1925, all in Osborn Correspondence.

35. W. D. Matthew to George Gaylord Simpson, 25 September 1929, George Gaylord Simpson Papers, series 1, American Philosophical Society; William King Gregory to Alfred Sherwood Romer, 31 May 1934, Alfred Sherwood Romer Papers, box 7, Harvard University Archives.

36. Clark Wissler, "Survey of the American Museum of Natural History, Made at the Request of the Management Board in 1942–43," 42–43, Central Archives.

37. DVP Annual Report, 1896; Osborn to Matthew, 22 August 1909, 26 January [1915], 5 April 1915, Matthew Correspondence. On Gregory see Osborn to Nicholas Murray Butler, 15 April 1916, 31 January 1921, 9 April 1924, Osborn Papers, Central Archives.

38. James W. Gidley to William Diller Matthew, 27 February 1905, Gidley Correspondence, Archives, DVP. O. A. Peterson to Osborn, 26 July 1904; Osborn to Peterson, 14 September 1904; 14 October 1904; Peterson to Osborn, 21 November 1906; Osborn to Peterson, 7 December 1906, all in Peterson Correspondence, Archives, DVP.

39. Henry Fairfield Osborn to John Bell Hatcher, 28 August 1890, Hatcher Correspondence, Archives, DVP.
40. No complete bibliography of Wortman's work exists. See his articles in *Bulletin of the American Museum of Natural History*, 1892–99. See also Rainger, "Collectors and Entrepreneurs"; G. Edward Lewis, "Memorial to Barnum Brown (1873–1963)," *Bulletin of the Geological Society of America*, 75 (1964): 19–27; George Gaylord Simpson, "Memorial to Walter Granger," *Proceedings of the Geological Society of America for 1941* (1942): 159–72. Matthew and Gregory are discussed in Chapters 8 and 9.
41. Lewis, "Brown." See also two autobiographies by his second wife, Lilian Brown, *I Married a Dinosaur* (New York: Dodd, Mead, 1950): idem, *Bring 'Em Back Petrified* (New York: Dodd, Mead, 1956).
42. Adam Hermann, "Modern Methods of Excavating, Preparing, and Mounting Fossil Skeletons," *American Naturalist*, 42 (1908): 43–47; idem, "Modern Laboratory Methods in Vertebrate Paleontology," *Bulletin of the American Museum of Natural History*, 26 (1909): 283–331.
43. Czerkas and Glut, *Dinosaurs, Mammoths, and Cavemen*.
44. Osborn allowed Peterson to publish his field notes in Henry Fairfield Osborn, "Fossil Mammals of the Uinta Basin. Expedition of 1894," *Bulletin of the American Museum of Natural History*, 7 (1895): 71–105. Osborn acknowledged that Peterson left the museum in 1895 because he "had done a great deal of work without receiving due credit for it from all parties concerned." In attempting to rehire Peterson, Osborn proposed "to give you credit for all the geological and scientific observations which you make": Osborn to O. A. Peterson, 10 December 1899, Peterson Correspondence. Peterson also experienced problems with W. J. Holland, director of the Carnegie Museum. Holland claimed that Peterson could not write and sought joint authorship for a paper on *Chalicotherium* on which Peterson had done most of the work: W. J. Holland to Osborn, 17 July 1907, Osborn Correspondence; O. A. Peterson to Osborn, 21 November 1906, Peterson Correspondence.
     Osborn criticized Hay's 1905 annual report to the department: Osborn to Gregory, December 1905, Osborn Correspondence.
45. Department personnel files, box 1:7, Archives, DVP.
46. Henry Fairfield Osborn, "On the Structure and Classification of Mesozoic Mammalia," *Journal of the Academy of Natural Sciences of Philadelphia*, 2d ser., 9 (1888): 186–265. On examining specimens at the Peabody Museum see Osborn to William Berryman Scott, 7 July 1885, Osborn Papers, box 4, New-York Historical Society; Marsh to Osborn, 29 September 1887, and Osborn to Marsh, 1 August 1888, O. C. Marsh Correspondence, Archives, DVP.
47. The Biological Society of Washington refused to publish a paper that Osborn presented in 1891: Osborn to Edward J. Nolan, 4 March 1891, Academy of Natural Sciences Correspondence, Manuscript Collection 567, Academy of Natural Sciences of Philadelphia; Charles Doolittle Walcott to O. C. Marsh, 2 April 1891, O. C. Marsh Papers, microfilm edition, reel 17, Manuscripts and Archives, Yale University Library. On problems over publishing articles in the *Proceedings of the Academy of Natural Sciences* see Edward J. Nolan to Osborn, 28 January 1891, Nolan to Marsh, 10 June 1891, and Marsh to Nolan, 11 June 1891, 12 June 1891, Academy Correspondence.

48. Osborn to Hatcher, 15 August 1890, 28 August 1890, Hatcher Correspondence; Peterson to Osborn, 9 October 1891, 9 November 1891, Peterson Correspondence; Osborn to W. H. Utterback, 22 January 1891, 20 February 1891, 9 February 1892, Utterback Correspondence, all in Archives, DVP.
49. Osborn to Hatcher, 27 April 1891, which is included in Hatcher to Marsh, 13 May 1891, Marsh Papers, reel 8. On Osborn's expedition see Hatcher to Marsh, 21 November 1891, 7 January 1892, 12 February 1892, 2 May 1892, Marsh Papers, reel 8.
50. On Marsh's efforts to limit others see Marsh to M. P. Felch, 24 March 1885, Marsh Papers, reel 5; Hatcher to Marsh, 21 November 1891, 30 November 1891, Marsh Papers, reel 8. On Osborn's argument see Osborn to Jesup, 20 January 1892, Marsh Correspondence.
51. Morris K. Jesup to Marsh, 19 February 1892, Marsh Correspondence.
52. Morris K. Jesup to J. H. Winser, 7 March 1892, Central Archives. See also Minutes of American Board of Trustees, 29 January 1892, 11 March 1892, Central Archives. On Jesup's threat of arbitration see Jesup to Marsh, 6 March 1892, Marsh Correspondence.
53. Peterson to Osborn, 11 November 1893, 12 December 1893, DVP Field Correspondence, box 2:3.
54. Morris K. Jesup to Hoke Smith, 9 December 1893, DVP Field Correspondence, box 2:3. See also Osborn to Smith, and William C. Whitney to Smith, 8 December 1893, DVP Field Correspondence, box 2:3. On the resolution of the problem see Wortman to Osborn, 7 June 1894, 13 June 1894, Wortman Correspondence.
55. Thomas G. Manning, *Government in Science: The U.S. Geological Survey, 1867–1894* (Lexington: University of Kentucky Press, 1967), 204–16.
56. Henry Fairfield Osborn to William B. Allison, 13 June 1892, Osborn Papers, Central Archives.
57. Marsh to John Wesley Powell, 16 June 1892, Marsh Papers, reel 13; Marsh letters of reference for Hermann, 1 September 1892, Marsh Papers, reel 9, and for Hatcher, 10 January 1893, Marsh Papers, reel 8. On Marsh's salary as honorary government vertebrate paleontologist see Charles Doolittle Walcott to Marsh, 30 June 1893, Marsh Papers, reel 17. Much of Marsh's later research was on dinosaurs: O. C. Marsh, "The Dinosaurs of North America," *Annual Report of the United States Geological Survey*, 16, pt. 1 (1896): 133–244. He also purchased and sponsored research on fossil cycads, plants found in association with dinosaur bones: correspondence with H. F. Wells and G. R. Wieland, Marsh Papers, reel 17.
58. DVP Annual Report, 1893. On hiring Hatcher see Willard Thorp, "The Founding of the Princeton Graduate School: An Academic Agon," *Princeton University Library Chronicle*, 32 (1970–71): 8.
59. On the Canadian Geological Survey see Gale Avrith, "Lawrence Lambe, H. F. Osborn, and the Dinosaurs of the Red Deer River: The Development of Canadian Paleontology," 26 October 1990, Seattle, Washington. Osborn to Walcott, 4 January 1900; Walcott to Osborn, 8 June 1900, Walcott Correspondence, Archives, DVP. Walcott claimed that Osborn's offer to absorb all expenses about $3,500 was "a most generous one": Walcott to Secretary of Interior, 15 June 1900, Walcott Correspondence.
60. Hatcher to Osborn, 9 August 1903; Nelson Darton to Henry Fairfield Os-

born, 3 January 1901, 14 November 1901, 26 November 1904; T. W. Stanton to Osborn, 16 February 1905; Osborn to C. W. Hayes, 24 June 1905, 28 June 1905, all in Osborn Papers, Central Archives.

61. Osborn to Hatcher, 6 July 1900, Osborn Papers, Central Archives. On Lucas's appointment see Walcott to Secretary of Interior, 15 June 1900, Walcott Correspondence. Lucas transferred Marsh's government collections to the National Museum: Lucas correspondence, Marsh Papers, reel 11.

62. Osborn to Hatcher, 18 February 1901, Osborn Papers, Central Archives; Osborn conference with Beecher and Dana on 16 February 1901, Henry Fairfield Osborn Papers, box 24, New York Historical Society; Osborn to Charles Emerson Beecher, 3 April 1900, 11 February 1901, 25 March 1901, 28 January 1903, 22 September 1903, and Beecher to Osborn, 4 October 1900, Beecher Correspondence, Archives, DVP. On Hay's work at Yale see Hay to Charles Emerson Beecher, 7 April 1903, Osborn to Beecher, 10 April 1903, Beecher to Hay, 13 April 1903, Charles Emerson Beecher Papers, Charles Schuchert Papers, box 1, Manuscripts and Archives, Yale University Library.

63. Charles Schuchert to Richard Swann Lull, 6 January 1906, Schuchert Papers, box 31. Beecher laid down guidelines for Hay's examination of fossil turtles: Beecher to Hay, 13 April 1903, 2 February 1904, Beecher Papers.

64. W. J. Holland Correspondence, Archives, DVP. On exchanges with Barbour see Matthew to E. H. Barbour, 14 October 1913, 23 December 1915, 7 October 1918; Matthew to Osborn, 29 September 1915 [1918]; Osborn to Barbour, 22 January 1915, 10 October 1918; Barbour to Matthew, 15 December 1915, 17 February 1916, all in Barbour Correspondence, Archives, DVP. On the La Brea specimens see Rachael H. Nichols, "Skeletons and Restorations of Fossil Vertebrates in the American Museum of Natural History," box 1:7, Archives, DVP.

65. "Casts, Models, Photographs, and Restorations of Fossil Vertebrates" (1898), unpublished manuscript, Archives, DVP. See also Henry Fairfield Osborn, "Models of Extinct Vertebrates," *Science*, 7 (1898): 841–45. On Knight's paintings see DVP Annual Reports, 1897–99. Riggs participated on expeditions in 1896–97, Lull in 1899 and 1902, and Loomis 1900–02: DVP Annual Reports, 1896–1902. See also Matthew to Charles Schuchert, 24 February 1905, Schuchert Papers, box 3.

66. On purchases of the *Ichthyosaur* and other specimens see DVP Annual Reports and correspondence of A. Hauff, Charles H. Sternberg, and Handel T. Martin. Archives, DVP. See also Nichols, "Skeletons and Restorations of Fossil Vertebrates." On negotiations with Barbour see n. 64 above.

On Osborn's negotiations to work at Agate see John Adams to Osborn, 29 July 1907, and Osborn to James Cook, 30 July 1907, DVP Field Correspondence, box 2:3; Matthew to Osborn, 3 July 1908, 11 July 1908, and Osborn to Matthew, 8 July 1908, W. D. Matthew Correspondence. Albert Thomson's excavations at Agate from 1907 to 1922 had important consequences for Matthew's work: W. D. Matthew, "Third Contribution to the Snake Creek Fauna," *Bulletin of the American Museum of Natural History*, 50 (1924): 59–210. See also Harold J. Cook, *Tales of the '04 Ranch: Recollections of Harold J. Cook, 1887–1909* (Lincoln: University of Nebraska Press, 1968).

67. William Berryman Scott, "The Development of American Vertebrate Pa-

leontology," *Proceedings of the American Philosophical Society*, 66 (1927): 409–29; Joseph T. Gregory, "North American Vertebrate Paleontology, 1776–1976," in Cecil J. Schneer, ed., *Two Hundred Years of Geology in America: Proceedings of the New Hampshire Conference on the History of Geology* (Hanover, N.H.: University Press of New England, 1979), 303–35.

68. W. J. Holland, "Heads and Tails: A Few Notes Relating to the Structure of the Sauropod Dinosaurs," *Annals of the Carnegie Museum*, 9 (1915): 273–78. S. W. Williston and O. P. Hay, "The Society of the Vertebrate Paleontologists of America," *Science*, 18 (1903): 827–28. See also Joseph Allen Cain, "George Gaylord Simpson's 'History of the Section of Vertebrate Paleontology in the Paleontological Society,'" *Journal of Vertebrate Paleontology*, 10 (1990): 40–48.

69. On the Hay incident see Osborn letters condemning Hay, 1 August 1922, 14 February 1923, Osborn Papers, Central Archives. See also Osborn to Matthew, 15 August 1922, 8 September 1922, Osborn Papers, Central Archives; Charles Schuchert to Osborn, 20 February 1923, and Osborn to Charles Schuchert, 23 February 1923, Schuchert Papers, boxes 37 and 17 respectively.

70. Schuchert to W. D. Matthew, 23 March 1905, box 31; Schuchert to William Berryman Scott, 11 April 1924, box 37; Schuchert to John Mason Clarke, 26 May 1925, box 18, all in Schuchert Papers.

71. Wortman to Osborn, 29 June 1892, Wortman Correspondence; Osborn to Peterson, 17 November 1893, 15 February 1894, DVP Field Correspondence, box 2:3.

72. William Diller Matthew, "Fossil Vertebrates of the Department of Vertebrate Paleontology," unpublished manuscript, Matthew Correspondence. See also DVP Annual Reports, 1895–1900.

73. Charles R. Knight, "Autobiography," Charles R. Knight Papers, box 4, New York Public Library. Knight noted that in the early 1890s he frequently visited the museum and conferred with the taxidermist John Rowley.

74. Henry Fairfield Osborn, "Prehistoric Quadrupeds of the Rockies," *Century Magazine*, 52 (1896): 705–15. Knight painted illustrations for *McClure's Magazine* and for museums besides the American Museum: Czerkas and Glut, *Dinosaurs, Mammoths, and Cavemen*, 6–23.

75. Charles Coleman Sellers, *Mr. Peale's Museum: Charles Willson Peale and the First Popular Museum of Natural Science and Art* (New York: Norton, 1980). On Hawkins and *Hadrosaurus* see *Proceedings of the Academy of Natural Sciences of Philadelphia*, 20 (1868): 204, 304–5; Edward J. Nolan, "History of the Academy of Natural Sciences," Manuscript Collection 463, Library, Academy of Natural Sciences of Philadelphia, 366–67, 519–43. See also Richard C. Ryder, "America's First Dinosaur," *American Heritage* (March 1988): 68–73. On the *Hadrosaurus* and Ward's specimens at the E. M. Museum see Arnold Guyot to Board of Trustees, College of New Jersey, 24 June 1876; "Report of Department of Natural History of the School of Science, 1882"; and F. C. Hill and R. H. Rose, "Sketches and Photos of Mounted Fossils; Geology Museum at Princeton," all in E. M. Museum File, Princeton University Archives, Seeley G. Mudd Library, Princeton University.

76. In 1893 Charles Doolittle Walcott requested that Marsh produce restorations of fossil vertebrates for the Columbian Exposition in Chicago. They were constructed by Marsh's assistants Hugh Gibb and Thomas Bostwick but were not displayed because they were too large for the available space: Walcott to Marsh, 14 March 1893, 25 April 1893, 30 June 1893, and Marsh

to Walcott, 10 April 1893, 28 June 1893, Marsh Papers, reel 17. On an earlier occasion Walcott asked Marsh to develop displays for a geological conference. That work was done in Washington and apparently Gibb was the only member of Marsh's staff who participated: Walcott to Marsh, 15 January 1891, Marsh Papers, reel 17; Lucas to Marsh, 30 March 1891, 17 July 1891, 29 September 1891, Marsh Papers, reel 11.

77. Knight claimed that Osborn had to push Hermann to develop new techniques: Knight, "Autobiography," box 5, folder 4. See also DVP Annual Report, 1894.

78. DVP Annual Reports, 1894–95, *Annual Report of the American Museum of Natural History*, 27 (1896).

79. Schuchert and LeVene, *Marsh*, 91. See also Frederic A. Lucas, "Restorations of Extinct Animals," *Smithsonian Institution Annual Report for 1900* (1901): 479–93. On Chubb see D. R. Barton, "The Story of a Pioneer 'Bone-Setter,'" *Natural History*, 41 (1938): 224–27.

80. DVP Annual Reports, 1895–96.

81. Ludwig Rütimeyer, "Beitrage zur Kenntniss der fossilen Pferd und zur vergleichenden Odontographie der Hufthiere uberhaupt," *Verhandlungen der Naturforschenden Gesellschaft in Basel* (1863): 558–696; Vladimir Kovalevsky, "Sur l'*Anchitherium Aurelianese Cuv.* et sur l'histoire paléontologique des chevaux," *Mémoires de l'Académie Impériale des Sciences de St.-Pétersbourg*, 7th ser., 20 (1873): 1–70; idem, "Monographie der Gattung *Anthracotherium Cuv.* und Versuch einer natürlichen Classification der fossilen Hufthiere," *Palaeontographica*, 3 (1873): 131–210; 4 (1874): 211–90. See also O. C. Marsh, "Fossil Horses in America," *American Naturalist*, 8 (1874): 288–94.

82. On donations by those men and others see folders 221 and 424, Central Archives. See also Henry Fairfield Osborn, *The Horse Past and Present in the American Museum of Natural History* (New York: Irving Press, 1913).

83. W. D. Matthew, *The Evolution of the Horse, American Museum Guide Leaflet,* no. 9 (New York: American Museum of Natural History, 1903). James W. Gidley, "A New Species of Pleistocene Horse from the Staked Plains of Texas," *Bulletin of the American Museum of Natural History*, 13 (1900): 111–16; idem, "Tooth Characters and Revision of the North American Species of the Genus *Equus*," *Bulletin of the American Museum of Natural History*, 14 (1901): 91–142; idem, "A New Three-toed Horse," *Bulletin of the American Museum of Natural History*, 19 (1903): 465–76. On Chubb see Barton, "Pioneer 'Bone Setter.'"

84. Osborn to William C. Whitney, 12 November 1903, Osborn Papers, Central Archives; Osborn to Frank Sturgis, 7 January 1909, Osborn Papers, Central Archives; DVP Annual Report 1901. See also folder 424, Central Archives.

85. Henry Fairfield Osborn, "Origin and History of the Horse," an address delivered to the New York Farmers, part of the prestigious Metropolitan Club. That address and papers by Osborn and Matthew for *Horse and Driver* are in Henry Fairfield Osborn Collected Papers, Osborn Library, DVP. On his subscription to the *Horseman* and other periodicals see Osborn Papers, package 31, Archives, DVP. See also prefaces to Spencer Borden, *The Arab Horse* (New York: Doubleday, Page, 1906); Osborn, *Age of Mammals*.

86. William King Gregory to Osborn, 9 July 1920, William King Gregory Papers, box 14, Central Archives.

87. On Morgan's sponsorship of Proboscidea see folder 236, Central Archives.

88. DVP Annual Reports, 1895, 1896. In 1896 Osborn used Wortman's idea that a North American mammal, *Psittacotherium*, was ancestral to the South American fauna to justify the expedition: Jacob L. Wortman, "*Psittacotherium*, A Member of a New and Primitive Suborder of the Edentata," *Bulletin of the American Museum of Natural History*, 8 (1896): 259–62.

89. George Gaylord Simpson, *Discoverers of the Lost World: An Account of Some of Those Who Brought Back to Life South American Mammals Long Buried in the Abyss of Time* (New Haven: Yale University Press, 1984). Ameghino and others are discussed in Chapter 8.

90. DVP Annual Report, 1895.

91. Howard K. Beale, *Theodore Roosevelt and the Rise of America to World Power* (Baltimore: Johns Hopkins University Press, 1984); Richard H. Collin, *Theodore Roosevelt, Culture, Diplomacy and Expansion: A New View of American Imperialism* (Baton Rouge: Louisiana State University Press, 1985); Howard Copeland Hill, *Roosevelt and the Caribbean* (New York: Russell and Russell, 1965). On Phelps-Dodge Corporation's expansion into Latin America see Robert Glass Cleland, *A History of Phelps Dodge* (New York: Knopf, 1952), 129–50.

92. William Berryman Scott, "Memoirs," William Berryman Scott Papers, box 5, notebook 3, Firestone Library, Princeton University. On Brown's salary see "Understanding Between Prof. Henry F. Osborn and Mr. Barnum Brown," 6 December 1898; Osborn to Brown, March 1899, 12 January 1900, Brown Correspondence.

93. Morris K. Jesup to Osborn, 26 December 1906, DVP Field Correspondence, box 2:3; Henry Fairfield Osborn, "The Geological and Faunal Relations of Europe and America during the Tertiary Period and the Theory of the Successive Invasions of an African Fauna," *Science*, 11 (1900): 561–74.

94. Brown worked for Williston and participated in a museum expedition in 1896: "Brief Record of Field Expeditions for the American Museum of Natural History, New York, done by Dr. Barnum Brown," Barnum Brown Papers, box 2:5, carton 1, Archives, DVP. See also Osborn to Brown, 24 March 1897; Brown to Osborn, 30 March 1897; Samuel Wendell Williston to Osborn, 31 March 1897, Brown Correspondence.

95. Trustee Minutes, 9 November 1895, 30 December 1895, Central Archives.

96. The quotations are from Brown to Osborn, 8 May 1897, Brown Correspondence, and Wilbur C. Knight to O. C. Marsh, 10 July 1898, Marsh Papers, reel 10.

97. DVP Annual Report, 1897.

98. DVP Annual Reports for 1898–1905; DVP Field Correspondence, box 2:3, 1898–1905; Wortman Correspondence for 1897–98. On Nine Mile Gulch see DVP Annual Report, 1899. On Six Mile Gulch see DVP Annual Report, 1901; William H. Reed Correspondence, Archives, DVP; Walter Granger to Osborn, 20 September 1902, DVP Field Correspondence, box 2:3. See also Colbert, *The Great Dinosaur Hunters*, 149–54; John S. McIntosh, "The Second Jurassic Dinosaur Rush," *Earth Sciences History*, 9 (1990): 22–27.

99. DVP Field Correspondence, box 2:3, especially Wieland to Osborn, 24 December 1900.

100. DVP Field Correspondence, box 2:3; DVP Annual Report, 1900. On Hell Creek see DVP Annual Reports, 1902, 1903; Brown to Osborn, 12 August 1902, 13 September 1902, DVP Field Correspondence, box 2:3. See also

Barnum Brown, "The Hell Creek Beds of the Upper Cretaceous of Montana," *Bulletin of the American Museum of Natural History*, 23 (1907): 823–45. On additional discoveries by Brown and Kaisen see Brown, "A Brief Record of Field Expeditions for the American Museum," Brown Papers, box 2:5.

101. DVP Annual Reports, 1897, 1899. Osborn hired Hay to work on the Cope collections of fossil reptiles and batrachians: Henry Fairfield Osborn to Oliver P. Hay, 13 December 1899, Hay Correspondence. On Hay's later work on dinosaurs see Hay to Osborn, 18 July 1905, Hay Correspondence; n. 29 above. On Gregory see DVP Annual Reports, 1901, 1902, 1906–9; William King Gregory, "The Weight of the *Brontosaurus*," *Science*, 22 (1905): 572. See also Chapter 9.

102. DVP Annual Reports, 1897–99; Trustee Minutes, 27 January 1898, 3 February 1899, 19 January 1900.

103. Wilbur C. Knight, "The Wyoming Fossil Fields Expedition of July 1899," *National Geographic Magazine*, 11 (1900): 449–63. On the dinosaur hall see folders 1160.1, 1175, 1178.4, Central Archives.

104. Ryder, "America's First Dinosaur." On the E. M. Museum see n. 75 above; Marsh, "The Dinosaurs of North America." One of Marsh's dinosaurs was mounted in 1901: Charles Emerson Beecher, "The Reconstruction of a Cretaceous Dinosaur, *Claosaurus annectens*, Marsh," *Transactions of the Connecticut Academy of Sciences*, 11 (1901): 311–24. Beecher also supervised the mount of the legs and pelvis of *Apatosaurus* at the Peabody Museum in 1901: Richard Swann Lull, "Reminiscences of the Vertebrate Paleontology Collection at the Peabody Museum, 1906–1946" [1946], Alfred Sherwood Romer Papers, box 11, Harvard University Archives.

105. *Report of the Field Museum of Natural History*, 5 (1898–99): 364.

106. Colbert, *The Great Dinosaur Hunters*, 164. On Wortman's role see John Bell Hatcher, "*Diplodocus* Marsh, Its Osteology, Taxonomy, and Probable Habits, with a Restoration of the Skeleton," *Memoirs of the Carnegie Museum*, 1 (1901): 1–63; W. J. Holland, "Dr. Jacob L. Wortman," *Annals of the Carnegie Museum*, 17 (1926): 199–201. On *Diplodocus* see W. J. Holland, "John Bell Hatcher," *Annals of the Carnegie Museum*, 2 (1904): 602.

107. Osborn to Walter Granger, 18 May 1899, 28 May 1899, 8 June 1899, DVP Field Correspondence, box 2:3; Osborn to Morris K. Jesup, 8 January 1901, DVP Annual Report 1899. On staff size see DVP Annual Reports, 1899, 1900.

108. W. D. Matthew, "The Pose of Sauropod Dinosaurs," *American Naturalist*, 44 (1910): 547–60. On staff members involved in those efforts see Nichols, "Skeletons and Restorations of Fossil Vertebrates."

109. Osborn published over twenty-five articles on dinosaurs and named *Tyrannosaurus rex*, *Ornitholestes*, and a great many others. See Osborn, *Fifty-Two Years*, 78–79.

110. On Brown see Lewis, "Barnum Brown," 25–27. On Mook see Edwin H. Colbert, "Charles Craig Mook, (1887–1966)," *Proceedings of the Geological Society of America for 1966* (1967): 313–15. Matthew, "The Pose of Sauropod Dinosaurs"; idem, "The Mounted Skeleton of *Brontosaurus* in the American Museum of Natural History," *American Museum Journal*, 5 (1905): 65–75; idem, "The *Tyrannosaurus*," *American Museum Journal*, 10 (1910); 3–8; idem, *Dinosaurs*, American Museum Handbook, no. 5 (New York: American Museum of Natural History, 1915).

111. Matthew, "*Brontosaurus*"; idem, "*Tyrannosaurus*"; idem, *Dinosaurs*. Barnum

Brown, "The *Trachodon* Group," *American Museum Journal*, 8 (1908): 51–56; idem, "*Tyrannosaurus*, the Largest Flesh-Eating Animal that Ever Lived," *American Museum Journal*, 15 (1915): 271–90; idem, "*Monoclonius*, A Cretaceous Horned Dinosaur," *American Museum Journal*, 17 (1917): 135–40. Henry Fairfield Osborn, "The 'Ostrich' Dinosaur and the 'Tyrant' Dinosaur," *American Museum Journal*, 17 (1917): 5–13. See also W. D. Matthew, "The *Brontosaurus*," *The Independent*, 58 (1905): 777–81; Barnum Brown, "Finding the *Tyrannosaurus*," *The Independent*, 63 (1907): 545–52.

112. Walter L. Beasley, "A Carnivorous Dinosaur: A Reconstructed Skeleton of a Huge Saurian," *Scientific American*, 97 (14 December 1907): 446; idem, "*Diplodocus*—The Greatest of All Earthly Creatures," *Scientific American*, 96 (15 June 1907): 491–92; idem, "A Wonderful Dinosaur Mummy: A Relic of the Prehistoric Past," *Scientific American*, 104 (20 May 1911): 262–63. Issues with Knight's paintings on the covers included *Scientific American*, 94 (3 February 1906): 105, 113–14; *Scientific American*, 97 (14 December 1907): 437, 446–47. The *New York Times* provided illustrated coverage of *Tyrannosaurus rex*, 3 December 1905, sec. 3, p.1, and of the mummified dinosaur skin, 21 March 1909, sec. 1, p. 4, col. 1.

113. See Henry Fairfield Osborn, "A Great Naturalist: Edward Drinker Cope," *Century Magazine*, 55 (1897): 10–15; William H. Ballou, "Strange Creatures of the Past: Gigantic Saurians of the Reptilian Age," *Century Magazine*, 55 (1897): 15–23. On Knight's paintings see Czerkas and Glut, *Dinosaurs, Mammoths, and Cavemen*, figures 40–49, pp. 40–45.

114. Glyn Daniel, *The Idea of Prehistory* (New York: World, 1963), 71–73; Alan Houghton Broderick, *Father of Prehistory, Abbé Breuil: His Life and Times* (New York: Morrow, 1963).

115. Marcellin Boule, "L'homme fossile de La Chapelle-aux-Saints," *Annales de paléontologie*, 6 (1909): 109–72; 7 (1910): 18–56, 85–192; 8 (1911): 1–71. On Piltdown see Ronald Millar, *The Piltdown Men: A Case of Archaeological Fraud* (London: Gollancz, 1972); J. S. Weiner, *The Piltdown Forgery* (London: Oxford University Press, 1955).

116. Henry Fairfield Osborn, "Men of the Old Stone Age. With an Account of a Motor Tour Through the Principal Cavern Regions of Southwestern Europe," *American Museum Journal*, 12 (1912): 279–95. Gregory's work is discussed in Chapter 9.

117. Roy Chapman Andrews, *Across Mongolian Plains: A Naturalist's Account of China's Great "Northwest"* (New York: Appleton, 1921).

118. The quotations are from Andrews, *New Conquest*, 5; idem, *On the Trail of Ancient Man: A Narrative of the Field Work of the Central Asiatic Expeditions* (Garden City, N.Y.: Garden City, 1926), 17.

119. On the donations see Andrews, *New Conquest*, 5–6. On the Central Asiatic Expeditions see folder 1214.1, Central Archives.

120. Osborn, *Fifty-Two Years*, 41–46. Many of the telegrams and releases he sent out are in the Osborn Papers, Central Archives.

121. Knight's painting of *Baluchitherium* is reproduced in Andrews, *New Conquest*, plate XXXIV, opposite p. 140. On the mount see William King Gregory, "Building a Super-Giant Rhinoceros," *Natural History*, 35 (1935): 340–43. Elizabeth Fulda's restoration of a nesting ground that depicted several adult and juvenile Protoceratopsians is in Andrews, *New Conquest*, plate

L, opposite p. 194. The mounted skeleton of *Protoceratops andrewsi* by Peter Kaisen is in the same work, 194.

122. Roy Chapman Andrews, *Under a Lucky Star: A Lifetime of Adventure* (New York: Viking, 1943), 162–78. The contributors, over 650 from thirty-six states and eight countries, are listed in Andrews, *New Conquest*, 631–44. Osborn told Andrews that he kept a diary for keeping track of his meetings and for keeping in mind potential patrons for projects: Osborn to Andrews, 27 April 1935, Osborn Papers, Central Archives.

123. The quotations are from Andrews, *Trail of Ancient Man*, 13 and Andrews, *New Conquest*, 9–10. Andrews used such language throughout *Trail of Ancient Man*.

124. Andrews, *New Conquest*, 572. See also Davidson Black, "Asia and the Dispersal of Primates," *Bulletin of the Geological Society of China*, 4 (1925): 133–83. Osborn's chapter in Andrews's book, 190–207, exaggerated the importance of *Baluchitherium*.

125. Raymond Dart, "*Australopithecus africanus:* The Man-Ape of South Africa," *Nature*, 115 (1925): 195–99.

126. Andrews, *New Conquest*, 177.

127. Andrews, *Trail of Ancient Man*, 65. On Dodge Cars see Andrews, *New Conquest*, 12–14, 179–80, 228–29. On typewriters see Andrews to Corona Typewriter Company, 10 January 1924, in *Asia*, 24 (1924): 239. See also Warren I. Cohen, *America's Response to China: An Interpretive History of Sino-American Relations*, 2d ed. (New York: Wiley, 1980); Robert McClellan, *The Heathen Chinee: A Study of American Attitudes Toward China 1890–1905* (Columbus: Ohio State University Press, 1971); Emily S. Rosenberg, *Spreading the American Dream: American Economic and Cultural Expansion, 1890–1945* (New York: Hill and Wang, 1982).

128. Andrews, *New Conquest*, 417–23. See also John Michael Kennedy, "Philanthropy and Science in New York City: The American Museum of Natural History, 1868–1968" (Ph.D. dissertation, Yale University, 1968), 156–222; Donna Haraway, *Primate Visions: Gender, Race, and Nature in the World of Modern Science* (New York: Routledge, 1989), 26–58.

5. The Museum, the Zoo, and the Preservation of Nature

1. T. J. Jackson Lears, *No Place of Grace: Anti-Modernism and the Transformation of American Culture 1880–1920* (New York: Pantheon 1981); David I. Macleod, *Building Character in the American Boy: The Boy Scouts, the YMCA, and Their Forerunners, 1879–1920* (Madison: University of Wisconsin Press, 1983), 29–59.

2. Henry Fairfield Osborn, "Biology and other Science in the Schools," *Report of the Schoolmasters Association of New York and Vicinity* (1892–93): 37.

3. Ibid., 35.

4. Henry Fairfield Osborn, *Creative Education in School, College, University and Museum: Personal Observation and Experience of the Half-Century 1877–1927* (New York: Scribners, 1927), 65.

5. Henry Fairfield Osborn, *Impressions of Great Naturalists* (New York: Scribners, 1924), 76.

6. Ibid., p. 22. Osborn emphasizes that point throughout his discussion of Roosevelt, 253–76.
7. Henry Fairfield Osborn, "Zoology at Columbia," *Columbia University Bulletin*, 18 (1897): 5.
8. Ibid., 6–7.
9. On zoology see Keith R. Benson, "American Morphology in the late Nineteenth Century: The Biology Department at Johns Hopkins University," *Journal of the History of Biology*, 18 (1985): 163–205; Hamilton Cravens, "The Role of Universities in the Rise of Experimental Biology," *Science Teacher*, 44 (1977): 33–37; Jane Maienschein, "Whitman at Chicago: Establishing a Chicago Style of Biology?" in Ronald Rainger, Keith R. Benson, and Jane Maienschein, eds., *The American Development of Biology* (Philadelphia: University of Pennsylvania Press, 1988), 151–82; Philip J. Pauly, "The Appearance of Academic Biology in Late Nineteenth-Century America," *Journal of the History of Biology*, 17 (1984): 369–97.
10. W. K. Brooks, *The Foundations of Zoology* (New York: Macmillan, 1899); C. O. Whitman, "The Naturalist's Occupation," *Biological Lectures Delivered at the Marine Biological Laboratory at Woods Hole for 1890* (1891): 27–52; Whitman, "Natural History Work at the Marine Biological Laboratory, Wood's Holl," *Science*, 13 (1904): 538–40. See also Pauly, "Academic Biology," 395–97.
11. Robert B. Downs, *Heinrich Pestalozzi: Father of Modern Pedagogy* (Boston: Twayne, 1975); Gerald Lee Gutek, *Pestalozzi and Education* (New York: Random House, 1968).
12. John Dewey, *School and Society* (Chicago: University of Chicago Press, 1900), 24. See also Lawrence A. Cremin, *American Education: The Metropolitan Experience, 1876–1980* (New York: Harper and Row, 1988).
13. Osborn, *Creative Education*, 8.
14. Henry Fairfield Osborn to Lucretia Perry Osborn, 22 June 1897, and letters throughout 1899, Henry Fairfield Osborn Papers, box 6, New-York Historical Society. See also Henry Fairfield Osborn to Morris K. Jesup, 26 May 1899, Henry Fairfield Osborn Papers, Central Archives, Library, American Museum of Natural History.
15. Osborn, *Creative Education*, 215.
16. Correspondence between Jesup and Adolf Bandelier, James Terry, and Appleton Sturgis to have the museum sponsor their work or purchase their anthropological collections is in Central Archives, 1888–91. Jesup agreed to sponsor Carl Lumholtz's explorations at a trustee meeting on 28 March 1890, American Museum Board of Trustees Minutes, Central Archives. Jesup's correspondence with Peary is in Central Archives, 1889–1905. On Jesup's donations and role as president of the Peary Club see "Jesup, Morris K," *Dictionary of American Biography* (New York: Scribners, 1932), 10: 61–62.
17. Osborn, "Zoology at Columbia," 3. On college museums see Sally Gregory Kohlstedt, "Museums on Campus: A Tradition of Inquiry and Teaching," in Rainger, Benson, and Maienschein, *American Biology*, 15–47; idem, "Curiosities and Cabinets: Natural History Museums and Education on the Antebellum Campus," *Isis*, 79 (1988): 405–26.
18. *Annual Report of the American Museum of Natural History*, 19 (1886): 10.
19. Thomas Bender, *Toward an Urban Vision: Ideas and Institutions in Nineteenth-Century America* (1975; reprint ed., Baltimore: Johns Hopkins University

Press, 1982), 159–87. Little evidence exists to link Jesup's ideas directly to Olmsted's, but the two men were acquainted: Laura Wood Roper, *FLO: A Biography of Frederick Law Olmsted* (Baltimore: Johns Hopkins University Press, 1973), 128, 334–35. On the museum as a Garden of Eden see Donna Haraway, *Primate Visions: Gender, Race, and Nature in the World of Modern Science* (New York: Routledge, 1989), 26–58.

20. Macleod, *Building Character in the American Boy*; Peter J. Schmitt, *Back to Nature: The Arcadian Myth in Urban America* (New York: Oxford University Press, 1969). See also William L. Bowers, *The Country Life Movement in America, 1900–1920* (Port Washington, N.Y.: Kennikat Press, 1974).

21. Roderick Nash, *Wilderness and the American Mind*, 3d ed. (New Haven: Yale University Press, 1982), 143–45. See also Stephen Fox, *John Muir and his Legacy: The American Conservation Movement* (Boston: Little Brown, 1981), 108–50; John F. Reiger, *American Sportsmen and the Origins of Conservation* (New York: Winchester Press, 1975).

22. Lears, *No Place of Grace*; Macleod, *Building Character in the American Boy.*

23. *Annual Reports of the American Museum of Natural History*, (1882–85). See also John Michael Kennedy, "Philanthropy and Science in New York City: The American Museum of Natural History, 1868–1968" (Ph.D. dissertation, Yale University, 1968), 82–84; L. P. Gratacap, "History of the American Museum of Natural History," chap. 4, Central Archives.

24. Sargent authored volume 9 of the tenth census, *Report on the Forests of North America* (Washington, D.C.: Government Printing Office, 1884). On Sargent see Stephen Fox, *John Muir and his Legacy*, 109; Frank Graham, Jr., *The Adirondack Park: A Political History* (New York: Knopf, 1978), 97–105. Correspondence between Sargent and Jesup is in Central Archives.

25. Graham, *Adirondack Park*, 102. The Jesup quotation is from his address of 6 December 1883 to the New York State Chamber of Commerce and is cited in Graham, *Adirondack Park*, 99.

26. Morris K. Jesup, "Report to the Trustees," 1882, Central Archives.

27. Joel Asaph Allen, *History of North American Pinnipeds: A Monograph of the Walruses, Sealions, Sea-Bears and Seals of North America* (1880; reprint ed., New York: Arno, 1974).

28. Joel Asaph Allen, "The American Bisons Living and Extinct," *Memoirs of the Museum of Comparative Zoology*, 4 (1876): 1–246. Allen's articles on bird protection include "On the Decrease of Birds in the United States," *Penn Monthly Magazine* (December 1876): 931–44; "Present Wholesale Destruction of Bird-Life in the United States," *Science*, 7 (1886): 191–95; "Destruction of Birds for Millinery Purposes," *Science*, 7 (1886): 196–97; "Protection of Birds by Legislation," *Forest and Stream*, 17 (1886): 304–5.

29. On conservation see Allen to Jesup, 15 December 1896, 4 February 1897, 12 November 1897, 24 November 1897, Central Archives. In the last letter Allen referred to Jesup's "keen interest . . . in the subject of bird protection" and stated that Jesup "proposed the formation of an Audubon Society, . . . lent the movement the countenance of your name, and suggested that it be organized in cooperation with the American Museum." On Allen's role in the development of the American Ornithologists' Union, the Audubon Society, and other organizations see Joel Asaph Allen, *Autobiographical Notes and a Bibliography of the Scientific Publications of Joel Asaph Allen* (New York: American Museum of Natural History, 1916), 41, 45. On the museum expe-

ditions and mammal hall see Joel Asaph Allen, *North American Ruminants, American Museum of Natural History Guide Leaflet,* no. 5 (New York: American Museum of Natural History, 1902).

30. Frank M. Chapman, "What Constitutes a Museum Collection of Birds?" *Proceedings of the IVth International Ornithological Congress,* (1905): 148.

31. Frank M. Chapman, "The Educational Value of Bird Study," *Educational Review,* (1899): 242. Chapman's guide books include *The Bird Rock Group, American Museum of Natural History Guide Leaflet,* no. 1 (New York: American Museum of Natural History, 1901); *The Habitat Groups of North American Birds in the American Museum of Natural History, American Museum of Natural History Guide Leaflet,* no. 28 (New York: American Museum of Natural History, 1930). See also Frederic A. Lucas, "The Story of Museum Groups, Part II," *American Museum Journal,* 14 (1914): 51–65.

32. Chapman, *Bird Rock Group,* 5, 13.

33. In 1891 Jesup sent S. D. Dill, the curator of the Hall of North American Woods, to California to obtain a Sequoia specimen; he brought back a tree dubbed "Mark Twain": S. D. Dill to Morris K. Jesup, 12 December 1891, Central Archives. See also George H. Sherwood, *The Sequoia: A Historical Review of Biological Science, American Museum of Natural History Guide Leaflet,* no. 8 (New York: American Museum of Natural History, 1902).

34. Franz Boas to Morris K. Jesup, 21 March 1898, Franz Boas Papers, American Philosophical Society. See also Boas to Jesup, 2 March 1897, 3 June 1897, 15 June 1897, Central Archives.

35. For accounts of the Jesup North Pacific Expedition see Franz Boas, "The Jesup North Pacific Expedition," in George W. Stocking, *A Franz Boas Reader: The Shaping of American Anthropology, 1883–1911* (Chicago: University of Chicago Press, 1974), 107–16; idem, "The Jesup North Pacific Expedition," *Thirteenth International Congress of Americanists* (1902): 91–100. See also Stanley A. Freed, Ruth S. Freed, and Laila Williamson, "Capitalist Philanthropy and Russian Revolutionaries: The Jesup North Pacific Expedition (1897–1902)," *American Anthropologist,* 90 (1988): 7–24.

36. Wilbur C. Knight, "The Wyoming Fossil Field Expedition of July 1899," *National Geographic,* 11 (1900): 449–65. See also William H. Goetzmann and Kay Sloan, *Looking Far North: The Harriman Expedition to Alaska, 1899* (Princeton: Princeton University Press, 1982). On Curtis see Edward S. Curtis, *The North American Indian,* 20 vols. (Cambridge: Cambridge University Press, 1907–30).

37. Osborn presented resolutions for museum endorsement of conservationists: Trustee Minutes, 10 May 1909, Central Archives.

38. Theodore Roosevelt and George Bird Grinnell, *American Big-Game Hunting: The Book of the Boone and Crockett Club* (New York: Forest and Stream, 1893), 10.

39. "What Constitutes a True Sportsman," *American Sportsman,* 2 (1872), cited in Reiger, *American Sportsmen and Conservation,* 29.

40. Reiger, *American Sportsmen and Conservation;* John F. Reiger, ed., *The Passing of the Great West: Selected Papers of George Bird Grinnell* (New York: Scribners, 1972).

41. Reiger, *American Sportsmen and Conservation,* 139. On Grinnell's role in the formation of the Audubon Society see Reiger, 68–75. Allen, *Autobiographical*

Notes, 45, indicates that he and five others established that society in New York in 1886.

42. Theodore Roosevelt, *An Autobiography* (New York: Macmillan, 1914), 26. On Roosevelt's early association with Frederick Osborn see Paul Russell Cutright, *Theodore Roosevelt: The Making of a Conservationist* (Urbana: University of Illinois Press, 1985), 89.

43. Theodore Roosevelt, *Ranch Life and the Hunting Trail* (New York: Century, 1888); idem, *Hunting Trips of a Ranchman* (New York: Putnam, 1885).

44. Ibid. See also Roosevelt, *An Autobiography*, 29–54.

45. Theodore Roosevelt, "The Strenuous Life," in Theodore Roosevelt, *The Strenuous Life: Essays and Addresses by Theodore Roosevelt* (New York: Century, 1901), 21. See also several other essays in that book. On the characterization of Roosevelt's statements see Edmund Morris, *The Rise of Theodore Roosevelt* (New York: Ballantine, 1979), 467.

46. Theodore Roosevelt, "Race Decadence," *Outlook*, 97 (1911): 763–69; idem, "A Premium on Race Suicide," *Outlook*, 105 (1913): 163–64. See also Thomas G. Dyer, *Theodore Roosevelt and the Idea of Race* (Baton Rouge: Louisiana State University Press, 1980), 142–67.

47. Kennedy, "Philanthropy and Science," 102–4. Osborn became an honorary member of the Boone and Crockett Club in 1899. Henry Fairfield Osborn, *The Preservation of the Wild Animals of North America* (New York: Boone and Crockett Club, 1904).

48. Henry Fairfield Osborn, "Address of Welcome at the Opening of the New York Zoological Park," *Fourth Annual Report of the New York Zoological Society* (1900): 77.

49. Madison Grant, "The Origins of the New York Zoological Society," in Theodore Roosevelt and George Bird Grinnell, *Trail and Camp Fire: Book of the Boone and Crockett Club* (New York: Forest and Stream, 1897), 320.

50. Madison Grant, *The Passing of the Great Race, Or the Racial Basis of European History* (New York: Scribners, 1916); idem, *The Conquest of a Continent, Or, the Expansion of Races in America* (New York: Scribners, 1933).

    William Temple Hornaday, *Our Vanishing Wildlife: Its Extermination and Preservation* (New York: New York Zoological Society, 1913); idem, *Thirty Years for Wild Life: Gains and Losses in the Thankless Task* (New York: Scribners, 1931). Hornaday frequently condemned "members of the lower class of southern Europe [who] are a dangerous menace to our wildlife": *Our Vanishing Wildlife*, 100. On pages 101–4 of that same work, he also criticized liberal immigration policies as a threat to nature.

51. Osborn, *Creative Education*, 162.

52. Ibid., 28.

53. Ibid., 26–49.

54. Ibid., 260.

55. Osborn, "Zoology at Columbia," 6–7.

56. Osborn, *Impressions of Great Naturalists*, 253–76. See also Osborn, "Theodore Roosevelt, Naturalist," *Natural History*, 19 (1919): 9–10. On Butler see Osborn, *Impressions of Great Naturalists*, 223–26.

57. Henry Fairfield Osborn, *Fifty-Two Years of Research, Observation and Publication, 1877–1929: A Life Adventure in Breadth and Depth* (New York: Scribners, 1930), 151. On the romance of paleontology see the following by Osborn:

"Fossil Wonders of the West, the Dinosaurs of Bone-Cabin Quarry, Being the First Description of the Greatest 'Find' of Extinct Animals Ever Made," *Century Magazine*, 68 (1904): 680–94; "Fossil Wonders of the West: The Evolution of the Horse in America," *Century Magazine*, 69 (1904): 3–17; "Western Explorations for Fossil Vertebrates," *Popular Science Monthly*, 67 (1905): 561–68; "Hunting the Ancestral Elephant in the Fayûm Desert: Discoveries of the Recent African Expedition of the American Museum of Natural History," *Century Magazine*, 74 (1907): 815–35; "The Discovery of an Unknown Continent," *Natural History*, 24 (1923): 133–49; "Why Central Asia?" *Natural History*, 26 (1926): 263–69; and many other articles on the Central Asiatic Expeditions. In 1926 the editors of *Natural History* devoted an entire issue to the romance of fossil hunting; W. D. Matthew, Richard Swann Lull, and several other Osborn associates contributed articles.

58. Osborn, *Fifty-Two Years*. On Osborn's inflated idea of his own self-importance see George Gaylord Simpson, *Concession to the Improbable: An Unconventional Autobiography* (New Haven: Yale University Press, 1978), 39–41; Edwin H. Colbert, *A Fossil Hunter's Notebook: My Life with Dinosaurs and Other Friends* (New York: Dutton, 1982), 67–82; Geoffrey Hellman, *Bankers, Bones and Beetles: The First Century of the American Museum of Natural History* (Garden City, N.Y.: Natural History Press, 1968), 193–206.

59. Kennedy, "Philanthropy and Science in New York City," 156–222; Haraway, *Primate Visions*, 26–58. Besides the Central Asiatic Expeditions, other major explorations that Osborn promoted included: Vilhjalmur Stefansson and Lincoln Ellsworth to the North Pole, Herbert Lang and James Chapin to the Congo, Carl Akeley to Africa, and William King Gregory and Harry Raven to Central Africa. Information on each of the expeditions and the exhibits associated with them is filed under the individual topic in Central Archives.

60. Osborn, *Creative Education*, 40–44.

6. Osborn, Nature, and Evolution

1. Henry Fairfield Osborn to William Henry Osborn, 27 February 1891, Henry Fairfield Osborn Papers, box 5, New-York Historical Society.

2. Peter J. Bowler, *The Eclipse of Darwinism: Anti-Darwinian Evolution Theories in the Decades Around 1900* (Baltimore: Johns Hopkins University Press, 1983); Wolf-Ernst Reif, "The Search for a Macroevolutionary Theory in German Paleontology," *Journal of the History of Biology*, 19 (1986): 79–130. See also Ronald Rainger, "The Continuation of the Morphological Tradition: American Paleontology 1880–1910," *Journal of the History of Biology*, 14 (1981): 129–58.

3. August Weismann, *Essays Upon Heredity and Kindred Biological Problems*, ed. E. B. Poulton, Selmar Schonland and Arthur E. Shipley, 2 vols. (Oxford: Oxford University Press, 1891–92); *The Germ Plasm: A Theory of Heredity*, trans. W. Newton Parker and Harriet Ronfeldt (London: Scott, 1893); Henry Fairfield Osborn, "Evolution and Heredity," *Biological Lectures Delivered at the Marine Biological Laboratory at Woods Hole for 1890* (1891): 131–40.

4. Henry Fairfield Osborn, "Are Acquired Variations Inherited?" *American Naturalist*, 25 (1891): 205. See also Osborn, "Evolution and Heredity"; Henry Fairfield Osborn, "The Present Problem of Heredity," *Atlantic Monthly*, 67 (1891): 353–64.

5. Osborn, "The Hereditary Mechanism and the Search for the Unknown Factors of Evolution," *Biological Lectures Delivered at the Marine Biological Laboratory at Wood's Hole for 1894* (1895): 79–81. See also Frederick B. Churchill, "The Weismann-Spencer Controversy over the Inheritance of Acquired Characters," *Proceedings of the 15th International Congress on the History of Science* (1978): 451–68.

6. Osborn, "The Present Problem of Heredity," 363.

7. Henry Fairfield Osborn and Jacob L. Wortman, "Fossil Mammals of the Wahsatch and Wind River Beds, Collection of 1891," *Bulletin of the American Museum of Natural History*, 4 (1892): 85. The term *modernization* referred to the change from archaic mammals with no modern representatives, to more recent mammals that have modern analogues.

8. Henry Fairfield Osborn, "Rise of the Mammalia in North America," *Proceedings of the American Association for the Advancement of Science*, 42 (1894): 227.

9. Henry Fairfield Osborn, *From the Greeks to Darwin: An Outline of the Development of the Evolution Idea* (New York: Macmillan, 1894), 188–201, 221–66, 303–48.

10. Osborn, "The Hereditary Mechanism," 95.

11. Henry Fairfield Osborn, "Ontogenic and Phylogenic Variation," *Science*, 4 (1896): 788. See also Henry Fairfield Osborn, "Organic Selection," *Science*, 6 (1897): 583–87.

12. James Mark Baldwin, "A New Factor in Evolution," *American Naturalist*, 30 (1896): 411–51, 536–53; Conwy Lloyd Morgan, "Of Modification and Variation," *Science*, 4 (1896): 733–40. See also Robert J. Richards, *Darwin and the Emergence of Evolutionary Theories of Mind and Behavior* (Chicago: University of Chicago Press, 1987), 398–404, 480–84.

13. Henry Fairfield Osborn, "A Mode of Evolution Requiring neither Natural Selection nor the Inheritance of Acquired Characters," *Transactions of the New York Academy of Sciences*, 15 (1896): 141–42, 148.

14. Richards, *Darwin and Evolutionary Theories of Mind and Behavior*, 486–95.

15. Henry Fairfield Osborn, "Tetraplasy, the Law of the Four Inseparable Factors of Evolution," *Journal of the Academy of Natural Sciences of Philadelphia*, 2d ser., 15 (1912): 275–309.

16. Henry Fairfield Osborn, "Orthogenesis as Observed from Paleontological Evidence Beginning in the year 1889," *American Naturalist*, 56 (1922): 134–43; idem, "Aristogenesis, the Creative Principle in the Origin of Species," *American Naturalist*, 68 (1934): 228–29. Osborn often contrasted his ideas to Henri Louis Bergson, *Creative Evolution*, trans. A. Mitchell (New York: 1910), who believed that only a vital impulse could explain the causes and direction of evolution.

17. Henry Fairfield Osborn, "'Mutations' of Waagen, 'Mutations' of De Vries and 'Rectigradations' of Osborn," *Science*, 33 (1911): 328; "Aristogenesis," 193–235.

18. See the following by Osborn: "Phylogeny of the Rhinoceroses of Europe," *Bulletin of the American Museum of Natural History*, 13 (1900): 229–67; "The Origin of the Mammalia," *American Naturalist*, 32 (1898): 91–109; "Fossil Wonders of the West: The Evolution of the Horse in America," *Century Magazine*, 69 (1904): 3–17.

19. Henry Fairfield Osborn, *The Age of Mammals in Europe, Asia and North America* (New York: Macmillan, 1910), 30–31. Examples of Osborn's phylogenies are in *The Titanotheres of Ancient Wyoming, Dakota, and Nebraska*, 2 vols.

(Washington, D.C.: Government Printing Office, 1929) and *Proboscidea. A Monograph of the Discovery, Evolution, Migration and Extinction of the Mastodonts and Elephants of the World*, 2 vols. (New York: American Museum Press, 1936, 1942).

20. Osborn, *Proboscidea*, passim. See also Henry Fairfield Osborn, "The Thirty-Nine Distinct Lines of Proboscidean Descent and the Migration into all Parts of the World except Australia," *Proceedings of the American Philosophical Society*, 74 (1934): 273–85.
21. Osborn, *The Titanotheres*, 2: 810–28, especially 819.
22. Henry Fairfield Osborn, "Geological and Faunal Relations of Europe and America during the Tertiary Period and the Theory of the Successive Invasions of an African Fauna," *Science*, 11 (1900): 563–64. See also Henry Fairfield Osborn, "The Law of Adaptive Radiation," *American Naturalist*, 36 (1902): 353–63.
23. Osborn, "Tetraplasy"; Osborn, *The Age of Mammals*, 22–39. See also Henry Fairfield Osborn, "Homoplasy as a Law of Latent or Potential Homology," *American Naturalist*, 36 (1902): 259–71.
24. Charles Darwin, *On the Origin of Species By Means of Natural Selection, or the Preservation of Favoured Races in the Struggle for Life* (1859; reprint ed., Cambridge, Mass.: Harvard University Press, 1964), 131–70, 254–60. See also Dov Ospovat, *The Development of Darwin's Theory: Natural History, Natural Theology, and Natural Selection, 1838–1859* (Cambridge: Cambridge University Press, 1981), 3, 20–23.
25. Louis Dollo, "Les lois d'évolution," *Bulletin de la Société Belge de Géologie, Paléontologie et d'Hydrologie*, 7 (1893): 164–66. See also Stephen Jay Gould, "Dollo on Dollo's Law: Irreversibility and the Status of Evolutionary Laws," *Journal of the History of Biology*, 3 (1970): 189–212.
26. Gould, "Dollo on Dollo's Law," 207; William King Gregory, "Williston's Law Relating to the Evolution of Skull Bones in Vertebrates," *American Journal of Physical Anthropology*, 20 (1935): 123–52. On Cope's law see Edward Drinker Cope, *The Primary Factors of Organic Evolution* (Chicago: Open Court, 1896).
27. Henry Fairfield Osborn, *Evolution and Religion* (New York: Scribners, 1923), 16.
28. Henry Fairfield Osborn, "Origin of Single Characters as Observed in Fossil and Living Animals and Plants," *American Naturalist*, 49 (1915): 210; idem, "Paleontology Versus Genetics," *Science*, 72 (1930): 2; idem, "Biological Inductions from the Evolution of the Proboscidea," *Proceedings of the National Academy of Sciences*, 19 (1933): 160–61.
29. Henry Fairfield Osborn, "Darwin and Palaeontology," in American Association for the Advancement of Science, *Fifty Years of Darwinism* (New York: Henry Holt, 1909), 240–41.
30. The quotations are from Osborn, *Evolution and Religion*, 11; Henry Fairfield Osborn, *Creative Education in School, College, University and Museum: Personal Observation and Experience of the Half-Century 1877–1927* (New York: Scribners, 1927), 252; idem, *Evolution and Religion in Education: Polemics of the Fundamentalist Controversy of 1922 to 1926* (New York: Scribners, 1926), 7.
31. Osborn, *Evolution and Religion in Education*. See also Henry Fairfield Osborn, *The Earth Speaks to Bryan* (New York: Scribners, 1925).
32. See Garland E. Allen, *Life Science in the Twentieth Century* (1975; reprint ed.,

Cambridge: Cambridge University Press, 1978), 1–19; Ronald Rainger, Keith R. Benson, and Jane Maienschein, "Introduction," in Ronald Rainger, Keith R. Benson, and Jane Maienschein, eds., *The American Development of Biology* (Philadelphia: University of Pennsylvania Press, 1988), 4–6.

33. Allen, *Life Science*, 21–72; Philip J. Pauly, *Controlling Life: Jacques Loeb and the Engineering Ideal in Biology* (New York: Oxford University Press, 1987). Roux's work is reprinted in Benjamin H. Willier and Jane M. Oppenheimer, *Foundations of Experimental Embryology* (Englewood Cliffs, N.J.: Prentice Hall, 1964), 2–37.

34. T. H. Morgan, *Regeneration* (New York: Macmillan, 1901); and idem, *Embryology and Genetics* (New York: Columbia University Press, 1934). See also Jane Maienschein, "Experimental Biology in Transition: Harrison's Embryology," *Studies in History of Biology*, 6 (1983): 107–27; and idem, "Heredity/Development in the United States, circa 1900," *History and Philosophy of the Life Sciences*, 9 (1987): 79–93.

35. On genetics see Garland E. Allen, *Thomas Hunt Morgan: The Man and His Science* (Princeton: Princeton University Press, 1978); William B. Provine, *The Origins of Theoretical Population Genetics* (Chicago: University of Chicago Press, 1971). On the relationship between morphology and experimental biology see the articles in *Journal of the History of Biology*, 14 (1981): 89–191; Joel B. Hagen, "Experimentalists and Naturalists in Twentieth-Century Botany: Experimental Taxonomy 1920–1950," *Journal of the History of Biology*, 17 (1984): 249–70.

36. Osborn's lectures at the MBL were "Evolution and Heredity," "Unknown Factors of Evolution," "A Student's Reminiscences of Huxley," *Biological Lectures Delivered at the Marine Biological Laboratory at Woods Hole for 1895* (1896): 29–42. An outline of Osborn's activities as president of the MBL board is in Henry Fairfield Osborn Papers, box 19, New-York Historical Society. His support of the MBL as a research center is noted above in Chapter 3. Henry Fairfield Osborn to Seth Low, 31 May 1895, Seth Low Papers, Central Record Files, Low Memorial Library, Columbia University, recommended Henry E. Crampton for doing work at Woods Hole. William King Gregory refers to working at Woods Hole in 1906 in miscellaneous biographical notes in William King Gregory Papers, box J, Central Archives, Library, American Museum of Natural History.

37. Correspondence between Osborn and Wilson is in Henry Fairfield Osborn Correspondence, Archives, Department of Vertebrate Paleontology, American Museum of Natural History; Henry Fairfield Osborn Papers, Central Archives. Correspondence with Sumner is in the Osborn Papers, Central Archives. See also Henry Fairfield Osborn to E. B. Poulton, 11 February 1919, Osborn Papers, box 9, New-York Historical Society.

38. On Wilson see Maienschein, "Shifting Assumptions in American Biology: Embryology, 1890–1910," *Journal of the History of Biology*, 14 (1981): 99–101; idem, "Cell Lineage, Ancestral Reminiscence, and the Biogenetic Law," *Journal of the History of Biology*, 11 (1978): 139–46. On Sumner see William B. Provine, "Francis B. Sumner and the Evolutionary Synthesis," *Studies in History of Biology*, 3 (1979): 224–28.

39. William Bateson, *Materials for the Study of Variation, treated with especial Regard to Discontinuity in the Origin of Species* (London: Macmillan, 1894).

40. Hugo de Vries, *Die Mutationstheorie*, 2 vols. (Leipzig, 1901, 1903). On the

reaction to de Vries's theory see Diane B. Paul and Barbara A. Kimmelman, "Mendel in America: Theory and Practice, 1900–1919," in Rainger, Benson, and Maienschein, *American Biology*, 281–310; Garland E. Allen, "Hugo de Vries and the Reception of the 'Mutation Theory,'" *Journal of the History of Biology*, 2 (1969): 55–87.

41. Gregor Mendel, "Experiments on Plant Hybrids," in Curt Stern and Eva R. Sherwood, eds., *The Origin of Genetics: A Mendel Sourcebook* (San Francisco: W. H. Freeman, 1966), 1–48.

42. William Bateson, *Mendel's Principles of Heredity: A Defence* (Macmillan, 1902). On Bateson see Allen, *Life Science*, 50–52; and Provine, *Theoretical Population Genetics*, 56–70. See also Frederick B. Churchill, "William Johannsen and the Genotype Concept," *Journal of the History of Biology*, 7 (1974): 5–30.

43. T. H. Morgan, A. H. Sturtevant, H. J. Muller, and C. B. Bridges, *The Mechanism of Mendelian Heredity* (New York: Henry Holt, 1915). On Morgan's later efforts see Garland E. Allen, "T. H. Morgan and the Split between Embryology and Genetics, 1910–1935," in T. J. Horder, J. A. Witkowski, and C. C. Wylie, eds., *A History of Embryology* (Cambridge: Cambridge University Press, 1985), 113–46; and Scott Gilbert, "Cellular Politics: Ernest Everett Just, Richard B. Goldschmidt, and the Attempt to Reconcile Embryology and Genetics," in Rainger, Benson, and Maienschein, *American Biology*, 311–46.

44. T. H. Morgan, *A Critique of the Theory of Evolution* (Princeton: Princeton University Press, 1916), 25–26.

45. The quotation is from T. H. Morgan to Henry Fairfield Osborn, 4 June 1918, Osborn Papers, Central Archives. On Morgan's criticisms of Osborn's speculative views see Garland E. Allen, "T. H. Morgan and the Emergence of a New American Biology," *Quarterly Review of Biology*, 44 (1969): 168–88.

46. John Michael Kennedy, "Philanthropy and Science in New York City: The American Museum of Natural History, 1868–1968" (Ph.D. dissertation, Yale University, 1968).

47. On Gregory's problems with Morgan see "Fifty Years in the Department of Zoology, 1896–1946," unpublished manuscript, Gregory Papers, box J; William King Gregory to Edwin H. Colbert, 15 September 1928, Gregory Papers, box 4. Osborn turned to Wilson and Columbia President Nicholas Murray Butler to support Gregory: Osborn to Wilson, 8 March 1913, 10 March 1913, Osborn Papers, Central Archives; Osborn to Nicholas Murray Butler, 14 April 1916, 18 April 1916, 31 January 1921, 8 February 1921, 18 February 1921, and 9 April 1924, Osborn Papers, Central Archives.

48. Osborn to Nicholas Murray Butler, 14 February 1921, 23 February 1921, 10 May 1923, 24 July 1924, Nicholas Murray Butler Papers, Central Record Files, Low Memorial Library, Columbia University.

49. Henry Fairfield Osborn, "The Continuous Origin of Certain Unit Characters as Observed by a Palaeontologist," *Harvey Society*, 7 (1912): 202.

50. Henry Fairfield Osborn, "Origin of Single Characters," 193–240. On the split between naturalists and experimentalists see Garland E. Allen, "Naturalists and Experimentalists: The Genotype and the Phenotype," *Studies in History of Biology*, 3 (1979): 179–209; and Ernst Mayr, "Prologue: Some Thoughts on the History of the Evolutionary Synthesis," in Ernst Mayr and William B. Provine, eds., *The Evolutionary Synthesis: Perspectives on the Unification of Biology* (Cambridge, Mass.: Harvard University Press, 1980), 1–48.

51. Osborn, "Unknown Factors of Evolution," 86.
52. Henry Fairfield Osborn, "Evolution as it Appears to the Paleontologist," *Science*, 26 (1907): 745.
53. Osborn, "Darwin and Palaeontology," 228.
54. Keith R. Benson, "From Museum Research to Laboratory Research: The Transformation of Natural History into Academic Biology," in Rainger, Benson, and Maienschein, *American Biology*, 49–83; Robert E. Kohler, *From Medical Chemistry to Biochemistry: The Making of a Biomedical Discipline* (Cambridge: Cambridge University Press, 1982); Pauly, *Controlling Life*. On that impact in an organizational context see Toby A. Appel, "Organizing Biology: The American Society of Naturalists and its 'Affiliated Societies,' 1883–1923," in Rainger, Benson, and Maienschein, *American Biology*, 87–120.
55. Osborn, "The Unknown Factors of Evolution," 79–80; idem, "The Origin of Single Characters," 235–38; and idem, *Evolution and Religion in Education*, 9–10, 216–17.
56. Osborn to Bateson, 30 March 1894, and 12 April 1894, Bateson Correspondence, Archives, DVP. Henry Fairfield Osborn, "Law vs. Chance," unpublished manuscript, Osborn Papers, Central Archives. See also "Paleontology Versus Genetics," and "Paleontology versus De Vriesianism and Genetics in the Factors of the Evolution Problem," *Science*, 73 (1931): 547–49. On changing ideas on mutations see Provine, *Theoretical Population Genetics*, 114–78.
57. Osborn, *The Origin and Evolution of Life on the Theory of Action, Reaction and Interaction* (New York: Scribners, 1917). Morgan's critique was analyzed by Allen in "T. H. Morgan." On Loeb see Pauly, *Controlling Life*; and Nathan Reingold, "Jacques Loeb, the Scientist: His Papers and His Era," *Library of Congress Quarterly Journal of Current Acquisitions*, 19 (1962): 119–30. The quotation is from Osborn, *Evolution and Religion in Education*, 90–91.
58. Timothy Lenoir, *The Strategy of Life: Teleology and Mechanism in Nineteenth-Century German Biology* (Dordrecht: Reidel, 1982); Sharon Kingsland, "Toward a Natural History of Man: C. M. Child, C. J. Herrick, and the Dynamic Study of Behavior at the University of Chicago," in Keith R. Benson, Jane Maienschien, and Ronald Rainger, eds., *The Expansion of American Biology* (New Brunswick, N.J.: Rutgers University Press, 1991).
59. Osborn, *Evolution and Religion in Education*, 13, 62. In a letter to the German vertebrate paleontologist Frederick von Huene of 26 July 1934, Osborn stated that "The argument from Design is far stronger than it was in Darwin's time; certainly, also, there is no 'Chance' in bio-mechanical evolution," Osborn Papers, Central Archives.
60. David Hammack, *Power and Society: Greater New York at the Turn of the Century* (New York: Columbia University Press, 1987), 78.
61. Henry Fairfield Osborn, "Report to Trustees, May 1908," unpublished manuscript, Central Archives.
62. Osborn, "Origin of Single Characters," 237. See also Henry Fairfield Osborn, "William Bateson on Darwinism," *Science*, 55 (1922): 194–99; and clippings and unpublished comments in the Bateson file, Osborn Papers, Central Archives.
63. The quotations are from Osborn, *Evolution and Religion in Education*, 73; and Osborn, *Creative Education*, 201. See also Gregg Mitman, "Evolution as Gospel: William Patten, the Language of Democracy, and the Great War," *Isis*, 81 (1990): 446–63.

64. Osborn, *Evolution and Religion in Education*, 73.
65. Henry Fairfield Osborn, "Biological Inductions from the Evolution of the Proboscidea," *Proceedings of the National Academy of Sciences*, 19 (1933): 161.
66. Henry Fairfield Osborn, "Eighteen Principles of Adaptation in Alloiometrons and Aristogenes," *Palaeobiologica*, 6 (1935): 273–302.
67. Osborn, "Biological Inductions from the Evolution of the Proboscidea," 161.
68. Osborn, *Evolution and Religion in Education*, 54.
69. Osborn, "Unknown Factors of Evolution," 79–81.
70. Benson, "From Museum Research to Laboratory Research"; Appel, "Organizing Biology."
71. Osborn, "Origin of Single Characters," 236–37.
72. Osborn, *From the Greeks to Darwin*. See also Osborn, "Unknown Factors of Evolution."
73. Osborn, *Creative Education*, 3–34, 39–49. Osborn referred to the impact of the museum on an associate, James Terry, on 14–15.
74. Osborn, *Evolution and Religion in Education*, 48.
75. Osborn, *Creative Education*, 96–98, 288–90, 298–308. Osborn disparaged the income tax in letters of the same date to Hamilton Fish and Royal S. Copeland, 24 July 1935, Osborn Papers, box 10, New-York Historical Society.
76. In the *Age of Mammals* Osborn devoted pages 374–509 to a discussion of the Pleistocene; however, he only examined questions on the antiquity of humans on pages 494–500.
77. Henry Fairfield Osborn, "Men of the Old Stone Age, with an Account of a Motor Tour Through the Principal Regions of Southwestern Europe," *American Museum Journal*, 12 (1912): 279–95. A map indicating the places that Osborn stopped on that tour is appended to Henry Fairfield Osborn, *Men of the Old Stone Age: Their Environment, Life and Art* (New York: Scribners, 1915).
78. The comment was made by Harry L. Shapiro and is included in Geoffrey Hellman, *Bankers, Bones and Beetles: The First Century of the American Museum of Natural History* (Garden City, N.Y.: Natural History Press, 1968), 203. In a letter to William King Gregory, Nelson noted that he devoted over one year's work to *Men of the Old Stone Age*: Nels C. Nelson to William King Gregory, 29 October 1932, Gregory Papers, box 7.
79. Osborn, *Men of the Old Stone Age*, 72–84, 95–103.
80. Ibid., 144.
81. Ibid., 257; Marcellin Boule, *Les Hommes Fossils: éléments de paléontologie humaine* (Paris: Masson, 1921); Arthur Keith, *The Antiquity of Man*, 2d ed., 2 vols. (London: Williams and Norgate, 1925). See also Peter J. Bowler, *Theories of Human Evolution: A Century of Debate, 1844–1944* (Baltimore: Johns Hopkins University Press, 1986), 87–100; and Michael Hammond, "The Expulsion of the Neanderthals from Human Ancestry: Marcellin Boule and the Social Context of Scientific Research," *Social Studies of Science*, 12 (1982): 1–36.
82. Osborn, *Men of the Old Stone Age*, 260–502. The decline of races after Cro-Magnon is discussed on pages 456, 486–87, 489, and 501.
83. Ibid., 261, 489. See also Osborn, "The Geological and Faunal Relations of Europe and America during the Tertiary Period," 561–74.
84. Osborn, *Men of the Old Stone Age*, 489, 491.
85. William Z. Ripley, *The Races of Europe: A Sociological Study* (London: Kegan Paul, Trench, Trubner and Co., 1900); Paul Topinard, *Anthropology*, trans.

Robert T. H. Bartley (London: Chapman and Hall, 1898). See also Bowler, *Theories of Human Evolution*; Nancy Stepan, *The Idea of Race in Science: Great Britain 1800–1960* (Hamden, Conn.: Archon, 1982).

86. Franz Boas, *Race, Language and Culture* (New York: Macmillan, 1940). See also George W. Stocking, "The Persistence of Polygenist Thought in Post-Darwinian Anthropology," in George W. Stocking, *Race, Culture and Evolution: Essays in the History of Anthropology* (New York: Free Press, 1968), 42–68.

87. Henry Fairfield Osborn, *Impressions of Great Naturalists* (New York: Scribners, 1924), 238.

88. Osborn, *Men of the Old Stone Age*, 264, 479, 492, 497.

89. Osborn, *Creative Education*, 26–30, 39–49. See also Henry Fairfield Osborn, *Man Rises to Parnassus: Critical Epochs in the Prehistory of Man* (Princeton: Princeton University Press, 1927).

90. Hammack, *Power and Society*; Alan M. Kraut, *The Huddled Masses: The Immigrant in American Society, 1890–1921* (Arlington Heights, Ill.: Harlan Davidson, 1982); and John Higham, *Strangers in the Land: Patterns of American Nativism, 1860–1925* (New Brunswick, N.J.: Rutgers University Press, 1955).

91. Osborn to Grant, 27 June 1928, Osborn Papers, Central Archives. The comment on Italians as "bootleggers" was made at a Galton Society meeting of 5 May 1925, Galton Society Folder, Charles Benedict Davenport Papers, American Philosophical Society. See also Henry Fairfield Osborn, "Birth Selection versus Birth Control," *The Forum*, 88 (1932): 83.

92. Osborn, *Impressions of Great Naturalists*, 243. See also his essays on Cope and Roosevelt in that same work.

93. On the eugenics movement see Daniel J. Kevles, *In the Name of Eugenics: Genetics and the Uses of Human Heredity* (New York: Knopf, 1985). Osborn's support of Davenport is referred to in letters in the Osborn Folder, Davenport Papers. On his support of Laughlin see Osborn's letters to Gregory, Gregory Papers, box 5. On negative eugenics and immigration restriction see Osborn to Grant, 23 December 1919, Grant Folders, Osborn Papers, Central Archives; and Osborn's correspondence with Senator Albert Johnson, Immigration File, Osborn Papers, Central Archives.

94. Osborn's preface to Madison Grant, *The Passing of the Great Race, Or the Racial Basis of European History* (New York: Scribners, 1916), vii–ix. On Osborn's support of Mussolini see Osborn to Grant, 1932, Osborn Papers, Central Archives, American Museum. In 1933 Osborn traveled to Germany to accept an honorary Ph.D. from the University of Heidelberg. That Osborn supported Hitler's policies is referred to in Osborn to Gregory, 23 March 1935, Gregory Papers, box 13; and Gregory to Raymond Pearl, 6 May 1935, Galton Society Folder, Raymond Pearl Papers, American Philosophical Society.

95. Osborn, *Creative Education*, 314. On his opposition to birth control see Henry Fairfield Osborn, "Birth Selection vs Birth Control," 79–83; Osborn to James R. Angell, 2 July 1929, Osborn File, Davenport Papers.

96. Osborn, *Creative Education*, 250–55, 309–14. See also Henry Fairfield Osborn, "The American Museum and Citizenship," *Annual Report of the American Museum of Natural History*, 54 (1923): 1–32. His wife, Lucretia Perry Osborn, also took up such concerns. Her book, *Washington Speaks for Himself* (New York: Scribners, 1927), emphasized patriotic values and democratic ideals.

97. Osborn, *Creative Education*, 311.
98. On Osborn's belief in human progress see *Creative Education*, 40–44, 144–46; *Evolution and Religion in Education*, 39–53, 124–28, 189–211; and *Men of the Old Stone Age*, xii.
99. Higham, *Strangers in the Land*; Kraut, *The Huddled Masses*; and Barbara M. Solomon, *Ancestors and Immigrants: A Changing New England Tradition* (Chicago: University of Chicago Press, 1972).

7. Representing Nature

1. John Michael Kennedy, "Philanthropy and Science in New York City: The American Museum of Natural History" (Ph.D. dissertation, Yale University, 1968); Minutes of the American Museum Board of Trustees, 10 May 1909, Central Archives, Library, American Museum of Natural History.
2. Henry Fairfield Osborn, "The American Museum and Public Health" (1913), Henry Fairfield Osborn Collected Papers, Osborn Library, Department of Vertebrate Paleontology, American Museum of Natural History. See also B. E. Dahlgren, *The Malaria Mosquito, American Museum Guide Leaflet*, no. 17 (New York: American Museum of Natural History, 1908); Charles-Edward Amory Winslow, *Protection of River and Harbor Wastes from Municipal Wastes, American Museum Guide Leaflet*, no. 33 (New York: American Museum of Natural History, 1911). On immigration restriction see Henry Fairfield Osborn, *Creative Education in School, College, University and Museum: Personal Observation and Experience of the Half-Century 1877–1927* (New York: Scribners, 1927), 264–66, 311.
3. Material on the Roosevelt Memorial is in Henry Fairfield Osborn Papers, Central Archives, Library, American Museum of Natural History; Henry Fairfield Osborn, *Fifty-Two Years of Research, Osbservation and Publication, 1877–1929: A Life Adventure in Breadth and Depth* (New York: Scribners, 1930), 113–14; Donna Haraway, *Primate Visions: Gender, Race and Nature in Modern Science* (New York: Routledge, 1989), 26–58.
4. Frank M. Chapman, *The Bird Rock Group, American Museum Guide Leaflet*, no. 1 (New York: American Museum of Natural History, 1901); idem, *The Habitat Groups of North American Birds in the American Museum of Natural History, American Museum Guide Leaflet*, no. 28 (New York: American Museum of Natural History, 1930); idem, *Birds and Man* (1943).
5. D. R. Barton, "Story of a Pioneer Bone-Setter," *Natural History*, 41 (1938): 224.
6. Julie Ann Miller, "A Celebration of Bones," *Science News* (13 April 1985): 232–33. On Osborn's support of Chubb see Osborn Papers, Central Archives.
7. S. Harmsted Chubb, "How Animals Run," *Natural History*, 29 (1929): 544–51.
8. Henry Fairfield Osborn, *The Horse Past and Present in the American Museum of Natural History* (New York: Irving Press, 1913), 12.
9. Henry Fairfield Osborn, "Fossil Wonders of the West: The Evolution of the Horse in America," *Century Magazine*, 69 (1904): 3.
10. Adrian Desmond, "Designing the Dinosaur: Richard Owen's Response to

Robert Edmond Grant," *Isis*, 70 (1979): 224–34. See also the reproductions of Hawkins's work in Sylvia J. Czerkas and Everett C. Olson, eds., *Dinosaurs Past and Present*, 2 vols. (Seattle: University of Washington Press, 1987), 1: xiii–xvi.

11. O. P. Hay, "On the Habits and the Pose of Sauropodous Dinosaurs especially of *Diplodocus*," *American Naturalist*, 42 (1908): 672–81; idem, "On the Manner of Locomotion of the Dinosaurs, especially *Diplodocus*, with remarks on the Origins of Birds," *Proceedings of the Washington Academy of Sciences*, 12 (1910): 1–25; Gustav Tornier, "Wie war der *Diplodocus carnegiei* wirklich gebaut," *Sitzberichte Gesellschaft Naturforschender Freunde zu Berlin* (1909): 193–209.

12. Henry Fairfield Osborn, "Fore Limbs and Hind Limbs of Sauropoda from the Bone Cabin Quarry," *Bulletin of the American Museum of Natural History*, 14 (1901): 199–208; idem, "A Skeleton of *Diplodocus*," *Memoirs of the American Museum of Natural History*, 1 (1899): 191–214; W. D. Matthew, "The Pose of Sauropod Dinosaurs," *American Naturalist*, 44 (1910): 547–60; William King Gregory, "The Weight of the *Brontosaurus*," *Science*, 22 (1905): 572.

13. William King Gregory, "William Diller Matthew, 1871–1930," *Natural History*, 30 (1930): 664.

14. Adam Hermann, "Modern Laboratory Methods in Vertebrate Paleontology," *Bulletin of the American Museum of Natural History*, 26 (1909): 310–15. The Christman drawings are in the DVP Photo Files, Drawer 1, Archives, DVP.

15. On Ditmars see Henry Fairfield Osborn, "*Tyrannosaurus*, Restoration and Model of the Skeleton," *Bulletin of the American Museum of Natural History*, 32 (1913): 91–92. Henry Fairfield Osborn and C. C. Mook, "Characters and Restoration of the Sauropod Genus *Camarasaurus* Cope," *Proceedings of the American Philosophical Society*, 58 (1919): 386–96.

16. The quotations are from Barnum Brown, "The *Trachodon* Group," *American Museum Journal*, 8 (1908): 51; and William Diller Matthew, "*Allosaurus*, a Carnivorous Dinosaur and its Prey," *American Museum Journal*, 8 (1908): 5.

17. Osborn, "*Tyrannosaurus*, Restoration and Model of the Skeleton," 92.

18. W. D. Matthew, "*The Tyrannosaurus*," *American Museum Journal*, 10 (1910): 7.

19. Barbara Novak, *Nature and Culture: American Landscape and Painting, 1825–1875* (New York: Oxford, 1980), 66–77, 221. Church gave advice to the Osborns on building Castle Rock: article from the *New York Daily News*, 26 October 1977, in Henry Fairfield Osborn Papers, box 1, New-York Historical Society.

20. On Chapman see above, n.4. See also *The Stokes Paintings Representing Greenland Eskimos*, American Museum Guide Leaflet, no. 30 (New York: American Museum of Natural History, 1909). The murals by Will S. Taylor are still up in the museum's Northwest Indian Hall.

21. Sylvia Massey Czerkas and Donald F. Glut, *Dinosaurs, Mammoths and Cavemen: The Art of Charles R. Knight* (New York: Dutton, 1982), figs. 40, 42–49, pp. 40–45.

22. Ibid., p. 10, and figs. 46–49, pp. 44–45. On Osborn's role on dinosaur paintings see Knight to Osborn, 28 June 1908, and August 1908; Osborn to Knight, 28 July 1908; and Osborn to Mary C. Dickerson, 11 May 1914, Knight Correspondence, Archives, DVP.

23. Osborn, "A Skeleton of *Diplodocus*." See also Czerkas and Glut, *Dinosaurs*,

298   *Notes to Pages 162–169*

Mammoths and Cavemen, fig. 44, p. 42; and Walter L. Beasley, *"Diplodocus—The Greatest of All Earthly Creatures,"* *Scientific American,* 96 (15 June 1907): 491–92.

24. On Yale see Richard Swann Lull, "Reminiscences of the Vertebrate Paleontology Collections at the Peabody Museum, 1906–1946" [1946], Alfred Sherwood Romer Papers, box 11, Harvard University Archives; W. J. Holland, "The Osteology of *Diplodocus* Marsh, with Special Reference to the Restoration of the Skeleton of *Diplodocus carnegiei* Hatcher," *Memoirs of the Carnegie Museum,* 2 (1906): 225–78. See also Helen J. McGinnis, *Carnegie's Dinosaurs: A Comprehensive Guide to Dinosaur Hall of the Carnegie Museum of Natural History, Carnegie Institute* (Pittsburgh: Carnegie Institute, 1982), 11–26.

25. Charles W. Gilmore, "Mounted Skeleton of *Camptosaurus,"* *Proceedings of the United States National Museum,* 41 (1912): 695. See also G. Edward Lewis, "Memorial to Charles Whitney Gilmore," *Proceedings of the Geological Society of America for 1945* (1946): 235–43. On the dinosaur mountings at the National Museum see Charles W. Gilmore, "A History of the Division of Vertebrate Paleontology in the United States National Museum," *Proceedings of the United States National Museum,* 90 (1941): 343–44. On Knight's restorations see Czerkas and Glut, *Dinosaurs, Mammoths and Cavemen,* figs. 88, 89, 91–118, pp. 70–88.

26. Coggeshall was in the DVP from 1896 to 1899 and Horne from 1903 to 1905, DVP Annual Reports, 1895–1905. Charles Schuchert to H. E. Gregory, 18 February 1905, Yale Archival Records, YRG 14 P, Accession 12/35, Manuscripts and Archives, Yale University Library; Schuchert to E. S. Dana, 3 October 1905; and Schuchert to Richard Swann Lull, 1 December 1905, 6 January 1906, Charles Schuchert Papers, box 31, Manuscripts and Archives, Yale University Library. On Lull see George Gaylord Simpson, "Memorial to Richard Swann Lull," *Proceedings of the Geological Society of America for 1957* (1958): 127–33.

27. Walter L. Beasley, "A Carnivorous Dinosaur: Reconstructed Skeleton of a Huge Saurian," *Scientific American,* 97 (14 December 1907): 446–47.

28. W. D. Matthew, "The Evolution of the Horse: A Record and its Interpretation," *Quarterly Review of Biology,* 1 (1926): 139–86; idem, "Exhibition Illustrating the Evolution of the Horse," *American Museum Journal,* 8 (1908): 117–22; George Gaylord Simpson, *Horses: The Story of the Horse Family in the Modern World and through Sixty Million Years of History* (New York: Oxford University Press, 1951).

29. Henry Fairfield Osborn, *The Titanotheres of Ancient Wyoming, Dakota and Nebraska,* 2 vols. (Washington, D.C.: Government Printing Office, 1929); 1: 250–304, 580–608.

30. Ibid., 2: 814.

31. On Knight's restorations of titanotheres see "List of Photographs of American Museum Restorations of Fossil Vertebrates," Personnel Files, box 1:7, Archives, DVP. William King Gregory, "A New Restoration of a Titanothere," *American Museum Journal,* 12 (1912): 15–17; DVP Annual Reports, 1901–4.

32. Gregory, "A New Restoration."

33. Henry Fairfield Osborn, *The Age of Mammals in Europe, Asia and North America* (New York: Macmillan, 1910), fig. 100, p. 212.

34. Osborn, *Titanotheres,* 2: 883.

35. Ibid., 805–94. See also William Berryman Scott, "On the Osteology of

Mesohippus and *Leptomeryx*, with Observations on the Modes and Factors of Evolution in the Mammalia," *Journal of Morphology*, 5 (1891): 371; and Edward Drinker Cope, *The Primary Factors of Organic Evolution* (Chicago: Open Court, 1896), 170–73.

36. Osborn to J. P. Morgan, Jr., 28 September 1916, 15 December 1916, Folder 249 C, 249 D, Central Archives; W. D. Matthew, "The Ground Sloth Group," *American Museum Journal*, 11 (1911): 113–19; idem, "The Asphalt Group of Fossil Skeletons," *American Museum Journal*, 12 (1912): 291–97; idem, "The Grim Wolf of the Tar Pits," *American Museum Journal*, 16 (1916): 45–47.

37. Henry Fairfield Osborn, *The Hall of the Age of Man, American Museum of Natural History Guide Leaflet*, no. 52 (New York: American Museum of Natural History, 1920). On McGregor see Henry Fairfield Osborn, *Men of the Old Stone Age: Their Environment, Life and Art* (New York: Scribners, 1915), 79–82, 140–45, 300–301; and folder 209 A, Central Archives.

38. J. Howard McGregor, "Restoring Neanderthal Man," *Natural History*, 26 (1926): 287–93; with quotation, 293.

39. Osborn, *Hall of the Age of Man*, 8.

40. Osborn, *Men of the Old Stone Age*, xii.

41. Henry Fairfield Osborn to Charles R. Knight, 28 July 1919, Osborn Papers, Central Archives. See also Charlotte M. Porter, "The Rise of Parnassus: Henry Fairfield Osborn and the Hall of the Age of Man," *Museum Studies Journal*, 1 (1983): 26–34.

42. Osborn, *Men of the Old Stone Age*, 358–60.

43. Osborn, *Hall of the Age of Man*, 31.

44. Osborn, *Creative Education*, 39–42.

45. Kennedy, "Philanthropy and Science," 242–47; and Clark Wissler, "Survey of the American Museum of Natural History Made at the Request of the Management Board in 1942–43," Central Archives, American Museum, 92, 224; Robert Lowie to Henry Fairfield Osborn, 19 June 1922, Osborn Papers, Central Archives. On Jennings see correspondence in Herbert Spencer Jennings Papers, Henry Fairfield Osborn folder, American Philosophical Society; and T. H. Morgan to Henry Fairfield Osborn, 14 June 1920, Charles B. Davenport Papers, Henry Fairfield Osborn folder, American Philosophical Society.

46. On Gregory see Galton Society folders 1267, 1269, Central Archives; and Davenport Papers, Gregory folders. See also discussion in Chapter 9. Gregory proposed Matthew for membership in Gregory to Davenport, 7 May 1920, Davenport Papers, and Matthew is listed as a member of the Galton Society in a 1927 list of members, Davenport Papers; W. D. Matthew, "Social Evolution: A Paleontologist's Viewpoint," *Natural History*, 20 (1920): 376.

47. *Annual Report of the American Museum of Natural History*, 54 (1923): 41.

48. Elof A. Carlson, *Genes, Radiation and Society: The Life and Work of H. J. Muller* (Ithaca: Cornell University Press, 1981), 15; Stephen Jay Gould, personal communication.

49. "The American Museum of Natural History," *Fortune*, 15 (April 1937): 124.

8. Organisms in Space and Time

1. Georges Cuvier, *Recherches sur les ossemens fossiles de quadrupeds, où l'on rétablit les caractères de plusieurs espèces d'animaux que les revolutions du globe paroissent avoir détruites*, 4 vols. (1812; reprint ed., Brusseles: Culture et Civilisation,

1969). See also Toby A. Appel, *The Cuvier-Geoffroy Debate: French Biology in the Decades Before Darwin* (New York: Oxford University Press, 1987). On Owen see Adrian Desmond, *Archetypes and Ancestors: Palaeontology in Victorian London 1850–1875* (Chicago: University of Chicago Press, 1984).

2. E. C. Case, "Oecological Features of Evolution," *Bulletin of the Wisconsin Natural History Society*, 3 (1905): 169–80; idem, "American Paleontology and Neo-Lamarckism," *Annual Report of the Michigan Academy of Sciences*, 11 (1909): 18–23; John C. Merriam, "Synopsis of Lectures in Paleontology I: Principles Involved in a Discussion of the History of Life," *University of California Syllabus Series*, no. 20 (1910); idem, "Relationship of *Equus* to *Pliohippus* Suggested by Characters of a New Species from the Pliocene of California," *University of California Publications in Geology*, 9 (1916): 525–34.

3. Henry Fairfield Osborn, "Memorial to William Diller Matthew," *Bulletin of the Geological Society of America*, 42 (1931): 55–95. See also Matthew to Hermann von Ihering, 24 March 1911, von Ihering Correspondence, Archives, Department of Vertebrate Paleontology, American Museum of Natural History.

4. DVP Annual Reports, 1896–99, 1901, 1902, box 1:1, Archives, DVP. His paper was "A Revision of the Puerco Fauna," *Bulletin of the American Museum of Natural History*, 9 (1897): 259–323.

5. W. D. Matthew, "A Provisional Classification of the Freshwater Tertiary of the West," *Bulletin of the American Museum of Natural History*, 12 (1899): 19–75; idem, "Is the White River Tertiary an Aeolian Formation?" *American Naturalist*, 33 (1899): 403–8.

6. On the development of the use of fossils for stratigraphy see Martin J. S. Rudwick, *The Great Devonian Controversy: The Shaping of Scientific Knowledge Among Gentlemanly Specialists* (Chicago: University of Chicago Press, 1985); and James A. Secord, *Controversy in Victorian Geology: The Cambrian-Silurian Dispute* (Princeton: Princeton University Press, 1986).

7. Leidy did little on biostratigraphy or correlation. On E. D. Cope see "The Relations of the Horizons of Extinct Vertebrata of Europe and North America," *Bulletin of the United States Geological and Geographical Survey of the Territories*, 5, no. 1 (1879); idem, "Vertebrata of the Tertiary Formations of the West," *Report of the United States Geological Survey of the Territories*, 3 (1883): 1–45. On Marsh see "Introduction and Succession of Vertebrate Life in America," *American Journal of Science*, 3d ser., 14 (1877): 337–78; and idem, "Geological Horizons as Determined by Vertebrate Fossils," *Comptes rendus de congress géologique internationale*, (1891): 156–59. On Scott see William Berryman Scott, "The Mammalia of the Uinta Formation," *Transactions of the American Philosophical Society*, n.s., 16 (1890): 461–504. On Hatcher see "The Ceratops Beds of Converse County, Wyoming," *American Journal of Science*, 3d ser., 45 (1893): 135–44; idem, "The Titanotherium Beds," *American Naturalist*, 27 (1893): 204–21; idem, "Origin of the Oligocene and Miocene Deposits of the Great Plains," *Proceedings of the American Philosophical Society*, 41 (1902): 113–31.

8. Henry Fairfield Osborn, "Correlation between Tertiary Mammal Horizons of Europe and America," *Annals of the New York Academy of Sciences*, 13 (1900): 5.

9. A copy of the "Trial Sheet of the Typical and Homotaxial Tertiary Horizons

of Europe" is attached to a letter from Osborn to W. B. Scott, 14 July 1897, Henry Fairfield Osborn Papers, box 6, New-York Historical Society.

10. J. B. Hatcher and T. W. Stanton, "The Stratigraphic Position of the Judith River beds and Their Correlation with the Belly River beds," *Science*, 18 (1903): 211–12. Hatcher's work for Osborn rekindled the antagonism that had existed between them in the early 1890s. See J. B. Hatcher, "A Correction of Professor Osborn's note entitled 'New Vertebrates of the mid-Cretaceous,'" *Science*, 16 (1902): 831–32. See also Ronald Rainger, "Collectors and Entrepreneurs: Hatcher, Wortman, and the Structure of American Vertebrate Paleontology circa 1900," *Earth Sciences History*, 9 (1990): 14–21.

On Darton see "Preliminary Report on the Geology and Underground Water Resources of the Central Great Plains," *United States Geological Survey Professional Paper*, no. 32 (1906): 1–433; idem, "Geology of the Bighorn Mountains," *United States Geological Survey Professional Paper*, no. 51 (1906): 1–129. Darton described his work in a letter to Osborn of 25 June 1901, Darton Correspondence, Archives, DVP. Some of Darton's maps are in the DVP Archives.

11. Henry Fairfield Osborn to W. D. Matthew, 14 July 1902, 31 July 1902, DVP Field Correspondence, box 2:3, Archives, DVP. See also Matthew's field diaries for 1902 and 1904, DVP Field Diaries, box 6:2, Archives, DVP.

12. Henry Fairfield Osborn, "Cenozoic Mammal Horizons of Western North America," *Bulletin of the United States Geological Survey*, no. 361 (1909): 1–138.

13. W. D. Matthew, "The Carnivora and Insectivora of the Bridger Basin, Middle Eocene," *Memoirs of the American Museum of Natural History*, 9 (1909): 293–97; and William King Gregory, "A Review of William Diller Matthew's Contributions to Mammalian Paleontology," *American Museum Novitates*, no. 473 (1932): 1–23.

14. T. W. Stanton to H. F. Osborn, 30 January 1914, 10 May 1918, Henry Fairfield Osborn Papers, Library, Central Archives, American Museum of Natural History. Matthew remained critical of the Geological Survey's emphases and claimed that the DVP's work was "sound and permanent to a degree that the Survey work is not." He also criticized Osborn for accepting Stanton's recommendation that the monograph employ generic names to distinguish localized facies of faunal zones. Matthew's comments attached to Osborn to Stanton, 8 October 1918, Henry Fairfield Osborn Papers, package 19, Archives, DVP.

15. George P. Merrill, *The First One Hundred Years of American Geology* (New Haven: Yale University Press, 1924), 515–17, 579–83. W. D. Matthew, "Evidence of the Paleocene Vertebrate Fauna on the Cretaceous-Tertiary Problem," *Bulletin of the Geological Society of America*, 25 (1914): 381–402. See also Ronald Rainger, "W. D. Matthew, "Fossil Vertebrates and Geological Time," *Earth Sciences History*, 8 (1989): 159–66.

16. F. H. Knowlton, "Cretaceous-Tertiary Boundary in the Rocky Mountain Region," *Bulletin of the Geological Society of America*, 25 (1914): 325–40.

17. Matthew, "Cretaceous-Tertiary Problem," 390.

18. Those papers, including one by T. W. Stanton, are in *Bulletin of the Geological Society of America*, 25 (1914): 321–80. Sinclair's paper was published separately: W. J. Sinclair, "Paleocene Deposits of the San Juan Basin, New Mex-

ico," *Bulletin of the American Museum of Natural History*, 33 (1914): 297–316. On the modern interpretation of the Cretaceous-Tertiary boundary see R. A. Robinson and Curt Teichert, eds., *Treatise on Invertebrate Paleontology. Part A: Introduction: Fossilization (Taphonomy), Biogeography and Biostratigraphy* (Boulder, Colo.: Geological Society of America, 1979), A500.

19. Henry Fairfield Osborn and W. D. Matthew, "Geological Correlation Through Vertebrate Paleontology by International Cooperation," *Annals of the New York Academy of Sciences*, 19 (1909): 41–44; and Henry Fairfield Osborn, "The Paleontologic Correlation through the Bache Fund," *Science*, 31 (1910): 407–8.

20. Matthew translated and published Louis Dollo, "The Fossil Vertebrates of Belgium," *Annals of the New York Academy of Sciences*, 19 (1909): 99–119; and "Patagonia and the Pampas Cenozoic of South America: A Critical Review of the Correlations of Santiago Roth," *Annals of the New York Academy of Sciences*, 19 (1910): 149–60.

21. George Gaylord Simpson, *Discoverers of the Lost World: An Account of Some of Those who Brought Back to Life South American Mammals Long Buried in the Abyss of Time* (New Haven: Yale University Press, 1984), 88; Florentino Ameghino, "L'âge des formations sédimentaires de Patagonie," *Anales de la Sociedad cientific argentina*, 50 (1900): 109–30, 146–65, 209–29; 51 (1901): 20–39, 65–91; 52 (1901): 189–97, 244–50; 54 (1902): 161–80, 220–49, 283–342; idem, "Les formations sédimentaires du Crétacé supérieur et du Tertiare de Patagonie," *Anales del Museo nacional de historia natural, Buenos Aires*, 8 (1906): 1–568. See also Santiago Roth, "Beitrag zur Gliederung der Sedimentablagerungen in Patagonien und der Pampasregion," *Neues Jahrbuch für Geologie, Mineralogie and Paläontologie*, 26 (1908): 92–150.

22. Simpson, *Discoverers of the Lost World*, 61–66, 71; Carlos Ameghino, "Le *Pyrotherium*, l'étage pyrothéréen et les couches à *Notostylops*. Une réponse à Mr. Loomis," *Physis*, 1 (1914): 446–60.

23. Florentino Ameghino, "Enumération synoptique des espèces de mammiferès fossiles des formations éocènes de Patagonie," *Boletin de la Academie nacional de ciencias Córdoba*, 13 (1892): 594–863; and idem, "Mammifères crétacés de l'Argentine. Deuxième contribution à la connaissance de la faune mammalogique des couches à *Pyrotherium*," *Boletin del Institutio geografica argentino*, 18 (1897): 301–461.

24. William Berryman Scott, gen. ed., *Reports of the Princeton University Expeditions to Patagonia, 1896–1899*, 8 vols. (Princeton: Princeton University Press, 1903–32), vol. 1: *Narrative of the Expeditions: Geography of Southern Patagonia*, by John Bell Hatcher.

25. John Bell Hatcher, "On the Geology of Southern Patagonia," *American Journal of Science*, 4th ser., 4 (1897): 330, 341; and idem, "Sedimentary Rocks of Southern Patagonia," *American Journal of Science*, 4th ser., 9 (1900): 85–108.

26. Matthew, "Patagonia and the Pampas Cenozoic of South America."

27. W. D. Matthew, "Climate and Evolution," *Annals of the New York Academy of Sciences*, 24 (1915): 193–202.

28. Ibid., 195.

29. Henry Fairfield Osborn, "Geological and Faunal Relations of Europe and America during the Tertiary Period and the Theory of the Successive Invasions of an African Fauna," *Science*, 11 (1900): 566; Philip L. Sclater and W. L. Sclater, *The Geography of Mammals* (London: K. Paul, Trench, Trubner, 1899);

Richard Lydekker, *A Geographical History of Mammals* (Cambridge: Cambridge University Press, 1896).
30. Osborn, "Geological and Faunal Relations," 568–69.
31. Ibid., 565; Joseph Dalton Hooker, *The Botany of the Antarctic Voyage of Her Majesty's Discovery Ships "Erebus" and "Terror" in the years 1839–1843. Under the Command of Sir James Clark Ross. Pt. 1 Flora Antarctica,* 2 vols. (London: 1844–47); *Pt. 2 Flora Novae Zelandiae,* 2 vols. (London: 1853–1855). See also Ludwig Rütimeyer, *Ueber die Herkunft unserer Thierwelt Eine Zoogeographische Skizze* (Basel and Geneva: 1867). See H. O. Forbes, "Antarctica: A Vanished Austral Land," *Smithsonian Institution Annual Report for 1894* (1895): 297–316. See also A. E. Ortmann, "The Geographical Distribution of Fresh Water Decapods: Bearing upon Ancient Geography," *Proceedings of the American Philosophical Society,* 41 (1902): 267–400.
32. Osborn, "Geological and Faunal Relations," 566.
33. Henry Fairfield Osborn, *The Age of Mammals in Europe, Asia and North America* (New York: Macmillan, 1910), 80.
34. W. D. Matthew, "Hypothetical Outlines of the Continents in Tertiary Times," *Bulletin of the American Museum of Natural History,* 22 (1906): 353–83.
35. Ronald L. Numbers, *Creation by Natural Law: Laplace's Nebular Hypothesis in American Thought* (Seattle: University of Washington Press, 1977).
36. Matthew relied on Chamberlin's article, "A Group of Hypotheses Bearing on Climatic Changes," *Journal of Geology,* 5 (1897): 653–83.
37. T. C. Chamberlin, "A Systematic Source of Provincial Faunas," *Journal of Geology,* 6 (1898): 597–608.
38. The quotation is from an unpublished manuscript prefaced with a statement by Charles L. Camp, Matthew's colleague at Berkeley, that the paper is probably the lecture that Matthew delivered to the Linnaean Society of London on 14 January 1902, William Diller Matthew Papers, vol. 4, Earth Sciences Library, University of California at Berkeley.
39. Matthew, "Climate and Evolution," 175.
40. The quotations are from Charles Darwin, *On the Origin of Species By Means of Natural Selection, or the Preservation of Favoured Races in the Struggle for Life* (1859; reprint ed., Cambridge, Mass.: Harvard University Press, 1964), 353 and 309, respectively.
41. Ibid., 356–65.
42. Martin Fichman, "Wallace: Zoogeography and the Problem of Land Bridges," *Journal of the History of Biology,* 10 (1977): 45–63.
43. Alfred Russel Wallace, *The Geographical Distribution of Animals,* 2 vols. (New York: Hafner, 1962), 1: 36–37, 46–49.
44. Darwin, *Origin of Species,* 379.
45. Wallace, *Geographical Distribution,* 173–74.
46. Ibid., 105–70.
47. Matthew, "Hypothetical Outlines of the Continents in Tertiary Times."
48. Ibid., 361.
49. Matthew, "Climate and Evolution," 236.
50. Ibid., 269. The reference to work by Dederer and Broom is on 267–68.
51. Ibid., 274.
52. Scott, *Princeton Expeditions to Patagonia,* vol. 4, pt. 2: *Tertiary Invertebrates,* by A. E. Ortmann, 311.
53. Rütimeyer, *Ueber die Herkunft unserer Thierwelt;* Forbes, "Antarctica." See also

Charles Hedley, "A Zoogeographic Scheme for the mid-Pacific," *Proceedings of the Linnaean Society of New South Wales*, 24 (1895): 391–417.

54. Ortmann, *Tertiary Invertebrates*, 315.

55. Hermann von Jhering, "The History of the Neotropical Region," *Science*, 12 (1900): 857–58. See also von Ihering's paper "On the Ancient Relations Between New Zealand and South America," *Transactions of the New Zealand Institute*, 24 (1891): 431–35.

56. Scott, *Princeton Expeditions to Patagonia*, vol. 3, pt. 3: *The Fresh-Water Fishes of Patagonia and An Examination of the Archiplata-Archhelenis Theory*, by Carl H. Eigenmann.

57. Matthew, "Climate and Evolution," 307–13. Matthew's comments on Wegener's work are part of a manuscript entitled "Note on the Wegener Hypothesis, etc., Supplementary to 'Climate and Evolution,'" which Edwin H. Colbert appended to the second edition of *Climate and Evolution* (New York: New York Academy of Sciences, 1939), 164–69. The quotation is from Matthew to von Ihering, 24 March 1911, von Ihering Correspondence.

58. Matthew, *Climate and Evolution*, 169. Matthew criticized Hans Gadow, *The Wanderings of Animals* (Cambridge: Cambridge University Press, 1913); R. F. Scharff, *Distribution and Origin of Life in America* (New York: Macmillan, 1912).

59. Matthew, "Climate and Evolution," 314.

60. Ibid., 307.

61. Ibid., 194–97. See also Osborn, *The Age of Mammals*, 39–47.

62. Matthew, "Climate and Evolution," 299–301. On Eigenmann see *Fresh-Water Fishes of Patagonia*, 293–374.

63. Matthew, "Climate and Evolution," 196.

64. Charles Schuchert wrote a critical review of "Climate and Evolution" in the *American Journal of Science*, 4th ser., 40 (1915): 83–85. Matthew defended his interpretation in a letter to Schuchert, 4 September 1915, Charles Schuchert Papers, box 10, Manuscripts and Archives, Yale University Library. William Morton Wheeler, the American student of insects and ethology, stated that the evidence of invertebrates and plants would not support Matthew's theory, Wheeler to Schuchert, 7 June 1915, Schuchert Papers, box 10. Thomas Barbour, "Some Remarks Upon Matthew's 'Climate and Evolution,'" *Annals of the New York Academy of Sciences*, 27 (1916): 1–15.

65. Osborn, *The Age of Mammals*, passim.

66. Karl P. Schmidt, "Animal Geography," in Edward L. Kessel, *A Century of Progress in the Natural Sciences* (New York: Arno Press, 1974), 777–78.

67. Ibid., 780–81; Philip J. Darlington, Jr., "The Origin of the Fauna of the Greater Antilles, with Discussion of Dispersal of Animals over Water and Through the Air," *Quarterly Review of Biology*, 13 (1938): 274–300; and idem, "The Geographical Distribution of Cold-Blooded Vertebrates," *Quarterly Review of Biology*, 23 (1948): 1–26, 105–23. George Myers, "Fresh-water Fishes and West Indian Zoogeography," *Annual Reports of the Smithsonian Institution for 1937* (1938): 339–64; and idem, "Fresh-water Fishes and East Indian Zoogeography," *Stanford Ichthyology Bulletin*, 4 (1949): 11–21.

68. George Gaylord Simpson, "Mammals and Land Bridges," *Washington Academy of Sciences*, 30 (1940): 142, 154–56. On Simpson see Henry Frankel, "The Paleobiogeographical Debate over the Problem of Disjunctively Distributed Life Forms," *Studies in History and Philosophy of Science*, 12 (1981): 232–44;

and Léo F. Laporte, "Wrong for the Right Reasons: George Gaylord Simpson and Continental Drift," *Geological Society of America Centennial Special Volume* (Boulder, Colo.: Geological Society of America, 1985), 273–85.

69. In 1914 Matthew and Gregory made detailed criticisms of an Osborn manuscript on evolution: W. D. Matthew to Osborn, 8 December 1914, 9 December 1914; William King Gregory to Osborn, 14 May 1914, 11 December 1914, 14 December 1914, 21 December 1914, Osborn Papers, Central Archives. Osborn suggested that he publish his paper with their dissenting comments, but neither Matthew nor Gregory wanted to disagree with him in print and therefore declined. Gregory to Osborn, 20 May 1917, Osborn Papers, Central Archives.

70. Henry Fairfield Osborn, "Darwin and Palaeontology," in American Association for the Advancement of Science, *Fifty Years of Darwinism* (New York: Holt, 1909), 209–50; idem, "The Continuous Origin of Certain Unit Characters As Observed by a Palaeontologist," *Harvey Society*, 7 (1912): 153–204. See also Henry Fairfield Osborn, "Paleontology Versus Genetics," *Science*, 72 (1930): 1–3. On the debate over the nature of variations see William B. Provine, *The Origins of Theoretical Population Genetics* (Chicago: University of Chicago Press, 1971).

71. W. D. Matthew, "New Canidae from the Miocene of Colorado," *Bulletin of the American Museum of Natural History*, 16 (1902): 286–87.

72. Ibid., 287.

73. Matthew, "Lecture to the Linnaean Society of London."

74. W. D. Matthew, "Time Ratios in the Evolution of Mammalian Phyla: A Contribution to the Problem of the Age of the Earth," *Science*, 40 (1914): 233.

75. Frederick B. Loomis, "Momentum in Variation," *American Naturalist*, 39 (1905): 839–43; W. B. Scott, *A History of Land Mammals in the Western Hemisphere* (New York: Macmillan, 1913), 535–41.

76. W. D. Matthew, "The Phylogeny of the Felidae," *Bulletin of the American Museum of Natural History*, 28 (1910): 306. See also W. D. Matthew, "Fossil Mammals of the Tertiary of Northeastern Colorado," *Memoirs of the American Museum of Natural History*, 1 (1901): 353–447.

77. Matthew, "Phylogeny of the Felidae," 307.

78. Ibid.

79. W. D. Matthew and S. H. Chubb, *The Evolution of the Horse in Nature*, American Museum Guide Leaflet, no. 36 (New York: American Museum of Natural History, 1913), 14.

80. Ibid., 30. See also W. D. Matthew, "The Evolution of the Horse: A Record and its Interpretation," *Quarterly Review of Biology*, 1 (1926): 171–78.

81. W. D. Matthew to F. A. Bather, n.d., Matthew Papers, vol. 26, Earth Sciences Library, University of California at Berkeley.

82. See Ronald Rainger, "Paleontology and Philosophy: A Critique," *Journal of the History of Biology*, 18 (1985): 267–87.

83. Ernst Mayr, "Prologue: Some Thoughts on the History of the Evolutionary Synthesis," in Ernst Mayr and William B. Provine, eds., *The Evolutionary Synthesis: Perspectives on the Unification of Biology* (Cambridge, Mass.: Harvard University Press, 1980), 1–48. See also Ernst Mayr, *Systematics and the Origin of Species* (New York: Columbia University Press, 1942), 108–22; and "Species Concepts and Definitions," in Ernst Mayr, ed., *The Species Problem*

(Washington, D.C.: American Association for the Advancement of Science, 1957), 1–22.
84. Estimates of the DVP's holdings by that time can be found in DVP Annual Report, 1922, Archives, DVP.
85. W. D. Matthew and Walter Granger, "Revision of the Lower Eocene Wasatch and Wind River Faunas. Part I. Order Ferae (Carnivora), Suborder Creodonta," *Bulletin of the American Museum of Natural History*, 34 (1915): 1.
86. Ibid., 101. See also W. D. Matthew and Walter Granger, "A Revision of the Lower Eocene Wasatch and Wind River Faunas. Part IV. Entelonycha, Primates, Insectivora," *Bulletin of the American Museum of Natural History*, 34 (1915): 434–35.
87. W. D. Matthew, "Contributions to the Snake Creek Fauna," *Bulletin of the American Museum of Natural History*, 38 (1918): 184.
88. W. D. Matthew, "Third Contribution to the Snake Creek Fauna," *Bulletin of the American Museum of Natural History*, 50 (1924): 154.
89. In a letter to W. B. Scott, Osborn noted that "I find my conclusions so different from those of Doctor Matthew, for example, that I could not write a joint work with him. All of his conceptions of evolution are quite different from mine and probably from yours also." Osborn to W. B. Scott, 5 February 1921, Osborn Papers, box 9, New-York Historical Society. Osborn's study was "Equidae of the Oligocene, Miocene, and Pliocene of North America, Iconographic Type Revision," *Memoirs of the American Museum of Natural History*, n.s., 2 (1918): 1–217. Matthew criticized Osborn's work in "Three-toed Horses," *Natural History*, 20 (1920): 473–78. The author has discussed this issue in "Just before Simpson: William Diller Matthew's Understanding of Evolution," *Proceedings of the American Philosophical Society*, 130 (1986): 474, n. 74.
90. W. D. Matthew to Francis B. Sumner, 8 May 1925, Sumner Correspondence, Archives, DVP. See also W. D. Matthew to William J. Sinclair, 19 October 1921, Sinclair Correspondence, Archives, DVP.
91. W. D. Matthew, "Critical Observations on the Phylogeny of the Rhinoceroses," *University of California Publications in Geology*, 20 (1931): 5.
92. W. D. Matthew, "Range and Limitations of Species as Seen in Fossil Faunas," *Bulletin of the Geological Society of America*, 41 (1930): 271–74.
93. Mayr, "Prologue: Some Thoughts on the History of the Evolutionary Synthesis," 9–28. See also Garland E. Allen, "Naturalists and Experimentalists: The Genotype and the Phenotype," *Studies in History of Biology*, 3 (1979): 179–209.
94. The quotations are from W. D. Matthew to T. H. Morgan, 6 August 1925, Morgan Correspondence, Archives, DVP; and Matthew to Sumner, 8 May 1925.
95. W. D. Matthew, "The Pattern of Evolution: A Criticism of Doctor Austin Clark's Thesis," *Scientific American*, 143 (September 1930), 193.
96. Matthew, "Critical Observations on the Phylogeny of Rhinoceroses," 5–6. Matthew's studies of orthogenesis and parallelism include "Critical Observations on the Phylogeny of Rhinoceroses," 5–7; "The Pattern of Evolution." 192–96; "The Phylogeny of Dogs," *Journal of Mammalogy*, 2 (1930): 117–38; "A Review of the Rhinoceroses with a Description of *Aphelops* material from the Pliocene of Texas," *University of California Publications in Geology*, 22 (1932): 411–82; and two papers with R. A. Stirton, "Osteology and Af-

finities of *Borophagus*," *University of California Publications in Geology*, 19 (1930): 171–216 and "Equidae from the Pliocene of Texas," *University of California Publications in Geology*, 19 (1930): 349–96.

97. The quotations are, respectively, from Simpson's "Autobiographical Notes," for 1933 and 1954, George Gaylord Simpson Papers, American Philosophical Society. See also George Gaylord Simpson, *Concession to the Improbable: An Unconventional Autobiography* (New Haven: Yale University Press, 1978), 33–39. Much of the Matthew-Simpson correspondence is in the George Gaylord Simpson Correspondence, Archives, DVP.

98. George Gaylord Simpson, *Tempo and Mode in Evolution* (New York: Columbia University Press, 1944). Although Simpson originally referred to Matthew as a neo-Darwinian in the turn-of-the-century sense, he later changed his assessment and claimed that Matthew's views on evolution and his awareness of extensive variation as a natural characteristic of species made him one of the forerunners of the new systematics. Ernst Mayr, "G. G. Simpson," in Mayr and Provine, *The Evolutionary Synthesis*, 454; George Gaylord Simpson, *Why and How: Some Problems and Methods in Historical Biology* (New York: Pergamon, 1980), 175. Stephen Jay Gould in a personal communication with the author commented that Simpson idolized Matthew and that Matthew profoundly influenced the younger man.

99. Osborn to Scott, 5 February 1921.

9. Fossils and Function

1. On Cuvier see Martin J. S. Rudwick, *The Meaning of Fossils: Episodes in the History of Palaeontology*, 2d ed. (Chicago: University of Chicago Press, 1985), 101–15. Vladimir Kovalevsky, "Monographie der Gattung *Anthracotherium Cuv.* und Versuch einer natürlichen Classification der fossilen Hufthiere," *Palaeontographica*, 3 (1873): 131–210; 4 (1874): 211–90; 5 (1874): 291–346. Louis Dollo, "La Paléontologie éthologique," *Bulletin de la Société Belge de Géologie, Paléontologie, et d'Hydrologie*, 23 (1909): 377–421. D. M. S. Watson, "The Evolution of the Tetrapod Shoulder Girdle and Fore-limb," *Journal of Anatomy and Physiology*, 52 (1917–18): 1–63.

2. Department of Vertebrate Paleontology, Annual Reports, 1901, 1902, box 1:1, Archives, Department of Vertebrate Paleontology, American Museum of Natural History.

3. Edwin H. Colbert, "William King Gregory," *Biographical Memoirs National Academy of Sciences*, 46 (1975): 91–133. See also Ronald Rainger, "What's the Use: William King Gregory and the Functional Morphology of Fossil Vertebrates," *Journal of the History of Biology*, 22 (1989): 103–39. On the influence of Bashford Dean see William King Gregory, "Memorial of Bashford Dean (1867–1928)," *Bulletin of the Geological Society of America*, 41 (1930): 16–25.

4. Henry Fairfield Osborn, "Rise of the Mammalia in North America," *Proceedings of the American Association for the Advancement of Science*, 42 (1894): 191. On Cope see "The Method of Creation of Organic Forms," in Edward Drinker Cope, *On the Origin of the Fittest: Essays in Evolution* (New York: Appleton, 1887), 173–214; "The Relation of Animal Motion to Animal Evolution," in Cope, *Origin of the Fittest*, 350–58.

5. Henry Fairfield Osborn, "Angulation of the Limbs of Proboscidea, Dinocerata and Other Quadrupeds in Adaptation to Weight," *American Naturalist*,

34 (1900): 94. See also Henry Fairfield Osborn, "*Oxyaena* and *Patriofelis* Restudied as Terrestrial Creodonts," *Bulletin of the American Museum of Natural History*, 13 (1900): 270–71.
6. Henry Fairfield Osborn, *The Titanotheres of Ancient Wyoming, Dakota, and Nebraska*, 2 vols. (Washington, D.C.: Government Printing Office, 1929), 2: 731–59. Gregory wrote the sections on the musculature and restoration of the titanotheres, 703–26, and a section on the principles of leverage and muscular action, 727–31. On the influence of Osborn's teaching and interpretations see William King Gregory, "Origin of Human Limb Proportions through Change of Function," *Bulletin of the New York Academy of Medicine*, 2d ser., 4 (1928): 239.
7. William Diller Matthew to Henry Fairfield Osborn, 4 January 1904, William Diller Matthew Correspondence, Archives, DVP.
8. William King Gregory, "William Diller Matthew 1871–1930," *Natural History*, 30 (1930): 664.
9. W. D. Matthew, "The Mounted Skeleton of *Brontosaurus* in the American Musuem of Natural History," *American Museum Journal*, 5 (1905): 68. See also W. D. Matthew, "The Pose of Sauropod Dinosaurs," *American Naturalist*, 44 (1910): 547–60.
10. See W. D. Matthew, "The Ground Sloth Group," *American Museum Journal*, 11 (1911): 113–19; "A Tree Climbing Ruminant," *American Museum Journal*, 11 (1911): 162–63; and "The Grim Wolf of the Tar Pits," *American Museum Journal*, 16 (1916): 45–47.
11. On Charles R. Knight's reconstructions see Sylvia Massey Czerkas and Donald F. Glut, *Dinosaurs, Mammoths, and Cavemen: The Art of Charles R. Knight* (New York: Dutton, 1982), 10–39. See also William King Gregory, "A New Restoration of a Titanothere," *American Museum Journal*, 12 (1912): 15–17.
12. William King Gregory, "Erwin S. Christman, 1885–1921, Draughtman, Artist, Sculptor," *Natural History*, 21 (1921): 620–25. DVP Annual Reports, 1901, 1902, and 1906. The Christman drawings of *Apatosaurus* in motion are in the DVP Photo Files, drawer 1, Archives, DVP.
13. William King Gregory, "The Weight of the *Brontosaurus*," *Science*, 2 (1905): 572.
14. William King Gregory, "Notes on the Principles of Quadrupedal Locomotion and on the Mechanism of the Limbs in Hoofed Animals," *Annals of the New York Academy of Sciences*, 22 (1912): 269.
15. William King Gregory, "The Orders of Mammals," *Bulletin of the American Museum of Natural History*, 27 (1910): 112–13, 277–88, 396.
16. Ibid., 226.
17. William King Gregory, "Present Status of the Problem of the Origin of the Tetrapoda, with Special Reference to the Skull and Paired Limbs," *Annals of the New York Academy of Sciences*, 26 (1915): 317–83.
18. J. H. McGregor, "The American Museum and Education in Science," *Columbia University Quarterly*, 19 (1917): 317–27. The relations between the museum and the zoo are referred to in Osborn's correspondence with W. T. Hornaday, Raymond Ditmars, and W. Reid Blair, Henry Fairfield Osborn Papers, Central Archives, Library, American Museum of Natural History. See also William Bridges, *Gathering of Animals: An Unconventional History of the New York Zoological Society* (New York: New York Zoological Society, 1974), 333–35.

19. *Annual Report of the American Museum of Natural History*, 53 (1921): 33–34. Subsequent reports provide listings of the department's staff.

20. William King Gregory and L. A. Adams, "The Temporal Fossae of Vertebrates in Relation to the Jaw Muscles," *Science*, 41 (1915): 764.

21. Roy W. Miner, "The Pectoral Limbs of *Eryops* and other Primitive Tetrapods," *Bulletin of the American Museum of Natural History*, 51 (1925): 151–52.

22. William King Gregory and C. L. Camp, "Studies in Comparative Myology and Osteology, No. III," *Bulletin of the American Museum of Natural History*, 38 (1918): 553.

23. Alfred S. Romer, "The Locomotor Apparatus of Certain Primitive Mammal-like Reptiles," *Bulletin of the American Museum of Natural History*, 46 (1922): 517–606.

24. Miner, "The Pectoral Limbs of *Eryops*," 300.

25. On Romer see "Crocodilian Pelvic Muscles and their Avian and Reptilian Homologues," *Bulletin of the American Museum of Natural History*, 48 (1923): 533–52; "The Pelvic Musculature of Saurischian Dinosaurs," *Bulletin of the American Museum of Natural History*, 48 (1923): 605–17; "Pectoral Limb Musculature and Shoulder-Girdle Structure in Fish and Tetrapods," *Anatomical Record*, 27 (1924): 119–43; "The Pelvic Musculature of Ornithischian Dinosaurs," *Acta Zoologica*, 8 (1927): 225–75.

26. Gregory and Camp, "Studies in Comparative Myology," 519, 520.

27. Ibid., 521.

28. William King Gregory, "The Dawn Man of Piltdown, England," *American Museum Journal*, 14 (1914): 189–200. See also Henry Fairfield Osborn, *Men of the Old Stone Age, Their Environment, Life and Art* (New York: Scribners, 1915), 130–44; and W. D. Matthew, "Appendix B. Note on the Association of the Piltdown Skull and Jaw," in William King Gregory, "Studies on the Evolution of Primates, Part II, Phylogeny of Recent and Extinct Anthropoids, with Special Reference to the Origin of Man," *Bulletin of the American Museum of Natural History*, 35 (1916): 348–50.

    Although Osborn and Matthew did not at first accept Piltdown as a fossil hominid, the discovery of additional fragments led them to change their minds. William King Gregory to T. Wingate Todd, 18 November 1921, William King Gregory Papers, box 17, Central Archives. See also Henry Fairfield Osborn, *Man Rises to Parnassus: Critical Epochs in the Prehistory of Man* (Princeton: Princeton University Press, 1927), 45–69.

29. William King Gregory, "On the Relationship of the Eocene Lemur *Notharctus* to the Adapidae and to Other Primates"; and "On the Classification and Phylogeny of the Lemuroidea," which appeared in *Bulletin of the Geological Society of America*, 26 (1915): 419–46. See also William King Gregory, "On the Structure and Relations of *Notharctus*, an American Eocene Primate. Studies on the Evolution of Primates. Part III," *Memoirs of the American Museum of Natural History*, n.s., 3 (1920): 49–243.

30. Gregory, "Studies on Evolution of Primates. Part II."

31. Ibid., 294, 341.

32. William King Gregory, "The Origin of Man from the Anthropoid Stem—When and Where," *Proceedings of the American Philosophical Society*, 66 (1927): 456. On Keith see "Man's Posture: Its Evolution and Disorders," *British Medical Journal*, 1 (1923): 451–54, 499–502, 545–48, 587–90, 624–26, 699–702. On Grafton Elliot Smith see *The Evolution of Man* (New York: Oxford Univer-

sity Press, 1918); and *Essays on the Evolution of Man* (New York: Oxford University Press, 1924).

33. William King Gregory, "The Origin of Man from the Anthropoid Stem"; idem, "Were the Ancestors of Man Primitive Brachiators?" *Proceedings of the American Philosophical Society*, 67 (1928): 129–50; idem, "The Upright Posture of Man: A Review of its Origin and Evolution," *Proceedings of the American Philosophical Society*, 67 (1928): 339–77.

34. William King Gregory and Milo Hellman, "Evidence of the Australopithecine Man-Apes on the Origin of Man," *Science*, 88 (1938): 615–16; idem, "The Dentition of the Extinct South African Man-Ape *Australopithecus (Plesianthropus) transvaalensis* Broom: A Comparative and Phylogenetic Study," *Annals of the Transvaal Museum*, 19 (1939): 339–72.

35. Gerrit S. Miller, "Conflicting Views on the Problems of Man's Ancestry," *American Journal of Physical Anthropology*, 3 (1920): 213–45. Miller never accepted the Piltdown specimens as genuine. Gerrit S. Miller, "The Piltdown Jaw," *American Journal of Physical Anthropology*, 1 (1918): 25–52.

36. Dudley J. Morton, "Evolution of the Human Foot. Part I," *American Journal of Physical Anthropology*, 5 (1922): 305–36; "Evolution of the Human Foot. Part II," *American Journal of Physical Anthropology*, 7 (1924): 1–50; Adolph Schultz, "Studies on the Growth of Gorilla and Other Higher Primates with Special Reference to a Fetus of Gorilla, Preserved in the Carnegie Museum," *Memoirs of the Carnegie Museum*, 11 (1927): 1–88.

37. William King Gregory, "A Critique of Professor Frederic Wood-Jones's Paper: 'Some Landmarks in the Phylogeny of Primates,'" *Human Biology*, 2 (1930): 101–4; idem, "The Transformation of Organic Designs: A Review of the Origin and Deployment of the Earlier Vertebrates," *Biological Reviews of the Cambridge Philosophical Society*, 11 (1936): 316–17.

38. Gregory, "Were the Ancestors of Man Primitive Brachiators?" 133. See also "The Evolution of Primates. Part II," 329–33.

39. Gregory, "Origin of Man from the Anthropoid Stem," 458.

40. Gregory, "The Evolution of Primates. Part II," 333.

41. Ibid., 340.

42. Ibid., 273.

43. Gregory, "Were the Ancestors of Man Primitive Brachiators?" 136.

44. Gregory, "The Evolution of Primates, Part II," 316–17.

45. Ibid., 308.

46. Gregory, "A Critique of Professor Wood-Jones's Paper." William King Gregory's book *Man's Place Among the Anthropoids* (Oxford: The Clarendon Press, 1934) was organized around his opposition to Wood Jones's hypothesis that man had evolved from an advanced tarsioid.

47. See George W. Stocking, "The Persistence of Polygenist Thought in Post-Darwinian Anthropology," in George W. Stocking, *Race, Culture and Evolution: Essays in the History of Anthropology* (New York: Free Press, 1968), 42–68; and Nancy Stepan, *The Idea of Race in Science: Great Britain, 1800–1960* (Hamden, Conn.: Archon, 1982), 83–139.

48. William King Gregory to Madison Grant, 20 October 1930, Osborn Papers, Central Archives. Gregory resigned from the Galton Society in 1935 because of his disagreement with Osborn's support of the racial policies of Nazi Germany. Osborn to Gregory, 23 March 1935, Gregory Papers, box 13. See also William King Gregory to Clarence C. Campbell, 6 May 1935, and Raymond

Pearl to William King Gregory, 8 May 1935, both in Raymond Pearl Papers, Galton Society Folder, American Philosophical Society.

49. William King Gregory, *Our Face From Fish to Man* (New York: Putnam's, 1929). See also William King Gregory and M. Roigneau, *Introduction to Human Anatomy: Guide to Section 1 of the Hall of the Natural History of Man*, American Museum of Natural History Guide Leaflet, no. 86 (New York: American Museum of Natural History, 1934), 44, fig. 15. See also Gregory's display in Henry Fairfield Osborn, *Hall of the Age of Man, American Museum of Natural History Guide Leaflet*, no. 52, 6th ed. (New York: American Museum of Natural History, 1932), 32–38.

50. See Gregory's reviews of Ronald B. Dixon, *The Racial History of Man*, and Hermann Klaatsch, *The Evolution and Progress of Mankind*, in *Yale Review*, 14 (1925): 598–602.

51. Osborn, *Man Rises to Parnassus*. On Osborn's "Dawn Man" see "Fundamental Discoveries of the Last Decade in Human Evolution," *Bulletin of the New York Academy of Medicine*, 2d ser., 3 (1927): 513–21; "Recent Discoveries Relating to the Origin and Antiquity of Man," *Science*, 65 (1927): 481–88; and "Is the Ape-Man A Myth?" *Human Biology*, 1 (1929): 2–16.

52. The statement on science and religion is in *Science*, 57 (1923): 630–31. Osborn's views on science and religion are discussed in *Evolution and Religion* (New York: Scribners, 1923); "Evolution and Daily Living," *The Forum*, 73 (1925): 169–77; *The Earth Speaks to Bryan* (New York: Scribners, 1925); "Wants Old Religion Taught in the Schools," 24 January 1926, *New York Herald-Tribune*; and *Evolution and Religion in Education. Polemics of the Fundamentalist Controversy of 1922 to 1926* (New York: Scribners, 1926).

53. Henry Fairfield Osborn, "Recent Discoveries Relating to the Origin and Antiquity of Man," *Proceedings of the American Philosophical Society*, 66 (1927): 382.

54. William King Gregory to D. M. S. Watson, 3 January 1927, Gregory Papers, box 18. The comment on the anti-evolutionists is in William King Gregory, "The Bearing of the Australopithecinae upon the Problem of Man's Place in Nature," *American Journal of Physical Anthropology*, n.s., 7 (1949): 485–87.

55. Osborn, *Men of the Old Stone Age*, 489. See also his diagram of the evolution of the human races on page 491 of that work.

56. Osborn, "Recent Discoveries Relating to the Origin and Antiquity of Man," 389.

57. Ibid., 376.

58. Gregory to Watson, 3 January 1927, Gregory Papers, box 18. Gregory's hesitation in attacking Osborn is referred to in letters to Osborn, 21 April 1927, Henry Fairfield Osborn Papers, Archives, DVP, and 2 January 1928, Gregory Papers, box 13.

59. The tables of evidence that Gregory and McGregor presented at meetings of the Galton Society in 1928 are in the Osborn Correspondence, Archives, DVP. See also William King Gregory to Henry Fairfield Osborn, 18 November 1927, 26 November 1927, Gregory Papers, box 13.

60. William King Gregory, "Two Views of the Origin of Man," *Science*, 65 (1927): 602. The contrast is evident in Osborn, *Hall of the Age of Man*; and Gregory and Roigneau, *Guide to Section 1 of the Hall of the Natural History of Man*. Although Gregory edited later editions of Osborn's guide, he emphasized that all races belonged to the species *Homo sapiens* and had evolved from

primates. Osborn, *Hall of the Age of Man*, 32–38. On the lack of acceptance of Osborn's theory see Jeanette May Lucas to Henry Geiger, 10 November 1941, Osborn Papers, package 29, Archives, DVP.

61. Osborn, "Is the Ape-Man a Myth?" See also Henry Fairfield Osborn, "The Discovery of Tertiary Man," *Science*, 71 (1930): 6–7.

62. Gregory, "Origin of Man from the Anthropoid Stem"; idem, "A Critique of Professor Osborn's Theory of Human Origin," *American Journal of Physical Anthropology*, 14 (1930): 133–64.

63. Osborn, "Is the Ape-Man a Myth?"

64. Gregory, "A Critique of Professor Osborn's Theory of Human Origin," 155.

65. Louis Dollo, "Les lois d'évolution," *Bulletin de la Société Belge de Géologie, Paléontologie, et d'Hydrologie*, 7 (1893): 164–66. See also William King Gregory, "The Roles of Undeviating Evolution and Transformation in the Origin of Man," *American Naturalist*, 69 (1935): 385–404; and idem, "On the Meaning and Limits of Irreversibility of Evolution," *American Naturalist*, 70 (1936): 517–28. For an interpretation of Dollo's law and the misunderstandings it has created see Stephen Jay Gould, "Dollo on Dollo's Law: Irreversibility and the Status of Evolutionary Laws," *Journal of the History of Biology*, 3 (1970): 189–212.

66. Gregory, "The Origin, Rise and Decline of *Homo sapiens*," *Scientific Monthly* (December 1934): 481–96.

67. Gregory, "Two Views of the Origin of Man," 602.

68. Gregory, "Is the Dawn Man a Myth?" 162.

69. William King Gregory to Robert Broom, n.d. [1933], Gregory Papers, box 3.

70. William King Gregory to W. P. Pycraft, 8 June 1936, Gregory Papers, box 7.

71. Gregory, "The Transformation of Organic Designs," 339.

72. William King Gregory, "On Design in Nature," *Yale Review*, 13 (1924): 344–45.

73. Gregory to Broom, n.d. [1933], Gregory Papers, box 3.

74. On Gregory's influence on Colbert see Edwin H. Colbert, *A Fossil-Hunter's Notebook: My Life with Dinosaurs and Other Friends* (New York: Dutton, 1982), 67–70.

75. George Gaylord Simpson to William King Gregory, 22 May 1933, George Gaylord Simpson Papers, Series 1, American Philosophical Society.

76. William King Gregory to George Gaylord Simpson, 16 November 1936, Simpson Papers. Simpson's paper was "Supra-Specific Variation in Nature and Classification," *American Naturalist*, 71 (1937): 236–67. See also Léo F. Laporte, "George G. Simpson: Vertebrate Paleontologist as Biologist," in Keith R. Benson, Jane Maienschein, and Ronald Rainger, eds., *The Expansion of American Biology* (New Brunswick, N.J.: Rutgers University Press, 1991). Simpson referred to Gregory's views on rates of evolution in "William King Gregory 1876–1970," *American Journal of Physical Anthropology*, 35 (1971): 159–60.

77. Gregory to Osborn, 21 April 1927, Gregory Papers, box 13.

78. Herbert O. Elftman, "Functional Adaptations of the Pelvis in Marsupials," *Bulletin of the American Museum of Natural History*, 58 (1929): 189–231; Harriet C. Waterman, "Studies on the Evolution of the Pelvis of Man and other Primates" (Ph.D. dissertation, Columbia University, 1929).

79. In addition to references in note 36, see Dudley J. Morton, *The Human Foot:*

Its Evolution, Physiology, and Functional Disorders (New York: Columbia University Press, 1935).

80. In addition to references in note 34, see William King Gregory and Milo Hellman, "The Dentition of *Dryopithecus* and the Origin of Man," *American Museum of Natural History Anthropological Papers*, 28, pt. 1 (1926): 1–123. Correspondence between Ashley-Montagu and Gregory is in Gregory Papers, box 1.

81. Adele Hast, "Nelson, Nels Christian," *Dictionary of American Biography* (New York: Scribners, 1982), 7th supplement, 569–71.

82. J. H. McGregor, "Recent Studies on the Skull and Brain of *Pithecanthropus*," *Natural History*, 25 (1925): 295–44; idem, "A Dissenting Opinion as to the Dawn Man and Ape Man," *Natural History*, 26 (1926): 270–71; and idem, "Restoring Neanderthal Man," *Natural History*, 26 (1926): 287–93. Frederick Tilney, *The Brain from Ape to Man: A Contribution to the Evolution and Development of the Human Brain* (London: H. K. Lewis, 1928); and "The James Arthur Lecture on the Evolution of the Human Brain," *Natural History*, 32 (1932): 219.

83. On Hrdlička see Frank Spencer, "Introduction," in Frank Spencer, ed., *A History of American Physical Anthropology 1930–1980* (New York: Academic Press, 1982), 1–10; and Frank Spencer, "The Rise of Academic Physical Anthropology in the United States, 1880–1980: An Historical Review," *American Journal of Physical Anthropology*, 56 (1981): 361–62. See also H. L. Shapiro, "Earnest A. Hooton," *American Journal of Physical Anthropology*, 56 (1981): 431–34.

10. The Osborn Legacy: Remnants and Reversals

1. Ronald Rainger, "Collectors and Entrepreneurs: Hatcher, Wortman, and the Structure of American Vertebrate Paleontology circa 1900," *Earth Sciences History*, 9 (1990): 14–21.

2. John Michael Kennedy, "Philanthropy and Science in New York City: The American Museum of Natural History, 1868–1968" (Ph.D. dissertation, Yale University, 1968), 215–32.

3. Gregory discussed the Galton Society's project with foundation officials Beardsley Ruml and Edwin R. Embree in 1924. Charles Benedict Davenport Papers, William King Gregory folder, American Philosophical Society. See also Geoffrey Hellman, *Bankers, Bones and Beetles: The First Century of the American Museum of Natural History* (Garden City, N.Y.: Natural History Press, 1968), 155. On philanthropy see Martin Bulmer and Joan Bulmer, "Philanthropy and Social Science in the 1920s: Beardsley Ruml and the Laura Spelman Rockefeller Memorial," *Minerva*, 19 (1981): 347–408; and Robert E. Kohler, "Science, Foundations, and American Universities in the 1920s," *Osiris*, n.s., 3 (1987): 135–64.

4. Much correspondence on the Proboscidea between Osborn and F. Trusbee Davison and Roy Chapman Andrews is in Henry Fairfield Osborn Papers, Central Archives, Library, American Museum of Natural History.

5. Clark Wissler, "Survey of the American Museum of Natural History Made at the Request of the Management Board in 1942–43," Central Archives, 43–44. Favoritisim toward Osborn was the basis of accusations made by museum director Hermon C. Bumpus in 1910: Bumpus to J. P. Morgan, Jr.,

13 June 1910, Henry Fairfield Osborn Papers, box 20, New-York Historical Society. Bumpus's accusations were well known among the museum's trustees and scientists and were the basis for his dismissal in 1910.

6. Wissler, "Survey of the Museum," 53, 65–66, 122–24.

7. Folders 1130, 1202, Central Archives; Wissler, "Survey," 214. See also Léo F Laporte, ed., *Simple Curiosity: Letters from George Gaylord Simpson to His Family, 1921–1970* (Berkeley: University of California Press, 1987), 233–43.

8. Although older interpretations, notably Kenneth Ludmerer, *Genetics and American Society* (Baltimore: Johns Hopkins University Press, 1972), suggested that most American scientists had abandoned eugenics by the 1930s, more recent studies have argued that eugenics was transformed and continued to be promoted under different guises and rubrics. See, for example, John Beatty, "Weighing the Risks: Stalemate in the Classical/Balance Controversy," *Journal of the History of Biology*, 20 (1987): 289–319; Diane B. Paul, "'Our Load of Mutations' Revisited," *Journal of the History of Biology*, 20 (1987): 321–35; Garland E. Allen, "Old Wine in New Bottles: From Eugenics to Population Control, in the Work of Raymond Pearl," in Keith R. Benson, Jane Maienschein, and Ronald Rainger, eds., *The Expansion of American Biology* (New Brunswick, N.J.: Rutgers University Press, 1991).

9. William Diller Matthew to J. H. McGregor, n.d. [1928], William Diller Matthew Papers, vol. 26, Earth Sciences Library, University of California at Berkeley.

10. Alfred Sherwood Romer, "Time Series and Trends in Animal Evolution," in Glenn L. Jepsen, Ernst Mayr, and George Gaylord Simpson, eds., *Genetics, Paleontology and Evolution* (Princeton: Princeton University Press, 1949), 103–20. Jepsen queried Osborn on his ideas about aristogenes in several letters in 1934–35. Osborn Papers, Central Archives. See also Huxley Correspondence with Osborn, Osborn Papers, Central Archives; and Julian S. Huxley, *Evolution: The Modern Synthesis* (London: Allen and Unwin, 1942), 486–555.

11. Jonathan Harwood, "National Styles in Science: Genetics in Germany and the United States between the Wars," *Isis*, 78 (1987): 390–414; Lynn Nyhart, "The Disciplinary Breakdown of German Morphology, 1870–1900," *Isis*, 78 (1987): 365–89; and Wolf-Ernst Reif, "The Search for a Macroevolutionary Theory in German Paleontology," *Journal of the History of Biology*, 19 (1986): 79–130.

12. See the letters to students in William King Gregory Papers, box 3, Central Archives. See also Gregory to Edwin H. Colbert, 15 September 1928, Gregory Papers, box 4. On his problems with Morgan see "Fifty Years in the Department of Zoology, 1896–1946," Gregory Papers, box J.

13. George Gaylord Simpson, *Tempo and Mode in Evolution* (New York: Columbia University Press, 1944).

Bibliography

Manuscript Sources

Academy of Natural Sciences of Philadelphia
  Academy Correspondence, Manuscript Collections 566 and 567
  Academy Minutes, Manuscript Collections 502A and B
  "History of the Academy of Natural Sciences," by Edward J. Nolan, Manuscript Collection 463
  Joseph Leidy Correspondence, Manuscript Collections 1 and 1A
American Museum of Natural History, Department of Vertebrate Paleontology
  Annual Reports
  Departmental Correspondence
  Field Correspondence
  Field Diaries
  Personnel Files
  Staff Meetings
American Museum of Natural History, Library
  Albert S. Bickmore, "Autobiography"
  Central Archives
  L.P Gratacap, "History of the American Museum of Natural History"
  Trustee Minutes
  Clark Wissler, "Survey of the American Museum of Natural History, Made at the Request of the Management Board in 1942–43"
George Baur Correspondence, Archives, Museum of Comparative Zoology, Harvard University
Franz Boas Papers, American Philosophical Society
Barnum Brown Papers, Archives, Department of Vertebrate Paleontology, American Museum of Natural History
T. C. Chamberlin Papers, Joseph Regenstein Library, University of Chicago

Columbia University, Low Memorial Library
  Nicholas Murray Butler Papers, Central Record Files
  Seth Low Papers, Central Record Files
  Trustee Minutes
Edward Drinker Cope Papers
  American Philosophical Society
  Department of Vertebrate Paleontology, American Museum of Natural History
  Quaker Collection, Haverford College
  University of Pennsylvania Archives, Alumni Records
Charles Benedict Davenport Papers, American Philosophical Society
William King Gregory Papers, Central Archives, American Museum of Natural
  History
Arnold Henry Guyot Papers, Firestone Library, Princeton University
William Rainey Harper Papers, Joseph Regenstein Library, University of Chicago
Charles R. Knight Papers, New York Public Library
Joseph Leidy Papers, University of Pennsylvania Archives, Alumni Records
James McCosh Papers, Firestone Library, Princeton University
O. C. Marsh Papers, Manuscripts and Archives, Yale University Library, Yale
  University
William Diller Matthew Papers, Earth Sciences Library, University of California,
  Berkeley
Henry Fairfield Osborn Papers
  Central Archives, American Museum of Natural History
  Department of Vertebrate Paleontology, American Museum of Natural His-
    tory
  New-York Historical Society
Princeton University, Seeley G. Mudd Library
  E. M. Museum Files
  Geological and Geophysical Sciences File
  John C. Green School of Science File
  Grounds and Buildings File
  William Libbey Files
  Henry Fairfield Osborn Files
  Princeton Science Club File
  Princeton Scientific Expeditions File
  William Berryman Scott Files
  Trustee Minutes
Alfred Sherwood Romer Papers, Harvard University Archives
Charles Schuchert Papers, Manuscripts and Archives, Yale University Library,
  Yale University
William Berryman Scott Papers, Firestone Library, Princeton University
George Gaylord Simpson Papers, American Philosophical Society
University of Chicago Archives, Joseph Regenstein Library
  Presidents' Papers
  Trustee Minutes
University of Pennsylvania Archives, Alumni Records
  Biology Department File, Geology Department File
  Trustee Minutes
Yale University, Peabody Museum of Natural History
  Accession Books

Charles Emerson Beecher Letters
John Bell Hatcher Diaries
O. C. Marsh File
O. C. Marsh Pocket Diaries
Records of the Board of Trustees

Primary Sources

Allen, Joel Asaph. "The American Bisons, Living and Extinct." *Memoirs of the Museum of Comparative Zoology* 4 (1876): 1–246.

———. *Autobiographical Notes and a Bibliography of the Scientific Publications of Joel Asaph Allen.* New York: American Museum of Natural History, 1916.

———. "The Geographical Distribution of the Mammals Considered in Relation to the Principal Ontological Regions of the Earth and the Laws that Govern the Distribution of Animals." *Bulletin of the United States Geological Survey of the Territories* 4 (1878): 313–77.

———. "The Geographical Origin and Distribution of North American Birds Considered in Relation to the Faunal Areas of North America." *Auk* 10 (1893): 97–150.

———. *History of North American Pinnipeds: A Monograph of the Walruses, Sealions, Sea-Bears, and Seals of North America.* 1880. Reprint ed. New York: Arno, 1974.

———. *North American Ruminants. American Museum of Natural History Guide Leaflet,* no. 5. New York: American Museum of Natural History, 1902.

Andrews, Roy Chapman. *Across Mongolian Plains: A Naturalist's Account of China's Great "Northwest."* New York: Appleton, 1921.

———. *Ends of the Earth.* Garden City, N.Y.: Garden City, 1929.

———. *On the Trail of Ancient Man: A Narrative of the Field Work of the Central Asiatic Expeditions.* Garden City, N.Y.: Garden City, 1922.

———. *Under A Lucky Star: A Lifetime of Adventure.* New York: Viking, 1943.

Boas, Franz. *Race, Language and Culture.* New York: Macmillan, 1940.

Boule, Marcellin. *Les Hommes Fossiles: éléments de paléontologie humaine.* Paris: Masson, 1921.

Broom, Robert. *The Coming of Man: Was It Accident or Design?* London: Witherby, 1933.

Brown, Barnum. "The Hell Creek Beds of the Upper Cretaceous of Montana." *Bulletin of the American Museum of Natural History* 23 (1907): 823–45.

———. "The Osteology of *Champsosaurus* Cope." *Memoirs of the American Museum of Natural History* 9 (1905): 1–26.

———. "The *Trachodon* Group." *American Museum Journal* 8 (1908): 51–56.

———. "*Tyrannosaurus,* the Largest Flesh-Eating Animal That Ever Lived." *American Museum Journal* 15 (1915): 271–90.

Burgess, John William. *Reminiscences of an American Scholar: The Beginnings of Columbia University.* New York: Columbia University Press, 1934.

Butler, Nicholas Murray. *Across the Busy Years: Recollections and Reflections.* 2 vols. New York: Scribners, 1939–40.

Chapman, Frank M. *Autobiography of a Bird-Lover.* New York: Appleton-Century, 1933.

———. *Bird-Life: A Guide to the Study of Our Common Birds.* New York: Appleton, 1897.

————. *The Bird Rock Group. American Museum of Natural History Guide Leaflet,*
no. 1. New York: American Museum of Natural History, 1901.

————. *Birds and Man. American Museum of Natural History Guide Leaflet,* no. 115.
New York: American Museum of Natural History, 1943.

————. *Birds' Nests and Eggs. American Museum of Natural History Guide Leaflet,*
no. 14. New York: American Museum of Natural History, 1904.

————. *Camps and Cruises of an Ornithologist.* New York: Appleton, 1908.

————. "The Department of Birds, American Museum: Its History and Aims."
Natural History 22 (1922): 306–18.

————. *The Habitat Groups of North American Birds in the American Museum of
Natural History. American Museum of Natural History Guide Leaflet,* no. 28.
New York: American Museum of Natural History, 1930.

————. "What Constitutes a Museum Collection of Birds?" *Proceedings of the
Fourth International Ornithological Congress* (1905): 144–56.

Clark, James Lippitt. *Good Hunting. Fifty Years of Collecting and Preparing Habitat
Groups for the American Museum.* Norman: University of Oklahoma Press,
1966.

Columbia College in the City of New York. Historical Sketch and Present Conditions.
New York, 1893.

Cope, Edward Drinker. "The Laws of Organic Development." *American Naturalist* 5 (1871): 593–605.

————. "The Mechanical Causes of the Development of the Hard Parts of the
Mammalia." *Journal of Morphology* 3 (1889): 137–290.

————. "On the Extinct Vertebrata of the Eocene of Wyoming." *Annual Report of
the United States Geological Survey of the Territories* 6 (1873): 545–649.

————. *On the Origin of the Fittest: Essays in Evolution.* New York: Appleton,
1887.

————. *The Primary Factors of Organic Evolution.* Chicago: Open Court, 1896.

————. "The Vertebrata of the Cretaceous Formations of the West." *Report of the
United States Geological Survey of the Territories* 2 (1875): 1–302.

————. "The Vertebrata of the Tertiary Formations of the West." *Report of the
United States Geological Survey of the Territories* 3 (1883): 1–1009.

Darwin, Charles. *On the Origin of Species by Means of Natural Selection, or the
Preservation of Favoured Races in the Struggle for Life.* 1859. Reprint. Cambridge, Mass.: Harvard University Press, 1964.

Darwin, Francis Edward, ed. *The Life and Letters of Charles Darwin.* 2 vols. New
York: Appleton, 1896.

————. *More Letters of Charles Darwin.* 2 vols. New York: Appleton, 1903.

Dollo, Louis. "Les lois d'évolution." *Bulletin de la Société Belge de Géologie, Paléontologie et d'Hydrologie* 7 (1893): 164–66.

————. "La Paléontologie éthologique." *Bulletin de la Société Belge de Géologie,
Paléontologie et d'Hydrologie* 23 (1909): 377–421.

Gidley, James W. "New or Little Known Mammals from the Miocene of South
Dakota. American Museum Expedition of 1903. Part 1. Geological notes;
Part III, Dicotylidae." *Bulletin of the American Museum of Natural History* 20
(1904): 241–46, 265–68.

————. "A New Species of Pleistocene Horse from the Staked Plains of Texas."
Bulletin of the American Museum of Natural History 13 (1900): 111–16.

————. "Revision of the Miocene and Pliocene Equidae of North America."
Bulletin of the American Museum of Natural History 23 (1907): 865–934.

————. "Tooth Characters and Revision of the North American Species of the

Genus *Equus.*" *Bulletin of the American Museum of Natural History* 14 (1901): 91–142.

Gilmore, Charles W. "A Nearly Complete Articulated Skeleton of *Camarasaurus,* a Saurischian Dinosaur from the Dinosaur National Monument, Utah." *Memoirs of the Carnegie Museum* 10 (1925): 347–84.

———. "On a Newly Mounted Skeleton of *Diplodocus* in the United States National Museum." *Proceedings of the United States National Museum* 81 (1932): 1–21.

———. "Osteology of *Apatosaurus,* with special reference to specimens in the Carnegie Museum." *Memoirs of the Carnegie Museum* 11 (1936): 175–300.

Granger, Walter, and William King Gregory. Protoceratops andrewsii, *a Pre-Ceratopsian Dinosaur from Mongolia. American Museum Novitates,* no. 72. New York: American Museum of Natural History, 1923.

———. "A Revision of the Eocene Primates of the Genus *Notharctus.*" *Bulletin of the American Museum of Natural History* 37 (1917): 841–59.

Granger, Walter, and W. D. Matthew. *New Carnivora from the Tertiary of Mongolia. American Museum Novitates,* no. 104. New York: American Museum of Natural History, 1924.

Grant, Madison. *The Conquest of a Continent, Or, the Expansion of Races in America.* New York: Scribners, 1933.

———. *The Passing of the Great Race; Or the Racial Basis of European History.* New York: Scribners, 1916.

Gregory, William King. "Basic Patents in Nature." *Science* 78 (1933): 561–66.

———. "The Bearing of Dr. Broom's and Dr. Dart's Discoveries on the Origin of Man." *Annual Proceedings, Associated and Technical Societies of South Africa* (1939): 25–57.

———. "The Bearing of the Australopithecinae upon the Problem of Man's Place in Nature." *American Journal of Physical Anthropology,* n.s. 7 (1949): 485–512.

———. "A Critique of Professor Frederic Wood-Jones's Paper: Some Landmarks in the Phylogeny of Primates." *Human Biology* 2 (1930): 99–108.

———. "A Critique of Professor Osborn's Theory of Human Origin." *American Journal of Physical Anthropology* 14 (1930): 133–64.

———. "The Dawn Man of Piltdown, England." *American Museum Journal* 14 (1914): 189–200.

———. *Evolution Emerging: A Survey of Changing Patterns from Primeval Life to Man.* 2 vols. New York: Macmillan, 1951.

———. "The Family Tree of Man." In Henry Fairfield Osborn, *The Hall of the Age of Man. American Museum of Natural History Guide Leaflet,* 6th ed., no. 52. New York: American Museum of Natural History, 1932, 36, 40–48.

———. "Genetics *versus* Paleontology." *American Naturalist* 51 (1917): 622–35.

———. "How Near is the Relationship of Man to the Chimpanzee-Gorilla Stock?" *Quarterly Review of Biology* 2 (1927): 549–60.

———. "Is the Pro-Dawn Man a Myth?" *Human Biology* 1 (1929): 153–65.

———. *Man's Place Among the Anthropoids.* Oxford: Clarendon, 1934.

———. "The Muscular Anatomy and the Restoration of the Titanotheres." In Henry Fairfield Osborn, *The Titanotheres of Ancient Wyoming, Dakota, and Nebraska.* 2 vols. Washington, D.C.: Government Printing Office, 1929. Vol. 2, 703–25.

———. "A New Restoration of a Titanothere." *American Museum Journal* 12 (1912): 15–17.

———. "Notes on the Principles of Quadrupedal Locomotion and on the Mechanism of the Limbs in Hoofed Animals." *Annals of the New York Academy of Sciences* 22 (1912): 267–94.

———. "On Design in Nature." *The Yale Review* 13 (1924): 334–45.

———. "On the Meaning and Limits of Irreversibility of Evolution." *American Naturalist* 70 (1936): 517–28.

———. "On the Structure and Relations of *Notharctus*, an American Eocene Primate. Studies on the Evolution of the Primates. Part III." *Memoirs of the American Museum of Natural History*, n.s., 3 (1920): 49–243.

———. "The Orders of Mammals." *Bulletin of the American Museum of Natural History* 27 (1910): 1–524.

———. *The Origin and Evolution of the Human Dentition.* Baltimore: Williams & Wilkins, 1922.

———. "Origin of Human Limb Proportions through Change of Function." *Bulletin of the New York Academy of Medicine*, 2d ser., 4 (1928): 239–42.

———. "The Origin of Man from the Anthropoid Stem—When and Where." *Proceedings of the American Philosophical Society* 66 (1927): 439–63.

———. "The Origin of Man from a Brachiating Anthropoid Stock." *Science* 71 (1930): 645–50.

———. *Our Face From Fish to Man.* New York: Putnam's, 1929.

———. "Principles of Leverage and Muscular Action." In Henry Fairfield Osborn, *The Titanotheres of Ancient Wyoming, Dakota, and Nebraska.* 2 vols. Washington, D.C.: Government Printing Office, 1929. Vol. 2, 727–31.

———. "The Roles of Undeviating Evolution and Transformation in the Origin of Man." *American Naturalist* 69 (1935): 385–404.

———. "Studies on the Evolution of Primates. II. Phylogeny of Recent and Extinct Anthropoids, with Special Reference to the Origin of Man." *Bulletin of the American Museum of Natural History* 35 (1916): 258–355.

———. "Supra-specific Variation in Nature and in Classification. IV. A Few Examples from Mammalian Paleontology." *American Naturalist* 71 (1937): 268–76.

———. "The Transformation of Organic Designs: A Review of the Origin and Deployment of the Earlier Vertebrates." *Biological Reviews of the Cambridge Philosophical Society* 11 (1936): 311–44.

———. "The Upright Posture of Man: A Review of its Origin and Evolution." *Proceedings of the American Philosophical Society* 67 (1928): 339–77.

———. "The Weight of the *Brontosaurus*." *Science* 22 (1905): 572.

———. "Were the Ancestors ot Man Primitive Brachiators?" *Proceedings of the American Philosophical Society* 67 (1928): 129–50.

Gregory, William King, and C. L. Camp. "Studies in Comparative Myology and Osteology. No.III." *Bulletin of the American Museum of Natural History* 38 (1918): 447–563.

Gregory, William King, and Milo Hellman. "The Dentition of *Dryopithecus* and the Origin of Man." *American Museum of Natural History Anthropological Papers* 28. pt. 1 (1926): 1–123.

———. "The Dentition of the Extinct South African Man-Ape *Australopithecus* (*Plesianthropus*) *transvaalensis* Broom. A Comparative and Phylogenetic Study." *Annals of the Transvaal Museum* 19 (1939): 339–73.

———. "The South African Fossil Man-Apes and Origin of the Human Dentition." *Journal of the American Dental Association* 26 (1939): 558–64.

Gregory, William King, and J. H. McGregor. "A Dissenting Opinion as to Dawn Men and Ape Men." *Natural History* 26 (1926): 270–71.

Gregory, William King, and C. C. Mook. *On Protoceratops, a Primitive Ceratopsian Dinosaur from the Lower Cretaceous of Mongolia.* American Museum Novitates, no. 156. New York: American Museum of Natural History, 1925.

Gregory, William King, and M. Roigneau. *Introduction to Human Anatomy: Guide to Section I of the Hall of Natural History of Man.* American Museum of Natural History Guide Leaflet, no. 86. New York: American Museum of Natural History, 1934.

Guyot, Arnold Henry. *Creation, or the Biblical Cosmogeny in the Light of Modern Science.* New York: Scribners, 1884.

———. *Earth and Man, or Lectures in Comparative Physical Geography in Its Relation to the History of Mankind.* Translated by C. C. Felton. Boston: Gould, Kendall and Lincoln, 1849.

Hatcher, John Bell. "The Ceratops Beds of Converse County, Wyoming." *American Journal of Science,* 3d ser., 45 (1893): 135–44.

———. "*Diplodocus* Marsh: Its Osteology, Taxonomy, and Probable Habits, with a Restoration of the Skeleton." *Memoirs of the Carnegie Museum* 1 (1901): 1–63.

———. "On the Geology of Southern Patagonia." *American Journal of Science,* 4th ser., 4 (1897): 327–54.

———. "Osteology of *Haplocanthosaurus,* with Description of a New Species, and Remarks on the Probable Habits of the Sauropoda and the Age and Origin of the Atlantosaurus Beds." *Memoirs of the Carnegie Museum* 2 (1903): 1–72.

———. "Sedimentary Rocks of Southern Patagonia." *American Journal of Science,* 4th ser., 9 (1900): 85–108.

———. "Structure of the Fore Limb and the Manus of *Brontosaurus.*" *Annals of the Carnegie Museum* 1 (1902): 356–76.

———. "The Titanotherium Beds." *American Naturalist* 27 (1893): 204–21.

Hay, Oliver Perry. "Dr. W. J. Holland on the Skull of *Diplodocus.*" *Science* 28 (1908): 517–19.

———. "Further Observations on the Pose of the Sauropodous Dinosaurs." *American Naturalist* 45 (1911): 398–412.

———. "On the Habits and the Pose of the Sauropodous Dinosaurs, especially of *Diplodocus.*" *American Naturalist* 42 (1908): 672–81.

———. "On the Manner of Locomotion of the Dinosaurs, especially *Diplodocus,* with Remarks on the Origin of the Birds." *Proceedings of the Washington Academy of Sciences* 12 (1910): 1–25.

———. "The Progress of Vertebrate Paleontology at the American Museum of Natural History, New York." *American Geologist* 35 (1905): 31–34.

Hermann, Adam. "Modern Laboratory Methods in Vertebrate Paleontology." *Bulletin of the American Museum of Natural History* 26 (1909): 283–331.

Holland, W. J. "The Osteology of *Diplodocus* Marsh, with Special Reference to the Restoration of the Skeleton of *Diplodocus carnegiei* Hatcher." *Memoirs of the Carnegie Museum of Natural History* 4 (1906): 225–78.

———. "A Review of Some Recent Criticisms of the Restorations of Sauropod Dinosaurs Existing in the Museums of the United States, with special reference to that of *Diplodocus carnegiei* in the Carnegie Museum." *American Naturalist* 44 (1910): 259–83.

Hornaday, W. T. *Our Vanishing Wildlife: Its Extermination and Preservation.* New York: New York Zoological Society, 1913.

Huxley, Julian S. *Evolution: The Modern Synthesis.* London: Allen & Unwin, 1942.

Huxley, Thomas Henry. *American Addresses, with a Lecture on Biology.* New York: Appleton, 1877.

———. *Evidence as to Man's Place in Nature.* London: Williams and Norgate, 1863.

———. "Palaeontology and the Doctrine of Evolution." In vol. 8 of *Collected Essays,* 340–88. New York: Verlag, 1970.

———. "Principles and Methods of Palaeontology." *Smithsonian Institution Annual Report for 1869* (1870): 363–88.

———. "Remarks on *Archaeopteryx lithographica.*" *Proceedings of the Royal Society of London* 16 (1868): 243–48.

Jepsen, Glenn L., Ernst Mayr, and George Gaylord Simpson, eds. *Genetics, Paleontology, and Evolution.* Princeton: Princeton University Press, 1949.

Jones, Frederic Wood. *Man's Place Among the Mammals.* London: Edward Arnold, 1929.

Keith, Arthur. *The Antiquity of Man.* 2d ed., 2 vols. London: Williams and Norgate, 1925.

Kovalevsky, Vladimir. "Monographie der Gattung *Anthracotherium Cuv.* und Versuch einer natürlichen Classification der fossilen Hufthiere." *Palaeontographica* 3 (1873): 131–210; 4 (1874): 211–90; 5 (1874): 291–346.

———. "On the Osteology of the Hyopotamidae." *Philosophical Transactions of the Royal Society of London* 163 (1874): 19–94.

———. "Sur l'*Anchitherium Aurelianese Cuv.* et sur l'histoire paléontologique des chevaux." *Mémoires de l'Académie Impériale des Sciences de St.-Petersbourg* 20 (1873): 1–73.

Leidy, Joseph. "The Ancient Fauna of Nebraska, Or, A Description of Remains of Extinct Mammalia and Chelonia from the Mauvaises Terres of Nebraska." *Smithsonian Contributions to Knowledge* 6 (1854): 1–126.

———. "Contributions to the Extinct Vertebrate Fauna of the Western Territories." *Report of the United States Geological Survey of the Territories* 1 (1873): 1–358.

———. "Cretaceous Reptiles of the United States." *Smithsonian Contributions to Knowledge* 14 (1865): 1–140.

———. *The Extinct Mammalian Fauna of Dakota and Nebraska. Including an Account of Some Allied Forms from other Localities, together with a Synopsis of the Mammalian Remains of North America.* 1869. Reprint. New York: Arno, 1974.

———. "A Flora and Fauna Within Living Animals." *Smithsonian Contributions to Knowledge* 5 (1853): 1–68.

Lucas, Frederic A. *Animals of the Past: An Account of Some of the Creatures of the Ancient World.* New York: American Museum of Natural History, 1913.

———. *Fifty Years of Museum Work: Autobiography, Unpublished Papers and a Bibliography of Frederic Augustus Lucas.* New York: American Museum of Natural History, 1933.

———. "Museum Methods: The Exhibition of Fossil Vertebrates." *Science* 3 (1896): 573–75.

———. "Restorations of Extinct Animals." *Smithsonian Institution Annual Report for 1900* (1901): 479–92.

———. "The Story of Museum Groups, Parts I and II." *American Museum Journal* 14 (1914): 1–15, 51–65.

Lyell, Charles. *Principles of Geology; Or the Modern Changes of the Earth and Its*

Inhabitants Considered as Illustrative of Geology. 3 vols. London: John Murray, 1830–33.

McCosh, James. *Christianity and Positivism: A Series of Lectures to the Times on Natural Theology and Apologetics.* New York: Robert Carter, 1871.

———. *The Development Hypothesis: Is it Sufficient?* New York: Robert Carter, 1876.

———. *Development: What Can it Do and What it Cannot Do.* New York: Scribners, 1883.

———. *The Religious Aspect of Evolution.* New York: Putnam, 1888.

Marsh, Othniel Charles. "American Jurassic Mammals." *American Journal of Science,* 3d ser., 33 (1887): 327–48.

———. *Dinocerata: A Monograph of an Extinct Order of Gigantic Mammals.* Washington, D.C.: Government Printing Office, 1886.

———. "The Dinosaurs of North America." *Annual Report of the United States Geological Survey* 16, pt. 1 (1896): 133–244.

———. "Fossil Horses in America." *American Naturalist* 8 (1874): 288–94.

———. *Odontornithes: A Monograph on the Extinct Toothed Birds of North America.* Washington, D.C.: Government Printing Office, 1880.

Matthew, William Diller. "*Allosaurus,* a Carnivorous Dinosaur and Its Prey." *American Museum Journal* 8 (1908): 1–5.

———. "The Carnivora and Insectivora of the Bridger Basin, Middle Eocene." *Memoirs of the American Museum of Natural History* 9 (1909): 291–567.

———. "Certain Theoretical Considerations Affecting Phylogeny and Correlation." *Bulletin of the Geological Society of America* 24 (1913): 283–92.

———. "Climate and Evolution." *Annals of the New York Academy of Sciences* 24 (1915): 171–318.

———. *Climate and Evolution,* 2d ed. New York: New York Academy of Sciences, 1939.

———. "The Collection of Fossil Vertebrates." *American Museum Journal* 3 (1903): 1–32.

———. "Critical Observations on the Phylogeny of the Rhinoceroses." *University of California Publications in Geology* 20 (1931): 1–9.

———. *Dinosaurs. American Museum of Natural History Handbook,* no. 5. New York: American Museum of Natural History, 1915.

———. "Evidence of the Paleocene Vertebrate Fauna on the Cretaceous-Tertiary Problem." *Bulletin of the Geological Society of America* 25 (1914): 381–402.

———. *The Evolution of the Horse. American Museum of Natural History Guide Leaflet,* no. 9. New York: American Museum of Natural History, 1903.

———. "The Evolution of the Horse; A Record and its Interpretation." *Quarterly Review of Biology* 1 (1926): 139–86.

———. "Exhibition Illustrating the Evolution of the Horse." *American Museum Journal* 8 (1908): 117–22.

———. "Fossil Carnivores, Marsupials and Small Mammals in the American Museum of Natural History." *American Museum Journal* 5 (1905): 22–59.

———. "Fossil Mammals of the Tertiary of Northeastern Colorado." *Memoirs of the American Museum of Natural History* 1 (1901): 353–447.

———. "The Hall of Fossil Vertebrates." *American Museum Journal* 2 (1902): supplement, 1–19.

———. "Hypothetical Outlines of the Continents in Tertiary Times." *Bulletin of the American Museum of Natural History* 22 (1906): 353–83.

————. "Is the White River Tertiary an Aeolian Formation?" *American Naturalist* 33 (1899): 403–8.

————. "Methods of Correlation by Fossil Vertebrates." *Bulletin of the Geological Society of America* 27 (1916): 515–24.

————. "The Mounted Skeleton of *Brontosaurus* in the American Museum of Natural History." *American Museum Journal* 5 (1905): 65–75.

————. "On the Osteology and Relationships of *Paramys* and the Affinities of the Ischyromyidae." *Bulletin of the American Museum of Natural History* 28 (1910): 43–72.

————. "Osteology of *Blastomeryx* and Phylogeny of the American Cervidae." *Bulletin of the American Museum of Natural History* 24 (1908): 535–62.

————. "Patagonia and the Pampas Cenozoic of South America: A Critical Review of the Correlations of Santiago Roth." *Annals of the New York Academy of Sciences* 19 (1910): 149–60.

————. "The Pattern of Evolution: A Criticism of Doctor Austin Clark's Thesis." *Scientific American* 143 (September 1930): 192–96.

————. "The Phylogeny of the Felidae." *Bulletin of the American Museum of Natural History* 28 (1910): 289–316.

————. "The Phylum in Zoology and Paleontology." *Science* 70 (1929): 142–43.

————. "The Pose of Sauropod Dinosaurs." *American Naturalist* 44 (1910): 547–60.

————. "A Provisional Classification of the Fresh-Water Tertiary of the West." *Bulletin of the American Museum of Natural History* 12 (1899): 19–75.

————. "Range and Limitations of Species as Seen in Fossil Mammal Faunas." *Bulletin of the Geological Society of America* 41 (1930): 271–74.

————. "A Review of the Rhinoceroses with a Description of *Aphelops* Material from the Pliocene of Texas." *University of California Publications in Geology* 22 (1932): 411–82.

————. "A Revision of the Puerco Fauna." *Bulletin of the American Museum of Natural History* 9 (1897): 259–323.

————. "Third Contribution to the Snake Creek Fauna." *Bulletin of the American Museum of Natural History* 50 (1924): 59–210.

————. "Three-Toed Horses." *Natural History* 20 (1920): 473–78.

————. "The *Tyrannosaurus*." *American Museum Journal* 10 (1910): 3–8.

Matthew, William Diller, and S. H. Chubb. *The Evolution of the Horse. American Museum of Natural History Guide Leaflet*, no. 36. New York: American Museum of Natural History, 1913.

Matthew, William Diller, and Walter Granger. "A Revision of the Lower Eocene Wasatch and Wind River Faunas. Part I. Order Ferae (Carnivora), suborder Creodonta." *Bulletin of the American Museum of Natural History* 34 (1915): 1–103.

————. "A Revision of the Lower Eocene Wasatch and Wind River Faunas. Part II. Order Condylarthra, family Hyopsodontidae." *Bulletin of the American Museum of Natural History* 34 (1915): 311–28.

————. "A Revision of the Lower Eocene Wasatch and Wind River Faunas. Part IV. Entelonycha, Primates, Insectivora." *Bulletin of the American Museum of Natural History* 34 (1915): 429–83.

————. "A Revision of the Lower Eocene Wasatch and Wind River Faunas. Part V. Insectivora, Glires, Edentata." *Bulletin of the American Museum of Natural History* 38 (1918): 565–657.

Matthew, William Diller, and R. A. Stirton. "Equidae from the Pliocene of Texas." *University of California Publications in Geology* 19 (1930): 349–96.

———. "Osteology and Affinities of *Borophagus.*" *University of California Publications in Geology* 19 (1930): 171–216.

Mayr, Ernst. *Populations, Species and Evolution.* Cambridge, Mass.: Harvard University Press, 1970.

———. *Systematics and the Origin of Species.* New York: Columbia University Press, 1942.

Miner, Roy W. "The Pectoral Limbs of *Eryops* and other Primitive Tetrapods." *Bulletin of the American Museum of Natural History* 51 (1925): 148–302.

Morgan, Thomas Hunt. *A Critique of the Theory of Evolution.* Princeton: Princeton University Press, 1916.

———. *The Scientific Basis of Evolution.* New York: Norton, 1932.

Morgan, T. H., A. H. Sturtevant, H. J. Muller, and C. B. Bridges. *The Mechanism of Mendelian Heredity.* New York: Henry Holt, 1915.

Morton, Dudley J. *The Human Foot: Its Evolution, Physiology, and Function Disorders.* New York: Columbia University Press, 1935.

Osborn, Henry Fairfield. "Additional Characters of the Great Herbivorous Dinosaur *Camarasaurus.*" *Bulletin of the American Museum of Natural History* 10 (1898): 219–33.

———. "Address of Welcome at the Opening of the New York Zoological Park." *Fourth Annual Report of the New York Zoological Society* (1900): 76–78.

———. "Address of Welcome to the Second International Congress of Eugenics." *Science* 54 (1921): 311–13.

———. *The Age of Mammals in Europe, Asia and North America.* New York: Macmillan, 1910.

———. "The Aim and Method of Science Study in Schools Below the College. Biological Work in the High School." *Regents Bulletin* 36 (1896): 62–64.

———. "The American Museum and Citizenship." *Annual Report of the American Museum of Natural History* 54 (1923): 1–32.

———. "The American Museum and the World." *Annual Report of the American Museum of Natural History* 55 (1924): 1–32.

———. "Angulation of the Limbs of Proboscidea, Dinocerata, and Other Quadrupeds in Adaptation to Weight." *American Naturalist* 34 (1900): 89–94.

———. "The Approach to the Immigration Problem Through Science." *Proceedings of the National Immigration Conference,* no. 26 (1924): 44–53.

———. "Are Acquired Variations Inherited?" *American Naturalist* 25 (1891): 191–216.

———. "Aristogenesis, the Creative Principle in the Origin of Species." *American Naturalist* 68 (1934): 193–235.

———. "Biology and other Science in the Schools." *Report of the Schoolmasters Association of New York and Vicinity* (1892–93): 35–42.

———. "Birth Selection versus Birth Control." *The Forum* 88 (1932): 79–83.

———. "The Born Naturalist." *Natural History* 25 (1925): 309–10.

———. "The Continuous Origin of Certain Unit Characters as Observed by a Palaeontologist." *Harvey Society* 7 (1912): 153–204.

———. "The Cornerstones of Learning." *Program of Dedication of the New Site, Morningside Heights* (1896). New York City, 2 May 1896.

———. "Correlation Between Tertiary Mammal Horizons of Europe and America." *Annals of the New York Academy of Sciences* 13 (1900): 1–72.

———. *Creative Education in School, College, University and Museum: Personal Ob-*

servation and Experience of the Half-Century 1877–1927. New York: Scribners, 1927.
———. "Credo of a Naturalist." *The Forum* 73 (1925): 486–94.
———. "Darwin and Palaeontology." In American Association for the Advancement of Science, ed., *Fifty Years of Darwinism*, 209–50. New York: Henry Holt, 1909.
———. "The Dawn Man of Piltdown, Sussex." *Natural History* 22 (1922): 577–90.
———. "Difficulties in the Heredity Theory." *American Naturalist* 26 (1892): 537–67.
———. "The Discovery of Tertiary Man." *Science* 71 (1930): 1–7.
———. *The Earth Speaks to Bryan*. New York: Scribners, 1925.
———. "Equidae of the Oligocene, Miocene, and Pliocene of North America, Iconographic Type Revision." *Memoirs of the American Museum of Natural History*, n.s., 2 (1918): 1–217.
———. "Eugenics—The American and Norwegian Programs." *Science* 54 (1921): 482–84.
———. "Evolution and Heredity." *Biological Lectures Delivered at the Marine Biological Laboratory at Woods Hole for 1890* (1891): 130–41.
———. *Evolution and Religion*. New York: Scribners, 1923.
———. *Evolution and Religion in Education: Polemics of the Fundamentalist Controversy of 1922 to 1926*. New York: Scribners, 1926.
———. "Evolution as it Appears to the Palaeontologist." *Science* 26 (1907): 744–49.
———. "The Evolution of Human Races." *Natural History* 26 (1926): 3–13.
———. "The Extinct Rhinoceroses." *Memoirs of the American Museum of Natural History* 1 (1898): 75–164.
———. *Fifty-Two Years of Research, Observation and Publication, 1877–1929: A Life Adventure in Breadth and Depth*. New York: Scribners, 1930.
———. "The Foetal Membranes of the Marsupials: The Yolk-Sac Placenta in Didelphys." *Journal of Morphology* 1 (1887): 373–82.
———. "Fore and Hind Limbs of Carnivorous and Herbivorous Dinosaurs from the Jurassic of Wyoming." *Bulletin of the American Museum of Natural History* 12 (1899): 161–72.
———. "Fossil Wonders of the West: the Dinosaurs of Bone-Cabin Quarry, Being the First Description of the Greatest 'Find' of Extinct Animals Ever Made." *Century Magazine* 68 (1904): 680–94.
———. "Fossil Wonders of the West: The Evolution of the Horse in America." *Century Magazine* 69 (1904): 3–17.
———. *From the Greeks to Darwin: An Outline of the Development of the Evolution Idea*. New York: Macmillan, 1894.
———. "Geological and Faunal Relations of Europe and America during the Tertiary Period and the Theory of the Successive Invasions of an African Fauna." *Science* 11 (1900): 561–74.
———. *The Hall of the Age of Man in the American Museum. American Museum of Natural History Guide Leaflet*, no. 52. New York: American Museum of Natural History, 1920.
———. "The Heredity Mechanism and the Search for the Unknown Factors of Evolution." *Biological Lectures Delivered at the Marine Biological Laboratory at Woods Hole for 1894* (1895): 79–100.

———. *The Horse Past and Present in the American Museum of Natural History.* New York: Irving Press, 1913.

———. "How to Teach Evolution in the Public Schools." *School and Society* 23 (1926): 25–31.

———. "Hunting the Ancestral Elephant in the Fayûm Desert: Discoveries of the Recent African Expedition of the American Museum of Natural History." *Century Magazine* 74 (1907): 815–35.

———. "Huxley on Education." *Science* 32 (1910): 569–78.

———. "The Ideas and Terms of Modern Philosophical Anatomy." *Science* 21 (1905): 959–61.

———. *Impressions of Great Naturalists.* New York: Scribners, 1924.

———. "The Influence of Habit in the Evolution of Man and the Great Apes." *Bulletin of the New York Academy of Medicine,* 2d ser., 4 (1928): 216–30.

———. "Is the Ape-Man a Myth?" *Human Biology* 1 (1929): 4–9.

———. "The Law of Adaptive Radiation." *American Naturalist* 36 (1902): 353–63.

———. "The Mammalia of the Uinta Formation. III. The Perissodactyla. IV. The Evolution of the Ungulate Foot." *Transactions of the American Philosophical Society,* n.s., 16 (1890): 505–572.

———. *Man Rises to Parnassus: Critical Epochs in the Prehistory of Man.* Princeton: Princeton University Press, 1927.

———. *Men of the Old Stone Age: Their Environment, Life and Art.* New York: Scribners, 1915.

———. "A Mode of Evolution Requiring neither Natural Selection nor the Inheritance of Acquired Characters." *Transactions of the New York Academy of Sciences* 15 (1896): 141–42, 148.

———. "The New York Zoological Park." *Science* 7 (1898): 759–64.

———. "Observations upon the Foetal Membranes of the Opossum and other Marsupials." *Quarterly Journal of Microscopical Science,* n.s., 23 (1883): 473–84.

———. "On the Structure and Classification of the Mesozoic Mammalia." *Journal of the Academy of Natural Sciences of Philadelphia,* 2d ser., 9 (1888): 186–265.

———. "Ontogenic and Phylogenic Variation." *Science* 4 (1896): 786–89.

———. "Organic Selection." *Science* 6 (1897): 583–87.

———. *The Origin and Evolution of Life on the Theory of Action, Reaction, and Interaction.* New York: Scribners, 1917.

———. "Origin and History of the Horse." Address before the New York Farmers. New York City, 19 December 1905.

———. "The Origin of the Corpus Callosum. A Contribution upon the Cerebral Commissures of the Vertebrata." *Morphologische Jahrbuch* 12 (1886): 223–51.

———. "Origin of Single Characters as Observed in Fossil and Living Animals and Plants." *American Naturalist* 49 (1915): 193–240.

———. "The 'Ostrich' Dinosaur and the 'Tyrant' Dinosaur." *American Museum Journal* 17 (1917): 5–13.

———. "Our Ancestors Arrive in Scandinavia." *Natural History* 22 (1922): 116–34.

———. "The Paleontologic Correlation Through the Bache Fund." *Science* 31 (1910): 407–8.

———. "The Paleontological Evidence for the Transmission of Acquired Characters." *American Naturalist* 23 (1889): 561–66.

————. "Paleontology Versus Genetics," *Science* 72 (1930): 1–3.

————. Preface to *The Arab Horse*, by Spencer Borden, vii–xiii. New York: Doubleday, 1906.

————. Preface to *The Passing of the Great Race*, by Madison Grant, vii–ix. New York: Scribners, 1916.

————. "The Present Problem of Heredity." *Atlantic Monthly* 67 (1891): 353–64.

————. *Preservation of the Wild Animals of North America*. New York: Boone and Crockett Club, 1904.

————. *Proboscidea. A Monograph of the Discovery of Evolution, Migration and Extinction of the Mastodonts and Elephants of the World*. 2 vols. New York: American Museum Press, 1936, 1942.

————. "Proving Asia the Mother of Continents." *Asia*, 22 (1922): 721–24.

————. "Race Progress in its Relation to Social Progress." *Journal of the National Institute of Social Science* 9 (1924): 8–18.

————. "Recent Discoveries Relating to the Origin and Antiquity of Man." *Science* 65 (1927): 481–88.

————. "Rise of the Mammalia in North America." *Proceedings of the American Association for the Advancement of Science* 42 (1894): 189–227.

————. *Sauropoda and Theropoda of the Lower Cretaceous of Mongolia*. American Museum Novitates, no. 128. New York: American Museum of Natural History, 1924.

————. "A Skeleton of *Diplodocus*." *Memoirs of the American Museum of Natural History* 1 (1899): 191–214.

————. "A Student's Reminiscences of Huxley." *Biological Lectures Delivered at the Marine Biological Laboratory at Woods Hole for 1895* (1896): 29–42.

————. "Tetraplasy, the Law of the Four Inseparable Factors of Evolution." *Journal of the Academy of Natural Sciences of Philadelphia*, 2d ser., 15 (1912): 275–309.

————. *The Titanotheres of Ancient Wyoming, Dakota, and Nebraska*. 2 vols. Washington, D.C.: Government Printing Office, 1929.

————. "To the Philosophic Zoologist." *Science* 29 (1909): 895–96.

————. "*Tyrannosaurus*, Upper Cretaceous Carnivorous Dinosaur." *Bulletin of the American Museum of Natural History* 22 (1906): 281–96.

————. "*Tyrannosaurus*, Upper Cretaceous Carnivorous Dinosaur." *Bulletin of the American Museum of Natural History* 22 (1906): 281–96.

————. "Vertebrate Paleontology in the American Museum." *Science* 2 (1895): 178–79.

————. "What is Americanism?" *The Forum* 75 (1926): 803–4.

————. "Why Central Asia?" *Natural History* 26 (1926): 263–69.

————. "William Bateson on Darwinism." *Science* 55 (1922): 194–97.

————. "The World's Debt to Biology." *The Chautauquan* 23 (1896): 564–69.

————. "Zoology at Columbia." *Columbia University Bulletin*, 18 (1897): 1–10.

Osborn, Henry Fairfield, and Harold Elmer Anthony. "Can We Save the Mammals?" *Natural History* 22 (1922): 388–405.

Osborn, Henry Fairfield, and Walter Granger. "Fore and Hind Limbs of Sauropoda from the Bone-Cabin Quarry." *Bulletin of the American Museum of Natural History* 14 (1901): 199–208.

Osborn, Henry Fairfield, and William Diller Matthew. "Cenozoic Mammal

Horizons of Western North America." *Bulletin of the United States Geological Survey*, no. 361 (1909): 1–138.

———. "Geological Correlation Through Vertebrate Paleontology by International Cooperation. Correlation Bulletin No. 1 Plan and Scope." *Annals of the New York Academy of Sciences* 19 (1909): 41–44.

Osborn, Henry Fairfield, and Charles Craig Mook. "*Camarasaurus, Amphicoelias,* and other Sauropods of Cope." *Memoirs of the American Museum of Natural History*, n.s., 3 (1921): 247–387.

Osborn, Henry Fairfield, and William Berryman Scott. "The Mammalia of the Uinta Formation." *Transactions of the American Philosophical Society*, n.s., 16 (1890): 461–572.

———. "On the Skull of the Eocene Rhinoceros, *Orthocynodon*, and the Relation of this Genus to Other Members of the Group." *Contributions of the E. M. Museum of Geology and Archaeology* 3 (1883): 1–22.

———. "Preliminary Account of the Fossil Mammals from the White River Formation contained in the Museum of Comparative Zoology." *Bulletin of the Museum of Comparative Zoology* 13 (1887): 151–71.

———. "Preliminary Account of the Fossil Mammals from the White River and Loup Fork Formations, contained in the Museum of Comparative Zoology, Part II." *Bulletin of the Museum of Comparative Zoology* 20 (1890): 65–100.

Osborn, Henry Fairfield, William Berryman Scott, and Francis Speir, Jr. "Paleontological Report of the Princeton Scientific Expedition of 1877." *Contributions of the E. M. Museum of Geology and Archaeology* 1 (1878): 7–106.

Osborn, Henry Fairfield, and Jacob L. Wortman. "Fossil Mammals of the Lower Miocene White River Beds. Collection of 1892." *Bulletin of the American Museum of Natural History* 6 (1894): 199–228.

———. "Fossil Mammals of the Wahsatch and Wind River Beds. Collection of 1891." *Bulletin of the American Museum of Natural History* 4 (1892): 81–147.

Owen, Richard. *Palaeontology; or a Systematic Summary of Extinct Animals and Their Geological Relations*. Edinburgh: Adam and Charles Black, 1860.

The Princeton Book: A Series of Sketches Pertaining to the History, Organization and Present Condition of the College of New Jersey. Boston: Houghton, Osgood, 1879.

Reeds, Chester A., gen. ed. *The Natural History of Central Asia*. 6 vols. New York: American Museum of Natural History, 1927–40. Vol. 1: *The New Conquest of Central Asia. A Narrative of the Field Work of the Central Asiatic Expeditions in Mongolia and China, 1921–1930*, by Roy Chapman Andrews.

Romer, Alfred Sherwood. "Crocodilian Pelvic Muscles and Their Avian and Reptilian Homologues." *Bulletin of the American Museum of Natural History* 48 (1923): 533–52.

———. "The Locomotor Apparatus of Certain Primitive Mammal-like Reptiles." *Bulletin of the American Museum of Natural History* 46 (1922): 517–606.

———. *Notes and Comments on Vertebrate Paleontology*. Chicago: University of Chicago Press, 1968.

———. "Pectoral Limb Musculature and Shoulder-Girdle Structure in Fish and Tetrapods." *Anatomical Record* 27 (1924): 119–43.

———. *Vertebrate Paleontology*. 3d ed. Chicago: University of Chicago Press, 1966.

Roosevelt, Theodore. *An Autobiography*. New York: Macmillan, 1914.

————. *Hunting Trips of a Ranchman*. New York: Putnam, 1885.

————. *Letters of Theodore Roosevelt*. Edited by Elting E. Morison. Cambridge, Mass.: Harvard University Press, 1951.

————. *Ranch Life and the Hunting Trail*. New York: Century, 1885.

————. *The Strenuous Life: Essays and Addresses by Theodore Roosevelt*. New York: Century, 1901.

Roosevelt, Theodore, and George Bird Grinnell. *American Big-Game Hunting: The Book of the Boone and Crockett Club*. New York: Forest and Stream, 1893.

————, eds. *Trail and Camp-Fire: The Book of the Boone and Crockett Club*. New York: Forest and Stream, 1897.

Scott, William Berryman. *A History of Land Mammals in the Western Hemisphere*. New York: Macmillan, 1913.

————. "On the Osteology of *Mesohippus* and *Leptomeryx*, with Observations on the Modes and Factors of Evolution in the Mammalia." *Journal of Morphology* 5 (1891): 301–406.

————. "On the Osteology of *Poebrotherium*. A Contribution to the Phylogeny of the Tylopoda." *Journal of Morphology* 5 (1891): 1–78.

————. "On Variations and Mutations." *American Journal of Science*, 3d ser., 48 (1894): 355–74.

————. *Some Memories of a Palaeontologist*. Princeton: Princeton University Press, 1939.

————, gen. ed. *Reports of the Princeton University Expeditions to Patagonia, 1896–1899*. 8 vols. Princeton: Princeton University Press, 1903–32. Vol. 1: *Narrative of the Expeditions: Geography of Southern Patagonia*, by John Bell Hatcher.

————, gen. ed. *Reports of the Princeton University Expeditions to Patagonia, 1896–1899*. 8 vols. Princeton: Princeton University Press, 1903–32. Vol. 3, pt. 3: *The Fresh-Water Fishes of Patagonia and An Examination of the Archiplata-Archhelenis Theory*, by Carl H. Eigenmann.

————, gen. ed. *Reports of the Princeton University Expeditions to Patagonia, 1896–1899*. 8 vols. Princeton: Princeton University Press, 1903–32. Vol. 4, pt. 2: *Tertiary Invertebrates*, by A. E. Ortmann.

Simpson, George Gaylord. *Concession to the Improbable: An Unconventional Autobiography*. New Haven: Yale University Press, 1978.

————. *Horses: The Story of the Horse Family in the Modern World and through Sixty Million Years of History*. New York: Oxford University Press, 1951.

————. *The Major Features of Evolution*. New York: Columbia University Press, 1954.

————. *The Meaning of Evolution*. New Haven: Yale University Press, 1949.

————. *Principles of Animal Taxonomy*. New York: Columbia University Press, 1961.

————. *Tempo and Mode in Evolution*. New York: Columbia University Press, 1944.

————. *Why and How: Some Problems and Methods in Historical Biology*. New York: Pergamon, 1980.

Smith, Sir Grafton Elliot. *The Evolution of Man: Essays*. Oxford: Oxford University Press, 1918.

Wallace, Alfred Russel. *The Geographical Distribution of Animals*. 2 vols. New York: Hafner, 1962.

Wortman, Jacob L. "The Ganodonta and their Relationship to the Edentata." *Bulletin of the American Museum of Natural History* 9 (1897): 59–110.
———. "Osteology of *Patriofelis*, a Middle Eocene Creodont." *Bulletin of the American Museum of Natural History* 6 (1894): 129–64.
Zittle, Karl Alfred von. *History of Geology and Paleontology to the End of the Nineteenth Century.* Translated by Marie M. Ogilvie-Gordon. London: W. Scott, 1901.

Secondary Sources

Adams, Mark B. "The Founding of Population Genetics: Contributions of the Chetverikov School, 1924–1934." *Journal of the History of Biology* 1 (1968): 23–39.
———. "Towards a Synthesis: Population Concepts in Russian Evolutionary Thought, 1925–1935." *Journal of the History of Biology* 3 (1970): 107–29.
Aldrich, Michele L. "American State Geological Surveys, 1820–1845." In *Two Hundred Years of Geology in America: Proceedings of the New Hampshire Bicentennial Conference on the History of Geology,* edited by Cecil J. Schneer, 133–43. Hanover, N.H.: University Press of New England, 1979.
Allen, Garland E. "The Eugenics Record Office at Cold Spring Harbor, 1910–1940." *Osiris,* n.s., 2 (1986): 225–64.
———. "The Introduction of *Drosophilia* into the Study of Heredity and Evolution: 1910–1940." *Isis* 66 (1975): 322–33.
———. *Life Science in the Twentieth Century.* 1975. Reprint. Cambridge: Cambridge University Press, 1978.
———. "The Misuse of Biological Hierarchies: The American Eugenics Movement, 1900–1940." *History and Philosophy of the Life Sciences* 5 (1983): 105–28.
———. "Naturalists and Experimentalists: The Genotype and the Phenotype." *Studies in History of Biology* 3 (1979): 179–209.
———. "T. H. Morgan and the Emergence of a New American Biology." *Quarterly Review of Biology* 44 (1969): 168–88.
———. "T. H. Morgan and the Split between Embryology and Genetics, 1910–1935." In *A History of Embryology,* edited by T. J. Horder, J. A. Witkowski, and C. C. Wylie, 113–46. Cambridge: Cambridge University Press, 1985.
———. *Thomas Hunt Morgan: The Man and His Science.* Princeton: Princeton University Press, 1978.
Appel, Toby A. *The Cuvier-Geoffrey Debate: French Biology in the Decades Before Darwin.* New York: Oxford University Press, 1987.
———. "Organizing Biology: The American Society of Naturalists and its 'Affiliated Societies,' 1883–1923." In *The American Development of Biology,* edited by Ronald Rainger, Keith R. Benson, and Jane Maienschein, 87–120. Philadelphia: University of Pennsylvania Press, 1988.
Avrith, Gale. "Lawrence Lambe, H. F. Osborn, and the Dinosaurs of the Red Deer River: The Development of Canadian Paleontology." Paper Delivered at History of Science Society Meeting, Seattle, Washington, 26 October 1990.
Baatz, Simon. *Knowledge, Culture and Science in the Metropolis: The New York*

Academy of Sciences, 1817–1970. New York: New York Academy of Sciences, 1990.

——. "Patronage, Science and Ideology in an American City: Patrician Philadelphia, 1800–1860." Ph.D. dissertation, University of Pennsylvania, 1986.

——. "Philadelphia Patronage: The Institutional Structure of Natural History in the New Republic, 1800–1833." *Journal of the Early Republic* 8 (1988): 111–38.

Baltzell, E. Digby. *Philadelphia Gentlemen: The Making of a National Upper Class.* Glencoe, Ill.: Free Press, 1958.

——. *The Protestant Establishment: Aristocracy and Caste in America.* New York: Random House, 1964.

Bannister, Robert C. *Social Darwinism: Science and Myth in Anglo-American Social Thought.* Philadelphia: Temple University Press, 1979.

Bender, Thomas. *New York Intellect: A History of Intellectual Life in New York City, from 1750 to the Beginnings of Our Own Time.* Baltimore: Johns Hopkins University Press, 1987.

——. *Toward an Urban Vision: Ideas and Institutions in Nineteenth-Century America.* Baltimore. 1975. Reprint. Johns Hopkins University Press, 1982.

Benson, Keith R. "American Morphology in the Late Nineteenth Century: The Biology Department at Johns Hopkins University." *Journal of the History of Biology* 18 (1985): 163–205.

——. "From Museum Research to Laboratory Research: The Transformation of Natural History into Academic Biology." In *The American Development of Biology*, edited by Ronald Rainger, Keith R. Benson, and Jane Maienschein, 49–83. Philadelphia: University of Pennsylvania Press, 1988.

——. "H. Newell Martin, W. K. Brooks, and the Reformation of American Biology." *American Zoologist* 27 (1987): 759–71.

——. "Problems of Individual Development: Descriptive Embryological Morphology in America at the Turn of the Century." *Journal of the History of Biology* 14 (1981): 115–28.

Bledstein, Burton J. *The Culture of Professionalism: The Middle Class and the Development of Higher Education in America.* New York: Norton, 1976.

Bowler, Peter J. "Darwinism and the Argument from Design: Suggestions for a Reevaluation." *Journal of the History of Biology* 10 (1977): 29–43.

——. *The Eclipse of Darwinism: Anti-Darwinian Evolution Theories in the Decades Around 1900.* Baltimore: Johns Hopkins University Press, 1983.

——. "Edward Drinker Cope and the Changing Structure of Evolution Theory." *Isis* 68 (1977): 249–65.

——. *Evolution: The History of an Idea.* Berkeley: University of California Press, 1984.

——. *Fossils and Progress: Paleontology and the Idea of Progressive Evolution in the Nineteenth Century.* New York: Science History, 1976.

——. *The Non-Darwinian Revolution: The Reinterpretation of a Historical Myth.* Baltimore: Johns Hopkins University Press, 1988.

——. "Theodore Eimer and Orthogenesis: Evolution by 'Definitely Directed Variation'." *Journal of the History of Medicine and Allied Sciences* 34 (1979): 40–73.

——. *Theories of Human Evolution: A Century of Debate, 1844–1944.* Baltimore: Johns Hopkins University Press, 1986.

Bridges, William. *Gathering of Animals: An Unconventional History of the New York Zoological Society.* New York: New York Zoological Society, 1974.

Brown, Lilian. *Bring 'Em Back Petrified.* New York: Dodd, Mead, 1956.

———. *I Married a Dinosaur.* New York: Dodd, Mead, 1950.

Brown, William Adams. *Morris Ketchum Jesup: A Character Sketch.* New York: Scribners, 1910.

Bruce, Robert V. *The Launching of American Science, 1846–1876.* New York: Knopf, 1987.

Burke, Colin B. "The Expansion of American Higher Education." In *The Transformation of Higher Learning 1860–1930: Expansion, Diversification, Social Opening, and Professionalization in England, Germany, Russia, and the United States,* edited by Konrad H. Jarausch, 108–30. Chicago: University of Chicago Press, 1983.

Burkhardt, Richard W., Jr. "Lamarckism in Britain and the United States." In *The Evolutionary Synthesis: Perspectives on the Unification of Biology,* edited by Ernst Mayr and William B. Provine, 343–52. Cambridge, Mass.: Harvard University Press, 1988.

Cain, Joseph Allen. "Moving Beyond Consistency: The Historical Significance of Simpson's *Tempo and Mode in Evolution.*" Master's thesis, University of Maryland, 1989.

Churchill, Frederick B. "In Search of the New Biology: An Epilogue." *Journal of the History of Biology* 14 (1981): 177–91.

Cohen, Michael P. *The Pathless Way: John Muir and American Wilderness.* Madison: University of Wisconsin Press, 1984.

Colbert, Edwin H. *Digging Up The Past: An Autobiography.* New York: Dembner, 1989.

———. *A Fossil Hunter's Notebook: My Life with Dinosaurs and Other Friends.* New York: Dutton, 1982.

———. *The Great Dinosaur Hunters and Their Discoveries.* 1968. Reprint. New York: Dover, 1984.

Coleman, William. *Biology in the Nineteenth Century: Problems of Form, Function, and Transformation.* New York: Wiley, 1971.

———. "Morphology Between Type Concept and Descent Theory." *Journal of the History of Medicine and Allied Sciences* 31 (1976): 149–75.

———. "Morphology in the Evolutionary Synthesis." In *The Evolutionary Synthesis: Perspectives on the Unification of Biology,* edited by Ernst Mayr and William B. Provine, 174–80. Cambridge, Mass.: Harvard University Press, 1980.

———. "Science and Symbol in the Turner Frontier Hypothesis." *American Historical Review* 72 (1966): 22–49.

Collins, Varnum Lansing. *Princeton.* New York: Oxford University Press, 1914.

Coon, Horace. *Columbia: Colossus on the Hudson.* New York: Dalton, 1947.

Crampton, Henry E. *The Department of Zoology of Columbia University, 1892–1942.* New York: Columbia University Press, 1942.

Cravens, Hamilton. "The Role of Universities in the Rise of Experimental Biology." *Science Teacher* 44 (1977): 33–37.

———. *The Triumph of Evolution: American Scientists and the Heredity-Environment Controversy, 1900–1941.* 2d ed. Baltimore: Johns Hopkins University Press, 1988.

Cremin, Lawrence A. *American Education: The Metropolitan Experience, 1876–1980*. New York: Harper & Row, 1988.

Cutright, Paul Russell. *Theodore Roosevelt: The Making of a Conservationist*. Urbana: University of Illinois Press, 1985.

Czerkas, Sylvia Massey, and Donald F. Glut. *Dinosaurs, Mammoths and Cavemen: The Art of Charles R. Knight*. New York: Dutton, 1982.

Delair, J. B., and W. A. S. Sargent. "The Earliest Discoveries of Dinosaurs." *Isis* 66 (1975): 5–25.

Desmond, Adrian. *Archetypes and Ancestors: Palaeontology in Victorian London 1850–1875*. Chicago: University of Chicago Press, 1984.

———. "Central Park's Fragile Dinosaurs." *Natural History* 83 (October 1974): 65–71.

———. "Designing the Dinosaur: Richard Owen's Response to Robert Edward Grant." *Isis* 70 (1979): 224–34.

———. *The Hot-Blooded Dinosaurs: A Revolution in Palaeontology*. London: Blond and Briggs, 1975.

Domhoff, G. William. *The Bohemian Grove and Other Retreats: A Study in Ruling-Class Cohesiveness*. New York: Harper & Row, 1974.

Dunlap, Thomas R. *Saving America's Wildlife*. Princeton: Princeton University Press, 1989.

Dupree, A. Hunter. *Science in the Federal Government*. 2d ed. Baltimore: Johns Hopkins University Press, 1986.

Dyer, Thomas G. *Theodore Roosevelt and the Idea of Race*. Baton Rouge: Louisiana State University Press, 1980.

Fox, Stephen. *John Muir and His Legacy: The American Conservation Movement*. Boston: Little, Brown, 1981.

Geiger, Roger L. *To Advance Knowledge: The Growth of American Research Universities, 1900–1940*. New York: Oxford University Press, 1986.

Geison, Gerald L., ed. *Physiology in the American Context, 1850–1940*. Bethesda, Md.: American Physiological Society, 1987.

Gerstner, Patsy A. "The Academy of Natural Sciences of Philadelphia, 1812–1850." In *The Pursuit of Knowledge in the Early American Republic: American Scientific and Learned Societies from Colonial Times to the Civil War*, edited by Alexandra Oleson and Sanford C. Brown, 179–97. Baltimore: Johns Hopkins University Press, 1976.

———. "The 'Philadelphia School' of Paleontology, 1820–1845." Ph.D. dissertation, Case Western Reserve University, 1967.

———. "Vertebrate Paleontology, an Early Nineteenth-Century Transatlantic Science." *Journal of the History of Biology* 3 (1970): 139–48.

Gilbert, Scott F. "Cellular Politics: Ernest Everett Just, Richard B. Goldschmidt, and the Attempt to Reconcile Embryology and Genetics." In *The American Development of Biology*, edited by Ronald Rainger, Keith R. Benson, and Jane Maienschein, 311–46. Philadelphia: University of Pennsylvania Press, 1988.

Gilmore, Charles W. "A History of the Division of Vertebrate Paleontology in the United States National Museum." *Proceedings of the United States National Museum* 90 (1941): 305–77.

Goetzmann, William H. *Exploration and Empire: The Explorer and the Scientist in the Winning of the American West*. 1967. Reprint. New York: Norton, 1978.

Gould, Stephen Jay. "Dollo on Dollo's Law: Irreversibility and the Status of Evolutionary Laws." *Journal of the History of Biology* 3 (1970): 189–212.

———. "Eternal Metaphors of Palaeontology." In *Patterns of Evolution as Illustrated by the Fossil Record*, edited by A. Hallam, 1–27. Amsterdam: Elsevier Scientific, 1977.

———. "G. G. Simpson, Paleontology, and the Modern Synthesis." In *The Evolutionary Synthesis: Perspectives on the Unification of Biology*, edited by Ernst Mayr and William B. Provine, 153–72. Cambridge, Mass.: Harvard University Press, 1980.

———. *Ontogeny and Phylogeny*. Cambridge, Mass.: Belknap, 1977.

———. *Wonderful Life: The Burgess Shale and the Nature of History*. New York: Norton, 1989.

Graebner, William. *The Engineering of Consent: Democracy and Authority in Twentieth-Century America*. Madison: University of Wisconsin Press, 1987.

Greene, Mott. *Geology in the Nineteenth Century*. Ithaca: Cornell University Press, 1983.

Gregory, Joseph T. "North American Vertebrate Paleontology, 1776–1976." In *Two Hundred Years of Geology in America: The Proceedings of the New Hampshire Bicentennial Conference on the History of Geology*, edited by Cecil J. Schneer, 305–35. Hanover, N.H.: University Press of New England, 1979.

Haller, Mark. *Eugenics: Hereditarian Attitudes in American Thought*. 2d ed. New Brunswick, N.J.: Rutgers University Press, 1984.

Hammack, David C. *Power and Society: Greater New York at the Turn of the Century*. New York: Columbia University Press, 1987.

Haraway, Donna. *Primate Visions: Gender, Race and Nature in the World of Modern Science*. New York: Routledge, 1989.

Harwood, Jonathan. "National Styles in Science: Genetics in Germany and the United States between the Wars." *Isis* 78 (1987): 390–414.

Hays, Samuel P. *Conservation and the Gospel of Efficiency: The Progressive Conservation Movement, 1890–1920*. Cambridge, Mass.: Harvard University Press, 1959.

Hellman, Geoffrey. *Bankers, Bones and Beetles: The First Century of the American Museum of Natural History*. Garden City, N.Y.: Natural History Press, 1968.

Higham, John. "The Reorientation of American Culture in the 1880s." In *The Origins of Modern Consciousness*, edited by John Weiss, 25–48. Detroit: Wayne State University Press, 1965.

———. *Send These to Me: Immigrants in Urban America*. Baltimore: Johns Hopkins University Press, 1984.

———. *Strangers in the Land: Patterns of American Nativism, 1860–1925*. New Brunswick, N.J.: Rutgers University Press, 1955.

Hoeveler, J. David, Jr. *James McCosh and the Scottish Intellectual Tradition: From Glasgow to Princeton*. Princeton: Princeton University Press, 1981.

Hofstadter, Richard. *Social Darwinism in American Thought*. 2d ed. New York: Braziller, 1955.

Horowitz, Helen Lefkowitz. "Animal and Man in the New York Zoological Park." *New York History* 55 (1975): 426–53.

Howard, Robert West. *The Dawnseekers: The First History of American Paleontology*. New York: Harcourt Brace Jovanovich, 1975.

Hull, David L. *Darwin and His Critics: The Reception of Darwin's Theory of Evolution by the Scientific Community*. Cambridge, Mass.: Harvard University Press, 1974.

Jaher, Frederic C. *The Urban Establishment: Upper Strata in Boston, New York,*

Charleston, Chicago and Los Angeles. Urbana: University of Illinois Press, 1982.

Jarausch, Konrad H., ed. *The Transformation of Higher Learning 1860–1930: Expansion, Diversification, Social Opening, and Professionalization in England, Germany, Russia, and the United States.* Chicago: University of Chicago Press, 1983.

Keating, James Martin. "Seth Low and the Development of Columbia University, 1889–1901." Ph.D. dissertation, Columbia University, 1973.

Kelly, Brooks Mather. *Yale: A History.* New Haven: Yale University Press, 1974.

Kennedy, John Michael. "Philanthropy and Science in New York City: The American Museum of Natural History, 1868–1968." Ph.D. dissertation, Yale University, 1968.

Keppel, Frederick Paul. *Columbia.* New York: Oxford University Press, 1914.

Kevles, Daniel J. *In the Name of Eugenics: Genetics and the Uses of Human Heredity.* New York: Knopf, 1985.

———. *The Physicists: The History of a Scientific Community in Modern America.* New York: Knopf, 1978.

Kingsley, William L., ed. *Yale College: A Sketch of its History.* New York: Henry Holt, 1879.

Kohler, Robert E. *From Medical Chemistry to Biochemistry: The Making of a Biomedical Discipline.* Cambridge: Cambridge University Press, 1982.

———. "Science, Foundations, and American Universities in the 1920s." *Osiris,* n.s., 3 (1987): 135–64.

Kohlstedt, Sally Gregory. "Curiosities and Cabinets: Natural History Museums and Education on the Antebellum Campus." *Isis* 79 (1988): 405–26.

———. *The Formation of the American Scientific Community: The American Association for the Advancement of Science, 1848–1860.* Urbana: University of Illinois Press, 1976.

———. "From Learned Society to Public Museum: The Boston Society of Natural History." In *The Organization of Knowledge in Modern America, 1860–1920,* edited by Alexandra Oleson and John Voss, 386–406. Baltimore: Johns Hopkins University Press, 1979.

———. "Henry A. Ward: The Merchant Naturalist and American Museum Development." *Journal of the Society for the Bibliography of Natural History* 9 (1980): 647–61.

———. "Institutional History." *Osiris,* n.s., 1 (1985): 17–36.

———. "Museums on Campus: A Tradition of Inquiry and Teaching." In *The American Development of Biology,* edited by Ronald Rainger, Keith R. Benson, and Jane Maienschein, 15–47. Philadelphia: University of Pennsylvania Press, 1988.

Kraut, Alan M. *The Huddled Masses: The Immigrant in American Society, 1890–1921.* Arlington Heights, Ill.: Harlan Davidson, 1982.

Laporte, Léo F. "George G. Simpson: Vertebrate Paleontologist as Biologist." In *The Expansion of American Biology,* edited by Keith R. Benson, Jane Maienschein, and Ronald Rainger. New Brunswick, N.J.: Rutgers University Press, 1991.

———, ed. *Simple Curiosity: Letters from George Gaylord Simpson to His Family, 1921–1970.* Berkeley: University of California Press, 1987.

———. "Simpson's *Tempo and Mode in Evolution* Revisited." *Proceedings of the American Philosophical Society* 127 (1983): 365–416.

Laudan, Rachel. *From Mineralogy to Geology: The Foundations of a Science, 1650–1830.* Chicago: University of Chicago Press, 1987.

Lears, T. J. Jackson. *No Place of Grace: Anti-Modernism and the Transformation of American Culture, 1880–1920.* New York: Pantheon, 1981.

Livingstone, David N. *Darwin's Forgotten Defenders: The Encounter Between Evangelical Theology and Evolutionary Thought.* Grand Rapids, Mich.: Erdmanns, 1987.

———. "The Idea of Design: The Vicissitudes of a Key Concept in the Princeton Response to Darwin." *Scottish Journal of Theology* 37 (1984): 329–57.

Lowitt, Richard. *A Merchant Prince of the Nineteenth Century: William E. Dodge.* New York: Columbia University Press, 1954.

Ludmerer, Kenneth M. *Genetics and American Society.* Baltimore: Johns Hopkins University Press, 1974.

Lurie, Edward. *Louis Agassiz: A Life in Science.* 2d ed. Baltimore: Johns Hopkins University Press, 1988.

———. *Nature and the American Mind: Louis Agassiz and the Culture of Science.* New York: Science History, 1974.

McCaughey, Robert A. "The Transformation of American Academic Life: Harvard University 1821–1892." *Perspectives in American History* 8 (1974): 239–332.

Maienschein, Jane. "Cell Lineage, Ancestral Reminiscence, and the Biogenetic Law." *Journal of the History of Biology* 11 (1978): 129–53.

———. *Defining Biology: Lectures from the 1890s.* Cambridge, Mass.: Harvard University Press, 1986.

———. "Experimental Biology in Transition: Harrison's Embryology." *Studies in History of Biology* 6 (1983): 107–27.

———. "Heredity/Development in the United States circa 1900." *History and Philosophy of the Life Sciences* 9 (1987): 79–93.

———. "History of Biology." *Osiris,* n.s., 1 (1985): 147–62.

———. "Shifting Assumptions in American Biology: Embryology, 1890–1910." *Journal of the History of Biology* 14 (1981): 89–113.

———. "Whitman at Chicago: Establishing a Chicago Style of Biology?" In *The American Development of Biology,* edited by Ronald Rainger, Keith R. Benson, and Jane Maienschein, 151–82. Philadelphia: University of Pennsylvania Press, 1988.

Maienschein, Jane, Ronald Rainger, and Keith R. Benson. Introduction to *The American Development of Biology,* edited by Ronald Rainger, Keith R. Benson, and Jane Maienschein, 3–11. Philadelphia: University of Pennsylvania Press, 1988.

———. "Were American Morphologists in Revolt?" *Journal of the History of Biology* 14 (1981): 83–87.

Maline, Joseph M. "Edward Drinker Cope (1840–1897)." Master's thesis, University of Pennsylvania, 1974.

Manning, Thomas G. *Government in Science: The U.S. Geological Survey, 1867–1894.* Lexington: University of Kentucky Press, 1967.

Martin, Edward Sanford. *The Life of Joseph Hodges Choate.* 2 vols. New York: Scribners, 1920.

Martyn, Carlos. *William E. Dodge: The Christian Merchant.* New York: Funk and Wagnalls, 1890.

Matthews, James Brander, et al. *A History of Columbia University 1754–1904.* New York: Columbia University Press, 1904.

Mayr, Ernst. "G. G. Simpson." In *The Evolutionary Synthesis: Perspectives on the Unification of Biology,* edited by Ernst Mayr and William B. Provine, 452–63. Cambridge, Mass.: Harvard University Press, 1980.

———. *The Growth of Biological Thought: Diversity, Inheritance and Evolution.* Cambridge, Mass.: Belknap, 1982.

———. "Prologue: Some Thoughts on the History of the Evolutionary Synthesis." In *The Evolutionary Synthesis: Perspectives on the Unification of Biology,* edited by Ernst Mayr and William B. Provine, 1–48. Cambridge, Mass.: Harvard University Press, 1980.

———. "The Role of Systematics in the Evolutionary Synthesis." In *The Evolutionary Synthesis: Perspectives on the Unification of Biology,* edited by Ernst Mayr and William B. Provine, 123–36. Cambridge, Mass.: Harvard University Press, 1980.

Mayr, Ernst, and William B. Provine, eds. *The Evolutionary Synthesis: Perspectives on the Unification of Biology.* Cambridge, Mass.: Harvard University Press, 1980.

Menard, Henry W. *Science: Growth and Change.* Cambridge, Mass.: Harvard University Press, 1971.

Merrill, George P. *The First One Hundred Years of American Geology.* New Haven: Yale University Press, 1924.

Merrill, Lynn L. *The Romance of Victorian Natural History.* New York: Oxford University Press, 1989.

Mitman, Gregg. "Evolution as Gospel: William Patten, the Language of Democracy, and the Great War." *Isis* 81 (1990): 446–63.

Moore, James R. *The Post-Darwinian Controversies: A Study of the Protestant Struggle to come to Terms with Darwin in Great Britain and America, 1870–1900.* Cambridge: Cambridge University Press, 1979.

Morris, Edmund. *The Rise of Theodore Roosevelt.* New York: Ballantine, 1979.

Nash, Roderick. *Wilderness and the American Mind.* 3d ed. New Haven: Yale University Press, 1982.

Nevins, Allen. *Abram S. Hewitt, With Some Account of Peter Cooper.* London: Harper, 1935.

Novak, Barbara. *Nature and Culture: American Landscape and Painting, 1825–1875.* New York: Oxford University Press, 1980.

Nyhart, Lynn. "The Disciplinary Breakdown of German Morphology, 1870–1900." *Isis* 78 (1987): 365–89.

Oleson, Alexandra, and Sanford C. Brown, eds. *The Pursuit of Knowledge in the Early American Republic: American Scientific and Learned Societies from Colonial Times to the Civil War.* Baltimore: Johns Hopkins University Press, 1976.

Oleson, Alexandra, and John Voss, eds. *The Organization of Knowledge in Modern America, 1860–1920.* Baltimore: Johns Hopkins University Press, 1979.

Osborn, Henry Fairfield. *Cope: Master Naturalist: The Life and Letters of Edward Drinker Cope with a Bibliography of His Writings Classified by Subject.* Princeton: Princeton University Press, 1930.

Ostrom, John H., and John S. MacIntosh. *Marsh's Dinosaurs.* New Haven: Yale University Press, 1967.

Outram, Dorinda. *Georges Cuvier: Vocation, Science, and Authority in Post-Revolutionary France.* Manchester: Manchester University Press, 1984.

Pauly, Philip J. "The Appearance of Academic Biology in Late Nineteenth-Century America." *Journal of the History of Biology* 17 (1984): 369–97.

——. *Controlling Life: Jacques Loeb and the Engineering Ideal In Biology.* New York: Oxford University Press, 1987.

——. "The World and All That Is In It: The National Geographic Society, 1888–1918." *American Quarterly* 31 (1979): 517–32.

Pfeifer, Edward J. "The Genesis of American Neo-Lamarckism." *Isis* 56 (1965): 156–67.

Porter, Charlotte M. *The Eagle's Nest: Natural History and American Ideas, 1812–1842.* Tuscaloosa: University of Alabama Press, 1986.

——. "The Rise of Parnassus: Henry Fairfield Osborn and the Hall of the Age of Man." *Museum Studies Journal* 1 (1983): 26–34.

Porter, Roy. *The Making of Geology: Earth Science in Britain, 1660–1815.* Cambridge: Cambridge University Press, 1977.

Provine, William B. Epilogue for *The Evolutionary Synthesis: Perspectives on the Unification of Biology,* edited by Ernst Mayr and William B. Provine, 399–411. Cambridge, Mass.: Harvard University Press, 1980.

——. "Francis B. Sumner and the Evolutionary Synthesis." *Studies in History of Biology* 3 (1979): 211–40.

——. *The Origins of Theoretical Population Genetics.* Chicago: University of Chicago Press, 1971.

——. *Sewall Wright: Geneticist and Evolutionist.* Chicago: University of Chicago Press, 1986.

Rainger, Ronald. "Collectors and Entrepreneurs: Hatcher, Wortman, and the Structure of American Vertebrate Paleontology circa 1900." *Earth Sciences History* 9 (1990): 14–21.

——. "The Continuation of the Morphological Tradition: American Paleontology, 1880–1910." *Journal of the History of Biology* 14 (1981): 129–58.

——. "Just Before Simpson: William Diller Matthew's Understanding o´ Evolution." *Proceedings of the American Philosophical Society* 130 (1986): 4,53–74.

——. "The Rise and Decline of a Science: Vertebrate Paleontology at Philadelphia's Academy of Natural Sciences, 1820–1900." *Proceedings of the American Philosophical Society* (forthcoming).

——. "Vertebrate Paleontology as Biology: Henry Fairfield Osborn and the American Museum of Natural History." In *The American Development of Biology,* edited by Ronald Rainger, Keith R. Benson, and Jane Maienschein, 219–56. Philadelphia: University of Philadelphia Press, 1988.

——. "W. D. Matthew, Fossil Vertebrates and Geological Time." *Earth Sciences History* 8 (1989): 159–66.

——. "What's the Use: William King Gregory and the Functional Morphology of Fossil Vertebrates." *Journal of the History of Biology* 22 (1989): 103–39.

Reif, Wolf-Ernst. "The Search for a Macroevolutionary Theory in German Paleontology." *Journal of the History of Biology* 19 (1986): 79–130.

Reiger, John F. *American Sportsmen and the Origins of Conservation.* New York: Winchester Press, 1975.

——, ed. *The Passing of the Great West: Selected Papers of George Bird Grinnell.* New York: Scribners, 1972.

Reingold, Nathan, ed. *Science in the American Context: New Perspectives.* Washington, D.C.: Smithsonian Institution Press, 1979.

————. *Science in Nineteenth-Century America: A Documentary History*. New York: Hill and Wang, 1964.

Reingold, Nathan, and Ida H. Reingold, eds. *Science in Twentieth-Century America: A Documentary History, 1900–1939*. Chicago: University of Chicago Press, 1981.

Richards, Robert J. *Darwin and the Emergence of Evolutionary Theories of Mind and Behavior*. Chicago: University of Chicago Press, 1987.

Romer, A. S. "Vertebrate Paleontology." In *Geology 1888–1938: Fiftieth Anniversary Volume of the Geological Society of America*. New York: Geological Society of America, 1941.

Rosenberg, Charles E. *No Other Gods: On Science and American Social Thought*. Baltimore: Johns Hopkins University Press, 1976.

Rosenberg, Emily S. *Spreading the American Dream: American Economic and Cultural Expansion, 1890–1945*. New York: Hill and Wang, 1982.

Rudwick, Martin J. S. *The Great Devonian Controversy: The Shaping of Scientific Knowledge Among Gentlemanly Specialists*. Chicago: University of Chicago Press, 1985.

————. *The Meaning of Fossils: Episodes in the History of Palaeontology*. 2d ed. Chicago: University of Chicago Press, 1985.

Rupke, Nicolaas A. *The Great Chain of History: William Buckland and the English School of Geology (1814–1849)*. Oxford: Clarendon, 1983.

Ruse, Michael. *The Darwinian Revolution: Science Red in Tooth and Claw*. Chicago: University of Chicago Press, 1979.

Russett, Cynthia Eagle. *Darwin in America: The Intellectual Response, 1865–1912*. San Francisco: Freeman, 1976.

Sapp, Jan. *Beyond the Gene: Cytoplasmic Inheritance and the Struggle for Authority in Genetics*. New York: Oxford University Press, 1987.

Satterlee, Herbert L. *J. Pierpont Morgan: An Intimate Portrait*. New York: Macmillan, 1939.

Schmitt, Peter J. *Back to Nature: The Arcadian Myth in Urban America*. New York: Oxford University Press, 1969.

Schneer, Cecil J., ed. *Towards A History of Geology*. Cambridge, Mass.: Harvard University Press, 1969.

————, ed. *Two Hundred Years of Geology in North America: Proceedings of the New Hampshire Conference on the History of Geology*. Hanover, N.H.: University Press of New England, 1979.

Schuchert, Charles, and Clara Mae LeVene. *O. C. Marsh: Pioneer in Paleontology*. New Haven: Yale University Press, 1940.

Secord, James A. *Controversy in Victorian Geology: The Cambrian-Silurian Dispute*. Princeton: Princeton University Press, 1986.

Sellers, Charles Coleman. *Charles Willson Peale*. New York: Scribners, 1969.

————. *Mr. Peale's Museum: Charles Willson Peale and the First Popular Museum of Natural Science and Art*. New York: Norton, 1980.

Shils, Edward. "The Order of Learning in the United States from 1865–1920: The Ascendancy of the Universities." In *The Organization of Knowledge in Modern America, 1860–1920*, edited by Alexandra Oleson and John Voss, 19–47. Baltimore: Johns Hopkins University Press, 1979.

Shor, Elizabeth Noble. *The Fossil Feud Between E. D. Cope and O. C. Marsh*. Hicksville, N.Y.: Exposition, 1974.

————. *Fossils and Flies: The Life of a Compleat Naturalist, Samuel Wendell Williston (1851–1918)*. Norman: University of Oklahoma Press, 1971.

Simpson, George Gaylord. *Discoverers of the Lost World: An Account of Some of Those Who Brought Back to Life South American Mammals Long Buried in the Abyss of Time*. New Haven: Yale University Press, 1984.

Sinclair, Andrew. *Corsair: The Life of J. Pierpont Morgan*. Boston: Little, Brown, 1981.

Soloman, Barbara M. *Ancestors and Immigrants: A Changing New England Tradition*. Chicago: University of Chicago Press, 1972.

Spencer, Frank, ed. *A History of Physical Anthropology, 1930–1980*. New York: Academic Press, 1982.

Stephens, Lester D. "Ancient Animals and Other Wondrous Things: The Story of Francis Simmons Holmes, Paleontologist and Curator of the Charleston Museum." *Contributions from the Charleston Museum* 17 (1985): 1–67.

Sterling, Keir B. *The Last of the Naturalists: The Career of C. Hart Merriam*. New York: Arno, 1974.

————, ed. *Selected Works in Nineteenth-Century North American Paleontology*. New York: Arno, 1974.

Stewart, Susan. *On Longing: Narratives of the Miniature, the Gigantic, the Souvenir, the Collection*. Baltimore: Johns Hopkins University Press, 1984.

Stocking, George W. *Race, Culture and Evolution: Essays in the History of Anthropology*. New York: Free Press, 1968.

Taylor, Francis Henry. *Pierpont Morgan as Collector and Patron, 1837–1913*. New York: Pierpont Morgan Library, 1957.

Thomas, Keith. *Man and the Natural World: A History of the Modern Sensibility*. New York: Pantheon, 1983.

Todes, Daniel. "V. O. Kovalevskii: The Genesis, Content, and Reception of His Paleontological Work." *Studies in History of Biology* 2 (1978): 99–165.

Veysey, Laurence R. *The Emergence of the American University*. Chicago: University of Chicago Press, 1965.

Wertenbaker, Thomas Jefferson. *Princeton, 1746–1896*. Princeton: Princeton University Press, 1946.

Williams, John Rogers. *The Handbook of Princeton*. New York: Grafton, 1905.

Wilson, Leonard. "The Emergence of Geology as a Science in the United States." *Journal of World History* 19 (1987): 416–37.

Winnick, Herbert C. "The Role of Personality in the Science and Social Attitudes of Five American Men of Science, 1876–1916." Ph.D. dissertation, University of Wisconsin, 1968.

Index

Academy of Natural Sciences: Edward Drinker Cope and, 12, 15; and expeditions, 252 (n. 26); fossil mountings, 9, 10, 27, 89, 97; Joseph Leidy and, 10; and vertebrate paleontology, 10, 15

Adams, L. A.: and William King Gregory, 222, 223

Agassiz, Alexander, 31; and O. C. Marsh, 261 (n. 56); and Henry Fairfield Osborn, 261 (n. 56); and William Berryman Scott, 261 (n. 56)

Akeley, Carl: expedition to Africa, 288 (n. 59); and Roosevelt Memorial, 153

Alexander, Annie Montague: and vertebrate paleontology at University of California, 21

Allen, Joel A.: and American Bison Society, 112; and American Museum, 4, 57, 58, 112–13; and American Ornithologists' Union, 112; and Audubon Society, 112; and *Bulletin of the American Museum*, 59; and evolution, 58; and exhibits, 112–13; and Hall of North American Mammals, 112; and Morris K. Jesup, 57, 59, 60, 109, 112; on Jesup, 285 (n. 29); and museum collections, 57, 58; on Henry Fairfield Osborn, 60; and preservation of nature, 4, 112, 163; scientific studies, 58; and vertebrate paleontology, 60

Ameghino, Carlos: and biostratigraphy, 189; discoveries, 189

Ameghino, Florentino: on biogeography, 93, 189–91, 200–2; on biostratigraphy

and correlation, 185, 189–90; on evolution, 93, 189–90, 200–1; John Bell Hatcher and, 190; William Diller Matthew and, 190–91, 200–1; Henry Fairfield Osborn and, 93, 185; reaction to, 93, 190–91, 200–1

American Museum of Natural History: Joel Asaph Allen and, 57–60, 109, 112–13; and American Ornithologists' Union, 112; and Audubon Society, 112; Albert Bickmore and, 33, 55, 56, 58; Central Asiatic Expeditions, 69, 72, 100–4; Frank M. Chapman and, 4, 57, 58, 112–14, 153, 160, 163; collections, 182–83, 209–11, 242, 247; and Columbia University, 61, 62, 221, 243; Cope collections, 63, 64, 68, 88, 96; Department of Comparative Anatomy, 217, 222; Department of Geology, 76; Department of Geology and Paleontology, 245; early history, 55–59; exhibits, 22, 58, 59, 60, 64, 68, 72, 74, 82, 109–12, 120, 144, 153–81, 220, 231, 243–44, 245; expeditions, 59, 62, 68–69, 72, 75, 81–82, 88–104 passim, 109, 112, 114, 121, 242–43, 288 (n. 59); financial status, 57, 244–45; and foundations, 244, 245; and functional morphology, 216–17; William King Gregory and, 217, 222, 225, 231, 239–41; habitat groups, 113, 153; Hall of Age of Man, 169–81, 225, 231, 245; Hall of Natural History of Man, 231; Hall of Public Health, 152–53; Morris K. Jesup and, 4,

About the Author

Ronald Rainger is Associate Professor of History, Texas Tech University. He received his bachelor's degree from Willamette University, a master's degree from the University of Utah, and a master's and doctorate from Indiana University.